LITERATURE AS COMMUNICATION

Pragmatics & Beyond New Series

Editor:
Andreas H. Jucker *(Justus Liebig University, Giessen)*

Associate Editors:
Jacob L. Mey *(Odense University)*

Herman Parret *(Belgian National Science Foundation, Universities of Louvain and Antwerp)*

Jef Verschueren *(Belgian National Science Foundation, Univ. of Antwerp)*

Editorial Address:
Justus Liebig University Giessen, English Department
Otto-Behaghel-Strasse 10, D-35394 Giessen, Germany
e-mail: andreas.jucker@anglistik.uni-giessen.de

Editorial Board:
Shoshana Blum-Kulka *(Hebrew University of Jerusalem)*
Chris Butler *(University College of Ripon and York)*; Jean Caron *(Université de Poitiers)*
Robyn Carston *(University College London)*; Thorstein Fraser *(University of Trondheim)*
Bruce Fretheim *(Boston University)*; John Heritage *(University of California at Los Angeles)*
Susan Herring *(University of Texas at Arlington)*; Masako K. Hiraga *(St. Paul's (Rikkyo) University)*
David Holdcroft *(University of Leeds)*; Sachiko Ide *(Japan Women's University)*
Catherine Kerbrat-Orecchioni *(University of Lyon 2)*
Claudia de Lemos *(University of Campinas, Brazil)*; Marina Sbisà *(University of Trieste)*
Emanuel Schegloff *(University of California at Los Angeles)*
Deborah Schiffrin *(Georgetown Univ.)*; Paul O. Takahara *(Kobe City Univ. of Foreign Studies)*
Sandra Thompson *(University of California at Santa Barbara)*
Teun A. Van Dijk *(University of Amsterdam)*; Richard J. Watts *(University of Berne)*

78
Roger D. Sell
Literature as Communication
The foundations of mediating criticism

LITERATURE AS COMMUNICATION

THE FOUNDATIONS OF MEDIATING CRITICISM

ROGER D. SELL
Åbo Akademi University

JOHN BENJAMINS PUBLISHING COMPANY
AMSTERDAM/PHILADELPHIA

∞ ™ The paper used in this publication meets the minimum requirements of American National Standard for Information Sciences — Permanence of Paper for Printed Library Materials, ANSI Z39.48-1984.

Library of Congress Cataloging-in-Publication Data

Sell, Roger D.
  Literature as communication : the foundations of meditating criticism / Roger D. Sell.
    p.   cm. -- (Pragmatics & beyond, ISSN 0922-842X ; new ser. 78)
  Includes bibliographical references and index.
  1. Criticism. 2. Literature--History and critisim. 3. Pragmatics. I. Title. II. Series.
PN81.S366   2000
801'.95--dc21   00-031142
ISBN 90 272 5096 0 (Eur.) / 1 55619 838 8 (US) (Hb. alk. paper)
ISBN 90 272 5097 9 (Eur.) / 1 55619 839 6 (US) (Pb. alk. paper)

© 2000 – John Benjamins B.V.
No part of this book may be reproduced in any form, by print, photoprint, microfilm, or any other means, without written permission from the publisher.

John Benjamins Publishing Co. • P.O.Box 75577 • 1070 AN Amsterdam • The Netherlands
John Benjamins North America • P.O.Box 27519 • Philadelphia PA 19118-0519 • USA

In loving memory
of
Arthur Philip Sell and Freda Marion Sell

Contents

Acknowledgements ix

1. Introduction 1
1.1. The need for a theory 1
1.2. Main features of the theory proposed 2
1.3. Interdisciplinarity 4
1.4. Postmodernity: the centrifugal and the centripetal 8
1.5. Positive mediation 12
1.6. Mediation and the discussion of literature 19
1.7. Wanted — an appropriate literary pragmatics 21

2. A-Historical De-Humanization 29
2.1. Modernist literary formalism 29
2.2. Structuralist linguistics 40
2.3. Alliances of literary formalism and linguistic thought 43
2.4. Speech act theory of literature 48
2.5. Formalist literary pragmatics 64
2.6. Some pros and cons 74

3. The Historically Human 77
3.1. The paradigm shift 77
3.2. Moves away from literary formalism 77
3.3. Late-twentieth-century linguistics 80
3.4. The written deed 83
3.5. From cultural structuralism and poststructuralism to postmodern stalemate 88
3.6. A historical yet non-historicist literary pragmatics 107

4. Literature as Communication 119
4.1. Proliferating contexts of reading 119
4.2. Social individuals and their co-adaptations 145
4.3. The protean self and communicative personae 158

5. Interactive Consequences — 177
5.1. Typology, hermeneutics, affect, ethics — 177
5.2. Generic co-adaptations through time — 178
5.3. Re-living biography and influence — 193
5.4. Changes in politeness — 207
5.5. Bi-dimensional beauties from history — 230

6. Mediating Criticism — 253
6.1. The theory for the practice — 253
6.2. Trajectories of mediation — 257
6.3. Inside and outside — 258
6.4. What medium for mediation? — 265
6.5. Dealing with conflict — 266
6.6. A future for literature? — 271
6.7. Scholarship and culture in symbiosis — 277

Glossary — 281
Bibliography — 303
Name Index — 333
Subject Index — 341

Acknowledgements

Robert Frost's "Spring Pools" is re-printed from *The Poetry of Robert Frost* (ed. Edward Connery Lathem), © 1928, 1969 by Henry Holt & Company, © 1956 by Robert Frost, with permission from Henry Holt & Company, LLC. W.B. Yeats's "Easter 1916" is re-printed from *Yeats's Poems* (ed. A. Norman Jeffares), Basingstoke, Macmillan, 1996, with permission from A.P. Wyatt Limited on behalf of Michael B. Yeats. Andrew Young's "An Old Road" is re-printed from *Selected Poems: Andrew Young* (eds. Edward Lowbury and Alison Young), Manchester, Carcanet Press Limited, 1998, with permission from Carcanet Press Limited.

Revised passages of my own earlier work are included from: *REAL: Yearbook of Research in English and American Literature,* "The Drama of Fictionalized Author and Reader: A Formalist Obstacle to Literary Pragmatics", 4: 291–316, © 1986, with permission from Mouton de Gruyter, Berlin; *Literary Pragmatics* (ed. Roger D. Sell), "The Politeness of Literary Texts", pp. 208–24, © 1991, with permission from Routledge, London; *Politeness in Language: Studies in its History, Theory and Practice* (eds. Richard J. Watts, Sachiko Ide and Konrad Ehlich), "Literary Texts and Diachronic Aspects of Politeness", pp. 109–29, © 1992, with permission from Mouton de Gruyter, Berlin; *Writing and Speaking: Language, Text, Discourse, Communication* (eds. Světla Čmejrková, František Daneš and Eva Havlová), "Literary Pragmatics and Speech Act Theory of Literature", pp. 125–35, © 1994, with permission from Günter Narr Verlag, Tübingen; and *Concise Encyclopedia of Pragmatics* (ed. Jakob Mey), "Literary Pragmatics", pp. 523–36, © 1998, with permission from Elsevier Science, Oxford.

During the twenty years or so I have been working on this book, the English Department of Åbo Akademi University has allowed me repeated study leaves for research in Britain. These trips have been generously financed from the H.W. Donner Fund of the Åbo Akademi Foundation, and the Foundation has also awarded me my present research chair, so enabling me to get the typescript into final form. Earlier on, a year's research leave was financed by the Academy of Finland, who for five years funded the Åbo Literary Pragmatics Project as well. For all this support I am very grateful.

I owe a special debt of gratitude to Nils Erik Enkvist, former Head of the Åbo Akademi English Department, under whose friendly guidance I first became interested in bringing together literary and linguistic thought, and whose patient comments on an earlier, extremely long typescript helped me to realize that I was writing not one book, but two. In separating these out from each other, I have received invaluable encouragement and many detailed suggestions from three other departmental colleagues, Anthony Johnson, John Smeds and Martin Gill, who all helped me fill some serious gaps as well. John was earlier a member of the Literary Pragmatics Project, and I have happy memories of working with him and Ilkka Joki, Peter Siegfrids and Iris Lindahl under those auspices.

During some terms, I have been based at Wolfson College Cambridge, Keble College Oxford, and the English Department of the University of Gothenburg. To friends in all three places I am grateful for unfailing support, and especially to Ed and Eva Johnson in Cambridge, to Nigel Smith and John and Rosemary Whitley in Oxford, and to Sanne Bildt and †Bo and Britta Gunnarsson in Gothenburg, for making sure I felt at home.

At present, my colleagues on a day-to-day basis are the members of the ChiLPA group, the Åbo project on "Children's Literature, Pure and Applied". I should like to thank them for all the fun we are having as we try to understand the implications of communicative pragmatics for the study of children's literature. And I am particularly grateful to Lilian Rönnqvist, Lydia Williams and Maria Nikolajeva for friendly and constructive comments on my typescript.

Librarians are usually thought of as having books in their care. Their role during the writing of books deserves far more recognition. The staffs of the National Library of Wales, Cambridge University Library, the Bodleian Library, and Åbo Akademi Library have not only supplied items on request, but gently advised on what to request.

I should like to express heartfelt thanks to my family and some close relatives. Without †Bo (L.), Kulti, Maxi, Tia, Sanne, Manne, Jyrkki, Catja, Cassandra, Jouni, Lotta, Toffe and Anna to cheer me on in times of concentration, and at other times to take my mind off things, I should never have reached this stage.

Acknowledgements

I dedicate the book to the memory of my mother and father. It was their love which first made me feel I had a place, and as time goes on I feel more and more drawn towards their values. In a way, the book has long been theirs already.

R.D.S.

We should look in society not for consensus, but for ineliminable and acceptable conflicts, and for rationally controlled hostilities, as the normal condition of mankind; not only normal, but also the best condition of mankind from the moral point of view, both between states and within states. This was Heraclitus's vision: that life, and liveliness, within the soul and within society, consists in perpetual conflicts between rival impulses and ideals, and that justice presides over the hostilities and finds sufficient compromises to prevent madness in the soul, and civil war or war between peoples. Harmony and inner consensus come with death, when human faces no longer express conflicts but are immobile, composed, and at rest.

(Hampshire 1992 [1989]: 189)

Members of one culture can, by the force of imaginative insight, understand (what Vico called *entrare*) the values, the ideals, the forms of life of another culture or society, even those remote in time or space. They may find these values unacceptable, but if they open their minds sufficiently they can grasp how one might be a full human being, with whom one could communicate, and at the same time live in the light of values widely different from one's own, but which nevertheless one can see to be values, ends of life, by the realisation of which men could be fulfilled.

(Berlin 1997: 9)

The large collective identities that call for recognition come with notions of how a proper person of that kind behaves: it is not that there is *one* way that gays or blacks should behave, but that there are gay and black modes of behavior. These notions provide loose norms or models, which play a role in shaping the life plans of those who make these collective identities central to their individual identities. ... Collective identities, in short, provide what we might call scripts: narratives that people can use in shaping their life plans and in telling their life-stories. In our society (though not, perhaps, in the England of Addison and Steele) being witty does not in this way suggest the life-script of "the wit". And that is why the personal dimensions of identity work differently from the collective ones.

(Appiah 1994: 159–60)

Chapter 1

Introduction

1.1. The need for a theory

In practice, one of the most valuable services performed by literary critics has been that of mediation. Often they have helped readers to understand and appreciate writings whose effect might otherwise have been unduly limited because of a certain strangeness, most typically the strangeness of literary works produced during some earlier historical period, or within some alien cultural tradition. Not that a mediating critic *reduces* a major text to its period or cultural tradition. That might be to overlook some of its most distinctive features, so lessening its interest to the very readers the critic is hoping to encourage. Nor can such readers themselves be regarded as simply the prisoners of their own time and milieu, since otherwise they could hardly be expected to take an interest in an old or alien text in the first place. Mediating critics do need, then, a delicate sense of balance.

For a long time now, this has been largely a matter of instinct. Even when critics have most successfully drawn on the riches of historical scholarship, their effort of mediation has not been underwritten by the main paradigms of twentieth century literary theory. Those paradigms, when they were new, entailed real advances in our understanding of literature, and in due course gave rise to much valuable commentary on particular texts. Yet literature is a multi-faceted phenomenon, and the theoreticians' main interest has not been in literary writing and reading as forms of interpersonal activity whose workings could sometimes be facilitated by mediation. The pragmatic conditions for literature as a genuine form of communication have been the main blindspot arising from literary theoreticians' particular kinds of focus.

Nowadays as much as ever, critics who hope to mediate will have to be knowledgeable, sensitive and fair-minded. But such personal qualities would always have been further enhanced by theoretical support, and in postmodern times may be very hard pressed without it. As a result of major social and political changes, many people now experience their own personal identity as intimately linked to some very precise positionality within a spectrum of cultural formations perceived as sharply heterogeneous and non-overlapping. Under such circumstances, the task of mediation can be not only urgently necessary, but problematic. Literary critics appealing to a liberal ideal of tolerance will not always win a hearing.

Yet if mediation were successful, individual readers would find a whole new range of interest and enjoyment, and relations between different groupings within society at large might be somewhat improved. This has encouraged me to try and develop the theoretical foundations which mediating critics at present do not have, an aim which is clearly reflected in this book's structure. What follows here is very much the work of a literary scholar who has turned to communicative pragmatics because of the blind-spot in twentieth century literary theory. The main line of argument runs from the difficulty faced by mediating critics in postmodern societies, *via* pragmatic considerations, to a vision of literary criticism as greatly strengthened by them.

1.2. Main features of the theory proposed

Perhaps the first thing to say about my proposal is that it involves a theory of communication in a full sense. Literary writing and reading are viewed as uses of language which amount to interpersonal activity, and which are thereby capable of bringing about a change in the status quo. This means that my references to communicative pragmatics will carry a strong echo of the Greek root *pragma* (= "deed"). As a further consequence, I shall have to explain what changes to the status quo can consist of.

A main assumption here will be that communicative situations are triangular. Two parties will always be in communication *about* some third entity. The basic situation can still be thought of in this way even when the two parties are the two halves of one and the same self-communing individual, as when we talk to ourselves or write a diary, and even when the third entity also includes one or both of the communicating parties, who in that case speak of "me" or "you" or "us". Equally well, the third entity can be somebody or something quite unconnected with the communicants themselves, and can actually involve an element of hypotheticality or even outright fiction, as with many jokes about celebrities, or as with most literature. But regardless of the precise way in which the communicational triangle happens to be realized, any change to the status quo will begin as a change in the communicants' perceptions and evaluations of this real, hypothetical or fictional entity under discussion. Communication can be thought of as a semiotic process by which people try, at least ideally speaking, to negotiate a balanced, and even shared view of that entity. In doing so, they inevitably open themselves to the possibility of mental re-adjustments, whose scope can range from the merely very minimal to the absolutely all-embracing. Directly or indirectly, what happens can also lead to actions of a tangibly physical kind, and ultimately may even contribute to changes in an entire communal thought- and life-world.

Then again, communicative pragmatics must also cover pragmatics in a sense with which linguists will be more familiar. One central concern will be with the consequences of the different kinds and degrees of contextual understanding which may be brought to bear by different communicants. While squarely recognizing literature's interactive potential, in other words, my theory will try to make explicit the possible need for mediation between any particularly positioned writer and any particularly positioned reader. In this way it will direct attention to avenues by which mediation may actually be able to proceed.

Here, too, the view of communicators as jointly negotiating within a basically triangular situation is crucial. Paradoxically enough, a more dualistic conception of communication might be far too weakly dialogical for a mediating critic's purposes. Expressed in binarisms of sender/receiver, speaker/hearer, writer/reader, narrator/narratee and so on, it could easily tend to prioritize the first terms in such pairings as agentive, and to associate the second terms with a kind of passivity after the event. Yet if communication is really to take place at all, the binarisms' second terms are clearly just as important as their first ones. Indeed, senders, speakers, writers, or narrators need not be physically present or even alive; instead, their words may be preserved in some form of legible or audible record. Even at its strongest, the role of such initiating participants can never be more decisive for how the communication actually turns out than the role of hearers, readers, receivers or narratees. Both kinds of role can be performed with either greater or lesser success, and the plain fact is that words can be taken in a very different way by one party from that intended by another. As speech-act theoreticians put it, perlocutionary effect may bear little relation to illocutionary act.

To the extent that such discrepancies are not wilful, they will derive from the differences of kind and degree of contextual understanding. A use of words representing one particular conjuncture of sociocultural history and circumstance, when processed at some different conjuncture, may offer a considerable challenge. It may well presuppose linguistic knowledge, more general knowledge, plus various kinds of evaluative and attitudinal overtones which, at the second conjuncture, cannot be taken for granted. On the contrary, many other items of knowledge, and some very different evaluative and attitudinal stances, may be far more readily accessible there. This is how the need for mediation most typically arises.

But although such facts of sociohistorical positionality will obviously come within a mediating critic's main focus of attention, human nature and behaviour are not entirely determined by them. For convenience, I shall be labelling the assumption that human beings *are* so determined as the historicist assumption, even though many scholars describing themselves as historicists would not embrace it to the full. If contexts really were as influential as historicism (in this strong sense) suggests, many attempts at communication would be complete non-starters, which mediators could never even hope to redeem. For communication between differently positioned people to stand any chance of satisfying both parties, the human imagination must be sufficiently autonomous to empathize with modes of being and doing that are different from the ones valorized within its most immediate milieu. The power of imaginative self-projection into otherness is in fact a kind of provisional independence of spirit which the mediating critic can seek to stimulate in readers, sometimes, we can hope, to lasting effect. True, a permanent change of outlook can never be simply foisted upon them, precisely because communication is negotiational. The empathizing sentiments so necessary to their grasp of an unfamiliar manner of thought, behaviour or feeling may well be closely accompanied by a degree of critical self-distancing. Even so, the mediating critic will always need to appeal to a certain heuristic flexibility of mind.

1.3. Interdisciplinarity

In elaborating such points, my discussion will entail a thorough-going interdisciplinarity between the fields of literary scholarship and linguistics. Many earlier attempts at "lang.-lit." interdisciplinarity, including some of the suggestions about literary pragmatics, were made within a framework of structuralist linguistics and literary formalism. Such research greatly improved our understanding of the text-types, styles and narratological organization of literary texts, but also involved a rather marked form of the blind-spot in twentieth-century literary theory. Literature was viewed as a use of language which was very special and not quite real. Today, both linguists and literary scholars are likely to find this too superficial. In linguistics, many of the most important developments are in the area of pragmatics, now seen as very much including matters of intention, meaning and value. In literary scholarship, ideas of literature's discoursal a-typicality have already been partly challenged by approaches such as new historicism, cultural materialism, feminist criticism, gay and lesbian criticism, postcolonial criticism, and ethnic criticism. By the same token, distinctions between linguistics and literary scholarship have begun to seem increasingly artificial. In developing a pragmatics of literature that is continuous with the pragmatics of communication in general, I shall merely be putting 2 and 2 together to make 4.

Some literary scholars may still need an immediate reassurance that I am not denying the obvious: that literary texts can have features of content, form and style which are not often found elsewhere, and that the experience of reading them can be pleasurable and valuable. As far as it goes, this is in perfect harmony with what I shall be saying. To view literature within the framework of a general theory of communication is certainly not to blind ourselves to its real character. On the one hand, literature does have a very great deal in common with other forms of communication, above all the fundamental fact of communicativeness itself. Even the features and functions usually thought of as most characteristically literary are not peculiarly so, being less a matter of law than tendency. In recognizing such points, my approach can be seen as a manifestation of postmodern non-elitism: as an attempt to explore aspects of writing and reading which the cultural politics underlying an earlier scholarship tended to marginalize. On the other hand, some more recent commentators, we shall see, have virtually reduced literature to a kind of anonymous orality, and this, too, is a serious distortion of the facts, motivated by considerations no less powerfully ideological. To say this is not to suggest that literary scholarship can ever be ideology-free. But in an adequate theory of literary pragmatics, the historical positionality of all readers, including literary scholars and critics themselves, will at least receive explicit prominence. This should encourage an openness of sociocultural self-consciousness from which a mediating criticism will especially benefit.

But even if my book does not confirm literary scholars' worst fears, both they and other readers may sometimes feel dissatisfied. In trying to synthesize two disciplines still often regarded as inevitably separate, I face a rhetorical problem. Linguists may well feel that long sections are from their point of view elementary, oversimplified, and arbitrarily selective, and that other sections say far too much about purely literary issues. Many other pages could seem just as unsatisfactory to literary scholars, whether because of the lengthy linguistic deliberations, or simply because my literary examples never give a clear idea of how to mediate texts or authors or periods in their entirety — a task which I am hoping to address in another book, completely devoted to mediating criticism in action. As for readers whose viewpoint is already closer to my own, they will probably find my advocacy of interdisciplinarity far too heavy-going throughout.

What I am trying to write is a basically theoretical book which will be of interest to a somewhat mixed audience. By making more concessions to any one type of reader, I might have reduced the attraction to readers of other types. I hope, though, that having frankly admitted this difficulty I can lodge a plea for patient understanding. In return, I may be able to offer some food for thought. The issues raised do need to be pondered by different types of mind, it seems to me, so that the areas of mental difference will eventually diminish. In such a process, we all may end up learning something.

One point perhaps worth stressing, for instance, is that an account of literary pragmatics is not necessarily a simple borrowing of ideas already current in general pragmatics. Pragmatic theory itself deserves to be kept under constant review, and can itself be developed with the help of ideas from literary scholarship, and through a study of literary examples. Much light is shed, for one thing, by literary-formalist and literary-structuralist insights into the implied writers and readers of, say, novels and poems. Any kind of linguistic interchange at all depends on textually constructed communicative personae which work in exactly the same way. And to take an even broader insight, literary phenomena clearly highlight the need for a general communicative theory that is historical without being historicist (in the deterministic sense).

By beginning with social tensions within the literary culture of the present, I may actually be able to suggest that historical considerations are not confined to what we think of as the past. That a historical pragmatics will often be dealing with communication as it took place during some earlier period or periods goes without saying. In addition, though, a historical pragmatics is a pragmatics which recognizes an unfolding historical dimension inherent to every act of communication *per se*. Once again, the binary terminologies of sender/receiver and so on can all too easily prioritize the situationality of the initiator, sometimes even to the extent of suggesting that the other communicant's situationality is somehow assimilated to it, and from the very outset. In point of fact, the current context of receiving is always different from the context of sending, quite regardless of whether the separating distance be one of whole centuries and wide oceans, or of only the very slightest shades of collocated awareness. The inevitable contextual disparity, moreover, has crucial implications for the way the current receiving really turns out in practice, and is also part of the reason for communicating in the first place. Often, differences of situationality are something human beings like to explore. Sometimes, they may positively *need* to explore them. It is only as the communicative act proceeds that the context of receiving may to a greater or lesser extent change, and if there happens to be a feedback channel, changes may also be registered to the context of sending as well. When completed, the negotiation taking place will have been a historical process by which the mental distance between the two contexts has perhaps been shortened.

As for the drawbacks of deterministic historicism, the issues are bound to become especially sharp in a discussion of literary phenomena, because for three or four decades now many literary theoreticians have been advocating philosophical alternatives to liberal humanism. Clearly, a liberal humanist pragmatics might almost be a contradiction in terms. Liberal humanists have sometimes come very close to suggesting that human individuals are too autonomous to be influenced by situationality at all. A historical yet non-historicist pragmatics, by contrast, will stop well short of this, but it will also qualify those recent kinds of literary theory in which the element of sociocultural determinism has been very strong.

A historical yet non-historicist pragmatics will indeed be an elastic and dynamic kind of pragmatics, not readily lending itself to formulation as a scientistic system. It will view human beings as profoundly affected by their different situationalities, yet as having the psychological endowments necessary to negotiate such differences through communication, even to the point at which situationality itself may be modified. A key concept here will be that of a certain *co-adaptability* between sociocultural siting and the human potential for a degree of imaginative independence. What liberal humanist literary critics used to call the imaginative creativity of literary authors is actually still observable today. The only, but important riders that need to be added are that authors' creativity has a more complexly social colouring than was apparent to a liberal humanist view, and that it can also alert us to the imaginative projections which take place in any kind of human communication at all.

So much for a historical yet non-historicist approach to pragmatics in general. More specifically literary phenomena will here be treated within this same framework of ideas. Unless I am mistaken, the resulting insights into literature's own typology, hermeneutics, affect and ethics will give just the kind of support that a critic needs in trying to mediate between different positionalities.

Nor is the relevance of such an approach confined to literature written under conditions of postmodernity. A sociohistorical difference is always a sociohistorical difference, irrespective of whether its main axis be synchronic or diachronic. The heterogeneities of several cultures or sub-cultures co-existing in our own present are no more complicated a challenge than are those of the earlier and later phases of a single cultural tradition throughout its history. British readers at the beginning of the third millennium, for instance, may well need a mediating critic to help them get the most out of Chaucer or Donne or T.S. Eliot. It so happens that this historical kind of challenge is the starting point for the other book I am hoping to complete — the one providing extensive demonstrations of mediating criticism in action. But in the present book, too, nearly all my literary examples are drawn from the past. Even though my proposal has a very urgently present occasion, I have wanted to avoid some of the dust and heat of postmodern controversies, in order to suggest that, both for a contemporary literature and for an older literature as well, principles of critical mediation are derivable from a single historical yet non-historicist theory of communicative pragmatics.

1.4. Postmodernity: the centrifugal and the centripetal

But to begin with the situation today, people representing different economic interests, classes, ethnic origins, religions, cultures, sub-cultures, gender identities and sexual orientations have become so sharply aware of themselves and of each other that many commentators speak of crisis. When they describe this as one aspect of the postmodern condition, the main meaning of "postmodern" is not "post-early-twentieth-century-artistic-Modern*ism*", but something more like "post-Enlightenment" and "post-imperialist". What they detect is a widespread scepticism as to grand narratives of scientific explanation and political teleology, and they are especially concerned with the political scepticism, which they say involves far-reaching problems of identity and legitimation.[1]

This type of analysis is already familiar, and fairly widely accepted. That very powerful centrifugal forces are leading to political, social and cultural fragmentation has become something of a commonplace. Judging by the jeremiads of some and the jubilation of others, any sense of a common human nature has now been seriously destabilized, and traditional power structures must be breaking down or getting more complicated.

Centrifugal phenomena are now a main stimulus to Western liberal philosophers, who tend to endorse the more jubilant response to them, speaking in Heraclitean or Blakean terms of the energies which can flow from a conflict of powerful opposites. Conflict, says Stuart Hampshire (1992 [1989]), makes for life and liveliness, both within the individual soul and within societies; it is quite frankly the normal and most healthy condition of human life. Hampshire's only proviso is that the hostilities must be controlled by rational justice.

This last point is well taken. After all, the many different kinds of people cohabit just the one planet, and often just some very tiny corner of it, roughly half the world's population now living in urban areas. As they all begin to insist on their own right to self-realization, the risk of friction, bigotry, injustice and violence is only too apparent. The philosophers' goal is accordingly to facilitate a politics of recognition, which would lay down clear guidelines as to the arrangements appropriate for each and every cultural grouping within particular jurisdictions (Taylor 1994).

---

1. See, for instance, Jean-François Lyotard, *The Postmodern Condition: A Report on Knowledge* (1984 [French original 1979]), Hal Foster (ed.), *Postmodern Culture* (1985), Steven Connor, *Postmodernist Culture* (1991), David Harvey, *The Condition of Postmodernity: An Inquiry into the Origins of Cultural Change* (1989), Fredric Jameson, *Postmodernism or the Logic of Late Capitalism* (1991), and Jonathan Rutherford (ed.), *Identity: Community, Culture, Difference* (1990). In even the titles of these key works, some slippage will be noted from "postmodern" to "postmodernist". In my own usage, I try to let "postmodernist" refer to developments in the arts which have come about since the time of Modernism, often by way of an extension of Modernist types of innovation and experiment. Needless to say, though, the latest phase of postmodernity can also be partly characterized in terms of postmodernist artistic phenomena, which often carry a very strong challenge to traditional types of legitimacy, sometimes by levelling distinctions between high-brow and low-brow. For comments on this, see Chapter 6 below.

It is a project which severely tests the liberal mind-set. For what can a politics of recognition actually entail? Central to liberalism is the Kantian ideal of a dignity which is to be respected in every single human being, quite irrespective of who he or she happens be (Kant 1998 [1785]). So Ronald Dworkin (1978) describes a liberal society as one which guarantees procedures for dealing fairly with all sorts and conditions of people, with no questions asked about their ideology and politics. In such a "difference-blind" society, any collective aspiration to some particular ideal of the good life would be fundamentally out of place. Rather, citizens would be free to cherish their own life-ideals, and as much as possible that freedom would be safeguarded by a scrupulous procedural impartiality on the part of the society's institutions. Charles Taylor (1994), on the other hand, though profoundly concerned for each individual's human dignity, thinks that the egalitarian principle may sometimes have to give way to the positive discrimination of those kinds of difference which have traditionally been downtrodden, or which may otherwise run the risk of extinction. For example, he takes no exception to a Quebec law which stipulates that francophones and immigrants may not send their children to English-language schools. He sees here a justification for granting a higher degree of recognition to the collective aim of preserving a French-language culture than to the individual freedom of Canada's inhabitants in general. For K. Anthony Appiah, by contrast, recognition on Taylor's terms comes embarrassingly close to compulsion. "[T]he desire of some Quebecois to require people who are 'ethnically' francophone to teach their children in French steps over a boundary", the boundary between public and private. Speaking from his own feelings as a gay, black male in the United States, Appiah similarly questions the identity which seems to be politically scripted for people such as himself. "If I had to choose between the world of the closet and the world of gay liberation, or between the world of *Uncle Tom's Cabin* and Black Power, I would, of course, choose in each case the latter. But I would like not to have to choose" (Appiah 1994: 163). In the best of imaginable worlds, he would be able to think of the sexual body and skin colour as belonging to the self's personal dimension. In practice, a coercive narrowing of the scope for human identity has all too often resulted from the very attempt to guarantee a common human dignity. The egalitarian politics of Rousseau, for instance, presupposed both an absence of differentiated social roles and a very strict common purpose; everyone would simply submit to the general will. Hence arose the standardizing Terror of the Jacobins, to which there have since been parallels in the totalitarian regimes of the twentieth century (Taylor 1994: 44–51).

If Appiah is beginning to find a postmodern politics of difference too intrusive, other commentators go still further, and see the entire phenomenon of postmodern disintegration as, precisely, a phenomenon: a good bit more apparent than real. Some our time's most powerful intellects are seeking to rehabilitate ideas of a commonality of human concerns which can lead to rational and progressive forms of co-existence, and without encroaching on the rights of individuals. For Habermas (1994), the choice between a procedurally difference-blind egalitarianism and the collective support of differentiated underprivilege is actually misconceived. In a democracy, he argues, we are the authors of our own laws, and those laws are always to be interpreted in the particular circumstances which apply in our society, and in particular cases. In effect, this means that we can have a common *political* culture which will be one of tolerance towards cultural differences on *other* levels.

Certainly, much of the way we live our lives presupposes that Enlightenment buzz-words such as expertise, responsibility, and cooperation still denote genuinely existing potencies for good. This is a recurrent theme in the writings of Raymond Tallis (1995, 1997), who among other things points to the justifiable confidence with which most people in the West submit to a hospitalization. In the same way, institutions such as law courts, ombudsmen, boards of arbitration, the International Court of Justice, and the United Nations all work on the assumption that, when differences between one individual or grouping and another become problematic, a just resolution can be negotiated. Peace Studies have long since become a major area of research,[2] and in some countries are already well established within secondary and even primary education as well.[3] And every once in a while, the lessons to be learnt are illustrated by our own time's history. After a careful process of discussion, as of Good Friday 1998 there at last seems to be a chance of new arrangements for Northern Ireland.

---

2. Peace Studies and Peace Research are partly a product of the Cold War. Often classified under International Relations, they were quick to develop in certain neutral countries (cf. Rytövuori-Apunen 1990), but their relevance was clearly recognized elsewhere as well (cf. *UNESCO* 1991; Boasson 1991). Recent contributions include: Otunnu and Doyle 1998; Pupesinghe 1998; Cortright 1997, and Doyle 1997.

3. See Hine and Parry 1989. As an example of a textbook, see Smoker, Davies and Munske 1990. For educational developments in a neutral country, see Pulkkinen1989. For the American tradition, see Stomfay-Stitz 1993.

Centripetal forces, in other words, have not exactly been neutralized. On the contrary, and to stay for a moment with Northern Ireland, although a major effect of the new order there would be to make that part of the world more centrifugally Irish, another of the new ideas would involve a forum — a so-called British-Irish Council — for the discussion of issues relating to the entire British archipelago as a larger sphere within Europe. This is characteristic of a broader trend. Knowledge, praxis and values are in several important areas tending to be globalized. If economic, informational and environmental developments are anything to go by, human beings are now linked together on a scale that is quite unprecedented.

If possible, the centrifugal and the centripetal should presumably be in balance. This is certainly the view of Ian Clark, who offers a fascinating assessment of twentieth century relationships between centrifugal domestic policy and centripetal foreign policy. Broadly speaking, he distinguishes four main phases: a pre-First-World-War phase of increasing internationalization; an inter-war phase of mutually destructive national projects; a post-Second-World-War phase of balance between the global order and the domestic welfare state; and a post-Cold-War phase of renewed internationalism, which is now increasing the pressure on domestic diversity. Looking into the future, his conclusion is emphatic:

> Precisely how the balance between globalization and fragmentation will be adjusted depends on the new role that states are able to form for themselves, and how successfully they manage to mediate between increasingly potent international pressures and the heightened levels of domestic discontent that will inevitably be brought in their wake.
> (Clark 1997: 202)

1.5. Positive mediation

A key word in Clark's prediction is "mediate". What hangs upon it is nothing less than the future peace and prosperity of the human race. The word's use in this kind of connection is not uncommon, and Clark's own work suggests the reason for it. If, in a particular society or in the world as a whole, mediation between the centrifugal and the centripetal were to be successful, human diversification would be energizing and constructive, and dialogue across perceived lines of difference would be illuminating and non-coercive. Contrary to the recommendations of Machiavelli, Hobbes and Rousseau, there would be no ironing out of difference in the name of stability or consensus, since, as Heraclitus and Stuart Hampshire both suggest, such a policy would be stultifying, dangerously repressive, and in the long run quite untenable. Hampshire, for his part, pins his hopes on "a recognisable basic level of common decency", which can feed into "a minimum procedural justice". On such a view, "evil, in the form of the drive to domination, consists in the uncompensated violation of this basic justice". When arbitration is necessary between conflicting moral claims and competing conceptions of the good, the minimum procedural justice should play "the role of the scales, while considerations derived from different conceptions of the good can be seen as the weights that have to be assessed" (Hampshire 1992 [1989]: 186).

Perhaps it is not too much to hope that widely various groupings of people will increasingly agree to weigh up conflicting considerations and, when necessary, settle for what Habermas (1993) calls "reasonable disagreement". But if this does happen, the type of mediation involved will have to be a good deal more positive than that still often discussed within Peace Studies, for instance. Ever since the early eighteenth century, mediation has been regarded as a special branch of diplomacy by which prestige accrues to mediating powers themselves. But it has not been thought of as an undertaking calling for much creativity and foresight. Its perceived scope has rather lain in the sorting out of conflicts already well under way, as Kalevi J. Holsti so bluntly notes: "there are no cases on record where formal mediation actually prevented a war" (Holsti 1991: 112). Given that the Cold War still belongs to the fairly recent past, there is a continuing preoccupation with *realpolitik*, so that terms like "positive diplomacy" refer mainly to the routine proffer of incentives, sops and threats (cf. Marshall 1997).

That this could indeed change is suggested by an increasing number of studies of the role which culture can play, not only in causing obstacles to agreement, but in offering unexpected opportunities for conflict resolution (e.g. Faure and Rubin 1993). Encouragingly enough, such more seriously hermeneutic mediation requires only the straightforward use of our ordinary human capacities, for our minds are actually capable of considerable flexibility. Although we seldom think about it, many different things can be going on in our heads at once. Some single emotion or attitude or state of affairs need never monopolize our psychic energy. For this, the best evidence is introspective: once we begin to scrutinize our own feelings and ideas, we soon notice a certain many-sidedness, not to say conflict. But from talking to other people we can deduce that they experience the same thing, and it has been much written about as well, especially by literary writers. Think only of King Lear's vacillation between extremes of wrath and self-abasement in face of Goneril and Regan. Support can also be drawn from biological and anthropological considerations. That the responses of human beings to each other, or to events and environment, can be so hesitant and complicated must help to explain our evolutionary success. Our species as a whole, never having set its heart on just some single future, can channel its energies according to circumstance, turning each and every situation to advantage. As individuals, too, we can often afford to "wait and see". We "keep our options open", "keep an open mind", "reserve judgement", or "look before we leap". The very currency of such idioms tends to corroborate our ready adaptability, a disposition which becomes problematic only if we crave for certainty — like King Lear — or feel under some obligation to choose, once and for all, between equally feasible courses of action. Otherwise, by being in more than one state of mind at a time we recognize that our impressions may be complex and slow to develop. As we wait, we can enjoy a kind of disinterestedness which stops us from becoming unsociably prickly, and which may have been an aspect of what Keats referred to as negative capability: that capability "of being in uncertainties, Mysteries, doubts, without any irritable reaching after fact and reason" (Keats 1954 [1817]: 53). True, there are situations in which by coolly refusing to decide or judge we could be letting other people down. Sometimes such epicureanism would hardly serve our own best interests either. But if negative capability should not be allowed to sap the readiness for swift and responsible action, the fact remains that when, even for quite unselfish or urgently practical reasons, we make our minds up, not only do certain possibilities get chosen, but certain others get rejected as well. As for the habit of forming opinions gratuitously, and the posture of always, immediately and emphatically knowing exactly what we mean and what we want, this is perhaps a symptom of spiritual insecurity.

It is when human beings do see, as we put it, different sides to an issue that a process of positive mediation can take place. When our thinking is in this mode, we look at a situation, an experience, an activity, both as seen by an observer from the outside, and as it is likely to seem to a person directly implicated on the inside. We deliberately weigh against each other the lifeworlds of different evaluations, frames of mind, styles of discussion. This is not a matter of irresponsible free-play. Nor is it an anaemic, lowest-common-denominator affair — a mere syncretic sinking of differences. We can still be critical, can still have our own opinion, and can even end up making a strong commitment on something. At the same time, our viewpoint certainly can move closer to somebody else's, and any strong commitment will bespeak, not a strident haste or a lazy stock response, but a solid grounding in relevant facts and considerations.

In saying "we" here, my appeal is once more to the very strongest kind of evidence, both for the human predisposition to mediation, and for mediation's beneficial effects: a direct appeal to introspection. Whether quite spontaneously, or whether on the prompting of some other person acting as a go-between, we have surely all known what it is to see things in more than one way at a time; have felt the satisfaction of improved understanding; have noticed that relationships can also be improved, even when complete agreement remains impossible; and have ourselves undergone a change of perceptions, attitudes and feelings. Clearly, my argument could also rely more heavily on third-person evidence, which would perhaps convey an impression of greater scientific objectivity. But if, as I suppose, most people will immediately know what I am talking about, this would be a waste of time. And after all, how should we recognize the significance of such objective evidence unless by introspection?

Once brought into focus, the process I have in mind can be thought of as a careful negotiation of differences, a trying on for spiritual size, a testing, a probing, a search for justice or a *modus vivendi*. Applied in particular situations, this kind of mediation is positive, in the sense that it is self-conscious, deliberately fair-minded, and purposefully future-oriented. Though not assuming the possibility or desirability of some all-embracing consensus, it nevertheless seeks to improve the chances of reasonable discussion, peace, and fairness. In a wholly constructive way, it builds on our adaptability, on our capacity for entering into widely different sets of circumstances without becoming inoperational, and, above all, on our ability to do so through an act of imagination — through what Isaiah Berlin once called "the force of imaginative insight" (Berlin 1997: 9).

As a small example of positive mediation in action, let me try to mediate some of Berlin's own phrasing. Even the title of his collection of essays, *The Proper Study of Mankind*,[4] could conceivably alienate some readers today,

---

4. It could be that the book's title was suggested by its editors, Henry Hardy and Roger Hausheer. Even so, it is in keeping with Berlin's own mind-style.

and so could the passage I have chosen as one of my epigraphs, with its mention of "values, ends of life, by the realisation of which men could be fulfilled". This manner of expression is now often seen as politically incorrect, in its alleged implication that men come closer than women to some ideal of human perfection. A more appropriate choice of words, it might be felt, would be "humankind" instead of "mankind", and "human beings" or just "people" instead of "men".

I myself, born in England in 1944, persisted in the same usage as Berlin well into the 1980s, and so did most of my contemporaries, female as well as male. As far as I am aware, I intended no sexist implication, and had no desire to cause offence. Then in 1988, a (male) editor who had commissioned an article from me pointed out that offence might indeed be taken, since which time I have gone in for different wording. Recognizing that the relationship between the two halves of the linguistic sign, the signified and the signifier, is arbitrary and conventional, I also know that meaning conventions can change in step with perceptions generally, and that if a thing cannot be said in one way then it can always be said in some other. On a cynical view of my overhauled phraseology, I have had nothing to lose. If anything, the risk would have been of losing some of my own listeners or readers by not accommodating. Seen more generously, I have responded to other people's sensitivities, and have merely accepted what, in the late twentieth century, were the linguistic consequences of my own political views. But either way, between myself and Isaiah Berlin there is a significant difference: until his recent death, Berlin had lived in England since 1921.

Rather than expecting such an old dog to learn new tricks, it makes better sense to take the full measure of an already impressive repertoire. What some less experienced readers may now be in danger of missing is his title's appeal to Pope, and to Pope's way of using the word "Mankind". Confronted with it in the passage from *The Rape of the Lock*,

> This Nymph, to the Destruction of Mankind,
> Nourished two Locks, which graceful hung behind
> In equal Curls ...,
> (Pope 1963 [1714]: 145)

young readers may at first even wonder which syllable to stress. Such hesitation can perhaps be retrospectively dispelled by the rhyme with the iambic "behind". A further consideration is that Pope, if he is playfully suggesting that Belinda's charms threaten more havoc to men than to women, could also

— though we shall never be sure! — be hinting at a latent sexism in the ostensibly neutral standard usage, a sexism which will of course look rather foolish when "Fair tresses Man's Imperial Race insnare" (*ibid.*). This irony at his own sex's expense would work most subtly by paying the standard usage a show of deference. The joke yielded by a trochaic pronunciation of "Mankind" would be a cheaper one, whereas an iambic pronunciation will still leave the males of the species with a dignity that can be eroded a little more slowly and enjoyably. Certainly that dignity is something with which Pope himself identifies only in describing its perennial collapse: "And Beauty draws *us* with a single Hair" (*ibid., my italics*). As for his injunction in *An Essay on Man*,

> Know then thyself, presume not God to scan,
> The proper study of Mankind is Man,
> (Pope 1963 [1733–1734]: 516)

this is even further away from what is now called male chauvinism, being more or less the most unmarked kind of usage possible. For the moment, the writing suggests neither patriarchal claims nor even the hint of a laconic challenge to such. The intention is nothing more and nothing less than to warn against vain and arrogant forms of speculative scholarship, in a spirit of benevolent concern for the entire race.

This was very much Berlin's wavelength, too, and his particular achievement was as one of the great champions of civil liberties. "The Pursuit of the Ideal", the essay from which my epigraph is taken, itself questions the assumption that only some single model of the human is valid. And although linguistic conventions certainly can facilitate the hegemonic tendency which political correctness seeks to nullify, Berlin at one and the same time adapted to the usage which was standard when he acquired his own English, and adapted *it* to his own liberatory purpose. What his essay gives us a glimpse of is actually a co-adaptation, between a social convention that may nowadays seem outmoded, and a personal trajectory that was always boldly individual. His writing does represent a particular situationality, but also tends to modify it. He does refer to the human race as "mankind", but in a way which throws in question any power structure for which that word may serve as ideological cement. As Aristotle might have put it, Berlin's continued use of the term actually makes him a skilful rhetorician, instinctively or deliberately meeting his audience half-way, and thereby improving his chances of altering their mind-set. Such co-adaptivity also recalls K. Anthony Appiah's distinction between the scripts for identity which are available to us publicly and our own private sense of self. A public script and a private self can be in a state of creative tension through which neither of them ultimately remains unchanged.

In Berlin's case, mediation need not be heavily laboured. Not even the readers most likely to object to his phrasing will be wilfully unjust. Like everybody else, they will be endowed with the empathetic capability of which he himself speaks, and can unproblematically apply it in their understanding of his idiom and argument.

No matter who the writer being mediated, such understanding is the more likely in that writers and readers ultimately also share our common human condition: we are born; we grow up; we become members of larger groupings and have relationships; we think that some things are more important than others; we have feelings; and we die. Here one really can say "we": these basics apply to everybody. To claim this is not to suggest that there is an unchanging human heart, that one set of value judgements and emotions is universal, that birth and relationships and death mean the same for everybody, that people are always and everywhere of a single pattern, or that they ought to be. The human basics cannot even be thought of except in some particular cultural version of them. Yet they do serve as a kind of meeting-point, and their culturally different manifestations can be of urgently personal interest to all and sundry. Every single human being has life, and therefore a potential interest in how it could be otherwise perceived, experienced, organized. Our curiosity about how the other half lives is only natural.

Together with the human capacity for imaginative self-projection into manifold mind-sets and scenarios, this sameness-that-is-difference of the human condition is precisely what underwrites our aptitude for interpersonal communication. For what is communication, if not a heuristic going-out from the self and its most immediate here-and-now? Certainly in a process of positive mediation, such dialogic versatility is at its most actively beneficial. Coming to terms with those who are not ourself, we gain a clearer idea of where we stand in the world, and are able to adjust accordingly. Sometimes we may even allow the existence and disposition of those who are "other" to change us in some way. Without waiving our own autonomy, without blandly accepting anything and everything, still agreeing to disagree when necessary, we nevertheless become more conscious about situationalities, developing, in particular, a strong sense of ourselves as seen from the outside, as *somebody else's* other.

1.6. Mediation and the discussion of literature

As much as in any other field of discussion, this turn of mind is needed in literary criticism, a genre of writing whose political dimension has in recent times been embittered and embattled. The immediate background to my present project is in the so-called culture wars besetting university literature departments during the era of new historicism, cultural materialism, feminist criticism, gay and lesbian criticism, ethnic criticism, and postcolonial criticism. If, as sometimes seems to be a risk, these current approaches involve reifying and judgemental distinctions between different groups or communities, then the "academic" culture wars must be aggravating the postmodern frictions within society at large. Some of the young or (by now) youngish exponents of such approaches do certainly indulge in what Edward Said (1993: 96) has called a rhetoric of blame, within which Habermas's idea of reasonable disagreement, let alone ideas of reconciliation and constructive compromise, have little breathing-space. Just as constricting is the response evoked by the rhetoric of blame from some more senior scholars, whose complaints against what one of them, Harold Bloom (1995: 31), sees as a whole new "School of Resentment" are hardly unresentful.

For the purposes of positive mediation between the different situationalities, critics will need to cultivate a distinctive tone. Although their alertness to difference will be very sharp, and while never for a moment sacrificing the highest standards of judgement, they will basically not be concerned to censure that which is other, but to improve understanding, so that standards of judgement will nevertheless be among the first topics for reasonable negotiation and, if necessary, for no less reasonable disagreement. As an exercise of critical intelligence, positive mediation is in any case fifty-percent self-critical, in that the self and the other are brought into full relationship. So mediating critics will be under no compulsion to say the last word, always preferring to let dialogue continue. This they will do in a spirit of good faith, and in the hope that it will eventually release new potentialities for self and other alike. Here their fundamental assumption will be Heraclitean: that a monomorphic stasis is not life.

Perhaps the best remedy for the culture wars is encapsulated in Gerald Graff's slogan, "Teach the conflicts!" (Graff 1992) And since nobody can view society or literature from some Archimedean point of non-involvement, critics could well make a virtue of necessity, by bringing into play the ambiguities already inherent in their own and every reader's personal formation. As Appiah's thoughtful introspection begins to hint, the postmodern tensions can be much more intimately problematic than we may publicly acknowledge. Any attraction we perhaps feel towards some recognizably hard and fast identity is likely to be strongly matched by a sense of ourselves as not only communal beings but individuals, or communal beings who belong to more than one community at once, or to a community that is itself many-faceted. Appiah, it will be remembered, describes himself as male, black, homosexual, and American. He is also, we might add, an intellectual.

Edward Said, who explicitly describes his own task as partly one of mediation (Said 1993: xxvi, xxxi), draws on his dual heritage as a Western-educated Arab. But mediators can also start from ambiguities apparently less extreme. Such inner dialogicality, of which the human mind is so eminently capable, is the mediating critic's main resource. It undercuts any sense of the self as either completely autonomous or culturally monomorphic, and is also the mind-style which the critic will seek to encourage in other readers as well. This will not be a matter of obliterating sociocultural differences, for these are both inevitable and potentially fruitful. The point is rather to prevent them from becoming overdramatized. Communication, understanding, and reasonable disagreement will be taken as real possibilities, and in practice there may even come to pass a greater or lesser amount of agreement or reciprocal influence.

In the same spirit, those who teach literature in schools and universities could well join forces with teachers of other subjects. By some means or other, public education must presumably seek to promote that "recognisable basic level of common decency" of which Hampshire speaks, and positive mediation could clearly have a central role here. If the banes of division are to become the blessings of diversity, then the centripetal and the centrifugal will have to be kept in reasonable balance. Especially dangerous now would be an education based on a nineteenth-century-style liberal humanism. As Hampshire and Berlin both warn, this, with concomitant ideals of harmony and consensus, might all too readily suggest that human identity is something rigidly unambiguous, to which all human beings should conform. No less dangerous would be an education drawing on the social determinism of some late-twentieth-century schools of thought, which fail to recognize that widely various groupings or communities can have qualities and interests in common, and can at the very least converse with each other.

On the one hand, sociocultural difference is a historical fact with very real consequences for all forms of human interaction. On the other hand, human beings have qualities and powers of mind which can prevent difference from becoming a *barrier* to interaction. As they successfully negotiate it, they will be revealing their readiness for co-adaptations between the mind-set of their own situationality, and perceptions or valuations falling well beyond its normal scope.

1.7. Wanted — an appropriate literary pragmatics

Between the liberal humanist Scylla and the determinist Charybdis, mediating literary critics must try to hold a firm course. Naturally they have their own intelligence, good judgement and magnanimity to fall back on. And they can often get help from scholars with a historical orientation. But historians of literature are sometimes historical purists, concerned mainly to insist on how a text would have been read in the there-and-then, and perhaps even a little unsympathetic to the thought-world of readers approaching it in the here-and-now. So critics also need, especially amid the tempests of postmodernity, a theory to steer by, and one which, while recognising the importance of context of writing, caters for the manifold contexts of current reading as well.

But where is such a theory to be found? In the earlier twentieth century, poetics was developed under historical circumstances quite unlike those of postmodernity, by scholars mostly desiring or expecting no such radically changed future, and sometimes rather indifferent to the past as well. Although much of their work remains permanently valid, they were not even trying to facilitate the negotiation of different situationalities, even though some sensitive criticism and learned literary history has in practice always performed that function. As for theoreticians of more recent times, some of them have been very concerned with situational difference indeed, but still without suggesting openings for its mediation.

Quite apart from the lack of an off-the-peg theory, there is perhaps another problem. Critics contemplating a mediating role within a situation of potentially dangerous multiculturalism may simply get cold feet. Bringing different kinds of people into contact is not the most obvious way of preventing them from doing each other harm. It may well seem that criticism has a more valuable role to perform as a kind of *cordon sanitaire*. Any such anxiety is certainly something which an appropriate theory will have to ease.

As a response to this entire complex of difficulties, a historical yet non-historicist theory of literary pragmatics should, I think, be adequate. It is very much a theory of communication, which, while facing up to the facts of situationality, does not embrace a rigid sociocultural determinism, but can envisage just the kind of individual and social changes necessary to rapprochement. The appropriate balance between its historical and non-historicist aspects will be a major theme in Chapter 4, my central chapter, where a slight difficulty of presentation arises because even non-literary communication is sometimes studied in a way that is either rather unhistorical or rather too historicist. What I shall have to hint, therefore, is the desirability, not only of a historical yet non-historicist pragmatics of literature, but of a similarly oriented general pragmatics as well, with which the literary pragmatics would be continuous. Fortunately for me, to describe the most important pragmatic factors that are common to communication of all kinds takes little technical finesse, since they are precisely the basic matters of situationality and psychological disposition. If they have not always been mentioned earlier, this may be partly because they are so obvious.

Many previous interdisciplinary discussions of literature as a use of language took a different tack, tending to see it essentialistically, as a use that was distinctly special and even rather unreal. This allowed a great many important discoveries to be made about literary textuality. But it did involve a rarefyingly a-historical and de-personalized view of literary authors and their readers. The account of literature to be offered here, by contrast, is non-essentialist, and views both writing and reading as at once historically positioned, voluntaristic and interpersonal. So when Chapter 5 deals with literature's typological, hermeneutic, affective and ethical dimensions, it does not speak in terms of exclusive properties, and will perhaps help mediating critics to make connections between their own work and constructive social commentary of other kinds.

The difficulties faced by mediating critics at present should become clearer from Chapters 2 and 3. Many earlier critics and literary theoreticians have had little call to address what, in the era of postmodernity, has become a central perception: that the writing, transmission and reading of literary texts really are human deeds, with a fully interpersonal valency. On the contrary, by the late nineteenth century the crass reductiveness of some types of historical and biographical criticism had provoked an understandable formalist reaction.

From the time of the Aesthetes and Symbolists onwards, there were theories of literature as representing an aesthetic autonomy that was basically impersonal and a-historical. This strand of thought, still central for Russian Formalism and Anglo-American literary Modernism,[5] was merely one instance of a de-historicizing and de-humanizing paradigm which was to dominate the humanities as a whole for well over half a century. Other prime examples were logical atomism and logical positivism in philosophy, and behaviourism in psychology and linguistics. As we shall see, then, linguists had reasons of their own for not questioning the literary formalists' assumptions about language. Behaviouristic linguistics and literary formalism could actually strike an alliance, in the shape of the rarefying "lang.-lit." interdisciplinarity just mentioned. Even the attempts to develop a speech act theory of literature, and even the earliest discussions of literary pragmatics, were so clearly marked by behaviouristic and formalist restrictions that our experience of reading literature within present-day multicultural societies is something they could never deal with. The author-reader relationship was systematically theorized away, both as a one-to-one matter between individuals, and in its collective implications as well. Marxist, feminist, postcolonial and other postmodern commentators may be tempted to blame the entire paradigm as a pre-emption of sociocultural difference in the interests of hegemonic repression. Certainly in the literary scholarship to which it gave rise, the very *need* for a mediating criticism was beyond the scope of theoretical formulation.

Nor was the interactive dimension of literature fully re-affirmed by critics' subsequent moves in the direction of cultural structuralism and poststructuralism.[6] Here the challenge to formalist accounts of aesthetic heterocosms was first and foremost a reminder of the roles played in human life by social construction, and by that proliferation of meaning which stems from the very differentiality of linguistic semiosis. Even more directly, the new paradigm was

---

5. Key examples of the latter would be Eliot's essays "Tradition and the Individual Talent"(1919), "*Hamlet*" (1919) and "The Metaphysical Poets" (1921), together with American New Critical works such as Cleanth Brooks's *The Well Wrought Urn: Studies in the Structure of Poetry* (1968 [1947]), René Wellek and Austin Warren's *Theory of Literature* (1963 [1949]), and W.K. Wimsatt's *The Verbal Icon: Studies in the Meaning of Poetry* (1979 [1955]). For specimens of Russian Formalism, see Lemon and Reis 1965.

6. Some of the main representatives of structuralist and poststructuralist thought are Roland Barthes, as for instance in his seminal essay, "The Death of the Author" (1977 [1968]) and Jacques Derrida, whose single most influential book has been *Of Grammatology* (1974 [1967]). Michel Foucault and Julia Kristeva are also very relevant (see bibliography).

a challenge to liberal humanist notions of the virtually autonomous individual self. As such, it remains of prime relevance for mediating critics. Without a historical focus on sociocultural difference, the task of mediation cannot even be conceptualized, and structuralist and poststructuralist assumptions as to the human being's fundamental and ongoing malleability in principle still leave scope for negotiation and rapprochement between the members of different groupings. In some versions, however, the new thinking has been rather restrictive, proposing a more or less total assimilation of the individual to the sociocultural formation, and in this way transferring agency and responsibility from real writers and real readers to pure abstractions. Roland Barthes's suggestive trope of the death of the author has sometimes been taken, perhaps by Barthes himself, a shade too literally, so leading to an obscurantist anthropomorphism, which sees writing and reading as performed by entities going under the name of culture, society, language or text. The fashion had already been anticipated by Claude Lévi-Strauss, in his controversial borrowing of Saussure's ideas from linguistics into cultural anthropology. "We are not ... claiming to show how men think the myths", said Lévi-Strauss (1970 [1964]: 46), "but rather how the myths think themselves out in the men and without men's knowledge". This remark is tellingly scrutinized by Raymond Tallis (1997: 249), whose opposition to such deterministic premises has been passionately sustained (see also Tallis 1988a, 1988b). When they are not resisted, and when emic differentiality is installed as the keystone of sociocultural theory, particular differences of formation come to be reified along lines that are tightly regimental. A person seen as belonging to a certain category of human beings is credited with insufficient autonomy to resist such a positioning, and with too little empathetic insight to approach, understand, and be influenced by a person belonging to some other category. Theoretically inexpressible here, in other words, is the *possibility* of mediating criticism. Instead, critics of this persuasion have sometimes gone in for a kind of principled divisiveness, a paranoiac pessimism, and the rhetoric of blame. Of the three modes, this last is the least harmful, in that the blaming at least springs from a re-awakening sense of writers' and readers' moral accountability. Yet in failing to envisage opportunities for reasonable interchange with otherness, it has reduced the potentialities for an extension of selfhood as well. This is the price to be paid for conceiving of the differentialities now so central to self-awareness and social recognition in terms that are too exclusively adversative.

Such stalemates are fairly common in recent literary criticism. But are there more fruitful responses to the postmodern tensions? Understandably enough, some critics try to defuse the situation by a strategy of political correctness — a *cordon sanitaire*, as I have put it. This too, though, can be a stalemate. As a way of counteracting demeaning stereotypes of various racial, religious, cultural, sexual, medical and age groups, political correctness has been another of the trends preparing the way for positive mediation. The risk is that it can degenerate into little more than a trick for calming people down. When this happens, the politically correct language and sentiments imply no genuine respect for the other person's difference, and not much self-respect either. They become a matter, not of expressing oneself in a way that is conciliatory, but of being conciliatory *without* expressing oneself. The commentator fundamentally refrains from dialogue, declining to enrich the other by giving, or to be enriched by the other's gift. What is thrown in doubt here, then, is not so much a theorizable need for, and a theorizable possibility of mediating criticism, as its *social advisability in practice*.

As for the open dialogue entailed by mediation at its most positive, this is certainly not for the squeamish and pusillanimous. But a historical yet non-historicist literary pragmatics, with its clear echo of the Greek root *pragma*, suggests that there is no wriggling out of it. The writing and reading of literary texts are seen as actions in a strong sense, with an interpersonal valency that cannot be fudged. Chaucer or Dickens or Emily Brontë or Oscar Wilde or W.H. Auden, no less than Isaiah Berlin in his philosophical essays, has presented us with a kind of challenge which invites a fully human response, and which may even affect our attitudes and actions. To try to euphemize it away is neither realistic, nor in the long term interests of either individual readers or their society. If a literary text can change us and our world for the better, we are foolish to prevent it. If it is potentially detrimental, the best course is again to face it head-on, since otherwise we shall be that much less prepared for threats of the same colour from other quarters.

Psychologically, the theory will explain literary interaction by stressing that human beings are very strongly social creatures, but that they also have their flexibility of empathetic imagination, and some degree of moral and temperamental autonomy as well. They are paradoxically *social individuals*, just as they were in the structuralist theory of Saussure before Lévi-Strauss's conversion of it, and just as they are now once again for K. Anthony Appiah and many other thoughtful contributors to present-day cultural and literary theory. In this connection I shall later be returning to Raymond Tallis, and shall also mention Frank Kermode, Ian A. Bell, Cheryl Walker, Emmanuel Levinas, Salman Rushdie, Wole Soyinka, Wilson Harris and Fred D'Aguiar.

On the one hand, there is history. In other words, the sociocultural formations and contexts between which writing and reading take place are crucially important for what goes on. As with communication in general, the situationality of sending and the situationality of current receiving are never completely coterminous. To a greater or lesser extent, the language and thoughtworld of a literary text, no less that those of, say, Berlin's *The Proper Study of Mankind*, may be substantively different from those of some particular current reader, so inviting from the latter a movement of imaginative self-projection. The perceptions and value systems of the two sitings will enter into dialogue, as it were, or even throw each other into question.

Yet on the other hand, there is our human capacity for negotiating history. People whose life experience takes place within different contexts can actually move closer together, the contextual disparity starting to diminish as they make the effort to understand each other. Even if they do not end up in complete agreement, there is a sense in which disagreement itself entails a kind of agreement: they cannot truly dissent from each other's views until they have tried them out in their own imagination. When their empathizing does result in a greater or lesser degree of more permanent personal change, communication will have been a process of self-alienation that results in self-discovery, perhaps ultimately making for co-adaptive changes to their entire milieu.

That changes are possible is something they always already know, through introspection, memory and imagination. Knowing that change can happen, moreover, has positive effects in itself. Consciously or unconsciously, the preparedness for change is what underlies genuine communication of any kind. And literary authors, having, like everybody else, no choice but to avail themselves of existing conventions and common-sense presuppositions, tacitly assume that conventions and common sense, as a result of their own intervention, may be somewhat modified. As much as any other kind of language use, literary texts can be seen as optimistically proposing some sort of shift, in which recipients may subsequently acquiesce. The writing of literature is itself a historical process, involving real agents, and an interpersonality which asks not to be sidestepped. Indeed, readers owe it to themselves to vindicate an author's faith in them.

Then there is a further point. Whereas readers, if they are going to be affected, must obviously be still alive, there is nothing to prevent them from being affected by a writer who is already dead, and by a cultural formation no longer extant. Contrary to certain extremist forms of cultural structuralism and poststructuralism, a literate culture, with all its riches of accurate historical and philological scholarship, is a very different phenomenon from an anonymous oral tradition of the folk. Those of its members who are no longer alive to defend themselves may still have their own personal names very clearly associated with particular deeds, not least with their particular deeds of writing. The authors of written texts are not merely a function constructed in the minds of readers. Nor is reading, as a channel of communication, an ethical anomaly. Authors, alive or dead, must be treated just as fairly as anybody else, not because their written work has ever been their own property, but because their deeds, non-verbal and verbal alike, are to be taken as those of a known human being, and admired or regretted accordingly. This is their fundamental human right, and it is no less absolute than the corresponding right of any reader, remaining just as binding even when their work's human value can be a value only to those who have come after them. Readers' unselfish efforts to be faithful and just to a dead author are nothing less than a way of valorizing life itself, and can only do themselves a favour. This has nothing to do with that narrow historical purism which undervalues a present-day reader's own response. Rather, it is related to that instinctive sense of the relative autonomy of both readers and writers which has always prompted the most helpful literary historians to engage in processes of mediation.

Even ordinary reading itself, similarly, is already a kind of mediation. Or to put this the other way round, and somewhat more accurately, mediating criticism represents ordinary reading at its best: at its most self-aware and principled, the principles being those made explicit by a historical yet non-historicist literary pragmatics.

So what difference can such criticism make? In my last chapter, I try to imagine a future in which mediating criticism becomes an integral part of multicultural social practice. The scenario is the more fascinating in that, as the result of postmodern scepticism towards traditional legitimations, bitter disputes are already taking place about what shall *count* as literature. The very category of literature itself is coming under frontal attack. In the last analysis, this represents the kind of social conflict which will always be with us, and there is every reason to try to keep it optimally manageable and, if possible, fruitful. In this regard, a mediating criticism strengthened by the kind of theory offered here could, I think, be of great service. Especially if it were able to enter into a kind of cultural symbiosis with the actual writing and reading of literature, those activities — even if the term "literature" were to fall out of fashion — might just conceivably become the centrifugal-centripetal phenomena *par excellence*. In that case, communication between a wide range of past and present writers and all the various kinds of living readers would end up channelling difference-in-sameness and sameness-in-difference with a controlled energy, and with a fullness of enthusiastic social endorsement, which would make the philosophers' dream of a basic common decency and minimal procedural justice seem unnecessarily modest. Otherness would be warmly embraced.

Chapter 2

A-Historical De-Humanization

2.1. Modernist literary formalism

My suggestion is, then, that a historical yet non-historicist pragmatics can provide foundations for the now so necessary work of mediating critics. In order to indicate how such a theory fills the gap, I must further explore some of the contrasts with other theoretical trends, both earlier and more recent. In particular, I shall have to be pointing out what previous scholars have *not* done, a line of discussion which is not intended as a negative judgement on their work as a whole. My concern here is with just the one particular angle: the serious consequences of their omissions for mediating criticism. Seen from other points of view, some of those same omissions were the prerequisites for valuable inclusions. "Omissions", indeed, can be a churlish misnomer. As a scholar hoping for positive mediation between different situationalities, the very least I can do is to acknowledge the relativities of scholarship's own sitedness. A mid-twentieth-century approach with little apparent relevance to a literary critic's problems today may well have been a most significant departure from what had gone before, permanently changing the climate of ideas. Even so, any adequate tribute to such achievements would certainly rather blur my present focus. In this and the next chapter, the main purpose is simply to clarify and familiarize the general bearings of my own proposal, before moving on to a more detailed discussion in Chapters 4 and 5.

One of my central claims is that literary writing is an act of communication with an ongoing interpersonal valency. So much so, that continuities arise between the pragmatics of literature and the pragmatics of communication in general. In this respect, however, my theory is perhaps not so new after all. As will emerge from the story to be told by Chapter 3, it can be seen as the latest of a whole series of reactions against one of the twentieth century's most powerful scholarly paradigms: the paradigm, so paradoxical in the humanities, of a-historical de-humanization.

Modernist literary formalism, in particular, was basically concerned with the proposition that literature is special, not least as regards its language, and the way its language is actually used. In the background here was Kant's idea of a distinctively aesthetic realm, more or less unaffected by either scientific truth-values or considerations of ethics. The alleged impersonality of literature was the impersonality of an art-work so conceived. Literary texts did not communicate the observations, ideas, feelings or wishes of authors to readers, but were imaginative creations within which descriptions of things, persons and events were strictly objectified, with little surrounding penumbra of that real world in which authors and readers actually live and become emotionally involved. If anything such did seem to register, it was preferably through the device of an objective correlative, and there was always a chance that any feelings apparently so admitted would be those, not of the work's real author, but of a merely fictional character or persona which the work dramatized. Seen this way, literature was not much implicated in historical human relationships at all, whether between individuals or whole groups.

In the pages of some Marxist and post-Marxist commentators, Modernist critics — the New Critics especially — have therefore figured as straw men, accused of de-historicizing literature as part of an ideological subterfuge. Such blanket disapproval is unfair, and a rehabilitation of the New Critics long overdue. That their lack of historical perspective had ideological ramifications cannot be denied, least of all in the age of our postmodern culture wars. Many literary texts now have such an obvious social thrust that to see them as timeless verbal icons would be none too easy. An interpersonalizing reading style will simply come more naturally, bringing with it a recognition of the individual or collectivity who offered the icon for consideration in the first place. All the same, the New Critical warning against reducing literature to life was a timely response to excessive forms of historical positivism and biographical criticism. Even today, we need ways to talk about literature's sometimes very wonderful beauties of language and form, and our reading styles can still include an element of de-personalization. Indeed, if we were under the impression that de-personalizing readings and interpersonalizing readings were mutually incompatible, this might say less about our genuine experience as readers than about our respect for the tidy pigeon-holes of literary theoreticians, whose grasp of reality is sometimes a good bit less than Johnsonian.[7] Literature, like any other form of communication, whether eyeball-to-eyeball or carried across time and space, can either be objectified as something in which individual involvement seems not directly mandatory, or be subjectified as coming to us here and now from somebody there and then. Although literary texts may seem to invite an objectifying reading insofar as they are not addressed to us personally, they are still not products of an anonymous oral tradition. Like many other written texts, they come to us with the author's personal name on them, and our minds will probably be quite flexible enough to objectify and subjectify simultaneously. The chances are that this is a fairly common kind of literary reading, and in its more objective aspect it will still be able to draw on the New Critics' detailed examination of literary textualities. Here, one might claim, their marginalization of real writers and readers is a decided asset, no less productive than the standard, and basically similar scientific procedure of reducing the number of variables in the interests of heuristic simplicity. Nor was it as if New Critical commentaries became obsolete overnight. New Critical de-personalization paved the way for the de-centering of the self in Anglo-American versions of literary structuralism. Also, the New Critical tradition of de-contextualized readings ensured a swift Americanization of poststructuralist deconstruction.

But even granting all this, the fact remains: according to the New Critics, whatever you might think about the interpersonality of writing in general, works of literature were different. The poem did not mean, but was. Literary works merely dramatized a relationship between a fictionalized speaker and a fictionalized reader, and any discussion of the real author's intention, and of the impact on real readers, involved a "psychologistic fallacy". As far as the genesis of literature went, "we ought to impute the thoughts and attitudes of the poem immediately to the dramatic *speaker*, and if to the author at all, only by an act of biographical inference". The phrasing here is from William Wimsatt's *The Verbal Icon* (1979 [1955]: 5), but the whole argument harks back to T.S. Eliot's dictum, "The more perfect the artist, the more completely separate in him will be the man who suffers and the mind which creates" (Eliot 1951[1919]b:18). Hence Wimsatt's distinction between "passion as objectified or embodied in poems — passion, that is, in its grounds and reasons as a public

---

7. Perhaps Johnson's best known protest against theoretical orthodoxy was that a play which observes the unities of time, place and action does not thereby achieve a more convincing verisimilitude than one which does not (Johnson 1960 [1765]: 38). See Section 4.1 below.

and negotiable 'thing', the poem — and passion, along with intentions and other thoughts, as the psychological source of the poem, its inspiration, or 'cause' in the efficient sense" (Wimsatt 1979 [1955]: 59). As for literature's reception, the formalist dogma was that nothing happened that was of any consequence in the real world. *Antony and Cleopatra* might, in its concretely dramatic presentation of situations of moral choice, "incline ... to a wrong answer" or, in plainer English, be immoral (Wimsatt 1979 [1955]: 98). But the fullness and imaginative power of the work's complex presentation could quite safely be preferred to a simpler and less artistic version along lines more ethically acceptable. Deviant "artistic language", though thought of as a disembodied medium not offering the same kind of truthful meanings as "ordinary language" or "the language of science", could paradoxically also mean a lot more, a "more" which under any other circumstances would be a threat to public morality. Potential assaults on the real reader's virtue, however, were parried by the fictionalized reader, and since the fictionalized reader was merely a textual construct, no harm was done at all. In short, literature revealed without revealing, influenced without influencing. It was non-communicative communication, non-interactive interaction. The New Critics spoke as if the writer and reader personae were hermetic seals between, on the one hand, the real worlds in which authors write and readers read and, on the other hand, a literary heterocosm.

This is the point at which the valuable formalist reaction against positivist and biographical reductionism can now seem overdone. That the exaggeration could seem plausible was partly thanks to a deep-rooted assumption that went right back to Plato. Many of the texts which had acquired literary status are fictional, and there was a strong tendency to think of fiction as "only" fiction: as not "serious" but essentially lying. From Kant and the Romantics onwards, the distinction between fact and fiction, between "science" and "imagination", was drawn even more sharply. For Coleridge, a poem is "that species of composition which is opposed to works of science by proposing for its *immediate* object pleasure, not truth" (Coleridge 1956 [1817]: 172, his italics), and many of those who would have accepted Coleridge's description of this opposition would not have placed as high a value as he upon a poem. Very prudently, too, if we think about it. Even if statements of truth were indeed as relative and conventionalized as American pragmatists, Austinian speech act theorists, Derridean poststructuralists and others have often claimed, the smooth running of human affairs would still require that notions of truth be respected, and that there be some consensus as to the protocols relevant for their formulation and application. In any given situation, we do need to know, at the very least, "what counts" as truth.

For a start, though, the postmodern age may be witnessing a reversion to criteria for literariness that are pre-nineteenth-century and more catholic. Either that, or we are watching the final demise of literature as a category. Certainly essentialistic definitions in terms of special functions, textual features or epistemological properties no longer seem to win acceptance. Nor do they provide the only way of discussing literary form, a type of interest which in the not too distant future could perhaps be rehabilitated, and without the Kantian ramifications. Be that as it may, my final chapter will suggest that a culture or sub-culture's literature consists of all the texts accorded literary status, such texts quite possibly having qualities which, within some other culture, would be re-described as valuable in some quite different way. As for my more immediate point, it is only that fictional texts, in the canons of many different groupings and communities, just happen to be in a majority. This need not mean that fictionality is a literary *sine qua non*.

Nor is fictionality peculiar to literature. Not only is there non-literary storytelling. Fictions can also be at work when story-telling is not apparently involved. In recent times, this point has been stated in a very strong form. When subjected to sceptical or nihilistic poststructuralist analysis, the writings of, say, journalists and historians get described as mere narratives, sharing basic compositional and epistemological characteristics with genres we think of as literary (cf. White 1978). But even in classical antiquity, a distinction was made between truth as humanly understood and any truth that may be actually real. Similarly, truth statements made from different points of observation have long been recognized to vary. Among other things, they can involve a selection, extrapolation, hypothesization and arrangement of details which, whether consciously or not, certainly draw on resources of creative imagination.

Conversely, even the most markedly fictional varieties of literary texts can be making a point about the world. Or rather, since this way of putting it copies the literary formalists' anti-pragmatic personification of texts, the *writer* of literary fiction can have a point to make: something to say about life, about people; something which, all being well, will indeed be transmitted to readers. Although the fiction will not be acceptable as the truth according to current truth-protocols, the kind of truth it lacks is merely episodic or specific truth: the narrated events never really happened. And at the price of episodic or specific truth, the writer may be able to implicate truth of some other kind. For one thing, there is general truth: the fiction may fit an Aristotelian account of literature, conveying the teller's honest sense of the things which most typically happen in life. For another, there is moral truth: in a heightened form, the fiction may convey an honest sense of what kind of behaviour is to be shunned and what to be followed, as Sir Philip Sidney put it (1973 [1595]: 88; cf. Leitch 1983). As for fictions offering exceptional case studies or fantastic alternative realities, the only way they can achieve their effect is by either challenging or strengthening their audience's sense of general and moral truth.

Even during the age of literary Modernism, some thinkers were already trying to develop a pragmatist semiotics which would see art and truth as much more closely linked. John Dewey, Charles Morris, Ernst Cassirer, and Susanne K. Langer all aimed at a philosophical unification of disciplines which would entail, among other things, an unashamedly down-to-earth attitude towards literature (cf. McGrath 1982). Symbolic languages would be grouped together as anthropologically central, even if they were not scientifically truthful in the Kantian sense. Dewey, in words quoted approvingly by Morris, foresaw a time "when it will be universally recognized that the differences between coherent logical schemes and artistic structures in poetry, music and the plastics are technical and special, rather than deep-seated" (Dewey 1931: 120–2, Morris 1971 [1939]: 427). Cassirer (1923–29) described both art and science as symbolic systems. Art, he said, gets at truth intuitively, but not irrationally. And Langer (1953), though retaining Coleridge's distinction between truth and a poem, described art as true to forms of feeling, which express themselves differently from propositional statement. Somewhat more recently, Nelson Goodman has said that science and art are equally truthful, at least if truth is a matter of appropriateness of fit to all the relevant circumstances. Like science, Goodman argues, the arts are "modes of discovery, creation, and enlargement of knowledge in the broad sense of advancement of the understanding". They suggest a way to integrate sense, emotion and intellect (Goodman 1978: 102–3).

The closest literary formalism came to this kind of thinking was perhaps in Jan Mukařovský's descriptively titled *Aesthetic Function, Norm and Value as Social Facts* (1970 [1936]). Mukařovský argued that one and the same physical object could be, not only a work of art, but a piece of communication or an ingredient in, say, a religious rite. But just as for Roman Jakobson, who joined him in the Prague Linguistic Circle and brought an infusion of ideas from Russian Formalism, so for Mukařovský, the aesthetic was still a potentially dominant function, and perhaps even a self-sufficient one. At times, too, Mukařovský perhaps belied his book's title, by seeming to imply that societies do not change, and that works of art do not have to be interpreted. He actually gave the impression that any particular work is inherently aesthetic, or inherently aesthetic and communicative, or inherently aesthetic and communicative and religious, eternally so, and always to exactly the same extent.

Other literary formalists with an interest in language and society have made similar moves. Geoffrey Leech (1983b) does recognize that Dr Johnson's famous letter to Lord Chesterfield had aims over and above that of being a piece of epistolary art: Johnson wanted to protest against the Earl's behaviour, and at the same time to remain civil. But Leech, unlike Tatyana Karpenko (1993), whose theory of literary pragmatics interestingly draws on him, usually reserves his sense of complex and conflicting discoursal goals for texts which are non-literary. In this particular case, Johnson's letter is very obviously just that: a letter, written by a certain individual under certain circumstances, and in order to be read by a certain other individual. It was not supposed to be a piece of published literature in the sense normally understood at the time — Chesterfield's own *Letters to His Son* did not come out until twenty years later —, and even less in any sense recognized by the nineteenth- and early-twentieth-century aesthetics which is still consonant with certain kinds of linguistic and stylistic enquiry. (Cf. Sections 2.2 and 2.3 below.)

Plato, by contrast, might have understood the pragmatist semiotics of Dewey and Goodman, for his attack on poetry was really two-pronged. It was not just a matter of poetry's communicating untruthfully. Poetry told its lies to undesirable effect upon the hearer's morals. This, too, has continued to fuel literary discussion down the ages, and certainly underpinned some expressions of New Critical literary formalism. Sidney had tried to refute the charge by suggesting that the golden world of art has an instructive simplicity; poetry's readers, thanks to its strongly idealizing contrasts between good and evil, can arrive at judgements which are morally sound. Plato might have countered, though, that the poet could well be of *unsound* judgement, in which case the poem's simplifying contrasts might lead some readers astray. Or instead of embodying the poet's faulty moral sense in idealized contrasts which less unwary readers would probably question, the poem might weave an experiential web that was more complex and imaginatively heightened than moral choices in life itself. In short, the poem might be *Antony and Cleopatra*

— assuming for the moment that *Antony and Cleopatra* does "incline ... to the wrong answer" — , which is precisely where the formalist de-contextualization of literature was such a useful ploy. Instead of fearing literature for its complex sophistication, the American New Critics stood Sidney on his head. Complexity was not to be simplified away, but positively cultivated and valued in its own right.

The reasoning here was very different from the psychological and communicative aesthetics of I.A. Richards, William Empson and F.R. Leavis. For these British scholars, literary complexity represented a challenge which was inseparable from a certain amount of pain and resistance on the reader's part. This alternative line of Modernist poetics expected great literature to be somewhat unpleasant and abrasive, mercilessly disturbing fixed and comfortable patterns of response, even if the new psychic organization towards which it urged readers was in the long run beneficial (cf. Trilling 1965). By comparison, the American New Critics might almost be said to have anaesthetized literary experience. For them, its complexity could never be very painful, since its inclination towards wrong answers in moral matters, and thereby any other stimulus it might offer to a change of mind or heart, were so clearly separated off from the real world in which writers write and readers read. The fictionalized writer and reader personae were seen as a kind of insulation.

Viewing such divergences in the light of a communicational theory of literature, we shall have to give the palm to Plato, and to the British Modernist critics who could face unpleasantness. There will be nothing at all to cushion us from the impact of literature on our moral lives except our own powers of judgement, even if the postmodern crisis of legitimacy now makes judgement very difficult. The impact of literature will be at least as direct and at least as great as that of any other discourse, and this will still be true of literature written on the extreme formalist premise of art for art's sake, whose abnegation of morality is itself a moral act. Plato even makes a kind of sense when he says that poetry should be placed under a ban. Although it would be impossible to curb immoral discourse of most other kinds, literature, which is arguably more influential because of its powerful rhetoric and its wide distribution, is at least readily identifiable.

Plato, one might say, is merely self-consistent, whereas the New Critics were perhaps instinctively closer to his insights than immediately appears. No less than the society in which he himself lived, Plato's ideal republic would have left large numbers of people quite blatantly without freedom. The politics of the New Critics, despite their roots in the American south, went nowhere near as far, and an education in their kind of literary formalism still seems much more attractive as a form of public control than censorship could ever be. After all, their account of fictionalized writers and readers still allowed the arts to go on flourishing. Yet their subordination of the ethical to the aesthetic may well have stemmed from a fear that real lines of communication between a literary writer and a reader might have unpredictable and dangerous consequences. By the time their influence was on the wane, the sense that they had knowingly chickened out of a moral responsibility had become fairly widespread, even among commentators such as E.D. Hirsch (1982), who could hardly be described as left-wing. In Hirsch's opinion, what the New Critics made fashionable was a "rarefied aesthetic approach to literature" which "insulated the teaching of literature from the political risk of culture-making".

On a communicational theory, anxieties about pernicious books cannot be shrugged aside, even if opinions may differ about which books are pernicious and in what ways, and even if there is a rather uncomfortable paradox to be faced: that the most pernicious book of all will presumably be a pernicious book bearing the seal of social approval. At the same time, a communicational theory can also pose the question: Need the potential damage actually be done? Even the most pernicious book of all still has to be read before it can have an impact, and everything depends on who does the reading, and how. In a pragmatic theory that is historical without being historicist, readers are seen as capable of a certain independence. They are social beings, but social *individuals*, whose stance *vis à vis* either the familiar or the alien can combine elements of both empathy and criticism. Sometimes they may sharply distance themselves from a writer, or even from their entire society's dominant norms. Not only can prohibition fail to control their thoughts. As Milton put it, a much better idea is to let them face temptations head-on.

> I cannot praise a fugitive and cloistered virtue, unexercised and unbreathed, that never sallies out and sees her adversary, but slinks out of the race, where that immortal garland is to be run for, not without dust and heat. Assuredly we bring not innocence into the world, we bring impurity much rather: that which purifies us is trial, and trial is by what is contrary. That virtue therefore which is but a youngling in the contemplation of evil, and knows not the utmost that vice promises to her followers, and rejects it, is but a blank virtue, not a pure; her whiteness is but an excremental [= superficial] whiteness; Which was the reason why our sage and serious poet Spenser, whom I dare be known to think

a better teacher than Scotus or Aquinas, describing true temperance under the person of Guion, brings him in with his palmer through the cave of Mammon and the bower of earthly bliss, that he might see and know, and yet abstain. (Milton 1925 [1644]: 290)

Let readers discriminate for themselves! Within the educational system and the media, let there be free and informed discussion! — the surest way for a society to valorize personal responsibility. Even if, as structuralist critics might say, choices are always made within a range of available options, choice is always choice, and sometimes the range of options can itself be co-adaptively modified.

So much for truth and morality. But twentieth-century notions of impersonal artistic form have also been underpinned by a less ancient, Symbolist assumption. This, though clearly evident in the work of Siegfried J. Schmidt (1982), for instance, was not always so explicitly spelt out. The basic idea went roughly as follows: Literary activity cannot be truly historical and interpersonal because literary texts are too open to interpretation. Their meaning radiates outwards in too many different directions to have any particular relevance for specific human relationships.

Nowadays pragmatic theory sharply qualifies arguments for hermeneutic scepticism in general. As Derrida and others have concluded from the arbitrariness and instability of the sign's signifier-signified relationship, the process of semiosis can in principle continue indefinitely. In practice, though, it probably never continues without interruption. Whether we are reading literature or simply living our everyday lives, we do not allow uncertainties to slow us down too much. There nearly always comes a point at which we momentarily freeze semiosis in its tracks. Drawing on all our knowledge and powers of contextual inference, for the time being we resolve that things have some particular meaning or meanings, so that we can then move on to the next interpretative challenge, even if it may retroactively change our mind about the present one.

This does not mean that a reader will understand a text in exactly the way its author understood it. A reader always brings to the interpretative process a greater or lesser ignorance of the author's historical life-world, plus types of information and evaluation which, though affecting the text's impact now, originally could have had no bearing at all. Even so, readers are not wholly confined to their own horizon. With the help of historical and philological scholarship, and by using the same inferential processes as they successfully use in life at large, they can try, as Gadamer would say, to merge their own and other horizons, and as a result will often approximate an authorial intention fairly closely. There is actually no way to make sense of a written text except as coming from the person or persons responsible for it, and readers are right to assume, consciously or unconsciously, that they can achieve at least some certainty on this score. Even a text read as a verbal icon is taken as being *offered* in that way.

As will be clear, this is still not an argument for historical purism. The certainty readers arrive at will be their own certainty, varying from reader to reader, and entering into unique reaction with each reader's own world-view. Nor is there any contradiction between the indeterminacy of literary meaning and my present argument's claims for literature's interpersonality. That a literary author's intentions are frequently debated, and that readers can actually go against an author's wishes, does not mean that literary texts form an exception to some general rule of communication. On the contrary, not only graphic texts of all kinds — including wills, constitutions and laws — but also all kinds of spoken texts — everything from famous last words to making a date — are no less open than literary texts to misinterpretation, deliberate or otherwise. Literary pragmatics is seamlessly continuous with general pragmatics.

Where does all this leave us, then? On the one hand, the formalists' tendency to de-historicize and de-humanize literature was not only a matter of strongly held aesthetic belief, but an understandable reaction against an earlier generation of critics' biographical and positivistic excesses. It was also a source of real heuristic power, so that formalist accounts of literary textuality can still greatly enrich our actual reading experience, especially since our mind can work in several ways at once. On the other hand, literary formalism could not possibly address our most urgent needs today, and it involved three lines of argument whose more extremist versions a historical yet non-historicist literary pragmatics will have to modify: the restriction of literature to a fictional universe without authors and readers; the concomitant attempt to undercut its real psychological impact; and the Symbolist point about its indeterminacy of meaning. The main modifications will be: that fictional texts are neither absolutely distinguishable from factual ones, nor capable of telling their stories to themselves; that even some Modernist critics — Richards, Empson, Leavis — recognized literature's affective dimension; and that literature is no more variously interpretable than other types of language use, or than human behaviour in general.

2.2. Structuralist linguistics

If modifications to extremist formalism are still worth suggesting today, sixty years ago they would have been almost unthinkable. For one thing, they would have won little support from the period's linguists. Modernist literary formalism and early-to-mid-twentieth-century structuralist linguistics actually went hand in hand, as part of that de-historicizing and de-personalizing paradigm which was so widespread.

No less than when we look back at New Criticism, in assessing that period's linguistic scholarship we cannot but admire the real achievements, especially when we bear in mind the circumstances under which they came about. The paradigm shift away from nineteenth century comparative philology was really momentous. Inevitably it meant that historical concerns no longer had quite such a high priority. But many issues central to an understanding of how a language actually hangs together at any given moment were focussed for the first time. True, in order to explore them linguists did concentrate on the generalities of *langue* at the expense of *parole*'s variation, individual and social. But there was no other way to go about the task, and any suggestion that Saussurian and Bloomfieldian structuralists positively turned their noses up at real-life communication would simply miss the point. Although a subsequent generation of linguists is now exploring *parole* very energetically, their work can only take place as a filling-in of their predecessors' masterly broad outline, a task in which they rely on technologies for the collection and analysis of authentic language corpora which Saussure and Bloomfield could only have dreamt of.

But once again, significant facts remain. If linguists had not concentrated on *langue*, the Symbolist assumption that literary meaning had a special kind of indeterminacy might have had less force. One point to bear in mind here is that linguists of that period often pieced together their accounts of language on the basis of introspection, sometimes making up their own illustrative examples for themselves. In principle this made good enough sense, since their instincts as informants were obviously at least as good as those of other people. Even the temptation to force the evidence to prove their own pet theories was something they could guard against, both through personal self-criticism, and by submitting their findings to each other as members of a scholarly community. The only real drawback was that this scholarly community was made up of individuals whose own use of language was highly articulate. Even the least tendentious of the examples it countenanced could create the impression that ordinary utterances are so successfully carried out that their meaning is always perfectly clear. In Per Linell's suggestive phrase, linguistics had a kind of "written-language bias" (Linell 1982), a bias towards the fluently perspicuous kind of writing produced by linguists themselves. In point of fact, and as the newer schools of corpus linguistics, conversation analysis, discourse analysis and pragmatics are now making very clear, *parole* is usually much more messy. At any moment, there may be communicative breakdowns or backfirings, so that ordinary everyday conversation could provide countless examples of utterances which leave people no less bemused than did some of the poetry valorized by Symbolist theory.

Still more fundamentally, structuralist linguists did little to challenge the literary formalists' tacit assumption that language does indeed lend itself to a use that is somehow non-personal. Now that literary canons have become so bitterly contested, and literature's interpersonal chemistry perhaps more apparent, the workings of literary texts are seen to be clearly different for different readers. If linguists, then, could shed light on the interpersonal dynamics of language use, their findings might be very useful to literary critics. Yet for much of the twentieth century, most Western linguists seemed to be implying that they either should not, or actually could not help here, which meant that notions of literary impersonality were likely to seem only the more convenient. It was not so much that linguists went along with the poetics of well wrought urns and verbal icons, though many of them had doubtless absorbed this as part of the literary education they were exposed to. It was more a case of their steering clear of interpersonality because they were interested in something else.

In this respect, at least, they took their cue from the previous century's comparative philologians. The *Junggrammatiker* had wanted to trace historical changes in the actual form of languages, and particularly sound changes. In order to do this, they had hypothesized laws which resembled the laws of the hard sciences. Although we are for ever in their debt for an amazing wealth of insights into the way languages have developed over time, they could never have isolated the features they discussed without to some extent de-humanizing linguistic activity. Their arrangement of languages into family trees was perhaps less than truly Darwinian in spirit, since it obscured those social and intellectual capacities which have made *homo sapiens* the creature best fitted to survive in various environments. The linguistic evolution was sometimes figured as ultimately rather like the geological, with animate agency reduced to a minimum.

Similarly, the efforts of twentieth-century linguists to describe language as a structure built up from various orders of small units suggested the forepresence of another, albeit more topical model from the hard sciences: the model of the atom. The similarity with Russell and Wittgenstein's logical atomism is rather striking, and the methodology by which *langue* was to be separated off from *parole* was inevitably rather behaviouristic. Though not necessarily endorsing the behaviourists' view of the human psyche as a mechanism of stimulus and response, linguists were certainly not greatly concerned with questions of intention and semantics. Why people might make a particular utterance under certain circumstances, or what they might mean by it, for a long time went largely by the board. As with New Criticism, then, we can speak of a mode of examination whose impressive findings were achieved by excluding humanity as the most erratic variable. It was not that linguists seriously believed there could be uses of language which were impersonal. Rather, in their preoccupation with formal structure they had placed the whole question of language *use* beyond the pale for discussion.

So with partial exceptions such as J. R. Firth, Western linguists of the early twentieth century did not explore topics such as language function, socio- and idiolect, language and ideology, language and history. Even less did they seek to develop a sociolinguistic poetics. That was rather the concern of Bakhtin, who was somewhat isolated in the Soviet Union as well (cf. Cook 1994). In Western linguistics, the exclusion of interpersonality was sometimes so complete that language was almost thought of as a kind of smoothly efficient machine. As for generative grammar (Chomsky 1957), its rejection of behaviouristic attitudes for a more mentalistic concern with deep structure was a crucial development, but to some extent more apparent than real. Not only did Chomsky's prioritization of "language competence" over "language performance" recapitulate the earlier prioritization of *langue* over *parole*. As Roy Harris puts it, Chomsky simply did not envisage a language "as needing human language-users at all, or a human brain to house it, as long as it has a machine to generate it". Its sentences were seen as serving "no social or communicational purpose of any kind". On the rare occasions when generative grammarians did treat language as a function of language users, the language users were "deprived of their status as human beings" (Harris 1987: 74–5).

If relatively few linguists raised interpersonal issues, moreover, even fewer raised them in connection with writing. Although so many linguists yielded to a written-language bias when making up their illustrative examples, in their actual theorizing they could be decidedly phonocentric, viewing written language as communication of a secondary, and perhaps even unauthentic form. This was eminently compatible with formalist poetics, an affinity which in turn was only one example of the world of learning's far more general marginalization of real language use in particular, and of human experience in general. Symptomatically, in philosophy there was a clear line from the logical atomists' rather chilling dream of an ideal language in one-to-one relation with observable facts to the logical positivists' dismissal of much ordinary communication, and especially of religious and ethical discourse, as loose, imperfect and metaphysically loaded expressions of mere feeling.

2.3. Alliances of literary formalism and linguistic thought

Formalism in literary scholarship and behaviouristic attitudes in linguistic scholarship proved to be long-lived. Much interdisciplinary work on the "lang.-lit." borderline has involved an alliance between the two, so falling full-square within the paradigm of a-historical de-personalization. At times, the restriction of the human variable has almost suggested a scientistic dream of unbending laws and system. Certainly the most important gains have been to our understanding of text-typical, stylistic and narratological regularities. As for the facilitating and strengthening of a mediating criticism, this was never one of the stated goals, and the possible need for such criticism could not have been formulated in the theory.

To begin with text-linguistics, contributions such as Robert de Beaugrande and Wolfgang Dressler's fine introduction to this field were crucial in moving linguistics on beyond the grammar of the single sentence. They brought a new sophistication to our understanding of entire stretches of speech and writing in various modes, literature being very much part of the total picture. One of de Beaugrande and Dressler's opening claims was that literary phenomena were bound up with the whole complex web of social action and interaction, and they drew many of their examples of linguistic processes from dialogue as represented in literary texts. At the same time, their typological aims perhaps made them particularly keen to borrow the literary formalists' Kantian distinction between literature and science. Literature's "world", they said, stands "in a principled *alternativity* relationship to the accepted version of the 'real world'" (de Beaugrande and Dressler 1981: 185–6, their italics). And by literature's world here, they meant nothing more than the intradiegetic world described by some literary texts — some of the fictional ones, that is. In a theory suitable for mediating criticism, by contrast, literature's world will be the world within which literature itself operates, which is the same world as for any other type of text: the real world, in which senders and receivers communicate. Even this way of putting it acquiesces in de Beaugrande and Dressler's "accepted version of the 'real world'", which tends to imply that everybody shares the world-view of some single spatiotemporal and sociocultural siting. In point of fact, the contexts of sending and receiving an utterance, including a literary text, are always, to however small an extent, different, quite possibly in terms of world-view as much as anything else. This is part of the reason why people communicate in the first place. It is also why mediation may be helpful.

As for stylistics, perhaps the strongest tradition has been that personified in Roman Jakobson and descending from the Russian Formalists through the Prague Linguistic Circle. Here the synthesis of a de-personalizing Modernist aesthetics and a synchronically oriented, behaviouristic structuralism has been particularly clear. Something of its emphasis was still to be heard in Geoffrey Leech and Mick Short's work on style in prose (1983), for instance. Seen in a British perspective, Leech and Short's achievement was to bring a new precision to that detailed discussion of the language of literary texts which had begun with Richards, Empson and Leavis, and to do so by means of a linguistic terminology which university students and ordinary readers would not find too intimidating. No less commendably, while pointing out the stylistic possibilities which the English language regularly offers, they seldom fell into the stylistician's trap of assuming that there is a regular one-to-one correlation between a particular stylistic device and a particular effect. They were sensitive, in other words, to the quiddities of individual writers, and to the particularities and totalities of each and every text. At the same time, this crucial effort of fidelity to writer and text is where their aims stopped short. The no less crucial effort of differently situated readers to be faithful to their own corner of the communicative triangle was beyond their sphere of interest. So much so, that they sometimes seemed to make the historically purist assumption that a good reader will read a text exactly and exclusively in the way its writer would have hoped. Given such an undialogical view of reading, their account of literary writers' actual impact was bound to be rather shadowy as well. Richards, Empson and Leavis's powerful sense that literature is "for real", that it can impinge on a reader's psychological, intellectual and moral life and even bring about changes there, was not something Leech and Short needed to develop for their particular purposes. If anything, they actually disagreed with it. Pretty much in key with the American New Critics, they claimed that the "function of literature" is "primarily aesthetic" (Leech and Short: 1983: 138). Treating the fictionalized writer and reader in more or less the same way as Wimsatt had done, they went on to state that a literary message does not "take effect" in the real world because there is a "sincerity gap"(Leech and Short 1983: 261). Like many earlier commentators, from literature's frequent fictionality they apparently drew the conclusion that a literary writer does not have genuine points to make for the consideration of real readers. That literature's "lies" could be very "serious", to use John Searle's adjective (cf. Section 2.4 below), had nothing to do with stylistics as they so helpfully developed it.

Poeticians of narrative, lastly, have drawn on structuralist linguistics for an analogical model. Their aim has been to see all the possibilities for story-telling as a *langue*-like system, of which any particular story will be a *parole*-like instantiation. And as with text linguistics and stylistics, there have been huge pay-offs in terms of descriptive precision and sophistication. Our terminology for the discussion of story elements and narrative architectonics is now very subtle and comprehensive, and scholars such as Seymour Chatman have also helped to clarify similarities and differences between narrative in literature and narrative in film. Yet again as with the other "lang.-lit." approaches, narratology has tended to overlook the real world in which literary intercourse actually takes place. So Robert de Beaugrande's diagrams of narrative transition networks traced nothing more than the "tracks" and "goals" of intradiegetic characters (de Beaugrande 1980: 271). A story's potential extradiegetic action, within relationships between the writer and readers, passed quite without comment. For Chatman (1978), similarly, the term "discourse" had a narrow sense, more or less equivalent to the Russian Formalists' *sjužet*. It was the shape given to an underlying story content, and had nothing at all to do with literature's intersubjective aspects. On the contrary, Chatman described the implied author and implied reader in the usual formalist manner, as conducting an interchange within an aesthetic universe, an interchange which could simply not "seduce" us. As so often with formalist approaches, this seemed to suggest that the story mysteriously had to happen for its own sake. Yet Chatman's account of irony, for instance, could have no psychological reality, unless the implied author and reader were internalized within real readers. What Chatman saw was a line of direct communication running from implied author through narrator and narratee to implied reader, with a line of ironical implicature moving from implied author to implied reader behind the narrator and narratee's backs. In other words, he said nothing at all about where communication really starts or really finishes.

That an author can create implied author and implied reader personae, and even narrator and narratee personae, is not in dispute. Far from it, for literature's construction of such sender and receiver personae is one of the features in which it resembles any other type of communication, by cashing in on the human psyche's heuristic flexibility of empathetic self-projection and self-dramatization. As Schlomith Rimmon-Kenan pointed out, however, Chatman made the formalist mistake of actually animating these textual constructs, as if it were between the constructs themselves that communication took place, an ontological error which Rimmon-Kenan herself, rather surprisingly, mirrored, by retaining a no less animate implied *reader*. She began well enough, by saying that the implied reader is an "it", not a "he" or a "she"; it is a theoretic construct, implied or encoded in the text, representing the integration of data and the interpretative processes "invited" by the text. What this left unclear, though, was how such a disembodied "it" can integrate and interpret in the way she then went on to claim:

> The hermeneutic aspect of reading consists in detecting an enigma (a gap), searching for clues, forming hypotheses, trying to choose among them and (more often than not) constructing one finalized hypothesis.
> (Rimmon-Kenan 1983: 128)

This is how we all really read. Such an "it", if it can be distinguished at all, functions by being internalized as one dimension of real human beings while they read. The implied reader, in other words, represents a role which the real writer has invited them to take upon themselves and try for size. In practice, they can both take it and leave it: for the purposes of communication, they can empathize while at the same time criticizing. The interpretative net result will reflect their degree of fidelity to the author in the context of writing, to their own situationality as readers, and to their own individuality.

This brings us very close to reader-response criticism and reception aesthetics, which as it happens throw an interesting side-light. Again rather surprisingly, they, too, show traces of the formalist-behaviourist affinity. Taken as a whole, these approaches have actually been rather self-contradictory. On the one hand, H.R. Jauss's reception theory did emphasize that reading habits change from one historical phase of culture to another (Jauss 1982), just as Stanley Fish's account of interpretative communities stressed a similar variation between different cultures or sub-cultures on a synchronic plane (Fish 1980). Fish actually opened the way for alliances between reader-response criticism and the cultural materialist, feminist, gay and lesbian, postcolonial, ethnic and cultural studies approaches so typical of postmodern polyvocality. On the other hand, even though Wolfgang Iser (1974) was at pains to emphasize the distinction between the implied reader and any real reader, reader activity as described in Iserian analysis often seemed to be a matter of all readers filling in the gaps in exactly the same way. In other parts of Jauss's work, similarly, there were signs of the puristic philologian's itch to outlaw ignorant misreadings, coupled, apparently, with a formalist's sense of the literary work as somehow immune to historical changes after all. In the third chapter of his *Toward an Aesthetic of Reception*, for instance, Jauss found it difficult to accept Renaissance and Romantic readings of mediaeval genres as part of the ever-unfolding meaning of mediaeval texts. As a follow-up to the same book's reception-theoretical prolegomenon, this was rather puzzling. It was also in strong contrast with another kind of approach to genres, which finds their tendency to break free from their original locus in life much less of a sticking point (cf. Section 5.2 below).

In a way, the contradictions within reader-response scholarship recall an ancient and very powerful Western dichotomy, between a nihilistic assumption that there is no such thing as truth, and a rationalistic assumption that there is a truth which is at once single and knowable. In reader-response scholarship, this stark epistemological dilemma seems to be transposed to the domain of textual interpretation, so that texts would have to have either no determinable meaning at all, or just some single, fixed meaning. The act of reading, one might conclude, is either chaotic or robotic.

A somewhat robotic regularity would be more in tune with the near-scientisms of earlier "lang.-lit." interdisciplinarities, for they did tend to reduce the variables in literary appreciation, overlooking differences both in sociocultural siting, and between individuals whose siting is more or less the same. Not that the only alternative is to see interpretation as chaotically irregular. Later on I shall be putting forward a kind of *tertium quid*, with

American pragmatist epistemology as a suggestive point of comparison, and with Gadamerian hermeneutic theory as an even more direct support. This will lead to a view of interpretation as a matter of irregularity and regularity intermixed, with the particular regularities sometimes predictable from the way people are historically situated. Yet at least by comparison with the older interdisciplinary alliances of literary formalism and behaviouristic linguistics, my more conspicuous emphasis will certainly be the "nihilistic" one on irregularity. This is simply the logical consequence of accepting the interpretative implications of situationality while at the same time rejecting a rigid historicist determinism. No two readers will ever read in exactly the same way. Granted, most readers presumably try to read what the writer has actually written, and to the extent that they are successful will come up will similar ideas about what the text means. But even at this most basic level, there may be different opinions, resulting from a *lack* of success on the part of either readers or the writer or both. Also, readers' own contributions to the communicative act can certainly vary a lot. The way they will value a text and feel that it affects their own lives is sometimes predictable, sometimes not. People sharing pretty much the same situationality tend to respond in the same fashion, but not always. They are social beings, but social individuals.

In sum, the "lang.-lit." interdisciplinarities gave an enormous boost to the detailed analysis of literary text-type, language, and narrative. But their advances went together with behaviouristic-formalist attitudes which at their most pronounced did tend to level readers to near-robots, not only in an assumed similarity of situation and response, but also in an assumed shallowness of response. As again in some reception aesthetics and reader-response criticism, there was little sense of the sheer variety of readers, or of literature's sheer importance in their lives, the two circumstances which will be uppermost in the mind of a mediating critic, and absolutely central in a pragmatic theory that is historical without being historicist.

2.4. Speech act theory of literature

Even in some very recent linguistic work, the attitudes and methodologies associated with the earlier structuralist linguistics still leave their trace. But it is often very faint, and much has changed. Not least, many linguists of the younger generation would insist that to speak of an impersonal *use* of language would be a contradiction in terms.

One of the first Western scholars to move in this direction was J.L. Austin, who pleaded for an explicit account of the relationships between words and thoughts, and, still more challengingly, between words and deeds. His proposals, and the discussion surrounding them, call for detailed examination here. Transferred to poetics, they might well seem to promise a theory of literature as contextualized interactivity, which would be just the kind of groundwork that a mediating critic needs. How, then, did his approach actually turn out?

Austin was a philosopher. His work harks back to the American pragmatism of Charles S. Peirce and to the language philosophy of the later Wittgenstein, both of whom emphasized in their different ways that the communication and interpretation of meaning rely on an interdependence of linguistic form and context of use. But Austin's own concerns go further than meaning. As indicated by the title of his most seminal work, his ambition is to explain how people actually *do* things with words. As a complement to linguists' behaviouristic quintessentialization of *langue*, this could not have been more radical. It brings *parole* into the very centre of attention, and raises mentalist questions of intention and understanding in a fuller form than they were raised by generative grammarians. Until we have considered how language really works between people, Austin is saying, until we have considered it as a contextualized *parole* that is positively interactive, our ideas about language will be inadequate.

His own account treats speech activity under three different aspects: as a locutionary act, i.e. speech as the act of producing a recognizably grammatical utterance; as an illocutionary act in the real world, i.e. speech as the asking or answering of a question, the giving of information, assurances or warnings, the announcing of a verdict or intention, etc., etc. (Austin is "not suggesting that ... [illocution] is a clearly defined class by any means" (Austin 1975: 99)); and as a perlocutionary act in the real world, i.e. speech as something which has an effect on the hearer.

Within this general set-up, his first step is to distinguish between two types of illocution: the constative and the performative. Whereas constatives purport to be a true representation of a state of affairs (e.g. "It's raining"), performatives perform an action (e.g. "With this ring, I thee wed"). In order to work properly, a performative requires a certain context within a community which recognizes it for what it is, but this has nothing to do with truth: a performative is felicitous only by actually doing something in the world. Its illocutionary force cannot necessarily be read off from its locutionary form, but is nevertheless partly conventional within the life of the community, so that people will sometimes even allow an apparent question to function as a request or an order. The standard example is "Could you open a window?" as addressed to a person with no obvious physical handicap. Such phenomena became known in the theory as indirect speech acts.

Austin's second step, having set up this binarism between language as saying and language as doing, is to deconstruct it. Even constatives are performatives, and faulty constatives fail because they do not fulfil communally recognized conditions. Constatives purport to tell the truth about a state of affairs. But Austin, like American pragmatists such as William James and Richard Rorty, was less interested in truth as a state of affairs obtaining independently of observers, than as the particular society's received notions about such a reality. So considered, truth behaves like a commodity: it is based on a socially agreed assessment from a particular point of view. For certain purposes it works to say that France is a hexagon, but for certain other purposes it does not work at all. Vice versa, obvious performatives also have a constative dimension, presupposing potential agreement as to states of affairs. And even this is an oversimplification, since the words "I'm sorry" will sometimes both constate a fact and perform an apology, will sometimes do neither of these things, and will sometimes do the one and not the other. In short, it is impossible to separate locution from the particular illocution in context. *Langue* is never realized except as *parole*.

Austin's alternative to the linguistic structuralists' abstraction of *langue* from *parole* points the way to more recent work in pragmatics, and speech-act theory is not at all the same thing as poststructuralist deconstruction. Although Austin's account of truth as a conventional linguistic construct is non-logocentric, and although he takes for granted the iterability of language utterances in a wide range of different contexts, he would take strong exception to Derrida or de Man's de-contextualizations of particular instantiations of utterances, precisely because they separate *langue* from *parole*. An example discussed by Sandy Petrey (1990: 131–46) concerns the young Rousseau, who notoriously accused a servant-girl of a crime he had committed himself. De Man (1979: 288–92) refuses to see Rousseau's accusation as an act. Quite regardless of whether Rousseau's accusation was true or false, or intended or unintended, de Man says that it was "merely" a piece of language. The unpleasant consequences for the girl he blames on the obtuseness of the presiding judges, who took Rousseau's words as something more than "just" words.

Petrey goes on to show that Derrida and de Man are not the only scholars unwilling to take on board the full social force of Austin's view of language. Emile Benveniste (1971), for one, hopes to reduce performatives to a structuralist account in purely formal terms (as first-person jussive verbs plus a dictum, e.g. "I order that the population be mobilized"), ironically enough contradicting himself by saying that a certain social hierarchy has to obtain as well. Austin, by contrast, leaves the question of linguistic form entirely open, since for him it is context that is far more decisive for meaning, and he perfectly understands that even social conventions themselves could change — as when the very first player of rugby, in the middle of what had so far been a football match, suddenly picked up the ball. Jerrold Katz (1977), to take a second example, tries to squeeze speech acts into a generative-grammar framework. Having first reconstructed the constative/performative distinction, he then leaves the performative dimension of language use entirely to one side. Whereas Austin's interest was in what we do with words within a community, Katz was hoping to reveal an innate language competence by which we classify and remember them.

After Austin, the other pioneers of speech-act theory are John Searle and H.P. Grice. Searle (1969) further sharpens the account of truth as a conventional construct, distinguishing between brute facts and institutional or discoursal facts, and firmly attacking the so-called descriptive fallacy: the idea that language simply describes reality. Searle also formalizes illocutionary acts into assertives, directives, commissives, expressives, and declaratives, and he greatly refines upon the felicity conditions for each type, i.e. the contextual circumstances which have to obtain in order for the act to have the particular illocutionary force. As for Grice (1991 [1967]), his proposal is that one general felicity condition underlies the production and interpretation of speech acts of every type. At issue here is a kind of fundamental principle of inference, or more specifically, a principle of cooperation involving four maxims, all of which have to be observed in any interchange. The maxim of quantity tells us to give just the amount of information necessary for the current purposes of the exchange. The maxim of quality tells us to be truthful, not saying what we believe to be false, and not saying that for which we lack evidence. The maxim of relation tells us to be relevant. And the maxim of manner tells us to be perspicuous: to avoid obscurity, ambiguity, prolixity and disorder. Grice further suggests that even when a speaker seems to flout a maxim, a hearer will nevertheless assume that the cooperative principle is still in force, and that the speaker is using the flouting in order to make a conversational implicature, perhaps for some special and striking effect — as with metaphorical flouting of the maxim of quality: "Queen Victoria was made of iron".

So far so good. And we shall gradually see that speech act theory, especially in this matter of the cooperative principle, has much to offer a historical yet non-historicist literary pragmatics. Yet can doing things with words be quite such a tidy business? In point of fact, uncertainties arise as to whether a scholarly mapping of speech onto interaction can ever be really close and comprehensive. Even speech act theoreticians themselves give the impression that the relationship between the said and the done is somehow inconsistent, as if interaction can go into abeyance or vary in strength. For indirect speech acts (e.g. "Could you open a window?"), a disregarding of the ostensible intention is actually consonant with the speaker's *true* intention. With direct speech acts, there seems to be little correspondence between an utterance's illocutionary force, allegedly calculable from the utterance itself in all the circumstances, and its actual perlocutionary effect. The hearers can refuse to comply with the speaker's wish, or simply misunderstand it, in either of which cases any act actually accomplished by the speaker is not going to be the act which the speaker intended. Austin himself perfectly realizes, so strong is his respect for *parole*, that in particular circumstances almost any utterance can work in ways that are quite unprecedented. The relationship between function (deed) and form (word) can be full of surprises.

To add to the complications, speech-act theoreticians are in some respects indistinguishable from the structuralist linguists they were hoping to enlighten. For one thing, they draw their examples of language use from their own intuition. As noted earlier, this procedure has much to be said for it. But it does mean that the language analysed in scholarship may be unusually articulate. In the case of speech act theoreticians, the risk is all the greater, given their background in philosophy and formal logic, fields traditionally very hospitable to invented examples, and encouraging unrepresentative levels of rationality as well. In the view of some corpus linguists and sociolinguists, this amounts to a serious let-down for speech act theory's central claim about the relation between speech and real activity. William Labov sees the theory's entire project as a typical example of philosophers' shadow-boxing. It tells us nothing at all, he says, about "the fundamental cohesion of discourse [,which] is not at the level of speech act but at the more abstract level of interaction where status and role are negotiated" (Labov 1981: 242).

In the last analysis speech act theoreticians, too, despite Austin's awareness of the pragmatist tradition, and despite their concern with context, come close to a methodology by which the vagaries, contingencies and inner feel of life are all diminished. Perhaps the underlying temper of their work is not all that different from that of their philosophical colleagues, the logical positivists. Subsequent work in pragmatics has certainly found Searle's categories too hard and fast, since illocutionary force is often ambiguous, only decidable — if at all — post-hoc (Leech and Thomas 1988; Mey 1993). As for perlocutory effect, its unpredictability has been clearly acknowledged from the start. Whether looked at from either the sender's or the receiver's end, then, the act performed by a piece of speech can be far less straightforward than speech act theoreticians perhaps originally envisaged. Their work acutely pinpoints the one-sidedness of structuralist linguistics, but without entirely redressing the balance.

Exactly as in other "lang.-lit." interdisciplinarities, moreover, so in speech act theory of literature, the trace of behaviouristic de-humanization is to be found alongside a trace of a-historical literary formalism. One might have expected a speech act theory of literature to argue that a literary use of language, provided that it is publicly recognized for what it is within a communal context, is experienced as some kind of interpersonal act. As it turns out, the speech act accounts of literature so far developed do not conceive of literary writing as either very speech-like or very act-like, and on the whole they tend to *de*-contextualize it. As a result, they do not quite provide the answer to a postmodern literary critic's most urgent need. To study them will rather be to gauge the scope for a fully historical yet non-historicist literary pragmatics by some interesting near-approximations to it.

Now Benveniste and Katz would hardly have attempted their respective reductions of speech acts to linguistic structuralism and generative grammar if speech act theory's foundational works had not already partly confirmed the paradigm of a-historical de-humanization. In the same way, the formalist trace in speech act theory of literature goes straight back to Austin. Austin was a great lover of literature, drawing on it for many of his examples. At the same time, he believed that literature was a non-illocutionary and parasitic use of language, an attitude which readily translates into formalist dogma about the poem not meaning but being.

The same attitude was reflected in Searle (1975), who did not accept that literature belongs to a genuine class of speech act. According to him, what really happens is that the literary author performs a series of illocutionary acts of representation during which the normal felicity conditions are "intersected". In passing, Searle did recognize that not everything in a text classified as fiction is necessarily fictional; there can also be perfectly factual chunks of history or geography. But his main interest was in saying that literary authors tell what amounts to a kind of undeceptive non-truth. In itself, this is an important observation, which in Section 2.1 I have already glossed in what were actually Gricean terms. Literary writers can flout the maxim of quality for a very good reason. By ignoring the protocols for episodic and specific truth, they can hope to *implicate* some general or moral truth. But Searle, not surprisingly in view of his formalist, anti-pragmatic account of literature, was merely puzzled that "non-serious" texts (by which he meant fictional texts) can communicate what somehow feels like a "serious" (non-fictional) speech act, even though the serious speech act communicated is not textually represented. "Almost any important work of fiction", as he puts it, "conveys a 'message' or 'messages' which are conveyed by but are not in the text". So like Plato, he was uncomfortable with literary works' fictionality, and saw it as much more significant than just trivial fibs. Yet he could still not bring himself to acknowledge the genuine sense in which literature can be experienced as interpersonal.

Where Searle argued that for a literary text the normal conditions for a speech act are intersected, Samuel Levin (1976) drew on the terminology of generative grammar, suggesting that a poem's illocutionary force is determined by an implicit higher sentence in its deep structure. This implicit higher sentence would have the form: "I imagine myself and invite you to conceive a world in which …". Levin thus saw the imagining of a world in which neither the author nor the reader really existed as poetry's definitive and exclusive property. In this way his account gave a further lease of life to the Kantian separation of the aesthetic from the scientific and ethical. The poetic act, sharply profiled by exclusive kinds of diction and phonetic patterning, was simply special — magical, inspired, vatic. Occasional poetry, didactic poetry, polemical poetry, and many other kinds of literature as well, were frankly not poetry in Levin's sense. He was speaking of poetry in what he regarded as its purest form, for which the real world underwent a sea-change, as the poet dreamed visions which had no real earthly counterpart. Seen this way, poetry is more or less wish-fulfilment, and many late nineteenth-century poems meet the requirements. But although a reader recognizing their convention can certainly read them in Levin's way, they can hardly stand as the type of all literature. Also, their authors' gesture of self-withdrawal was in any case an interactive move.

Richard Ohmann (1973) also offered a speech act theory of literature based on formalist presuppositions, but was rather more sensitive to historical considerations. On the one hand, he did not see the literary text itself as constituting a speech act. For him, speech acts came into the picture only because literary texts represent the illocutionary acts of their fictional characters, whose intradiegetic world readers have to build up through their understanding of the conventions for illocutionary acts in general. On the other hand, in doing this readers become implicated in that intradiegetic world, which they are forced to judge according to their own political and ethical convictions. According to Ohmann, they either like it, or they do not, and their response depends on their own situation. There is no ideal reader, in other words. The worlds in which writing and reading take place are divided along lines of sociohistorical difference.

Ohmann's account of the reader constructing the fictional worlds in which characters make their speech acts is very illuminating, and anticipates some of the most suggestive work on reader reception. Obviously, too, he is right to say that readers ultimately either like a work or do not like it, and that this will partly depend on their own disposition and circumstances. Like Searle, Ohmann could hardly have come closer to a fully pragmatic account of literary interpersonality without actually opening up the field himself. But like both Searle and Levin, he still thinks all literature is circumscribed by being merely fictional. The one move he does not make is to subsume the construction of fictional worlds, and the speech acts of the characters within them, under a speech act directed by the real writer to real readers. Instead, he speaks as if writers never conveyed any thoughts or feelings at all, whether about life in general or about the worlds and characters of their fiction.

In one of his articles, Ohmann perhaps gave a hint of at least *some* writer-reader communication. But this again seemed sharply qualified when, in broaching the idea, he simultaneously said that there are barriers to such communication.

> Although the writer is in a way hidden, so that we meet only his surrogate and carry on no intercourse with the author himself, through our sharing the act of mimesis we do get at something like the world he meant to create, and in this way we move close to his wishes and his fears. Although hidden, he gives us access to his imaginative worlds, and to that much of himself.
> (Ohmann 1972: 57)

True, a full account of the pragmatics of literature will make exactly these same concessions. Communication between a literary writer and a reader can certainly be far from straightforward. But there are further points as well. For one thing, access to the imaginative worlds of a *non*-literary writer or speaker can be just as unstraightforward. For another thing, a literary text, like many other types of utterance, can also offer intercourse with the sender that is altogether *closer* than this. Still implicit in Ohmann's thinking was the formalist view of the author and reader personae as fictions which seal off real authors from real readers.

I have already begun to suggest that author and reader personae can be accounted for very differently, as typical cases of sender and receiver personae to be found in any kind of linguistic communication at all. They are the point at which sender and receiver come into human contact, with implications that are fundamental for our experience of particular literary works. Take, for instance, two well-known poems which have already been discussed within the speech act theory framework: Shakespeare's "Sonnet 19" and Robert Frost's "Spring Pools".

> Devouring Time, blunt thou the lion's paws,
> And make the earth devour her own sweet brood;
> Pluck the keen tooth from the fierce tiger's jaws,
> And burn the long-lived Phoenix in her blood;
> Make glad and sorry seasons as thou flee'st,
> And do whate'er thou wilt, swift-footed Time,
> To the wide world and all her fading sweets;
> But I forbid thee one most heinous crime:
> O carve not with thy hours my fair love's brow,
> Nor draw no lines there with thine antique pen;
> Him in thy course untainted do allow
> For beauty's pattern to succeeding men.
> Yet do thy worst, old Time: despite thy wrong,
> My love shall in my verse ever live young.
> (Shakespeare 1996 [1609]: 42)

> Spring Pools
>
> These pools that, though in forests, still reflect
> The total sky almost without defect,
> And like the flowers beside them, chill and shiver,
> Will like the flowers beside them soon be gone,
> And yet not out by any brook or river,
> But up by roots to bring dark foliage on.

> The trees that have it in their pent-up buds
> To darken nature and be summer woods —
> Let them think twice before they use their powers
> To blot out and drink up and sweep away
> These flowery waters and these watery flowers
> From snow that melted only yesterday.
> (Frost 1972 [1928]: 245)

In analysing these texts Michael Hancher's concern, reminiscent of Ohmann's, is to define the illocutionary acts *imitated*. His conclusion is that "Sonnet 19" addresses Time, and moves from an act of conceding (Time's power) to a prohibition immediately reduced to a wish (that Time not harm the loved-one), then switching to a boast (about the poem's own power to immortalize the loved-one). As for "Spring Pools", it ends, not with a wish (that the trees think twice before drinking up the water of the pools) but with a warning (that winter will return all the sooner if the trees try to rush into the spring). Hancher then comments: "The speaker knows that the trees cannot act on his warning...; like Shakespeare's Time, they cannot do otherwise than they do" (Hancher 1980).

Precisely. The speech acts Hancher so accurately describes are an imitation within the poems, and they are unrealistic even at that. What kind of communicant is Time, what kind of eavesdropper a tree? — Frost does not actually address the trees directly. Poetry on Hancher's account, no less than on Levin's, becomes a kind of fantasizing. What he fails to recognize is that the poems' "speakers" shape their words for Time and for the trees to absolutely no purpose, unless as a clue to the thoughts and feelings of the "speakers" themselves. In turn, the "speakers" themselves are unreal constructs, of no earthly interest unless as a clue to the thoughts and feelings, or possible thoughts and feelings, of human beings, most obviously of the writers who constructed them, or of people who might reconstruct them in reading about them. Yet of the real Shakespeare and Frost addressing real readers Hancher says nothing at all. Writers and readers might just as well not exist, since on this view the poems convey no messages between them. If readers, while enjoying the poetry's superlative device and witty twists on ancient themes, also find themselves thinking, in one very intimate corner of their mind, about growing old, about their attempts to wrestle and come to terms with this process, about the proposition that love might not outlast youth, about the relative importance placed on youth and age in the particular cultures in which they live; if, in short, they feel some degree of fellow-feeling with, or self-distancing from Shakespeare or Frost's self-projection, and from the reader personae offered for themselves: then such readers are not reading like the reader envisaged in Hancher's speech act theory of literature.

As Martha Woodmansee puts it, such theories have some rather odd consequences. To take one of her examples, Elizabeth Barrett Browning's poems, if they are a declaration of her love for Browning, are suddenly not poems after all. Woodmansee comments: "To characterize literature by fictivity is ... debilitating .... Literature is thereby rendered mere make-believe. It becomes impossible to explain why — unless for sheer diversion — people should bother to read it at all." Taking up the issue which puzzled Searle, Woodmansee asks how, by means of *pretended* illocutions, serious messages could ever be communicated, or a connection made between literature and the world of experience outside the book — "the only connection", as she puts it, that is "capable of grounding the importance and effort we attach to literature" (Woodmansee 1978: 76, 83).

Her point is well taken. On the view adopted in the present work, literature does not involve pretended illocutions at all. Granted, within the fictional world an author will imitate speech acts as performed by the characters in the story. But real authors write for, and offer to engage in interaction with, real readers. And when, over and above the characters' imitated speech acts, authors also dramatize, as they always must, a relationship between implied writer and reader personae, they are doing what all communicators do: they are offering a representation of their relationship with their fellow communicant. This has nothing to do with pretending. It is absolutely for real. They make the offer in good faith, for their readers' convenience and use, and readers are well able to enter into the relationship as so represented, including all the implied attitudes, judgements and feelings. They can do so as a way of trying these on for spiritual size, just like they do with the implied relationships of any other piece of communication. What happens is the result of their astonishing, albeit everyday powers of imaginative empathy, and their readiness for it is easy enough to understand. What Woodmansee calls readers' world of experience outside the book is connected no less closely to their interpretation of the book than to their interpretation of ordinary everyday gossip. Their engagement in communication of any kind, oral or literate, non-literary or literary, is always driven by a directly personal interest in how the universal gift of life can be variously perceived, experienced, dealt with. Nor is their heuristic flexibility of mind to be confused with a gregarious impressionability. Their critical faculties are in no way overridden. In literary communication as much as in any other, the implied relationship with the other person is something they can simultaneously take and leave. This, too, has nothing to do with pretending. In the fullest sense, it is a matter of ethics.

Speech act theory of literature came somewhat closer to some such richly pragmatic view in the work of Mary Louise Pratt (1977). Cogently attacking the formalist dogmas that literature is autotelic and that literary language is special, Pratt stressed the importance of the address to the hearer in all narrative texts, whether colloquial or literary. She pointed out that, of the six components of colloquial narrative structure defined by the sociolinguists William Labov and Joshua Waletzky (1967), only two are strictly speaking "story", while the other four have to do with winning, sustaining and guiding the recipient's evaluative attention. She then demonstrated the same four interpersonal elements at work in classical novels. So the literary text performs a real speech act, taking place under definable conditions, with prefaces, chapter headings, and direct addresses all requesting a "turn", and with the literary institution guaranteeing that the text is definite, prepared and selected. The cooperative principle is also in operation, though without the bias towards episodic and specific truth. Even if a literary text grossly flouts the cooperative principle, Pratt claimed that readers go on reading it as if it were not doing so. They assume there is some element of implicature, as Grice would have said, and tolerantly interpret the difficulties away.

Given the date at which Pratt's ideas were published, they were a very bold pioneering effort. It is only from our present vantage point that her unsurprising remnants of formalist thinking can stand out at all clearly. One of the questions to arise is over this matter of implicature. The fruitfulness of her suggestion is clear enough. I myself am indebted to her, in my account of fiction as apparently flouting the maxim of quality while also implicating an indirect observance of it. Yet when it comes to floutings of the maxims of quantity, relevance and manner, readers are perhaps less patient than Pratt suggests, and may well dislike being steamrollered by authors they experience as impolite. The politeness of literary authors is a topic to which we must return.

A related question arises over Pratt's description of literary texts as "display" texts that are quite detachable from their contexts. Her account of literature stopped short, in fact, at tellability: a story's *raison d' être* or point. Perhaps this point was something readers could either take or leave. But Pratt gave the impression that they usually took it, perhaps rather automatically.

There was no suggestion of their evaluating it in some deeper sense, or of its somehow impinging on their lives, an omission which a mediating critic will certainly notice.

Sandy Petrey's work was published thirteen years after Pratt's. But he, too, seems to underestimate literature's sheer interactive force. As far as non-literary communication goes, his sense of the acts performed through language is very robust. This much is clear from his discussion of Rousseau's false accusation of the servant-girl, where his disagreement with Paul de Man is most eloquent. But as regards literary communication, he may actually be closer to Ohmann than to Pratt. Pratt sees the social nature of literary texts as coming close to orality, and consequently subordinates the text to the person who wrote it, almost as if he or she were actually present. Petrey would perhaps find this too full-blooded. He remarks, quite rightly, that written texts, of their nature, operate in the absence of their sender, as it were by proxy, and can in any case be read in many ways. But from this he draws the conclusion that authors' intentions are of no great importance. One of his opening claims is that the reception of a written text above all privileges the present context of the particular community within which reception is now taking place. Unsurprisingly in view of this, he has little to say about lyrical poetry, the literary genre most difficult to distinguish from ordinary self-expression, and the same kind of one-sidedness affects his discussion of drama. Authors, it would seem, cannot really expect to have much of a say. So presumably, any attempt by a critic to mediate between authors and their readers would be merely redundant.

Petrey does not mean that literary interpretation is a narcissistic free-for-all. In his view, the audience watching a play by Shakespeare or Molière, for instance, certainly have to keep their eyes and ears open. Just like the readers described by Ohmann, they must try to create a world in which the characters' words would actually work, and that world is one they have to build up from what is actually presented to them. What is felicitous, and what is accepted as truth, is a matter of the particular social context as created on the stage. So is Coriolanus superior to ordinary mortals, or is he not? Does Don Juan tell the truth, or does he not? It all depends. The social world bodied forth upon the stage actually changes, so that with the passing of theatre-time these two heroes' words and deeds are seen by other characters in a new light.

Petrey's demonstration of this is sensitive and valuable, and even tends to modify his initial prioritization of the current context of reception. His idea now is apparently that the audience moves into the stage world, so to speak, and makes it, temporarily at least, their own. Yet even the context formed by the world within the play is still not the same context as the one in which the dramatist was actually writing or, for that matter, the one in which the play was or is being staged and performed by those many intermediaries — producer, director, actors etc. — who can also contribute to its meaning. In my own account, by contrast, literary communication is seen as always a matter of at least three contexts, which in the act of communication are brought into interrelationship: the context of writing, the intradiegetic context within the world created by the writer, and the current context of reading. And even though there can also be the contexts of intermediaries to consider, a literary tradition is not at all the same thing as an oral tradition. The chain of literate transmission never completely eliminates the sense that the particular named writer, working in a particular context, was the originator from whom the act of communication still flows.

The closest Petrey comes to talking about literary writers being in communication with other people is in his mention of "themes". These themes, he says, are something which the audience of a play, for instance, detects (Petrey 1990: 112, 123). Since he does not explain who, apart from, say, Shakespeare and Molière, could have put them there, it almost begins to seem as if the writers' intentions are important after all. But when it comes to saying what the themes actually are, they turn out to be nothing other than those Austinian ideas about speech acts which Petrey expounds the plays as demonstrating. In effect, he is suggesting that Shakespeare and Molière succeeded in saying exactly the same thing as Austin says in *How to Do Things with Words*. Rather than engaging their audience's imagination, emotions and ethical sensibility in a consideration of Coriolanus and Don Juan as human beings, they were simply presenting speech act philosophy in fancy dress, although Petrey never gives them the credit for even this. Perhaps the Austinian themes are no more or less immanent in their plays than in any other use of language, in which case it would be Petrey himself, if anybody, who ought to be congratulated, for having winkled them out.

His account of Balzac's realism is somewhat similar, except that here he confines his remarks more explicitly to the responses of the first audience. Balzac's realism, he says, worked just like a human being's ordinary perception of the world. It did not describe or copy things referentially. Indeed, it constated them, in a way that Roland Barthes failed to grasp. In Petrey's view, Barthes's deconstruction of Balzac's *Sarrasine* in *S/Z* concentrated far too much on linguistic play; what Barthes overlooked was that Balzac's text also invited its first readers themselves to participate in the social construction of reality. Here, then, Petrey does begin to make literature sound more interactive, at least on its first reception, and his detailed textual commentary is customarily rich and thought-provoking. Once again, though, a main claim is that recipients ended up interpreting the texts as thematizing the insights of Austin, and Petrey still never asks who they believed to have put the insights there in the first place, or whether the texts might not also convey, and at a somewhat less philosophical pitch, their author's thoughts and feelings about human life and society.

Petrey is actually closer to Barthes than may at first appear, since Barthes, too, in both the structuralist and poststructuralist aspects of his project, was concerned to divert critical attention away from authors. Yet not even Barthes would have denied that readers do develop a sense of an author's personality and intention. He merely complained that an older type of criticism made this a pretext for seeing literature as a kind of indirect or allegorical autobiography. When Petrey criticizes Searle for making author intention the sole test of illocutionary force, he does have a point. An author may be unsuccessful in finding the form of words most likely to achieve the intended illocution under prevailing circumstances, in which case the text can well be read as representing some quite different illocution. That literary communication is very dependent on the way texts are actually processed by readers is exactly what *S/Z*, despite gestures towards linguistic determinism, so brilliantly demonstrates. Yet the point can be overstated. The intention of the speaker or writer remains a fact of all language use, and listeners or readers habitually try to work that intention out, perhaps even allowing themselves to be affected by it. In this respect as well, literary texts are not unusual. Not only do they offer imitations of speech acts within a fictional world. They are also real speech acts in themselves. Their illocutionary force and perlocutionary effects may be very difficult to pin down, and when their impact carries over into contexts of reading very different from the context of writing, the results can be even more unforeseeable than ever. But as the scholarly reactions to speech act theory clearly show, other kinds of communication are often just as difficult to categorize. Also, the sense that a known originator of a text must have at least something to do with what it can be taken to mean is very deeply rooted. If it were not, after all, our societies would be offering alarmingly little scope for any principle of justice. People could be quite freely blamed for meanings which they did not mean.

Not only does Petrey discount authors, however. In the last analysis his prioritization of the current context of reception is modified quite beyond recognition. The only people responsible for interpreting the speech acts he discusses are the groups of characters within Molière and Shakespeare's plays, and Balzac's first readers. Putting together his treatment of authors and his total neglect of readers or spectators contemporary with himself, we can conclude that literary tradition does not interest him. He simply has no sense of the classic text, either as originating from an author whose intentions have a continuing relevance, or as interpreted by succeeding generations for whom its valency nevertheless inevitably changes. Instead, his concentration on the interpretative conventions applied by characters in stage plays and by Balzac's first readers is reminiscent of the de-humanizing and synchronic orientation of behaviourist-structuralist linguistics. It tidies everything up into a watertight system, from which historical mutations in linguistic form, semantics, pragmatics, and world-view are quietly excluded.

As an alternative to this kind of approach, a historical yet non-historicist literary pragmatics will prioritize neither the context of writing, nor the intradiegetic context, nor the current context of reading. Communication has to do with the triangular interrelationship of all these types of context, and with the fusing of different horizons of expectations. As a matter of fact, horizons fuse quite regardless of whether the difference between them is a matter of time or place or both. People differently situated in any number of ways simply must, can, and do *negotiate* the differences. This is one of the central pragmatic considerations on which a positively mediating criticism can build, but which speech act theory of literature has so far not conceptualized.

Another main consideration is that a literary author really does engage in interpersonal activity, which, especially but not only across lines of marked sociocultural difference, can bring about change, whether to individual readers, or more widely within a climate of ideas. Plato's worry about the possible impact of poets on their audience's moral life is to this extent understandable, and so is Searle's puzzled suggestion that what literature conveys is in the end a "serious" message. Milton had an even stronger sense of this, and was more democratic into the bargain: even non-philosophers could be expected to develop powers of responsible judgement. This is an area of discussion in which speech act theory of literature has so far not engaged, and that is another reason why the approach can still not support the mediating critic. A-historically formalist in its poetics, and de-humanizingly behaviouristic in its methodology, it has left the ethical dimension of literary communication firmly to one side. The acts it has discussed have been treated as pseudo-acts.

2.5. Formalist literary pragmatics

But even pragmatics has sometimes been dealt with in a somewhat behaviouristic spirit. Human interaction can already sound rather mechanically regimented in the work of Charles Morris, the foundational figure. For him, pragmatics was to be one of three components of a proposed science of semiotic [*sic*], the other two being syntactics and semantics. Syntactics would deal with the relation of signs to each other, semantics with the relation of signs to the objects to which they are applicable, and pragmatics with "the relation of signs to interpreters" (Morris 1971 [1938]: 21). This last was to lead to the formulation of pragmatic rules stating the conditions to be met by interpreters in order for the sign vehicle actually to function as such. The communicative process was very ship-shape, by the sound of it, with little room for serendipity or whim.

This more narrowly systematic side of Morris's work underlies much scholarship on the pragmatics of specifically linguistic signs (see e.g. Davis 1991). Echoing Morris's subdivision of the field of semiotic, linguists have sometimes thought of pragmatics as a more or less separate component of linguistics with its own rules, though these can also have syntactical or semantic consequences, one main hypothesis being that there are "relations between language and context that are *grammaticalized*, or encoded in the structure of a language" (Levinson 1983: 9). In order to locate such rules and relations, linguistic analysis has had to be kept simple, with human variables restricted to a minimum. The contextualization of an utterance has been examined mainly in terms of mere co-text (the immediately adjacent parts of the same utterance), or of co-text plus only the most immediate circumstances of use. In keeping with this, discussion has in fact stayed fairly close to the syntax and semantics of mainstream linguistics, and even to philosophical logic.

These methodological limitations have had important heuristic pay-offs. There have been valuable studies of deixis, for instance, the linguistic means by which a text actually "points to" its own context, and much light has also been shed on listeners' and readers' processes of inferencing. Rather than everything being there "in the actual words", the receivers of an utterance have to disambiguate, to assign reference, to resolve vagueness or indeterminacy, to recover implicit content and/or attitudes, and, more generally, to know how to take things — ironically, metaphorically, symbolically or literally. That is why some of the most interesting research has been into presuppositions and implicatures.

From the point of view of would-be mediating critics, the most problematic limitation in much of this work has been an unquestioned, and sometimes merely implicit assumption that, for each and every participant in an interchange, the context is simultaneously present and basically the same. This unitary context assumption, quite at odds with the theory I am proposing here, involves an unhistorical idealization that is typical of much twentieth-century research in the humanities. It is entirely consonant with the aesthetics and ideology underlying the marginalization of sociocultural difference in formalist literary criticism.

The most controversial development in this tradition of pragmatics is relevance theory, in which the unitary context assumption seems in some ways to be taken for granted. Among relevance theory's main concerns are inferencing, presupposition and implicature, and strictly speaking it is a theory of cognition, coming close to cognitive psychology. It takes its starting point from Grice's idea that the interpretation of utterances must work according to a principle of inference that is broad and general. But whereas Grice's principle of cooperativeness resulted in maxims of quality, quantity, manner and relation, Dan Sperber and Deirdre Wilson (1986) subsume all four types of factor under relation, so arriving at the master principle of relevance. The idea is that, when we are interpreting an utterance, the principle of relevance tells us to choose those contextual assumptions, and to recover those implicatures, which for the particular utterance and its circumstances have the greatest number of consequences, and which involve the least amount of processing effort. By analyzing communication along these lines, relevance theoreticians have already offered many fascinating insights into the way our mental "black boxes" must be working. For the theory's critics, however, it all smacks too strongly of artificial intelligence (cf. Talbot 1998). The human mind is viewed as a "deductive mechanism" or information-processing "device", very like a computer, so that considerations of value, emotion, and the inner feel of life go largely by the board. Certainly for anyone interested in the tensions of postmodernity, and in avenues for a mediating intervention, a crucial question must be: Do relevance theoreticians pay enough attention to society and culture? More particularly, do they fully recognize the consequences of sociocultural differences between the cognitive environments of different individuals? (Cf. Mey and Talbot 1988.) Sperber and Wilson, in the second edition of their book (1995), seek to allay such worries, and have certainly always countered the mutual knowledge hypothesis, as they call it, by claiming that no two communicants can ever be sure they are aware of exactly the same contextual considerations, not even when a shared awareness would *prima facie* seem most likely. In practice, however, sociocultural difference has not been one of relevance theory's main preoccupations.

Fairly typical is the following illustration, used by Sperber and Wilson:

> *Mary*: What I would like to eat tonight is an osso-bucco. I'm ravenous. I had a great day in court. How was your day?
> *Peter*: Not so good. Too many patients, and the air conditioning was out of order. I'm tired.
> *Mary*: I'm sorry to hear that. O.K. I'll make it myself.
> (Sperber and Wilson 1986: 140)

Sperber and Wilson's discussion of this is very astute, well demonstrating the mental steps by which Peter hints and Mary guesses that he would rather not man the kitchen at the moment. Yet this little dialogue is in clear descent from the fabricated examples of speech act theoreticians and many philosophers, generative grammarians and structuralist linguists before them. It actually sounds rather unauthentic. Stylistically, "I'm sorry to hear that" seems too formal for this kind of situation, and more generally, middle-class professionals as smug as Mary about being middle-class professionals are surely such stuff as television soaps are made on. The sequence does rather read like a written script, in fact. Certainly the communication taking place is just as smoothly mechanical and successful as in many of the other examples arrived at by way of scholars' own written-language bias. Especially because Peter, too, is a middle-class professional, and because what he and Mary are engaging in is face to face conversation, the interchange is in any case unrepresentative of vast amounts of the communication that really goes on in the world. Dialogue like this can very well happen, albeit with more genuine language and attitudes, and perhaps some communicational hiccups as well. But communication often takes place across distances of time, space and culture, distances which can be either smaller or greater. One day, a career posting may physically separate Peter and Mary, so that their relationship really will have to rely on writing for a while. And who knows? Mary may even bump into somebody who is less clued up than Peter on osso-bucco.

Relevance theorists, unless I am mistaken, could deal with these possibilities as well. But so far, they have perhaps tended not to. Predictably, therefore, there are accounts of the pragmatics of literature whose orientation is just as markedly de-humanizing and a-historical as that of speech act theory of literature or the other "lang.-lit." interdisciplinarities. Once again, there is also an unmistakable trace of literary formalism. For one thing, there tends to be a rather narrow conception of context, which is furthermore taken to be unitary — i.e. identical for a text's writer and all its readers in whatever time and place. Examples would include Pilkington (1991, 1994 and 1996), Toolan (1994) and Clark (1996).

To give an idea of what this can mean in practice, I turn to Clark's relevance-theory account of "Little Things", a very short story by Raymond Carver (1981). Clark pays special attention to Carver's way of manipulating inferential processes so as to build up a kind of horror and suspense. In part, "Little Things" tells how, in a darkening room, a man who is on the point of walking out on a woman fights with her for possession of a baby (presumably theirs). With the woman pulling on one of the baby's arms with all her might, and with the man pulling very hard in the opposite direction on the other arm, the story ends with the words, "In this manner, the issue was decided."

The reason why Clark's analysis works so well is that, at least for the inferences he discusses, Carver and anybody likely to read him can only operate within cognitive environments that certainly do overlap. To a considerable extent, the story's real readers will have to follow in the footsteps of the text's implied reader, some of which Clark attentively re-traces. There can hardly be a culture in the world for which the room's growing darkness, given the other circumstances, would not have sinister connotations, and part of the moral implication of the struggle for the baby is just as general, and at least as ancient as the story of the two women whose maternal claims were decided by Solomon: a claimant who really loved the child, sooner than see it come to grief, would *renounce* all claim. That something very unbeneficial will happen to a baby if manhandled in the way Carver describes is again something that every reader will know, from universal laws of physics and biology. No less universally, readers would be likely to experience at least fear and horror at such a possibility.

In one sense it would be quite unfair to accuse Clark of downplaying the interactive element of reading. On the contrary, his discussion of Carver's economical sophistication brings out the build-up of tension very well. But rather as with Sperber and Wilson's example of Mary and Peter's negotiation of culinary arrangements, a question arises as to representativeness. Clark is seeking to illustrate, not only the artistry of Raymond Carver, but the appropriateness of relevance theory to the analysis of literature in general. Assuming that his description of Carver's story is adequate, then, are literary texts always more or less like this one? Or do some of them communicate something other than a universal shiver down the spine? More particularly, do not at least a fair number of them communicate on matters about which authors' and readers' presuppositions, thoughts and feelings may widely vary?

As it happens, even the kind of thing Clark finds in Carver may itself be open to a more critical assessment. Not that skilful and exciting entertainment is unwelcome. But perhaps "Little Things", from its title onwards, is a bit too slickly gruesome. Perhaps the thrill of its climax is rather cheap and primitive. And what about that enigmatic punchline? — "In this manner, the issue was decided." Is it too ponderously poker-faced? Is Carver playing fair? Or is he, under the cover of a mere *jeu d'esprit*, wriggling out of an assessment of the human probabilities — of whether one claimant will actually love the child enough to relinquish it? At least as represented in these details and as described by Clark, the story does little more than supply to order, as it were, a kind of frisson which we recognize from many earlier written texts and films, a frisson by which readers' view of both the world and themselves will be so little challenged that communication could be said to be at a minimum.

But then there is a further question: *Is* Clark's description of the story adequate? Or has he reduced it in such a way that the allegedly crucial inferences are simply the most universal ones? In point of fact, the story's action takes place, not in one room, but in three: a bedroom, a living room, and a kitchen. The last part, the struggle for the baby, happens in the kitchen, and this is mainly what Clark concentrates on. What he rather leaves to one side is the story's beginning, in the bedroom. The man is packing his suitcase on the bed. The woman comes in, very angry and upset, and says she is glad he is going. She then notices that one of the things he is about to pack is a picture of the baby. She seizes the picture and walks out with it through the living room. He asks for it back, but she just tells him to get out. He finishes packing, goes into the living room, and speaks to her as she stands in the doorway of the kitchen with the baby in her arms. What he now tells her is that he wants the baby itself. She says he must be crazy, after which the action moves to its violent climax in the kitchen.

This climax, though it obviously *is* a climax and has the powerful impact already noticed, in another sense merely sets a seal on what goes before. In itself, the climax would be far less interesting without that lead-up. For the question is, surely: How could things ever have got this far out of hand? Who did what? Who went wrong where? And why? The spiral of enmity has already begun when the story starts, with the man packing his suitcase. So *he*, at least, is not satisfied with the relationship. Then the woman seems to be far more passionately discontented. So has he been really dreadful to her? Or has she been extremely unreasonable, and he long-suffering up until now? When she grabs the baby's picture, in other words, is it, say, an act of outrage at his seeming to stake an interest in the one thing that still means something in her life? Or is it an act of spiteful pique, meanly refusing to recognize his genuine feelings for the child? These questions are clearly not immaterial, because whatever the truth of the matter, his demanding to have the baby itself rather than just the baby's picture seems like a gesture of retaliation. Either he is getting even nastier. Or the worm is finally turning. Unless, of course, and as may be just as likely, these disjunctions, and any such attempt to blame one party more than the other, are quite misguided. Perhaps Carver is hinting that the two of them are simply locked into something which, with the best will in the world, and no matter how ghastly the possible outcome, simply cannot be helped. Perhaps, in our efforts to make sense of the story, we must turn to the one glimpse it gives us of the world outside these claustrophobic three rooms, as the only available standard of comparison. The story's first paragraph says that the weather changed that day; that the snow was melting into dirty water; and that cars "slushed by in the street outside, where it was getting dark". And then, as if to confirm the possibility of comparison: "But it was getting dark on the inside too." If we do make the connection, it is surely something to the effect that what happens inside might be just as much a fact of nature as the changes of the snow to dirty water, and of day to night, all within a humanly rather empty cityscape, in which the motor cars, too, seem to take on a pre-programmed life of their own.

Paying attention to details such as these, a reader may well be in two minds at once, quite possibly disagreeing with many other readers, and with Carver himself as well. For what the story is very much about is responsibility. Is one of the human agents to blame? Are both of them to blame? Or is everything beyond their own control? Or only partly beyond their control? Carver does not alienate readers by spelling out his own opinions too clearly, and he actually dropped the story's original title, "Popular Mechanics", presumably because it made the element of deterministic naturalism too obvious. But the first paragraph's hint of that is still pretty strong, and on repeated readings will perhaps place itself ever more firmly in an American tradition going back to Dreiser, so giving the story a sadness of tight-lipped resignation in which some readers will acquiesce more readily than others, depending on their own situationality, world-view, temperament and personal experience.

Once again, the point is not that relevance theory is necessarily incapable of a richer and more complex approach. Clark himself is careful to underline that he is not analysing Carver's story exhaustively. He is merely illustrating the relevance of relevance for just some of its details, which he very helpfully explores, well highlighting certain likely aspects of readers' empathetic effort. All the same, he does stay very close to the unitary context assumption, concentrating only on those aspects of meaning which, because the cognitive environments involved are maximally universal, are least interestingly problematic. This in turn is related to a larger restriction: problematic disagreements are unlikely to arise, not only because of the assumedly unitary context, but because the writer-reader relationship is not thought of as one of human parity. Clark tends to suggest that readers merely take the writer's meaning and leave it at that. The possibility that they will have a response of their own, and perhaps a critical one, he does not reckon with.

This restriction, so reminiscent of the "lang.-lit." interdisciplinarites already discussed, is also fairly typical of formalist literary pragmatics. An understanding of literature that is historical and interpersonalizing in any very full sense is precluded. Often, indeed, the approach disempowers writers just as much as readers. If anything, a dichotomy is sustained between, on the one hand, a text's writer and readers in their assumedly unitary context and, on the other hand, the text itself in an autotelic literary universe of its own. So understood, literary pragmatics allows interesting explorations of textualities and imaginative worlds, but at times can also give the impression of transferring enunciation and agency from literature's real authors to entities which are entirely abstract: to the literary institution and its conventions. Obviously, the institution and conventions of literature do have a psychological reality with very definite implications for the way people write and read. So much so, that formalist literary pragmatics has considerable potential when it comes to describing literary genres, for instance. The risk, though, is of suggesting that the institution and conventions are prime movers which operate *through* human beings. As in any formalist poetics, communication between the writer and the current reader, whose situationalities in reality always differ from each other, tends to drop out of sight, precisely because of the way literariness itself is theorized, and because the contexts of writing and reading are methodologically assimilated. Literary works are seen as constituting aesthetic heterocosms, while writers, seen as situationally indistinguishable from their readers, are that much less interesting to them in human terms. Inevitably, the unitary context assumption suggests that a writer's words can arouse no curiosity as to the sameness-that-is-difference of the human condition, and will consequently provide little intrinsic stimulus to self-reassessment.

One way for formalist literary pragmaticists to cement the disjunction between the aesthetic world of literature and the real worlds of writers and readers is by restricting analysis to the discourse pragmatics of characters "*within* the story", rather like Petrey in his analysis of speech acts within plays by Molière and Shakespeare. Of this there are many examples (such as Wadman 1983; Doty 1984; Krysinsky 1984; van Stapele 1990), and it is probably what most linguists and literary scholars still think of when they come across the term "literary pragmatics". In cases such as Paul Simpson's analysis of the politeness of characters in a play by Ionesco, the approach can valuably concretize or test interpretations of the work's intradiegetic action (Simpson 1989). But the pragmatics of literature itself as communication remains unexplored.

As for formalist literary pragmaticists who do treat literature within a communication-theoretical framework, they still bring about the disjunction between the aesthetic and the real, though in a different way. Theirs is the argument descending from Russian Formalism. In a nutshell, the pragmatics of literature is said to involve a self-foregrounding deviation from ordinary language use, as when Rainer Grübel (1987) suggests that in poetic discourse the usual distinction between the first or second person and the third person can be collapsed. All such ideas about a peculiarly literary syntax culminate in the literary pragmatic theory of Ann Banfield (1982, 1992), who develops an idea put forward by Emile Benveniste. Benveniste had been trying to distinguish French forms of literary narrative (*histoire*) from ordinary communication (*discours*). The main conclusion he came to was that literary French does not use the *passé simple* tense in the first and second person, or in connection with spatial deictics. Banfield, in her turn, says that literary narrative, so often couched in third person forms, actually aspires to a condition of total impersonality. Her chief proposition is that literary works consist of what are really "non-person" forms, so giving rise to sentences which are "speakerless". Literature, as it were, speaks itself.

This suggestion has already come in for detailed scrutiny from, among others, Jon-K. Adams (1985: 17–18), who points out that the issue is *more fundamentally* pragmatic than Banfield allows. (See also Fludernik 1993: 367–97 and Sell 1995b.) Banfield's suggestion raises all the problems discussed in connection with extremist literary formalism in Sections 2.1–4 above, where I have also drawn the contrast with an approach that is historical yet non-historicist. If we take the pragmatics of literature to be continuous with the pragmatics of communication in general, then a sentence which has not been written or spoken by somebody is clearly seen for what it is: an impossibility that is quite unimaginable to listeners or readers. Any sentence purporting to be of this nature is in reality taken as having been presented that way by its producer. A sentence is not even the kind of entity that has the consciousness to purport something in the first place, and grammatical "anomalies" of the kind pointed out by Banfield are in any case rather common, as in the third-person expressions of this present sentence, which is just as "unspoken" as any sentence from *Madame Bovary*, yet does not magically increase in "speakability" when I hereby include a first-person pronoun. The entire sentence has been my personal responsibility from start to finish, as any readers it reaches will be well aware, not least those who may wish to disagree with it.

It is hard to imagine a narrower definition of context than one which would exclude a sentence's producer. But a formalist orientation is also to be found among literary pragmaticists defining context far more broadly, in terms of society or culture. In the early days there was actually a close link with formalistic speech act theory of literature, from which much of the terminology was drawn. This is how Teun van Dijk, for instance, re-phrased the essentialistic claim that literature is necessarily and peculiarly non-interactive and fictional, another of the formalist dogmas already scrutinized above (in Section 2.1). According to van Dijk, there are such things as literary speech acts, which are deviant because confessedly counterfactual; they are dominated by what he called a specific operator for irrealis (van Dijk 1972), a suggestion somewhat akin to Levin's idea of an implicit higher sentence. Or as Siegfried J. Schmidt (1976) put it, one aspect of literature's difference involves an "aesthetic" or non-factual reading convention, a point on which

Bennison Gray also agreed: this aesthetic reading convention resulted in society's acceptance of literary discourse

> as fiction even when it contains some true assertions. Literary pragmatics is thus to be the study of those norms or standards by which society agrees to accept certain discourses as fiction. ... The object is to be the discovery, analysis, and description of the means by which literature is created as fiction and understood as such.
> (Gray 1978: 194)

In developing this line of thought, van Dijk suggested that a literary utterance has no instrumental character in the control of interaction. Instead, it acquires an "object" character in a production-consumption process, with an assigned "value" which "depends (among many other factors) on the amount of (esthetic or other) 'pleasure' caused in the reader" (van Dijk 1976: 47). Since van Dijk did not specify his two parenthetical "others" here, the impression remained that literature is a form of harmlessly irresponsible hedonism. Later, he went on to describe literature as belonging to a class of "ritual" speech acts which also includes jokes and stories, with literary properties adjudicated with reference to the institutional social context (van Dijk 1981). Though still placing much emphasis on literature's difference from other language use, he did now see literature as intending to bring about a change in its recipient. On the other hand, this change was only with respect to the literary utterance itself, and was still largely a matter of the reader's coming to "like" it, such liking most probably attaching only to its fictional world. All sense of an author's "talking" *about* that world, or of the reader "listening" *to the writer* rather than simply contemplating the free-floating fiction, was quite absent, partly because literary pragmatics as developed by van Dijk and Schmidt always tended to throw doubt on the very possibility of definitive authorial meanings. This in turn was because their approach also endorsed yet another of the formalist dogmas examined above: the basically Symbolist idea that a literary text is unlike "ordinary" language use because it has manifold potential meanings. Schmidt (1982), who argued that readers by convention read literature in positive expectation of semantic polyvalence, was such a firm believer in literary deviance that he overlooked, not only the pragmatic likelihood that readers will come to think that a text's writer intends something in particular, but the possibility that literature is no more variously interpretable than life in general. More recently, Tony Bex (1992, 1994), who tempers formalist claims with Hallidayan sociosemiotics, sees the whole of literature as a single genre, which is read according to a convention including a deviantly indirect, yet socially recognized application of Sperber and Wilson's principle of relevance.

All in all, formalist literary pragmatics tends to make literature more extraordinary than it really is. It underestimates, not only what Deborah Tannen (1986, 1992) calls the poetry of ordinary talk, but the extent to which literature itself is a form of communication. The approach offers some of the clearest examples of that a-historically de-humanizing paradigm for the humanities which, though permanently enriching our understanding of many different areas, did not evolve as a response to the condition of postmodernity, and leaves us pretty helpless in the face of it.

2.6. Some pros and cons

Both as a matter of aesthetic belief, and as a methodological exclusion for the sake of heuristic simplicity, the approaches to literature discussed in this chapter have on the whole perpetuated a Kantian separation of art from both knowledge and ethics. In this way they have preserved a fact-fiction dichotomy which can nowadays seem rather naive in its rigidity, and have more or less marginalized considerations of literary interpersonality. For a critic hoping to mediate between real writers, readers and their communities, such approaches offer no real foothold. The impression they give is that human beings are always and everywhere the same, and that even if they were not, literature is somehow quite separate from human engagements.

To re-emphasize what I said at the outset, scholars studying literature within this earlier paradigm were neither stupid nor wilfully untruthful. The Kantian aesthetics they had inherited still made perfect sense within their own ideological structures, and they were seeking to develop two observations about literature which no adequate account can afford to overlook: that literature can seem to have its own kind of beauty, intimately bound up with observances of, and departures from linguistic and more broadly generic conventions; and that literature seems functionally distinctive as well, in that it tends not only to avoid the direct address to a known listener or reader that we associate with conversation or a letter, but to avoid certain kinds of role as well — the straightforwardly informational, mandatory, and utilitarian roles, for instance, that are filled by encyclopedias, sermons, and instruction manuals. Literature's beauty, and its formal and functional distinctiveness, are what many of these scholars permanently illuminated, not least with the help of some important descriptive refinements. Even though their more extreme theoretical positions neglected the communicative aspects of literature, their best insights still stand as valuable reminders of these other aspects, and could well prove recyclable within the non-Kantian aesthetics we may one day see. Given that the human mind is flexible enough to alternate between a mode of literary reading that is more de-personalizing and one that is more inter-personalizing, the formalist emphasis may in the end be reconciled with an approach that is historical and communicational. Indeed, by the end of the next chapter I shall be pointing to scholarship in which a reconciliation may already be taking place.

For the time being, my point is only that, compared with the approaches reviewed above, a historical yet non-historicist literary pragmatics of the kind needed by a mediating critic will give greater stress to considerations such as the following:

that a literary text is usually written by somebody in particular;

that the text is what it is as a result of having been written by that particular person, and at the particular time and place;

that in order for the work to be instantiated, it has to be read by a reader;

that even granting the fullest and most well-informed effort of empathy, the way it is instantiated partly depends on who that reader is, and on where and when the reading is taking place;

and that despite the inevitable lack of correspondence between the author's sense of the work and any particular reader's sense of it, and despite the lack of a feed-back channel, the act of reading can nevertheless be experienced as part of a process of communication, sometimes giving rise to strong antagonism, or even to self-reassessment or personal change, which may ultimately lead to social change as well.

Chapter 3

The Historically Human

3.1. The paradigm shift

As we have partly seen in connection with speech act theory, by the 1970s a paradigm shift was under way. There was a new interest in the historical and the human, and indeed in the historically human: in approaches to the humanities that are historical without being historicist (in the deterministic sense explained in Section 1.2). Paradigm shifts of course take time, and certain developments from cultural structuralism and poststructuralism have involved a de-humanizing loss of direction, so contributing to the stalemates of some postmodern literary criticism. All the same, there have been very clear moves away from literary formalism, plus major changes in scholarly approaches to both spoken and written language. Also, certain aspects of cultural structuralism and poststructuralism have actually been very beneficial, and there has already been some progress towards a historical yet non-historicist view of both general and literary pragmatics. All things considered, it should now be much easier to offer mediating critics some theoretical support.

3.2. Moves away from literary formalism

In literary scholarship, interesting new positions were developed by a number of scholars who, unlike text-linguists, Jakobsonian stylisticians, structuralist narratologists, speech act poeticians and formalist literary pragmaticists, began to recognize literature's interpersonality. They were also keen to build bridges between literary scholarship, linguistics and philosophy, and in a very different spirit from speech act theoreticians of literature. So in 1977 John Reichart argued against too systematic a poetics, proposing instead that literature has no one single function or quintessentially aesthetic property, but is basically like many different kinds of thing (Reichart 1977). Using language suggested by Wittgenstein, he described literature as an open-ended series of family resemblances. In addition, he saw it as "for real". Even if it involves the element of imitated illocution "in the story", there is also a genuine speech act as well, between writer and readers. The dramatized speaker of a literary work is not necessarily fictional, and we can always make some assessment of an author's intentions, and respond accordingly, even though new interpretations inevitably arise with the passing years.

Some of Reichart's points were taken further in four books published in 1981. In Susan Sniader Lanser's poetics of fictional point of view, the link with the new humanizing and historical trends within the humanities generally was only implicit (Lanser 1981). But in Charles Altieri's account of literature as act, in Roger Fowler's treatment of literature as social discourse, and in Richard J. Watts's pragmalinguistic approach to narrative, literary study was more explicitly drawing on the new tendencies in philosophy and linguistics (Altieri 1981; Fowler 1981; Watts 1981).

In retrospect it is easy enough to find some aspects of this work inadequate. Watts's narratological analysis of *Hard Times* can perhaps seem a shade too formalist, and Lanser's description of the literary speech act comes as something of a disappointment after her strong account of the real author. Literature, she says, is essentially hypothetical, setting up a world whose difference from the real world is what affects us. This is a view which could well have been re-worked in pragmatic terms, but as it stands it is rather close to Samuel Levin's implicit higher sentence. Altieri, too, sometimes makes literature sound rather static, and readers rather passive. He places great stress on formal organization and contemplative pleasures, and says that poems are essentially different from other types of discourse: that they evoke a special aesthetic response combining sympathy and distance.

Basically, though, these four scholars were certainly moving towards a view of literature as historical and interactive. Lanser, for instance, following in the footsteps of Robert Weimann (1977), searchingly questioned the formalists' de-contextualizing account of point of view. A literary text's point of view, she insisted, plays a crucial part in channelling a communicative act. Although, like some of the narratologists mentioned in Section 2.3 above, she said that narrators can exist at various levels, she was firm on three points: in the text we can define a voice that is extrafictional; this voice is the textual counterpart of the real author; and there are conventions by which we can deduce whether or not this authorial voice is identical with that of the narrator. There is, in fact, a whole spectrum of possibilities, from complete separation of author and narrator to complete identity. And in the absence of complete identity, a text enters into dialogue, so to speak, with its authorial, extrafictional voice. On Lanser's account, then, real authors maintain a high profile.

Altieri's work had something of the same tendency. Like Austin, Searle and Grice, he started out from the later Wittgenstein's explorations of the conventional use of language in context. To Wittgenstein he then added Grice in order to arrive at a theory of interpretation. His idea was that there can be an "expressive implicature" such that readers apprehend the qualities of the writer as part of a text's meaning. Literary speech acts are dramatistic, then, but not in the de-contextualizing manner suggested by New Criticism. We know by convention how to situate them and establish their authorial intention, because we belong to what amounts to a kind of readers' jury. Just as we assess people's actions in ordinary life as involving a practical purpose, a self-regarding purpose, or some larger and perhaps unconscious project, so with a literary text we can work from extension to intension. We can reconstruct the author and the author's purpose in order to account for local aesthetic choices, for stylistic patterns, and for something we sense as an interpretative presence within a historical or typological framework. As a result, literature gives us a kind of cognitive knowledge which can be used for good or for ill, and which is not necessarily a matter of episodic or specific truth values. Altieri would clearly sympathize with the line of pragmatist semiotics from Dewey to Goodman, and, somewhat like I.A. Richards, he suggested that literature offers us frameworks of thought, feeling, and attitude, and helps to develop our powers of response — our sensibility, taste, tact. In other words, a literary work can have a significance well beyond its own historical context, and can even have a major cultural role to play in prompting readers towards an adequate conception of their own potentialities. By this Altieri was not suggesting that literature is a conspiratorial form of social control. In his account, readers retained a certain autonomy, and so did writers. He insisted on differences, not only between writers of different periods, but between writers belonging to one and the same period.

Fowler, for his part, returned to the nineteenth-century pre-formalist assumption that authors do speak to us, yet he was able to subject such authorial discourse to detailed linguistic analysis. For him, "discourse" was a far broader concept than for Chatman, as emerged when he analysed George Eliot's presentation of Ladislaw. This showed that "there are discourse relationships between three vocalizable consciousnesses." *George Eliot* presents *Ladislaw* to *the reader*. Here, no less than in Lanser and Altieri, works of literature were seen as answerable — responsible. They are the utterances of a real speaker with a determinate and relevant ideological background, and are not basically different from other types of discourse. According to Fowler, literature simply cannot be "cocooned from an integral and mobile relationship with society". In his view, favourite formalist terms such as "implied author", "persona", "fiction", "stasis", "objectivity", "depersonalization", and "tradition" were all too often pure evasions (Fowler 1981: 94).

Similarly, in Watts's pragmalinguistic analysis of *Hard Times* speech act theory was involved, not, as in Ohmann, by way of limiting illocutionary force to the fiction-internal imitation, but with a sense of the asserting or representing illocution of the literary writing itself, which can therefore interest and stimulate the reader. Literary communication was also seen to involve discoursal turn-taking, Watts being perhaps the first scholar to point out that readers, despite the superficial asymmetry of the situation, can refuse to grant the writer a turn. They can leave a book unread. As for the writer's end of things, Watts followed Mary Louise Pratt in appealing to Labov and Waletzky's work on oral narratives, so emphasizing that narrators have the freedom to evaluate their own tales. They can do so either directly and omnisciently, or by "filtering in" their views through characters (Watts 1981: 69).

In their different ways, Reichart, Lanser, Altieri, Fowler and Watts were all directly addressing the interpersonality of literature. This, together with their sometimes very clear historical concerns, and their corresponding avoidance of scientistic universalizations, augured well.

3.3. Late-twentieth-century linguistics

Linguists' restriction of scope to a de-contextualized *langue* or linguistic competence came under challenge at roughly the same time as did literary formalism. Speech act theory was one instance of this. But scholars representing several other approaches and methodologies — functional linguistics, conversation analysis, discourse analysis, critical discourse analysis, anthropological linguistics, corpus linguistics — were also beginning to relate words to interaction. For the functionalists of the Halliday school, for instance, language had an interpersonal function, with which ideational and textual functions were in interplay. In fact a text's interpersonality was something which its ideational and textual dimensions served to actualize, and by way of structures which were not so much linguistic as sociosemiotic within the community. In order to plot the workings of this arrangement, the Hallidayans drew up flow-charts of particular real-life interchanges. And at least for dialogues between just two participants with clearly definable goals, such analysis was fairly manageable, as in Eija Ventola's study of simple service encounters in shops and post offices (Ventola 1987).

Other scholars tried to do the same kind of thing on a more ambitious scale. Willis Edmondson (1981), partly in response to speech act theory, claimed that *all* communication can be mapped onto interaction, provided that the inventory of different kinds of speech act is greatly expanded. One of his most important arguments was that there is really no such thing as an indirect speech act; there are simply some illocutions whose force is negotiable. Another of his conclusions was that not all interaction is verbally realized in any case, so that the turns of talk in a conversation are no true guide to what is happening. The linguistic surface can be deceptive, and both semantic and pragmatic analysis may be needed in order to pin the interaction down.

Geoffrey Leech (1983a), too, though a literary formalist in his poetics and stylistics, in his more purely linguistic work aimed at a detailed picture of interactional pragmatics. Borrowing Halliday's trilogy of ideational, textual and interpersonal functions, he based everything on an interplay between grammar (phonology, syntax, semantics) and pragmatics. He first worked out the ideation of sentences (i.e. their semantic representations), and then sought to show how hearers deduce the specific meaning and force of that ideation as used in the particular context. His suggestion was that they do this by heuristically applying principles derived from both a textual rhetoric and an interpersonal rhetoric, at which points his scheme became scarcely less complicated than Edmondson's.[8] Like Edmondson, too, Leech found Searle's list of illocu-

---

8. For the record, the textual rhetoric is made up of: a processability principle, with attendant maxims; a clarity principle; an economy principle; and an expressivity principle, with an attendant maxim. The interpersonal rhetoric is made up of: Grice's cooperative principle, with its maxims of quantity, quality, relation and manner; a politeness principle, with maxims of tact, generosity, approbation, modesty, agreement, and sympathy; an irony principle; a banter principle; an interest principle; and what Leech calls a pollyanna principle.

tionary forces too narrow, and wrote of speech acts whose force can be negotiated. Most interestingly of all, perhaps, having set up no fewer than ten pragmatic principles and various maxims, he then tried to show how one principle or maxim can be in tension with another, and even be outweighed by it. His work was a fascinating attempt to capture something of the complex processuality of language interaction in the real world. Traditional speech act theory can seem very undynamic by comparison.

Other linguists, it is true, have been sceptical of such projects. Stephen Levinson deemed Edmondson's attempt to write a grammar of behaviour based on clearly definable and structured acts, and to intermesh this with a grammar of language utterance, frankly unrealistic (Levinson 1983: 288–92), and Levinson and Penelope Brown reacted negatively to Leech's proposals (Brown and Levinson 1987 [1978]: 4–7). Hence Levinson's own conversation analysis did not try to plumb conversation's interactive depths. Instead, when describing those points in a conversation at which a new turn can start he entirely confined himself to empirical observations of surface features such as pausing. Similarly, although he, too, dispensed with indirect speech acts, he did so by means of a sequence of four utterances (I. "Could you open the window?" II."Yes." III. "Please open one then". IV. "Yes, of course.") of which two (II and III) are simply omitted as a matter of polite convention (Levinson 1983: 356–64, 296–302).

Nor is Levinson's caution hard to understand. Any grammar of underlying behaviour based on clearly definable and structured acts presupposes an affirmative answer to a very big question: Is human action "grammatically" structured? Yet even Ventola's flowchart for simple post-office encounters had to include options for the mixing, embedding and switching of genres, and for recursions, omissions and side-programming. This was because, in even the most rudimentary human intercourse, there is much that seems unpredictable. Although linguistic and behavioural norms are socially given, a human being is nevertheless a social *individual*, as I am putting it, whose adaptation to the socially given is not necessarily passive, since there is also the scope for resistance, or for creative *co*-adaptation. Then again, how many different goals, and how many different kinds of considerations or principles, can human beings keep in play simultaneously? Is Leech's model with its ten principles likely to be more accurate than a model with fifty, or with three, or — like relevance theory — with just one? Could not the four principles of Leech's textual rhetoric — processability, clarity, economy, expressivity —

be assimilated to the first principle of his interpersonal rhetoric — to Grice's cooperative principle, in fact? And so on. Perhaps a very close and comprehensive mapping of language on interaction will have to remain the scientistically minded linguist's unfulfilled dream.

These hesitations notwithstanding, human interactivity would never work without regularities and structures of some sort, however temporary and flexible, and we can already talk about at least some of the interpersonal dimensions of language use. In particular, over the past twenty years or so much has been learnt about linguistic manifestations of power, ideology, gender, and intercultural tension, and there has also been some valuable discussion of politeness phenomena. I shall later be suggesting that this kind of research, if developed in a sufficiently non-deterministic spirit, can serve as a stimulus to ideas about the interactivity of literature. (See esp. Section 5.4, on literary authors' politeness.)

3.4. The written deed

Another feature of the more recent linguistics is also relevant. Earlier linguists' hesitation to speak up for the interpersonality of literature reflected their methodological restrictions in describing language of any kind at all. But it also has to be said that they did think of *written* language — not just literary texts but written texts of every sort — as somehow less than fully communicational, a phonocentric prejudice which many lay people unquestioningly shared. Today, by contrast, many linguists would insist that writings are interactional deeds.

In oral cultures, obviously, language is always spoken language, and language spoken in a self-evident context. Walter J. Ong has shown that the intimate relationship between oral narrators and their listeners can affect the way a story gets told:

> Narrative originality lodges not in making up new stories but in managing a particular interaction with this audience at this time — at every telling the story has to be introduced uniquely into a unique situation, for in oral cultures an audience must be brought to respond, often vigorously.
> (Ong 1982: 41–2)

This is understandable, since the aim and result of oral narrative are not merely aesthetic:

> Performance of an oral epic ... can serve also simultaneously as an act of
> celebration, as *paideia* or education for youth, as a strengthener of group
> identity, as a way of keeping alive all sorts of lore — historical, biological,
> zoological, sociological, venatic, nautical, religious — and much else.
> (Ong 1982: 161)

Ong notes that writers active within literate cultures still wrote to be read aloud well down into the nineteenth century. His main argument, however, is that genuine author-audience interaction gradually lost its force: that thanks to the increasing hold of print, the author and the reader both became fictionalized and de-contextualized — became, in effect, the implied author and the implied reader, structures which Ong regards as a-historical and purely artistic. This view may well seem plausible enough, especially if we bear in mind the aesthetics of Realism and Modernism. Henry James's call for novels providing a maximally intense illusion of reality shifted attention right away from the act of enunciation to the enunciated itself — from "who says" to "what is said" — and the same goes for T.S. Eliot's early ideas about poetic impersonality, or for New Critical ideas about author and reader personae as hermetic seals between art and life.

Yet the residual orality of literate culture could well be stronger than Ong allows. He might have noted, for instance, that a nineteenth century writer such as Dickens not only wrote to be read aloud but, in serializing his novels, was also sensitive to feed-back. The woman on whom he modelled *David Copperfield*'s Miss Mowcher, the dwarfish travelling chiropodist and supplier of cosmetics, recognized herself from his descriptions, and wrote to complain that he had made her too grotesque and sinister. Dickens, having written a propitiatory reply, in later issues was careful to underline that Miss Mowcher's unprepossessing appearance and manner were merely the mask for some very high principles (Bentley, Slater and Burgess 1990: 171). To generalize the point: serious writers never merely give the public what it wants; but neither will they court rejection. Their audience can be a decisive presence for them.

Ong's account of the fictionalizing de-contextualization of writers and readers unquestioningly endorses the New Critical dogma which he presumably picked up at school or university. Basically, he does not recognize that there are sender and receiver personae in communication of all kinds, and that in literature they have the same interpersonalizing function as elsewhere. Not that there is no difference between speech and writing (cf. Čmejrková, Daneš and Havlová 1994). As far as surface features are concerned, writing tends to have a higher lexical density and simpler dependency structures (Halliday

1985: xxiv), to use "the" rather than "this" or "that" (Ochs 1979), and to have an infrequent use of so-called pragmatic particles or compromizers such as "you know" and "kind of" (Östman 1982, 1995; James 1983). Speech phenomena such as stuttering and hesitations have no equivalent in writing other than in transcripts of real or fictional conversations, while some types of written text correspond to nothing at all in normal speech — telephone directories, for example. Even so, many of the surface phenomena which, in spoken language, every linguist associates with interpersonal considerations of, say, politeness also occur in written language as well. This alone suggests that care should be taken not to overemphasize functional differences either.

True, there is a tradition going back at least as far as the Prague school of functional linguistics which sees speech as emotional, interpersonally involved, interactional, "warm", whereas writing would be detached, informational, "cold" (Vackek 1973: 15–16, Chafe 1982; Brown and Yule 1983: 13, Lakoff 1982). True, too, some scholars have argued that there are real cognitive differences in both encoding and reception, speech tending to be used in face-to-face situations, whereas writing tends to bridge gaps in time and space (Hildyard and Olson 1982; Olson and Hildyard 1983). But to take this last issue first, in the age of telephones, tape-recorders and e-mail it is easy enough to see that these situational tendencies are *only* tendencies. Still more to the point, some types of written text — laws, holy books, prayerbooks, cooking recipes, love-letters, business letters even — promote at least as much interaction between communal or individual sender and receiver as any speech does, and conversely, certain types of speech are analytically objective. Some speech is more ceremonial than many styles of writing, and some writing is more casual and colloquial than many styles of speech. Speakers and writers alike select from a wide variety of styles and tones, and their choice here — let alone their choice of what to say — immediately confronts hearers or readers as some particular kind of human approach.

One explanation for the phonocentric attitudes of Ong and the earlier linguists is suggested by Derrida (1974 [1967]), who sees a link with what he describes as the Western world's unexamined prioritorization of presence. Speech is assumed to be original and authentic, whereas writing is deemed derivative and more artificial. One of Derrida's own arguments is that speech and writing are both instances of language, and that both are equally operative in constructing a reality that bears no necessary relation to any world there might be "outside" of language. For him, speech and writing are equally far away from any such reality, including the possible reality of the persons producing and receiving the spoken or written utterance. Derrida would also say, though, that writing is not *less* authentically personal than speech, and that is the main point here. During an act of reading, the writer is usually physically absent, and may even be dead and buried. But during absence, or even after death, a person's influence on others may be stronger than ever before, and a piece of writing can be instrumental in this. "Has there been a book which has changed your life?" is a perfectly reasonable question to ask.

Another unexamined assumption may have been that writing is monologic, and that monologue is not interactive. If so, the assumption is hardly surprising, since it is only fairly recently that an interactive dimension has been recognized in extended *spoken* monologues. In this connection, some remarks by Schegloff were especially notable:

> The common discourse-analytic standpoint treats the lecture, or sermon, or story told in an elicitation interview, campfire setting, or around the table, as the product of a single speaker and a single mind; the conversation-analytic angle of inquiry does not let go of the fact that speech-exchange systems are involved, in which more than one participant is present and relevant to the talk, even when only one does any talking.
> (Schegloff 1981: 71–2)

Fortunately, however, and despite the difficulties of a comprehensive mapping of language on to interaction, such insights have already been applied to written texts.

One of the earliest attempts was by Bennison Gray (1977), who saw the main difference between speech and writing as little more than the degree of interactional explicitness. In both speech and writing, he labelled the main relations between one assertion and the next as either descriptive (continuing or contrasting), explanatory (supporting or concluding), or rhetorical (questioning or answering). In spoken dialogue, there are often fully-formed questions at the surface level, which rhetorically generate answering moves from one assertion to the next. In writing, every new move is a reply to a question that is more usually only implied. Gray was well aware that these catalytic questions are chosen by writers themselves, whereas in spoken dialogue it is the recipients who do this. Indeed, Gray suggested that these writer-selected questions stem from a large-scale sense-coherence framework that is also chosen by the writer, and that the entire composition can thus be seen as a single macro-assertion. But not even this amounts to an absolute difference between speech and writing, since in speech situations such as job interviews and classroom talk one participant can be much more in control than another. Gray's kind of approach was further developed by Edmondson (1981), moreover, who spotted an element of interactionally strategic anticipation in language use of any kind. Or as Lauri Carlson, borrowing an idea from Hintikka's game-theoretical semantics, put it, the interactivity of both written texts and spoken monologue can be traced with the help of interpolation:

> In order to reveal the implicit structure of a piece of discourse, extend it into a dialogue, by adding implicit dialogue steps which make the connections between the sentences of the text explicit.
> (Carlson 1983: 146)

Most strikingly of all, perhaps, the covertly dialogic nature of writing has for at least two decades been clearly grasped by applied linguists in the fields of composition and reading (Miller and Kintsch 1980, de Beaugrande 1982; Cooper 1982). A composition teacher's first duty is to help pupils see that "readability is an interactive relationship between the properties of a text and the reader who is processing it" (Miller and Kintsch 1980: 348). As we can all know from our own attempts to write, a writer is actually just as keen to hold the floor as a speaker, and perhaps more prone to anxiety about it. When writing, we cannot sit back and enjoy other people's contributions, and it can be unnerving to know that we shall never *see* and *hear* when a recipient stops attending to us. The fact that compromizing pragmatic particles ("kind of", "you know" and so on) do not generally occur in writing does not mean that as writers we never hesitate. We have more time to formulate our ideas than as speakers, but we are just as unwilling to risk rejection by forcing the pace. In the act of writing there is an unmitigated finalty that can be something of a burden. For although it is a type of communication which seems to travel on a one-way ticket, articulating no explicit exchange, at the reader's end this can only mean that the negotiation of otherness takes on a marked centrality. A writer's otherness can become very highly salient, and to repeat Watts's point, readers may even refuse to grant it much of a "turn". Few of them would go to the Johnsonian lengths of throwing an offending volume out of the window. But for readers to read most of the written language that is actually addressed to them, life is far too short. This means that writers do have to use the medium's foregrounding of their otherness to some effect, for they may never get a second chance. If readers are not won over, if readers themselves do not become truly involved, nothing can be said to be happening. Communication will simply not be taking place. With writing no less than with any other kind of communication, partnership in the interaction is not confined to overt linguistic production. Soldiers silently obeying an order, pupils who do not get to answer teacher's question, delegates who walk out in silent protest — they are all interacting. And so are people with their nose stuck in a book.

The only time when a piece of writing is not working interpersonally is when nobody is thinking about it. As long as somebody is in the process of writing, reading, listening to, or remembering it, interaction with its assumed author must be under way. Not all *language* is interpersonal. But all language *use* is interpersonal. A book on a shelf is not interpersonal, but does represent a potential to interpersonality. Whatever else it contains, its author could not fail to include a proposed relationship between the writer and reader personae, in some proposed configuration of time, space, culture, knowledge, ideology, attitude and feeling. This multidimensional model of the sender-receiver relationship is an invitation to empathy which anyone starting to process the book's language cannot fail to latch on to, even if they also come to criticize it. Such catalysts to interaction work in the same way for writing, including literary writing, as for speech. When they are being put there by a writer, or are found and used by a reader, then what is taking place is a form of interpersonal activity.

3.5. From cultural structuralism and poststructuralism to postmodern stalemate

From the 1970s onwards, then, the climate of ideas within the humanities has radically changed. Many scholarly approaches are now re-contextualizing human reality within history as a matter of course. In literary scholarship, however, the main boost to this did not come from the work of Reichart, Lanser, Altieri, Roger Fowler and Watts, excellent and suggestive though it was. Far more influential were Marxist criticism, cultural structuralism and poststructuralism, feminist criticism and, from a somewhat later date, cultural materialism and new historicism. These approaches boldly challenged formalist ideas about a timelessly aesthetic autonomy, emphasizing instead a kind of consubstantiality of literature with society, language and ideology, an argument representing the transmigration of structuralist thinking from linguistics via cultural anthropology. Since then, the same trend has been continued in approaches such as gay and lesbian criticism, postcolonial criticism, and ethnic criticism. All along, it has done much to fuel the postmodern critique of traditional norms and legitimations.

For the would-be mediating critic, these developments have been a mixed blessing. On the one hand, the new approaches have brought the facts of historical contextualization into sharper focus, and have in some respects positively emphasized the human being's capacity for moving between one sociocultural formation and another. As a result, it is easier to talk about situational difference, and without precluding the kind of imaginative self-projection which can help to negotiate it. On the other hand, there are also versions of the new thinking in which the likelihood of communication across lines of sociohistorical difference would be seriously underestimated. This is because they involve an element of sociocultural determinism, which directly encourages the stalemates of some postmodern critical discourse.

One representative figure was Roland Barthes, who, in opposition to nineteenth-century-style criticism of both the biographical and aestheticizing varieties, announced the death of the author (Barthes 1977 [1968]). To the extent that his project was structuralist, he was saying that neither authors nor anybody else could be thought of as having a strongly centred self. It was therefore not possible to speak of active individuals who were author-artists. There were only writer-workers, who were a more or less passive channel through which the society's common culture and language necessarily flowed. Given a poststructuralist twist, the argument was that such writer-workers were actually no more important than readers, who interpreted texts in many different ways. This, though, did not mean that readers won back a measure of centred identity and freedom, since interpretative variability was seen as another aspect of the workings of language itself. Language was strapped firmly into the driving seat, with the erratic process of semiosis as the only route map.

In both the structuralist and the poststructuralist modes, Barthes was so seminal for many of the critical approaches flourishing during the last quarter of the century that "Barthesian" is a convenient collective term. Here, too, I must mention my own indebtedness. Although his formulations could be deliberately provocative, perhaps nudging other critics towards stances of extremist determinism, his work is also very suggestive for mediating criticism, and for the type of theory on which it must be based. His emphasis on the productive role of reading can spur the historical yet non-historicist pragmaticist's effort to relate different styles of reading to the contexts in which they occur. No less valuable is his cultural structuralist's view of writers, since literary texts do have a kind of representativeness, the major ones no less than the undistinguished and derivative. In Barthes's account, such manifestations of social colour are not, as within the behaviouristic-formalist paradigm, lost sight of, but are very clearly distinguished, partly by means of the concept of intertextuality. That concept, moreover, and the wider de-centering strategy to which it was a contribution, will also support the pragmatist in resisting the older, formalist variety of de-personalization. According to the New Critics, the literature-lover's sense of being confronted by a writer's human personality was the result of an artistic illusion; a text's authorial persona bore no necessary relation to the author's personality "in reality". Barthes, by contrast, in suggesting that the psyche is open to social formation, sees it as so malleable and protean that no form of identity is more original or authentic than any other. I shall later have to qualify this point, by noting certain continuities of moral autonomy and temperament. But it is certainly the case that an author's literary personality need be no less complete or less genuine than any other version of personality an individual takes on. As Reichart long since pointed out, the dramatized speaker of a literary text is not necessarily fictional in any very meaningful sense. And readers, too, are no less labile than authors. For the purposes of communication, they are perfectly able to empathize with social formations that are different from their own current one, and may even allow themselves to be influenced in some way.

In some of the commentary influenced by Barthes and his *confrères*, however, the human being's psychological flexibility receives far less allowance. Whereas Modernist formalism had tended to dissociate literature from history, Barthesians not only insisted on the connection, but sometimes went as far as historicist reductionism. From a mediating critic's point of view, this did not represent an improvement. The Modernist dissociation and the Barthesian reduction were linked to two very different kinds of political and ideological motivation. But the accounts they offered of both human nature and literature were equally distorting and de-personalizing.

For Barthes, no less than for T.S. Eliot or the New Critics, the enemy, so to speak, was to be found in the middle classes, but by no means for the same reason. The early Eliot's anti-humanistic suspicion of personality and individuality reflected the influence of Charles Maurras, P. Lasserre and the ultraconservative *Action Française* movement, with its twin emphases on the human being's sinful imperfectability and the consequent need for discipline and order (Svarny 1988). Later on, similarly, the formalist dogma of impersonality was to help the New Critics avoid awkward questions about a writer's social background, so shoring up an agrarian myth of the classlessly democratic American republic. As for Barthes, his obituary on the author, no less than Eliot's influential essay "Tradition and the Individual Talent", can be read as an attack on the individualism of bourgeois capitalism, but from the opposite end of the political spectrum. Its association with the Paris of 1968 was symptomatic.

At both extremes, as it happens, the aesthetic doctrines which emerged were actually overstatements, applying more fully to certain forms of textual production than to others. For the early Eliot, impersonality would tend to be an impersonality of elitist aesthetic form, probably most fully realized in the poetry of the Symbolists and Imagists. For Barthes, impersonality was perhaps closer to an impersonality of the folk, as found in ballads, in nursery rhymes, in popular culture generally, and in its oral dimension in particular. In much post-structuralist cultural analysis, literacy, with all its potential for artistic creativity, for scholarship, for rational argument and, above all, for individual self-fashioning, is sometimes frowned upon as a kind of monologically repressive privilege of class, almost as if reading and writing were still not widely taught. Whereas Walter J. Ong perpetuated New Critical attitudes by playing literature's residual orality down, some Barthesian commentators have found no other way to praise literary texts except by overemphasizing it, a valorization which works by reducing a writer's authority.

With the movement from the older scholarly paradigm to the newer, then, what has sometimes happened is that the formalist type of impersonality has merely been rejected in favour of impersonality of a structuralist or poststructuralist type. This still leaves the impression that any interpersonal link between literary authors and their readers is an impossibility. The only difference between extremist versions of the older and newer orthodoxies is that, whereas formalism tended to suggest that literature was too *sui generis* to communicate anything at all, some cultural structuralists and poststructuralists have now seen literature as too mundane, too implicated in society's intertextualities in general, too closely analogous to a tradition of anonymously oral transmission, to communicate anything personally distinctive.

Some of their accounts have actually involved an obscurantist kind of animism, by which a wholesale transfer of responsibility for deeds of writing and reading is made from human beings to language or society or culture or ideology, by whose structures human identity and experience are taken to be completely determined. According to David Trotter (1988), for example, Dickens willy-nilly transmits the bourgeois discourse of economic modernity, as if he were only a mindless mouthpiece. More particularly, Trotter finds in Dickens an obsession with the notion of circulation. The scientific backing for this was in Adam Smith's advocacy of *laissez faire*, the theory that goods and services should be traded without any restrictions. But other areas of life, and other discourses, had also been affected. Trotter sees a direct link between Dickens's own restless mobility and his belief that people, air, and information should all flow about freely. He lived in constant fear of any kind of stagnation, physical or spiritual, and his association with the "Moral Police" was an attempt to bring about social reforms by dispelling concentrations of disease or ignorance, for instance by proper sanitation or circulating libraries. In his novels, prostitutes and secretive lawyers are among those who cause blockages, whereas the detective police and the science of physiognomy open things up by allowing meanings to circulate freely from signs. On all of which points Trotter is most helpfully perceptive, except in suggesting that this is the *only* way Dickens thinks. A more sophisticated account of Dickens's reaction to modernity is offered by Jeremy Tambling (1993), who sees the desire for openness, movement and progress as coming up against a conservative desire for concealment and preservation. So Dickens's fascination with railways as the means to mobility and change is complemented by a concern for those ways of life and forms of experience which the railways were destroying. Dickens could sympathize with two very different ideological strains, then, and had sufficient independence of mind to play them off against each other.

Barthesian commentary of the more de-humanizing variety, by depriving human beings of autonomy and moral initiative, has implied that neither an author nor a reader stands much chance of doing or thinking anything out of the ordinary. Authors are viewed as unable to write anything which anyone else of the same formation could not have written just as well, while readers are assumed to read only in certain culturally sanctioned ways. If this were indeed so, when a writer and a particular readership belonged to one and the same phase of the same culture, the writer's texts would not be truly communicative, so that the need for mediation would never arise. What took place between writer and readers would be a mere circularity of cultural production, the society talking to itself, as it were. As for a writer and a particular readership belonging to two different cultural constellations, even such empty circularity would be impossible. Instead, there would be sheer disjunction. Yet in both kinds of situation, what actually happens is clearly not like this at all. Readers whose cultural formation is ostensibly identical with that of a writer they are reading can indeed experience the shock of newness, and can also read in ways which would leave the writer quite non-plussed. As for readers reading an old or alien author, they can in fact register a very great deal, and may even find some of the styles of writing and reading practised within their own more immediate milieu much less attractive.

At their most de-humanizing, the Barthesians see authors as repeating something that has been done before, so that they are rather characterless. This is not a complete nonsense, since even the most obviously literary texts — poems, novels, plays — can often seem of a piece with other products of the contemporary culture, just as a ballad or nursery rhyme can make us feel that we are sharing in a kind of wisdom or humour that is somehow timelessly communal. Lyric poetry, however, the generic possibility tendentiously downplayed in Barthes's essay on the death of the author, can strike us as also very distinctive, and its entire *raison d'être* and effect can involve an element of perceptible self-expression. In ignoring this, de-personalization of a structuralist and poststructuralist variety is unrealistic at precisely the same point as was the late-nineteenth-century and Modernist aestheticism whose ideology it was supposed to replace. To see a poem such as "She dwelt among the untrodden ways" as the result of Wordsworth's social formation, or as a text which self-deconstructively undermines the reality of both its "she" and "me", is at least as much of a half-truth as to call it a verbal icon. Even *non*-lyrical works, moreover, are paradoxically representative and unique, and one of the things to emerge from the tension between the communal and the exceptional is nothing less than a matter of personality. That an author who makes an impact is positively recognizable is borne out by countless readers such as Jonathan Bate:

> I remember when I first read *Pericles* as a teenager, ignorant of authenticity disputes and putative collaborations. I couldn't put my finger on what it was, but something wasn't quite right about the language of the first two acts. Then the storm broke at the beginning of Act Three — "The god of this great vast, rebuke these surges,/Which wash both heaven and hell" — and suddenly the verse was humming, and I knew I was reading Shakespeare.
> (Bate 1997: 3)

Even if readers cannot always attribute a significant text to its author *prima vista*, they have little difficulty in relating hitherto unseen work to what they know already, just as connoisseurs of other forms of cultural production have corresponding abilities. The differences between one major author's writing and another's will be quite unmistakable, even if both of them have been active within one and the same literary genre during one and the same period. Christopher Marlowe, all historical similarities notwithstanding, could never be Shakespeare, Dickens never Thackeray, Frost's poems never Hardy's. Even the Brontë sisters are three very different novelists for readers who know them at all well. Although writers are social beings, they are actually social individuals, and by the same token the structuralist and poststructuralist concept of interextuality, for all its value to a pragmaticist seeking to focus the consequences of sociocultural situationalities, should not be used to de-center the human self too completely. Authors' own control over what they write is by no means unlimited. But they are not just wafted away on an intertextual flow. On the contrary, their dialogue with some of their predecessors and contemporaries can be quite conscious and even explicit. Their deliberate response to influences and sources, or their deliberate cultivation of, say, allusion and parody, can give rise to crucial types of newness, which may well stand in need of mediating criticism, not least within their own communal grouping.

So much for authors. As it affects the description of readers, the extremist type of determinism is equally unrealistic, which explains how it has become an ingredient in the culture wars of postmodern societies. In any true democracy, the political and social goals of most Barthesian commentators would in themselves be unimpeachable. Their structuralist and poststructuralist analyses have identified the linguistic and ideological concealments of time-honoured injustices, so adding yeast to the postmodern brew of sociocultural difference. Amid even the headiest excitement, a certain reasonableness has often prevailed, as critics representing different groupings have tried to understand each other and even form alliances. Much Barthesian criticism has also been genuinely lively, even if not matching Barthes's own lambent intelligence and sheer delight in language. Constitutionally incapable of being boring, Barthes himself was for ever racing on ahead to new insights, opening up every topic or text he ever discussed to a whole new range of enquiry. At the same time, though, his agility certainly was rather exceptional, since when human beings are faced with a wide array of sociocultural difference, they may very easily withdraw into the shell of what feels like a hard and fast identity. Given structuralist and poststructuralist theory at its most reductive, such a response is positively reinforced. The differences between one grouping and another come to seem inevitable and unsurmountable, since the individual's cultural formation is figured as virtually cast-iron. The kind of thing that gets lost from view is that human beings can have sufficient independence and flexibility of mind to criticize their own grouping; that even a monolingual can display an impressive facility of imaginative self-projection into manifold mind-sets and scenarios; and that a person who is proficient in several languages can only be so by contextualizing and interpreting their signified-signifier relationships within the cognitive environments of the different societies with which they are typically associated (Sell 1995a). Theoreticians and critics who overlook such considerations may well underestimate the sheer scope of human communication, so ending up in a kind of stalemate. For them, sociocultural differences merely tend to fuel a political struggle of the most bitterly unconstructive kind. As K. Anthony Appiah begins to hint, what happens is that self-definition takes the form of an undue self-limitation, through the insistence on certain human potentialities to the exclusion of far too many others. The polarities used to separate one readership from another become strategically exaggerated, and thereby over-rigid.

In discussion of this kind, the pessimistic social determinism is often coupled to a Foucauldian anatomy of power relations. Foucault's magisterial cultural histories of reason, madness, punishment and sexuality have been of crucial importance for several groupings thrown up into self-consciousness by the postmodern maelstrom, while for many of the scholars developing American new historicism, British cultural materialism, feminist studies, gay and lesbian studies, postcolonial studies, and ethnic studies he is little less than foundational. Very characteristic of his work, however, is a complete absence of that infectious personal exuberance by which, in Barthes, the account of social formation is so fascinatingly qualified. The pyrotechnics of Barthes's own mind-style always tends to confirm his suggestion that the psyche, having taken the impression of one social formation, is open to countless others. Foucault's own personal gloom, by contrast, is no less oppressive than the oppressions his analysis so tellingly exposes. He will write, for instance,

> We are accustomed to see in an author's fecundity, in the multiplicity of the commentaries, and in the development of a discipline [from such a major author's contribution] so many infinite resources for the creation of discourses. Perhaps so, but they are nonetheless principles of constraint; it is very likely impossible to account for their positive and multiplicatory role if we do not take into consideration their restrictive and constraining function. (Foucault 1996 [1971]: 248)

and his "Perhaps so" is seldom if ever elaborated into a fuller account of the "positive and multiplicatory role". For most of the time, he seems to labour under an obscurantist sense of various agentless forces, by which society restricts and constrains. Carried to its logical conclusion, this paranoiac defeatism can only throw in doubt his own and any other commentator's ability to challenge their society with a constructive and uncompromized critique. Just like anybody else, they would merely be society's brain-washed victims, and at one point he even asks,

> What, after all, is an education system, other than a ritualization of speech, a qualification and a fixing of the roles for speaking subjects, the constitution of a doctrinal group, however diffuse, a distribution and an appropriation of discourse with its powers and knowledges?
> (Foucault 1996 [1971]: 251)

Well, if we refuse to take this as a rhetorical question, some educational ventures really are less totalitarian. The irony is, though, that this — not least in his forcing through of the rhetorical question — is clearly how Foucault is trying to educate his own readers. And as I say, he has actually become foundational: an author in the constraining sense of the first quotation above, his success borne out by the vociferousness of his own doctrinal group. As for the dogmas, his radical challenge to public perceptions has been paradoxically inspiring and depressing. While invaluably highlighting patterns of power and control, he systematically underestimates the odds for the kind of originality which he himself so unexhibitionistically manifests.

Whether or not taking their cue from Foucault directly, many intellectuals working in the wake of structuralism and poststructuralism give voice to a similarly pessimistic determinism, which has already been discussed by, among others, J.C. Merquior (1986) and Raymond Tallis (1997). For John Hillis Miller (1995), for instance, sociocultural difference is "all the way down", and his response to the postmodern culture wars besetting American universities is therefore very different from that of Gerald Graff (cf. Section 1.3 above). Miller's call is for a "university of dissensus". For him, the centripetal is far more to be feared than the centrifugal. So his adepts at dissensus would spend their time questioning commonly accepted realistic representations, and subjecting ordinary uses of language to violent interrogation. To expose the assumptions hidden beneath common sense would be the way to combat what he sees as a very sinister commodifying hegemony.

Miller's anxieties are as understandable as Foucault's cultural histories are revealing. It is impossible to read his words without recognizing their intelligence and sincerity as one powerful thinker's response to the society in which he finds himself. Clearly, too, his feelings of dismay are by no means uninformed about the workings of human civilization in general. Even Foucault's severest critics would hardly deny that common sense can become the mask of human exploitation, not least because a vaunting of its commonness can so easily marginalize or quite erase any human formation regarded as unacceptable. That is why an all-embracing consensus would never be a possible or desirable outcome of mediating criticism. Stuart Hampshire's Heraclitean warnings against any such dream should be firmly borne in mind.

All the same, Miller does seem to be caught on the horns of the ancient Western dilemma mentioned earlier (in Section 2.3). Unless I have misread him, his response to scientism and judgemental certainties is in effect nihilism, which he apparently believes is the only viable alternative. Assuming, not without justification, that agreement on some universal truth and universal values will all too often result from force or fraud, he evidently thinks that common sense deserves no credence at all, and that negotiation between different viewpoints can never be *anything but* an ominous repression of difference. Even if he could entertain the idea of a relative truth of the kind recognized by American pragmatists and German hermeneuticians, he would probably have no faith in Habermas's vision of a reasonable dialogue *between* the relative truths of different groupings. He might even query Hampshire's belief in a "minimal procedural justice" springing from "a recognisable basic level of common decency". The possibility he seems to rule out is that members of one culture or subculture will, in Isaiah Berlin words, bring into play "the force of imaginative insight" and thereby "understand (what Vico called *entrare*) the values, the ideals, the forms of life" of some very different community (Berlin 1997: 9). Instead, his proposal for a university of dissensus not only involves a reification of self and other that seems rather static and essentialistic from such a perceptive deconstructionist, but splits up the university into a number of introverted ghettoes, so replicating the postmodern city at its most dysfunctional. The gesture connotes a hermeneutics of suspicion so intently concerned with the unveiling of hegemonic conspiracies that any idea of people getting together for reasons non-malign is quite excluded.

An altogether different view of the university's role emerges from Amy Gutman's description of the Princeton University Center for Human Values.

> Can people who differ in their moral perspectives nonetheless reason together in ways that are productive of greater ethical understanding? The University Center faces up to this challenge by supporting a university education that is centrally concerned with examining ethical values, the various standards according to which individuals and groups make significant choices and evaluate their own as well as other ways of life. Through the teaching, research, and public discussions that it sponsors, the University Center encourages the systematic study of ethical values and the mutual influences of education, philosophy, religion, politics, the professions, the arts, literature, science and technology, and ethical life. In no small part, the promise of ethical understanding lies in its educational practice. If universities are not dedicated to pushing our individual and collective reasoning about human values to its limits, then who will be?
> (Gutman 1994: xiii-xiv)

This is much closer to Graff's proposals for "teaching the conflicts". Nor need it be a recipe for a university — or a society — of gregarious zombies. Intellectually, such a programme could try to balance the centrifugal and the centripetal in the spirit of Habermas. Temperamentally, it would represent a cautious optimism, or a not excessive pessimism. Both intellectually and temperamentally, it would foster an ideal of conversation.

Yet if Miller, whether by temperament or intellect or both, were unable to accept such a vision, he could justly claim to be a lot more honest than some of those who profess to. There are a fair number of literary critics and other commentators who, though basically persuaded by our time's extremist cultural determinism that difference is "all the way down", still pay lip service to the conversational ideal. Understandably wishing to defuse conflicts, they purport to believe that communication will be successful as long as nobody says anything offensive. So arises the insincere kind of political correctness. When this comes into play, the opposed parties do not communicate in a way that is conciliatory, but are conciliatory *without* communicating. Whereas a political correctness stemming from a genuine respect for otherness will always welcome opportunities for dialogue, the phenomenon at issue here is a mere sham, beneath which atavistic suspicions, prejudices and antagonisms can only thrive with renewed vigour. The chances of genuine rapprochement will actually have worsened, and there is always the risk that the veil will be rudely torn asunder, with new intensities of linguistic or even physical abuse as the most likely sequel.

A case in point occurred in 1992, when Pat Buchanan, looking for votes in the southern primaries, thundered forth his intention to thrash the National

Endowment for the Arts (the NEA) for "subsidizing both filthy and blasphemous art". This outburst was part of a backlash occasioned by news of NEA funding awarded to Ramona Lofton (pen name: Sapphire) for the writing of a poem inaccurately reported as describing a homoerotic act by Jesus Christ. In fact, Lofton's "Wild Thing" is about a gang-rape carried out by black teenagers on a white female jogger in Central Park, though its main focus is on the severe social deprivation to which the rapists themselves have been exposed during their childhood and youth in Harlem. One of them, in whose mind the office of priesthood is associated with Christ, was once lured into an act of oral sex with a member of the clergy, and consequently feels victimized and contaminated by what he perceives as white America's privilege and hypocrisy. The poem is an indignant and powerful protest. But even to Anthony Hecht, no admirer of Pat Buchanan, it seems "poorly written, rife with clichés and weary repetitions, alternately sentimental and infuriated, and almost entirely limp and unimaginative in its use of language". Among the passages which Hecht re-prints as a sample are the following:

> My thighs pump
> thru the air
> like tires
> rolling down
> the highway
> big and round
> eating up the ground
> of America
> but I never been any
> further than 42nd St.
> Below that is as
> unfamiliar as my
> father's face.
> .....
> My sneakers glide off
> the cement like
> white dreams
> looking out at the world
> thru a cage of cabbage
> and my mother's fat,
> hollering don't do this
> don't do that
> .....
> Her welfare check buys me $85
> sneakers
> but can't buy me a father.

Hecht concludes that the poem's "single-minded posture of zeal and outrage" simplifies the moral and political issues in a way worthy of the fulminatory Buchanan himself (Hecht 1995: 168, 173). In the cross-fire between people like Buchanan's supporters and people like the admirers of Lofton, the NEA award proved to be a gesture of ingratiating short-term expediency which in the long run could do considerable damage. John Frohnmayer, head of the NEA, was eventually fired, and long-standing racial tensions can hardly have been alleviated.

When functioning as a form of pseudo-communication, political correctness is analogous to a poem as conceived by the New Critics. It works by *not* saying things. In literary criticism, it overlooks, not only shortcomings, as in the NEA approval of Ramona Lofton, but strengths as well. Nowadays there are critics who would fight shy of predicting that some contemporary work will become a world classic, and the books they themselves discuss often belong to the limited canon of their own culture or sub-culture. Some of them specialize in gay or lesbian books, or feminist books, or ethnic books, or "establishment" books, and so on, and books get marketed along these lines as well. In public discussion surrounding the Nobel Prize for Literature, similarly, there is an assumption, which may or may not correspond to the perceptions of the adjudicating panel, that they have to apply criteria similar to those for which one can perhaps blame John Frohnmayer, so that the award can only be thought of as a diplomatic gesture. This year, people say, it is such and such a continent or country's turn to get it.

Talk about literature is beginning to be culturally purist, in much the same way that some literary history from the nineteenth century onwards sought to be historically purist. We are reaching the point at which to turn to writers for what they might have to say to members of some grouping other than their own, or to judge them by the criteria of some such other grouping, or by criteria thought to be common to several different groupings, will be deemed an act of bad taste. Difference is thought of as "all the way down", and communication across perceived lines of difference as therefore impossible. Given this climate of discussion, John Frohnmayer might almost plead — perhaps he has done so already — that for him to have taken into consideration Anthony Hecht's way of reading Lofton's "Wild Thing" would have been quite unthinkable: that Hecht's criteria can be applied only to poets like Hecht himself.

If Frohnmayer actually sympathized with Hecht's viewpoint, such a plea would obviously be patronizing, implying not only that Lofton is inadequately educated, but that people like her are actually ineducable, and should therefore be allowed some kind of handicap in literary competitions. On the other hand, verse writing does take place within a wide variety of different styles and genres. So without denying that Hecht's strictures could have force even for readers not sharing his precise cultural background, we could still ask whether, in his scheme of things, *good* protest songs and popular verse are a real possibility. If they are, there is also the further question: Should they qualify for state patronage of the arts? For all I know, Hecht might answer affirmatively on both counts. But be that as it may, such speculation certainly brings home the postmodern crisis of authority, and some of its more detailed cultural implications.

Gestures of political correctness stemming from a pessimistic determinism similar to Miller's underestimate the human capacity for empathy, which is taken to weigh far lighter than the facts of historical situationality. This view comes closest to the truth when applied to human beings not enjoying a reasonable level of education and political liberty. Even they, though, need not be mentally confined to just one single grouping or context, and they, too, share with everybody else the sameness-that-is-difference of the human condition itself, into whose myriad cultural formations they may be willing to project themselves imaginatively. The self-projective ability is what underlies the power of interpersonal communication in the first place, and it is an ability of which people really can avail themselves, giving and taking across every conceivable cultural divide. They not only *can* be educated, but are magnificent autodidacts. Naturally entering into a process of self-discovery through self-alienation, they may even become different people as they go along. Although the distinction between self and other may well be experienced as the most profound distinction of all, it is not very hard and fast.

The claim I am making for the human predisposition to empathy, understanding and change will recur in Chapter 4, where I shall support it with Gadamerian considerations. For the time being, my main purpose is still to explore in a rather general way the similarities and contrasts between my own and certain other approaches. As at a similar point earlier on, moreover, I am far from disowning the element of gut-feeling and introspection in all this. Miller, as far as I can tell, is something of a pessimist, and his intellect tells him one thing. I myself am not so pessimistic, and my intellect tells me something different. Whether gut feeling and intellect can work independently of each other, or whether the one always influences the other, and in that case which influences which, are ancient questions I shall not presume to answer. But it is certainly the case that my somewhat optimistic claim can be rationally supported *with introspective gut feelings as evidence*. Even making allowances for bias of temperament, an individual's gut feelings must partly register an assessment of both self and others as hitherto observed. A perfectly rational empirical procedure would be to have a world-wide show of hands to see which kind of assessment is more typical. This is hardly feasible, needless to say. But if it were, it would have to be taken as the best indication we could ever get as to whether the pessimistic or the optimistic view of human capacities is the more realistic.

But even if it is *un*realistic, the determinist mind-set underlying both Miller's frank divisiveness and the harmonies of disingenuous political correctness could *become* realistic. Alternatively, its pessimism, if realistic already, could become even *more* realistic. The risk is that a pessimistic prophecy can become self-fulfilling, as may already be happening. Perhaps the world is ending up with too few people who *believe* that communication across perceived lines of difference is really possible, and consequently with too few mediators prepared to intervene when opposed groupings seriously misunderstand each other. Certainly the field now seems wide open for the rhetoric of blame, a discourse from which magnanimity, reasonableness and balanced judgement are conspicuously absent, so allowing free rein to the spirit of postmodern paranoia. Both "establishment" and "minority" commentators become implicated in this,[9] and although the disagreements can involve real issues, including understandable and very serious grievances, the mood of resentment is simply too intense to permit a genuine dialogue. Party x judges party y entirely on party x's own terms, and *vice versa*. Ironically, the parties' experience of difference is so intense that they refuse to make allowances for it — for the other person's difference, that is.

The fairest way to illustrate this might seem to be with examples from critics representing several different groupings. This, though, would come uncomfortably close to the routine gestures of insincere political correctness, and would take more space than it is worth. When I disagree with a critic representing a particular grouping, I show my respect. I show that I take both the critic and the grouping seriously enough to enter into frank dialogue. And

---

9. The inverted commas signal that the terms are relative to particular sets of circumstances.

since my aim here is not to offer a complete survey of contemporary criticism but to pinpoint a theoretical difficulty, a single example will be enough; a whole sequence of them would not further advance the argument. In the end, I have chosen a Jewish critic, not because Jewish critics behave worse than any others, "minority" or "establishment", but mainly because this particular case brings in T.S. Eliot again, who will also be important later on.

Anthony Julius's critique of Eliot (Julius 1995) seems rather like a speech by prosecuting counsel. His scholarship is wide-ranging, and highly illuminating in contextualizing Eliot's attitudes. Yet far from suggesting that the context makes Eliot's attitudes more understandable, Julius sometimes seems to suggest that the impact of the context on Eliot's thought was altogether weaker than the impact of Eliot's thought on the context. What this tells us is that the self-fulfilling prophecies of cultural pessimism have not only split everybody up into camps between which communication is assumed to be inevitably antagonistic. Paradoxically enough, that crude historicist determinism has also resulted in a critical culture within which a commentator belonging to party x's camp can diabolize somebody belonging to party y's camp by crediting that individual with powers that are entirely *superior* to history and society. With little sense of the individual and society's co-adaptive reciprocity, Julius has no time for historical mitigation, seeming much less concerned to be fair, than to get Eliot convicted. Writing as if most present-day readers were not already well aware of Eliot's anti-Semitic attitudes, he accuses Christopher Ricks (1994) of neutralizing and trivializing the issue, and he himself exaggerates it. That Eliot used anti-Semitic topoi and clichés, did not apologize for doing so, and never campaigned against anti-Semitism is all true enough. Especially from our own position in time, we can readily grant that the example he set was, to say the least, unenlightened here. If a figure of his stature had taken a stand against anti-Semitic attitudes, the world would have been a somewhat better place, in which those nurturing and acting upon such sentiments would have had even less excuse. At the same time, Eliot can hardly be accused of working for anti-Semitism's wider spread or intensification. Tainted in the same way as very many of his contemporaries, in some of his writings he nevertheless explored, as Ricks does carefully show, the operations of prejudice. Some of his later cultural criticism is more concerned than Julius's own book to see justice done.

To repeat, my focus is on a theoretical deficiency which Julius shares with contemporary critics of many other "minority" orientations, whether religious, sexual, ethnic or political, and which can just as strongly affect responses evoked from the "establishment" old guard. In much critical writing nowadays, the underlying theory is insufficiently pragmatic to hold the unfairnesses in check. More specifically, postmodern blame, time and time again, is fundamentally uncircumstantial and/or anachronistic, with critics of opposed parties aggravating their quarrels by ignoring important considerations of context. So arises the kind of slanging match for which, in an intellectual ambience of programmatic divisiveness and dystopian determinism, there is all too much warrant. Fairness can occur only by a fluke of generous character.

A typical product of this mental climate are Julius's twenty pages on "Dirge", a 22-line section of the original draft of *The Waste Land*, probably written in 1921, and opening with the lines,

> Full fathom five your Bleistein lies
> Under the flatfish and the squids.
> Graves' Disease in a dead jew's eyes!
> (Eliot 1971: 121)

After which, it goes on to describe the dead man's physical decomposition in spine-chilling detail. For me personally, the most obvious thing to say about Bleistein's originally so solid Jewish identity is that it makes the spectacle of his total annihilation a very powerful *memento mori*. But even if, more narrowly, one reads the strangely surrealistic horrors as a vindictive anti-Jewish fantasy, the fact is that Eliot never actually published it, except as the completely different "Death by Water" of the poem's official version. To imply, here, that he acted in such a way as to insult Jews would simply disregard the circumstances of his action. At the very most, he may possibly have had a nasty anti-Semitic impulse, which he did not follow through into his public behaviour. In which case, the critic to cast the first stone must be the one who has never had a shameful impulse to repress.

Another pragmatic factor downplayed by Julius is that, in 1921, a nasty anti-Semitic impulse, even if it had resulted in a public manifestation, would not have seemed particularly surprising. The frame of mind a reader brings to reading does have interpretative and affective implications, which is why Julius's comments on even the published poems can seem rather disingenuous. Accurately pointing out that some of the ones collected in *Poems 1920* contain ugly anti-Semitic clichés, he then claims that they belong to Eliot's most artistically impressive, and by implication most influential, achievements. In fact, the clichés were, precisely, clichés from the start, however much re-worked, and most readers have not been all that enthusiastic. Bernard Bergonzi's commentary of 1972 was fairly representative, arguing that "Gerontion", for instance, the poem which includes the lines,

> My house is a decayed house,
> And the Jew squats on the window sill, the owner,
> Spawned in some estaminet of Antwerp,
> Blistered in Brussels, patched and peeled in London,
> (Eliot 1969 [1920]: 37)

is an "echo chamber where there is much interesting noise but nothing can be clearly distinguished", and that the so-called quatrain poems, imitated from Gautier under the influence of Pound and also containing Jewish characters, are over-ingenious and trivial, in a vein where Eliot was not at ease (Bergonzi 1978 [1972]: 49–56; see also Bergonzi 1996). Julius's damning with loud praise will not quite work.

Julius also tends to speak of passages which "make a Jewish reader's face flush", and which "insult Jews: to ignore these insults is to misread the poems" (Julius 1995: 1–2). This reaction, though from our present point of view preferable to Modernist aestheticization in that it recognizes literature's inter-personality, is nevertheless just as unhistorical. The pragmatics of reception are fundamentally misrepresented by Julius's use of the present tense. Eliot has been dead for thirty years; the passages and poems in question were written even longer ago; and times and attitudes have changed. Without question, the expressions to which Julius objects, written or spoken today, would not only insult Jews, but would attract widespread condemnation for doing so. But Eliot did not write or speak them today. When he wrote them, they may well have been insulting to Jews but, however regrettably from Jews' own point of view, and from the point of view of any responsible person today, they would not have been so publicly unacceptable, and even many Jews might have taken them in their stride. To say this is in no sense to rehabilitate anti-Semitism, whether Eliot's or anybody else's. But it is certainly to insist that, morally speaking, a case such as Eliot's, though extremely regrettable, is different from, say, the case of Ezra Pound. Not only were Pound's anti-Semitic statements more blatant, comprehensive and vituperative. He was still making them in what could already be called our own epoch, at a time when the naivety or ignorance or hate or self-confidence which knew no better was even more obviously misplaced, as he himself may eventually have recognized — "Too late came the understanding" (Pound 1963).

Julius's verdict on Eliot, though by no means unaware of historical detail, falls into the habit of universalizing the values of here and now to a different milieu: to a milieu which mostly pre-dated the Holocaust by well over a decade. In our own time, and precisely because of the raised level of public awareness, anti-Semitism is likely to be more insidious, even if some of its manifestations are as crude as ever. Julius is excellently equipped to expose it, and deserves to be listened to with respect and concern. But the contemporary phenomenon would have to be dealt with in its contemporary form, and illustrated from present-day representatives, whom his strategy in *T.S. Eliot, Anti-Semitism, and Literary Form* lets off the hook. Eliot would be of interest only insofar as somebody here and now has been influenced by him.

Even this would risk oversimplification. Influence, I shall later argue, is a phenomenon to which twentieth-century literary criticism has paid too little attention. Yet any claim that Eliot is somehow responsible for what somebody else subsequently said or did will have to be carefully hedged. Most obviously, perhaps, influence always takes two: one person who is suggestive, and another who is suggestible. Then again, a writer's originality never bursts upon the world *ex nihilo*. For it to communicate its stimulus at all, it must emerge in co-adaptive reciprocity with cultural tradition; and Julius is himself at his most trenchant in showing that the history of the West has been completely riddled with anti-Semitism. But above all, perhaps, the passing of the years will once again affect the pragmatics of tense: of the present tense in sentences of the form "T.S. Eliot is an influence on x", where x is a writer living now. T.S. Eliot was responsible for what he did and said when he did and said it. If the acts of writing and publication extended his responsibility into the future, it was into a future which, if he had a duty to think about it, he did not have a supernatural capacity to foresee. What he would have done and said and written and published if he had been alive today we cannot know for sure.

Even if a pessimistic cultural determinism is blind to human beings' potential mobility between one sociohistorical formation and another, this is not to be compensated by an impatient and incriminatory blindness to the real consequences of situational disparity. Julius, like so many contemporary critics, has a great deal of historical knowledge, yet in forming his value judgements behaves as if there-and-then and here-and-now were indistinguishable. Even in the post-Barthes era, one of the most widespread theoretical errors is in making the unitary context assumption, the error so characteristic of formalist literary pragmatics as well, and of the entire earlier paradigm.

3.6. A historical yet non-historicist literary pragmatics

As an alternative to the postmodern stalemates, I am proposing a mediating criticism based on a theory of literary pragmatics for which the main desiderata will by now be clear. Most fundamentally, the theory will carry a resounding echo of the Greek root *pragma*. The writing of a literary text is a deed with an interpersonal valency across time and space, which can only be realized, furthermore, by a second kind of human act, an act of reading. What takes place between readers and writers has clearly affective and ethical dimensions, and the need for mediation can certainly arise.

The need can also be aggravated by some degree of cultural difference, on either a diachronic or a synchronic axis. But even when the sender and current receiver ostensibly belong to the same cultural constellation, their two contexts will be less than fully coterminous. There will always be some difference in awareness, in the minimal case because the receiver has not yet received, or has already forgotten, what the sender sends. This is true of both literary and any other kind of communication, and the inevitable contextual disparity, great or small, is what can make an act of communication at once difficult and worthwhile in the first place. It actually helps to constitute the act as a historical process, communication being a matter of negotiating the contextual disparity, and perhaps even lessening it. A literary pragmatic theory underlining this will strongly support mediating critics in their efforts to keep different situationalities in balance, whether in the discussion of historical authors, or in an effort to counteract our own time's anachronistic and uncircumstantial rhetoric of blame. The best Barthesian commentary will also be suggestive, by siting writers and readers inside the intertextualities of particular cultures.

In addition, the proposed theory will have to be sufficiently non-historicist to emphasize that contexts, for all their importance, are not completely determining. When the Barthesian arguments are driven to extremes, literary interpersonality is thought of as a non-individual matter of a society, language or ideology within whose single world-view both writers and readers are, as it were, imprisoned. This can lead, among other things, to the paranoiacally divisive notion that genuine communication across perceived lines of difference is impossible, which in turn may tempt lovers of a quiet life into the non-communicating type of political correctness. The pragmatic theory needed for mediating criticism, by contrast, though sharply distancing itself from extreme liberal humanist notions of an absolute human autonomy, will not endorse a total de-centering of the self. It will rather emphasize at least a relative autonomy, plus a power of intellectual and imaginative flexibility for which lines of sociocultural difference will not be too constraining. Here, too, the best work in the Barthesian mould is profoundly suggestive, in actually loosening up ideas of a fixed and settled self. This makes it easier to discuss an individual's transgression of contextual boundaries.

In point of fact, the theory needed will resemble a certain strand of American new historicism. Stephen Greenblatt, for instance, despite his strong indebtedness to Foucault, acknowledges that art can seem to have an aura of its own, as if it were lifted above its particular time and place. On the one hand, art objects are constructed by processes which leave them "resonant" with cultural-historical contingency. But on the other hand, they can also inspire "wonder": they are able "to stop the viewer in his tracks, to convey an arresting sense of uniqueness, to evoke an exalted attention" (Greenblatt 1996 [1990]: 276–7). A historical yet non-historicist literary pragmatics, similarly, will view men and women as beings who are at one and the same time social and individual; they are *social individuals*. Though certainly influenced by context, they are also partly independent of it, and can even change it, sometimes by means of literary communication. Of central importance here are the processes of co-adaptation through which the two modalities of the social individual can exert an influence *upon each other*. At one and the same time, individuals can be changed by society, and society by individuals.

Fortunately enough, a pragmatic theory of this kind is not without all precedent. Earlier work in general pragmatics has not been exclusively based on behaviourist universalism, and earlier work in literary pragmatics has not always represented an alliance of behaviouristic linguistics and Modernist formalism. Pragmaticists have already devoted a fair amount of attention to the significance of historical contextualization, and have sometimes been sufficiently humanizing in spirit to resist the scientific attractions of a rigid sociocultural determinism.

Perhaps rather surprisingly, this work is best reviewed by once again beginning with Charles Morris. In Section 2.5 above, I described Morris's behaviouristic systematicity as a decisive factor for literary pragmatics of a formalist orientation. Morris, however, was a many-sided figure, and his behaviourism was at times sufficiently down-played to dim the prospect of tight pragmatic rules. He also tended to undermine his account of the semiotic science's three components, partly by emphasizing the science's unity, and partly by speaking of a pragmatic perspective which is distributed throughout syntactics and semantics as well (Morris 1971 [1938]: 51–2, 1946: 219). In this connection he assigns pragmaticists the daunting task of dealing with "biotic aspects of semiosis": with "all the psychological, biological, and sociological phenomena which occur in the functioning of signs" (Morris 1971 [1938]: 43).

This aspect of his work, too, has inspired a whole tradition of later pragmaticists (e.g. Nunberg 1981; Verschueren 1987; Mey 1993: 278). For them, context is much broader and looser than for scholars in the other tradition, so that their discussion can have anthropological, sociolinguistic, and even ideological dimensions. Here pragmatic research does not aspire to the "exact" methods reminiscent of mathematics or physics, for the primary goal is not one of scientific explanation in the traditional sense, but of hermeneutic understanding (*verstehen*). Above all, pragmaticists are expected to imagine themselves in the same shoes as the people whose communication they are trying to examine. Especially in analyses of linguistic interaction between different communities, there is a clear recognition that the contexts of sending and receiving an utterance can be quite different enough to cause problems.

Even relevance theory, which I was earlier linking to the more behaviouristic tradition of pragmatics, can in some respects be related to this other line of descent from Morris. Up until now, relevance theoreticians have perhaps tended to avoid broad-context considerations of, say, ideology, and have in some ways come very close to the unitary context assumption. Basically, though, the store of encyclopaedic knowledge on which the principle of relevance is said to help listeners or readers draw in making their inferences is in itself unlimited. Not only that, but relevance theorists do point out the difficulties of the mutual knowledge hypothesis. Unless I am mistaken, then, they should also be able to deal with interchanges whose interpretation depends on context in the largest possible sense, and this would include interchanges calling for mediation because such macro-contextual knowledge is not shared. Before long I shall be singling out some relevance theoreticians whose discussion of literary texts is certainly very different from literary pragmatics of the formalist school.

An alternative school of literary pragmatics is in fact already discernable, clearly corresponding to the non-behaviouristic tradition in general pragmatics, even if not always fully aware of it. Jerome J. McGann would never claim to know much about Morris and his influence, being very much a literary scholar. But for him, literary pragmatics does embrace the sociohistorical study of the entire circumstances of writing, publication and reading. He has become particularly aware of its implications during his bibliographical work for scholarly editions (McGann 1991b). Whereas the mid-twentieth-century editorial theory epitomized by Fredson Bowers was as "technical, specialized, and a-historical as the formal and thematic hermeneutics that ran a parallel course in interpretative studies" — a clear reference to American New Criticism — , McGann's own editorial policy strongly emphasizes that to talk of different textual states of one and the same literary work is a contradiction in terms (McGann 1991a: 3). Rather, each new state — each revised version, each new edition — in effect constitutes a new work. No less emphatically, McGann insists that the contexts in which a text was first written and disseminated can be very different from some of the contexts in which it is currently being read. This is precisely the consideration which Julius's critique of Eliot overlooks, and McGann has illustrated its interpretative consequences in a series of major studies of English literary history.

One his discussions focuses on Tennyson's "The Charge of the Light Brigade" (McGann 1985: 173–203).

> The Charge of the Light Brigade
>
> Half a league, half a league,
> Half a league onward,
> All in the valley of Death
> Rode the six hundred.
> "Forward, the Light Brigade!
> Charge for the guns!" he said:
> Into the valley of Death
> Rode the six hundred
>
> "Forward, the Light Brigade!"
> Was there a man dismayed?
> Not though the soldier knew
> Someone had blundered:
> Theirs not to make reply,
> Theirs not to reason why,
> Theirs but to do and die:
> Into the valley of Death
> Rode the six hundred.

> Cannon to the right of them,
> Cannon to the left of them,
> Cannon in front of them
> Volleyed and thundered;
> Stormed at with shot and shell,
> Boldly they rode and well,
> Into the jaws of Death,
> Into the mouth of Hell
> Rode the six hundred.
>
> Flashed all their sabers bare,
> Flashed as they turned in air
> Sabring the gunners there,
> Charging the army, while
> All the world wondered:
> Plunged in the battery-smoke
> Right through the line they broke;
> Cossack and Russian
> Reeled from the sabre-stroke
> Shattered and sundered.
> Then they rode back, but not
> Not the six hundred.
>
> Cannon to the right of them,
> Cannon to the left of them,
> Cannon behind them
> Volleyed and thundered;
> Stormed at with shot and shell,
> While horse and hero fell,
> They that had fought so well
> Came through the jaws of Death,
> Back from the mouth of Hell,
> All that was left of them,
> Left of six hundred.
>
> When can their glory fade?
> O the wild charge they made!
> All the world wondered.
> Honour the charge they made!
> Honour the Light Brigade,
> Noble six hundred!
> (Tennyson 1987 [1854])

This poem, written in 1854, became very popular. Many people knew it by heart, and in Virginia Woolf's novel *To the Lighthouse* of 1927 the philosopher Mr Ramsay still chants it to himself, as he paces up and down in the hope of urging his mind to some boldly original flight of thought. Even today it is fairly well known; it can still rouse excitement; and its message seems straightforward enough. Yet for many readers now, its sentiments may well seem rather straightforwardly Victorian, and thereby platitudinous — just the kind of monument one would *expect* from a nation of empire-builders when some of its soldiers make the ultimate sacrifice.

McGann's point, however, is that in 1854 things were not so simple. Nor was the poem published together with other poems and surrounded with an aura of art. It first appeared in a newspaper, along with reports of everyday public events, and of the continuing war in the Crimea. At the time, moreover, heroic death was the last thing many people would have predicted of British cavalry regiments, whose members were regularly lampooned as reactionary, overprivileged, and unsoldierly, less interested in fighting than in flaunting a lady-killing appearance in their splendid uniforms. Tennyson is not only making the point that the valour of the nation's young patricians can still be roused. He even represents them in just the kind of poses through which the painters of the French bourgeoisie had idealized Napoleon's non-élite *chasseurs*.

Alerted to all this, a reader of today can still not read the poem like a Victorian. It is more a question of reading it like a Victorian *and* like a person of our own time, so that the two life-worlds start to interact upon each other. So nowadays the total experience can be much more complex and more interesting than it could have been for the first readers. The poem can no longer strike an emotional chord in quite the same way. But even for readers unimpressed by social rank and the trappings of empire, even for readers extremely unenthusiastic about the Victorians' wars, even for readers who feel that the First World War or Wilfred Owen's "Dulce et decorum est" finally dispelled the mystique of military honour and glory, there may still be something rather awe-inspiring about an age in which this kind of self-sacrifice was made so readily, even by those from whom it was perhaps not expected. It is all very well for us to think that our own ideals are far superior to those of the Victorians. But even if they are — and is it such a little "if"? —, are they so well articulated and so keenly held? How ready are we to follow where they lead?

McGann's adherence to the critical principles endorsed by a historical yet non-historicist pragmatics could not be more rewarding. In sending his readers' minds along these paths, he is already performing a service of mediation.

In illuminating earlier phases of a cultural tradition for the benefit of a later phase, he neither underestimates the difference between them, nor for a moment doubts that an act of communication really can take place, which will change the present-day reader's perceptions of both then-and-there and here-and-now.

Another literary scholar is Brian Caraher. For him, literary pragmatic research returns to a link with philosophical pragmatism that was hinted by Morris himself: more particularly, to a link with John Dewey's interest in the overlaps between reading and purposeful activity of other kinds, including communal activities. Caraher's belief in communication generally, and in the efficacy of literary *pragma* especially, could hardly be stronger. For him, there are "particular ways in which a real reader actively engages the text and ... ways in which the text acts on and guides that reader". For this reason he refuses to mourn, with Baudrillard, the dissolution of the social bond and the disappearance of unifying grand narratives. He is also less upset than Lyotard by the "spiritless hegemony of new discursive practices that remake the field of the knower and the known into a technologically mediated economy and circulation of discrete information" (Caraher 1991, 8, 10). Caraher's answer to such unsocial dystopias is that literature, at least, is a kind of human conversation which still works, a claim he seeks to substantiate through a discussion of Wordsworth.

For Geoff Cox (1986), to take a third example, literary pragmatic research can have a clearly Marxist slant. The scholar studies acts of reading in their context of social class, with special attention to inequalities in readers' educational background, and with a sharp sense of the literary book as a capitalist commodity. In this particular kind of mission, Cox's work is reminiscent of certain continental varieties of general pragmatics (e.g. Mey 1993: 283–330), and of Norman Fairclough's critical discourse analysis (Fairclough 1995), offering similar gratifications to the scholar's social conscience. According to Cox, the literary pragmaticist's aim is to root out injustices, and the ideological distortions that go with them.

Here the only risk is that Cox's strong reaction against formalist de-historicization could lead him to a kind of sociocultural determinism. This would correspond to some of the postmodern stalemates mentioned earlier, and would just as seriously distort the human being's paradoxically social individuality. On the one hand, if readers and other language users are to remain both relatively sane and acceptably undangerous to themselves and others, they will not indulge in incoherent solipsism. That is why it makes good scholarly sense to relate individuals to contexts in the first place. A total lack of conformity between individuals and the world around them is unthinkable. On the contrary, it is by considering the world around them that we seek to understand and commune with them as individuals, and Cox is clearly right to assume that readers may not notice when they are being placed under ideological pressure. On the other hand, if there were no scope for personal experience, and for a freedom of choice which even allows a relative originality, Cox himself would be unable to launch his critique. He would be just as gregarious as the readers he wants to rescue.

Not even the dichotomy between historical and formalist literary pragmaticists should be exaggerated. Predictably enough, relations between the two schools have been somewhat strained and subject to confusion.[10] But if the formalist school could only move away from Kantian aesthetics, from the behaviouristic assumption of human uniformity and mechanism, and from the unitary context assumption, and if the historical school could only hold back from a reductive social determinism, then the two approaches could easily flourish side by side in fruitful complementarity. The actual readers of literature are perfectly capable of reading it with a care for both what it *is* (formally speaking) and what it *does* (historically speaking).[11] True, in order to cope with the postmodern culture wars, we do urgently need a mediating criticism based on a pragmatic theory in which sociohistorical difference is at the centre. Yet nothing is more pleasant to imagine than a future in which, perhaps partly as a result of successful mediation, the interpersonality of literature

---

10. The Åbo Symposium on Literary Pragmatics (1988) was planned with a view to mapping out common ground. In introducing the published version of its papers (Sell: 1991a), I still had this aim in mind, though I also wrote at some length of emergent differences of emphasis. Some reviewers hinted that the differences might be too radical to promise genuine collaboration (see Wales 1994; Semino 1992; Cunico 1992). (Cf. the hesitations about literary pragmatics expressed by de Geest 1995.) But on the whole, the Åbo papers were welcomed in the exploratory spirit in which they were intended, and a number of them received very high praise (see especially Fowler 1993; Jucker 1995; Fludernick 1993: 749–57).

11. Incidentally, at Åbo Akademi University I am currently leading a research project entitled, "Children's Literature: Pure and Applied". Some of the project workers are literary scholars, some teachers and educationalists. Through cooperation, they are seeking to increase their understanding of what children's literature is by examining what it can do in educational contexts, and to increase their understanding of what it can do in educational contexts by examining what it is. The project is funded by the Finnish Ministry of Education.

would be less of a minefield, and its formal properties restored to fuller appreciation.

Even today, some commentators, weary of the rhetoric of blame, are harking back to the New Critics;[12] Helen Vendler's recent *The Art of Shakespeare's Sonnets* has been much praised for its loving attention to poetic effects (Fowler 1998); and there are already literary pragmaticists for whom the relationship between formalist and historical concerns is far from oppositional. Alexander Gelley (1987: 80–1), appealing to Bakhtin's account of the heteroglossia at work in prose fiction, exhorts literary pragmaticists to study the convergence of extra-literary and literary discourse practices in one and the same text. To similar effect, Tzvetan Todorov (1990 [1978]) says that both structural and functional definitions of literature are inadequate. One can only talk about many different genres of discourse, some of which are regarded as literary, and share many properties with non-literary ones; indeed, the literary genres *originate* in human discourse, and "ordinary" genres still underlie them. A third example would be Dominique Maingueneau (1990), who begins in the spirit of Morris's pragmatic laws by first stipulating the way discourse works. For him, communication depends on considerations of cooperativeness, relevance, sincerity, exhaustiveness, appropriateness, and politeness, and his initial claim is that literary activity proceeds by breaking such laws, an argument which echoes a Russian Formalist poetics of deviance. The more historical side of his approach emerges just as clearly, when he hastens to add, not only that a literary writer cannot risk such innovations without first earning a legitimating authority, but that the innovations, once they are established, affect the society's entire discoursal economy.

What Gelley, Todorov and Maingueneau are describing is basically a process of co-adaptation. What they are *not* saying is that literary text-type conventions are mysteriously immutable and above history. And within general pragmatic theory, there is already a body of work which, at least by implication, explains why such a claim would not stand up. Jef Verschueren (1987), for instance, resists Morris's streak of behaviouristic universalism precisely by noting the dynamic reciprocity of text and context. People say

---

12. A. W. Johnson's book about Ben Jonson and architecture, for instance, has been praised as "satisfyingly old-fashioned in one respect: he [A.W. Johnson] does not even mention Derrida or Foucault, and he seems to assume that the critic's job is to heighten appreciation of particular works of art by demonstrating the structural skill of the artist. In this critical aim he very much resembles an (old) New Critic." (McPherson 1997: 891)

and write things which are bound to take the status quo into account, but by which the status quo can itself be changed. So between the individual and society, any flow of stimulus and response will actually be bi-directional, a point also specially stressed by pragmaticists with anthropological interests. As Charles Godwin and Alessandro Duranti (1992: 31) put it,

> Instead of viewing context as a set of variables that statically surround strips of talk, context and talk are now argued to stand in a mutually reflexive relationship to each other, with talk, and the interpretive [sic] work it generates, shaping context as much as context shapes talk.

A corresponding sense of literary communication as a kind of dialogic negotiation between older and newer ways of viewing the world was already present in the pioneering book by Altieri. Among literary pragmaticists now working along similar lines are Norman Macleod (1992) and Ziva Ben-Porat (1991), who would probably be quite happy to replace the word "talk" in the passage from Godwin and Duranti with the phrase "literary text". Macleod's discussion of Dickens concludes that

> contexts are not monolithic; neither are they stable. A context can be altered by the very expression it contextualizes, just as much as the interpretation of an expression can depend on its context.
> (Macleod 1992: 157)

As for Ben-Porat, she suggestively speaks of a literary pragmatics that is "two-way", and offers some fascinating examples from Israeli poetry. For many years after the establishment of the actual state of Israel, writers' perceptions of that country's weather, and of the city of Jerusalem, were still influenced by European poetic traditions originating from the diaspora. Many a melancholy poem was written about the autumnal migration of birds to warmer climes, and much veneration was focussed on the dominating beauty of the Temple. Gradually, though, it was as if poets began to use their own eyes. Their writing now registered that Israel has only two seasons, the wet and the dry, both of them reasonably hospitable to birds, and that Jerusalem is also a sacred city of Islam and Christianity.

Both Dickens and Israeli poets found themselves in certain historical situations, had inherited certain ways of thinking, and were obviously shaped by them. Yet they were also sufficiently independent to contribute to social, conceptual and ideological change. And while Dickens and Israeli poets were themselves writers, the same co-adaptive interplay of social formation and individuality applies to readers as well. At both the writing end and the reading end, a historical yet non-historicist pragmatics will be a matter of neither under- nor over-emphasizing the facts of social construction. The approach seeks to avoid the pitfalls of extremist formalism and extremist historicism alike.

Consequently, it will never be a tidily systematic science. Comparative philologists, structuralist linguists, text-linguists, stylisticians, narratologists, speech act theoreticians, Barthesian cultural structuralists and post-structuralists, and both formalist literary pragmaticists and even a few historical ones as well have all tended, in their various ways, to speak of human activity as rule-governed. Their scholarly achievements have been prodigious, but have left something importantly human out of the picture. And the same goes for the regularities of primal scene and archetype detected by Freudian and myth criticism, which certainly re-introduced the human into literature, but in a somewhat universalized packaging. The theory proposed here, by contrast, is a kind of *media via* between scientism and intuition, a mixture of regularities and irregularities, and precisely because of its subject matter. Its most straightforward preoccupation is its historical concern with the effect on acts of writing and reading of their own situationality. Here, at least, there is a certain amount of system. But one complication is that the context of writing and the current context of reading are always to a greater or lesser extent heteromorphic. An act of reading can therefore have a confrontational dimension, even when both writer and reader are, in terms of *their own* sociocultural situations, at their most normal. This proliferation of reading contexts alone would have major consequences for the actual reading experience. Then there is the further point: that both writers and readers can behave in ways which, for their own time and place, are actually maverick. Although they are social beings, they are social individuals.

A historical yet non-historicist account of the basic pragmatic set-up of literary communication will have to focus on both of these chaotic features in turn: on the proliferation of "receiving" contexts, and on the individual's potential *resistance* to context. Otherwise, the account will be unable to clarify a third main feature: the discoursally proposed relationships into which "receivers" imaginatively project themselves across the situational divide, in order to pick up the interpersonal charge from the "sender".

Not only is literature no less interactive than other forms of communication. It also shares with them all these three features. One difficulty in trying to discuss them, however, is that they have not yet been widely dealt with by linguists working on the pragmatics of communication in general, with which the pragmatics of literature is on my account continuous. My next chapter, therefore, though basically concerned with literature, is also an indirect contribution to that larger growth area. My attempt to provide a theory for a mediating literary criticism emphasizes the need for a non-scientific, less-than-totally-systematizing, historical yet non-historicist theory of general pragmatics as well: the kind of theory for which predictions and explanations are not more important than an openness to the unexpected.

Chapter 4

Literature as Communication

4.1. Proliferating contexts of reading

In the previous two chapters I have stressed that literary writing is a deed of communication with an ongoing interpersonal valency. This explains how a need for mediating criticism can arise in the first place, and why such a criticism calls for a type of theory not hitherto available: an adequate theory of literary pragmatics. I have already indicated the main assumptions and claims of such a theory, which also apply for the pragmatics of communication in general, and two complementary emphases have emerged as especially important: the historical emphasis on the inevitable disparate sitedness of "sending" and "receiving", which can make communication at once problematic and worthwhile; and the non-historicist emphasis on human beings as social individuals endowed with a capacity for co-adaptations *between* the social and the individual, and with a fairly protean power of empathetic self-projection, such that disparate sitedness is not in itself an insuperable obstacle to communication.

In exploring the theory in greater detail, the present chapter will sometimes have to point out communicative facts which in earlier linguistic and literary scholarship have not always held a central place. And to begin with communication's disparate sitedness, many other approaches have tended to rest on a quite different premise: the unitary context assumption. I have already discussed this at some length. But given its pivotal position in the approaches I am seeking to qualify, it now calls for more precise definition and further examination.

By context, then, I here mean a cognitive environment or mental condition: more specifically, everything which a person can recall or is aware of, either consciously or in a more automated manner, while speaking, writing, reading, hearing or remembering a particular utterance. Much of this knowledge will be intimately bound up with beliefs and value judgements, many of them widely shared within the person's sociocultural grouping. As for a *unitary* context, this would be such a context which, during the production and reception of a particular utterance, was identical for the two or more people involved, perhaps even from the beginning.

Now certainly, two people can at least come very close to sharing a context, which will mean that communication between them is that much easier. This in turn makes it easier for present-day linguists, in the interests of heuristic simplicity, to follow in their structuralist forbears' footsteps: more particularly, to indulge a phonocentric predilection for synchronized presence, paradoxically coupled to a "written-language bias" in the kind of examples offered. In Sperber and Wilson's Peter-and-Mary vignettes, for instance, the two communicants are engaged in face to face conversation, which seems to work with the same fluent articulacy as Sperber and Wilson's own commentaries on it. If Peter and Mary did not to a large extent share a context as two middle-class professional people in Britain, the dialogues Sperber and Wilson make up for them would seem even less authentic.

Yet even in the Peter-and-Mary type of case, the context is not entirely shared. Sperber and Wilson's rejection of the mutual knowledge hypothesis does firmly recognize this, so that communication can be seen as a process by which, among other things, contextual disparities are negotiated. Between any two communicants, there will always be differences of recall or awareness or attitude, however slight, which make communication at once desirable, worthwhile, and sometimes problematic. The negotiation of such differences is exactly what constitutes the communicative act as a historical process that can change the status quo. Before Peter and Mary have had their conversation about osso-bocco, for instance, their cognitive environments differ from each other in at least the following ways: neither of them knows whether the other is hungry, and, if so, what kind of meal would be welcome, or whether the prospect of actually having to cook it would be appealing. During the course of communication, Peter and Mary's contexts do become coterminous on all these points. But their mutual understanding will never be exhaustively complete, and the need for communication will not have come to an end. Before long they will notice other contextual discrepancies they wish to eliminate.

Such discrepancies can be so infinitesimal that the communicants themselves are quite unaware of their existence, and of having to negotiate them. At the risk of written-language bias, I can perhaps invent an example of my own. Suppose that George asks his twin brother, Fred, to come and help him repair his vintage car. Fred turns up at the workshop at the time agreed, and the first thing he says, nodding towards the car, is "Gorgeous!" Linguists usually describe such remarks as phatic communication, pointing out that they seem to contribute very little new knowledge. Yet they do communicate something, and in interpersonal terms it can be very important, generally tending to make people's time together pass more cheerfully. Even if George knew as much about Fred as one man can ever know about another, and even if they both knew everything there was to know about the car, Fred's enthusiastic cliché would still help them both to orientate themselves within the situation a little more comfortably. Indirectly, Fred is confirming something about which George might otherwise have had a slight uncertainty. His exclamation is a way of saying that he is perfectly happy to come and help today. If a linguist actually drew this to the brothers' attention as an item of information which has passed between them, they would probably be rather non-plussed. But the linguist would be right. Their unanimity is not total and static. It involves a constant process of contextual monitoring and re-alignment.

The fact that Fred sensed the need to indicate his willingness illustrates that contexts of sending and receiving are never quite unitary, even in cases where unitariness would *prima facie* seem most likely. As for other kinds of case, to think in terms of a unitary context is even more seriously counterproductive to an understanding of interpersonal experience. A lot of communication is not even face to face, and takes place across sometimes very considerable distances of time, space or culture. This is especially true of written communication, even though the mental distances may be very significantly reduced, or for the time being apparently quite eliminated, while communication is actually taking place.

And no matter how great or small the mental distance is between the contexts of the sender and receiver, an act of communication always involves another context as well. In Section 1.2, I explained the sense in which communicative situations can be thought of as triangular. To take Fred's exclamation, "Gorgeous!", there is (1) George, and there is (2) Fred himself, who are in communication about (3) the car. In every kind of communication, oral or written, literary and non-literary, there is the context of the sender, the context of the receiver, and the communication-internal context of the real, hypothetical or fictional people, events and things under discussion. This third type of context has a distinctive ontological status, which is easiest to recognize when the third entity is a hypothetical or fictional human being, an abstraction, or an inanimate object such as a car. In these kinds of case it is quite obvious that the third context does not correspond to a context which really exists for a really existing mind. It can only obtain in the minds of the people who are currently in communication. Even when the third entity is some other person who really exists or has existed, his or her context can still only be that context as reconstructed by the current communicants.

Whenever we say or write something, we indicate our sense of the communicative situation that actually prevails, or is likely to prevail, in the real world. We do this partly through the assumptions we make about our addressees' range of knowledge and system of values, and partly through the way we use person-, space-, time- and politeness (or social) deixis. "Deixis" is a Greek word meaning "a pointing to", "a pointing out", "an indicative gesture", and linguists have borrowed it as a label for all those aspects of texts which "point out" the communicative situation as the speaker or writer takes it to be.[13] Together with the presuppositions as to knowledge and values, deictic expressions *imply* a situation, and this situation is closely associated with the sender and receiver personae, which are also inevitably implied by any text. Put another way, any piece of language to some extent has to model the triangular situation of its own use. It provides a kind of replica of what is going on, so that communicants can empathize their way into each other's general life-world, and into the particular negotiation. One can speak, then, of a kind of textualization that is also contextualization: a textualization-cum-contextualization, as I shall be calling it.

But to continue with Fred's exclamation "Gorgeous!", for instance, his situation-modelling can be minimal. He does not even articulate the car in the third person as a noun or pronoun; he similarly takes for granted that George will not need first- or second-person pronouns or indications of time and space to help him; and, with no words implying either disrespect or deference towards George, and with no expressions of either humility or superiority on his own part, he is merely glowingly complimentary about the car itself, simultaneously assuming that George will apply the same aesthetic criteria as he himself. This economy of textualization-cum-contextualization is possible because the three context positions his words need to imply in fact all replicate

---

13. A helpful general account of deixis is to be found in Levinson 1983: 54–96. Literary deixis is discussed in Sternberg 1983; Engler 1987; Sell 1987; Green 1995.

one and the same spatio-temporal, sociocultural and informational juncture in the real world. Fred is an "I" talking directly to a "you" (George) in one and the same here-and-now about an "it" (the car) which shares that same siting with them. His little piece of phatic communication merely narrows down the differences in cognitive environment still further, even though as soon as either he or George says something new, it will be because some other contextual discrepancy has begun to make itself felt.

Another communicative possibility is that the three implied context positions replicate real-world junctures which overlap a good deal less completely than this. For example, an "I" and a "you" can converse in one and the same here-and-now, but about a "her" in some quite other time and place. Then again, all three implied context positions may replicate junctures which in the real world are quite distinct from each other. An "I" can write a letter to be read by a "you" in some other time and place, and the letter can describe what a "she" did in some third time and place. This, we should note, is the most common type of arrangement for literary texts. Authors, writing in their own milieu, portray characters in some different milieu, for the benefit of readers in some third milieu.

Or *is* it just some single third milieu? Well, to judge from certain kinds of literary scholarship, yes, it is. In much of the research conducted within the frameworks of the "lang.-lit." interdisciplinarities — speech act theory of literature, and the various other alliances of literary formalism and structuralist behaviourism, including the formalist versions of literary pragmatics — the putatively single milieu of readers is not even distinguished from the milieu of the real writer, which in turn is sometimes thought to correspond to a single milieu shared by the implied writer and implied reader as well. It is in this form that the unitary context assumption underlies Billy Clark's analysis of the most primitively universal appeal of Raymond Carver. The possibility which Clark does not allow for is that readers might respond to something else, and might be differently placed and differently disposed both from Carver himself, from the characters in the story, and from each other.

A considerable amount of literary pragmatic research does claim to examine the way in which literary writers actually exploit the difference between internal contexts and the context of the reader or audience. Hans-Jürgen Diller (1991) has looked at the pragmatics of the actor-audience relationship from the mystery cycles to the early Tudor comedies. Before the advent of indoor theatres with lighting and a "fourth-wall" view of the stage, the separation of players from audience was not so clear, and the audience might even have been noisy. So how, under those circumstances, was the dichotomy between the ordinary world and the world of the drama actually handled? One technique was to frame the dramatic action by means of a presenter character; another was homiletic, with a character from within the play preaching at the audience; and a third involved characters who ambiguously straddled both worlds, sometimes even drawing the audience into the drama, as when the devil Tityvillus tells spectators to be quiet while he whispers falsehoods into the ear of the sleeping Mankynde. Maingueneau (1990: 141–61), too, has a brilliant chapter on what he calls the duplicity of drama, his point being that the meaning and value of words spoken in a play can be quite different for the characters on stage from what they are for the audience. This observation, in its turn, is close to Cynthia Bernstein on the pragmatics of Browning's dramatic monologues: on the fact that the reader is able "both to see 'My Last Duchess' as poetry and to hear it as conversation .... [T]he same words may have different purposes, depending on who is perceived to be speaking and listening" (Berstein 1990: 128). What *Browning* presents to *the reader* is the *Duke* speaking to the *Count's messenger*.

Yet such studies, very illuminating in their way, are closer to the formalist branch of literary pragmatic research than to the historical. As in the reader-response criticism associated with Wolfgang Iser, scholarly attention is mainly directed to the implied reader or audience as an aspect of literary form. The underlying assumption, dating back to some of the ancient Greeks, is that there is only one, universal kind of truth, rationality, morality, politics, beauty and so on, because there is only one way of being human. Hence there is only one way of reading: in effect, that of the text's implied or ideal receiver as apprehended by the particular commentator.

Not that such approaches represent a current commentator as necessarily very powerful — or any other current reader, for that matter. On the contrary, all the versions of the unitary context hypothesis so far mentioned are strongly weighted in favour of the person who actually initiates the communication. Raymond Carver or the writer of a morality play or Robert Browning are all thought of as not only supplying the text, but as surrounding it with an obligatory context, in practice the implied context of the implied reader, which real readers or spectators are thought of as having to re-create for themselves. They are figured as confining themselves within its framework, responding only in the way the author would have wished.

Certain types of linguistic scholarship work in the same way. Because many linguists still combine ostensibly phonocentric attitudes with a written-language bias in their choice of examples, an immediately present speaker is often figured as having total control. Not only do linguists tend to apply a merely dualistic — sender/receiver — model of communication. They can also do this in such a way that the current sender comes across as exclusively active in face of a more or less absolute docility in the current receiver. Even in the processual pragmatics of Geoffrey Leech, which captures so much of human interaction's complexity and dynamism, the flow of communication is largely unidirectional (see especially Leech 1983a: 58–62). Consequently many of his examples stop short after a single turn of speech or, if a second person does get a word in, still leave the initiator of communication as very much king of the castle. The following case is typical:

> A: Have you got any matches?
> B: Yes. *Here you are. (Gives matches.)*
> (Leech 1983: 98, his italics)

Here B's choice of options is apparently between "Yes" and the italicized "Here you are"; it would be unusually childish to say, "Yes. But you can't have any." One of the only two ways in which A's wishes would not be fulfilled would be if B did not actually have any matches at the moment, and this is as much beyond B's control as A's, since B either has matches or does not. As for the other possibility, B, even though possessing matches at the moment, might say something such as "No. Sorry, I haven't," so telling a lie, and letting A be without them. But this, the only scenario which would recognize that B is no less ethically empowered than A, represents conditions of dialogic parity from which linguists have somewhat averted their gaze.

A fair proportion of traditional literary criticism, by contrast, though also making a unitary context assumption, applies it the other way round. Here it is the the initiator — the author — who is disempowered, because critics arrogate a universal legitimacy to their own interpretation and value judgements. The single discourse community presupposed is not that of the author's there-and-then, but of the critic's own here-and-now.

Perhaps the most obvious examples are from formalist criticism, which as part of the Aesthete-Symbolist-Modernist reaction against nineteenth-century historical positivism and biographical reductionism tended to decontextualize literature altogether. The reaction was more than understandable, and promoted new directions in literary activity, and new ways of appreciating it. But this development, too, could be taken to extremes, in effect re-instating the critical practices of the early eighteenth-century Augustans. Augustan critics had seen only the smallest segment of the past as something still to be emulated; had set up a canon of great works which they took to be instantly and universally apprehensible as such; and had then demonized the rest of history as a grotesquely Gothic antithesis to a kind of eternal present, the domain of their own good selves and the ancient Greeks and Romans. Modernist critics, applying criteria which were not Augustan, arrived at a non-Augustan canon. Yet in terms of actual procedure, it was as if the intervening ages of criticism, with all their remarkable advances in historical understanding and hermeneutic sophistication, had never been. The second edition of Thomas Warton's *Observations on the Fairy Queen of Spenser*, probably the first piece of English criticism to stress the importance of considering "the customs and genius of ... [the writer's] age", might just as well never have been written (Warton 1762: II 263–4).

Warton had "searched his [Spenser's] contemporary writers, and examined the books on which the peculiarities of his style, taste, and composition, are confessedly founded" (*ibid.*). He readily conceded that Spenser, like Ariosto before him, did not completely raise himself above "Gothic ignorance and barbarity"; that he reflected the "romantic manner of poetical composition introduced and established by the Provencal bards"; and that he accordingly recounted "unnatural events, the machinations of imaginary beings, and adventures entertaining only as they were improbable". These were objections which Warton himself, very much a child of his own time, could only endorse. Yet more unusually, he also had the flexibility of mind to see that a neo-classical taste drawing its legitimation from Homer and Aristotle — from the "example and precept of antiquity" — represented only one set of possible criteria.

> If the FAIRY QUEEN be destitute of that arrangement and œconomy which epic severity requires, yet we scarcely regret the loss of these while their place is so amply supplied, by something which more powerfully attracts us: something which engages the affections [*sic*; ? ^ and] the feelings of the heart, rather than the cold approbation of the head. If there be any poem, whose graces please, because they are situated beyond the reach of art, and where the force and faculties of creative imagination delight, because they are unassisted and unrestrained by those of deliberate judgement, it is this. In reading Spenser if the critic is not satisfied, yet the reader is transported.
> (Warton 1762: I 1–2)

In effect, Warton's entire argument was a sophisticated exercise in positive mediation. In the language of Gadamerian hermeneutics, he wanted to establish Spenser's horizon of expectations. By fostering a self-consciousness about the preconceptions of his (Warton's) own age, he hoped to counteract their inhibiting effect on literary appreciation. Gently reprimanding Pope for reading even Shakespeare too much through Augustan spectacles, he commented: "If Shakespeare is worth reading, he is worth explaining" (Warton 1762: II 265).

> [T]he commentator whose critical enquiries are employed on Spenser, Jonson, and the rest of our older poets, will in vain give specimens of his classical erudition, unless, at the same time, he brings to his work a mind intimately acquainted with those books, which though now forgotten, were yet in common use and high repute about the time in which his authors respectively wrote, and which they consequently must have read.
> (Warton 1762: II 264)

Similarly, it was all very well to say that Caxton was "rude and uncouth". But "in an illiterate and unpolished age he [Caxton] multiplied books, and consequently readers" (Warton 1762: II 266).

In its full context, this last remark, with its continuing clear fondness for neoclassical preconceptions, does not come across as patronizing towards Caxton, since Warton has so unashamedly opened himself to the imaginative power of that earlier age's literature as well. Modernist critics, by contrast, can seem rather narrowly self-absorbed, giving the impression that only a fairly small range of earlier writers is still of interest. A conspicuous example was the early Eliot, for whom the golden age of English literature was immediately prior to the dissociation of sensibility he saw setting in with Milton and Dryden. Writers of the more recent past — the Romantics and Victorians — came to figure as the most old-fashioned and irrelevant of all, and new writing, despite Eliotian apophthegms on tradition and the continuing relevance of Dante and the Metaphysicals, was expected to break with the past quite noticeably. Dante and the Metaphysicals were seized upon only insofar as they seemed to offer a solution to a twentieth-century problem — only insofar as they belonged to the "usable past". The full extent of their otherness remained unexplored. No matter how civilized Modernist critics may have been as private individuals, the view of history encouraged by some of their public statements, and not only by statements of a Futurist cast, could actually be somewhat Fordian. Even critics in the Richards-Empson-Leavis tradition, though far more focussed on literature's psychological impact than critics in the Aesthete-Symbolist tradition, tended to universalize human nature itself, expecting all writers and all readers to share complex, adult and not always particularly pleasant experiences of exactly the same twentieth-century kind. Leavis excluded Fielding from his great tradition of the English novel on the grounds that to "a mind ... demanding more than external action", he is superficial, i.e. totally deficient in "marked moral intensity" (Leavis 1962 [1948]: 11–12). Leavis clearly thought that mature readers of any time and place ought to agree with him, and that Fielding himself ought to have known better than to write as he did. Such criticism has no Wartonian intuition of what its own time's literary sensibility may be blind to.

By the 1950s, this obliviousness of cultural relativities had become very widespread in at least the English-speaking world's educational establishments, where it was transmitted through the pedagogical use of practical criticism. The seminal text here, I.A. Richards's *Practical Criticism: a Study of Literary Judgement* (1929), had examined how a number of readers responded or failed to respond to the linguistic detail of particular literary texts. In drawing attention to the way such texts are worded, Richards was offering an invaluable antidote to self-indulgent "appreciation" and the excesses of biographical and historically positivist criticism. So if I now have to mention the excesses of an institutionalized practical criticism, this is by no means to question the value of careful close reading. On the contrary, present-day new historicists and others cannot afford to relapse into the old pre-Modernist sloppiness. But over and above his general universalization of a twentieth-century mind-set, Richards's more particular shortcoming was to imply that good readers receive no benefit from information about a text's provenance, and should be able to manage without it. The student guinea-pigs who produced the readers' protocols from which he drew his evidence were given nothing to go on apart from the literary texts themselves: not the author's name, and not even the date of composition or publication. Many teachers drew the conclusion that the literature classroom could profitably become a kind of laboratory, artificially insulated from history, as if readers could confront texts in a kind of eternal present. In not a few colleges and university departments, survey courses on the literary tradition were simply scrapped.

As part of the more general reaction against nineteenth century historical preoccupations, the Modernist deracination of literature is comparable to the shift in Western linguistic scholarship from comparative philology to

Saussurian and Bloomfieldian structuralism, approaches which in seeking to refine *langue* from the dross of *parole* were not concerned with the diachronic variation of which *parole* is both the motor and exponent. The synchronic focus on a single state of the language was as much a part of linguistic structuralism's de-humanizing methodology as was its behaviouristic disregard of meaning and intention. Linguists knew perfectly well that the linguistic signifier's relation to the signified is a matter of arbitrary convention, and that its interpretation therefore depends on contextualization in a particular time and place. But the structuralist methodology left this, the historical side of things, unresearched.

Richards, who also knew about contextualization, who in his work on non-literary language actually started to investigate it, and who so strongly insisted on the real psychological impact of literature's models of attitudinal organization, was in other respects more like a literary formalist — the similarity with Austin is very striking. In particular, he saw poetic language as non-referential and self-legitimating. What this overlooked was that the need for contextualization attaches to the language of literature no less than to any other language. If readers have no preparedness to move inside contexts of writing, and inside literature's internal contexts, they will turn the texts they read into something either vaguely universal or largely personal to themselves. In the undergraduate protocols Richards quotes in *Practical Criticism*, such idiosyncratic redeployments occurred time and time again. As a well educated person he was appalled by them. But his unhistorical pragmatics of poetic language could not explain what had gone wrong.

More recently, literature has in an obvious sense been re-situated in history, thanks to Marxist criticism, feminist criticism, cultural structuralism, new historicism, cultural materialism, gay and lesbian criticism, post-colonial criticism, and ethnic criticism. Yet as I have suggested, the more deterministic forms of such approaches contribute to the climate of ideas in which the rhetoric of blame is now so rampant. Paradoxically, then, the historian's feel for sociocultural relativism is still not strengthened. Critics representing community or period x blame writers of community or period y entirely according to the criteria of community or period x. Anthony Julius, for instance, is not altogether unlike Leavis, in effect seeking to impose a here-and-now understanding on the there-and-then. In his discussion of Eliot, a pre-Holocaust moral universe is collapsed into one that is post-Holocaust.

Historians, literary historians and historically minded literary critics sometimes over-react to the unitary context assumption in this form by adopting it in its other form: they go in for the kind of historical or cultural purism which disempowers the current reader altogether, granting sole communicative responsibility to the author in the context of writing. But whichever way the unitary context assumption is applied, its proponents sometimes fail, not only to distinguish between the three context positions in themselves, but to recognize a further proliferation in the way all three context positions are actually filled. Both in real life contexts, and in a text's self-contextualizing replications of them, proliferation can in fact take place at any or all of the communicative triangle's apexes.

For one thing, an author's own conditions of writing can change during the course of communication, and a reader's attention may be drawn to this by the implied context of writing. The first versions of the first two volumes of Laurence Sterne's *Tristram Shandy* were published in New York in 1759, and the remainder of the novel in London between 1761 and 1767. During this entire period, its author came closer and closer to death, needless to say, a circumstance on which successive volumes regaled their readers with a kind of metafictional running commentary. The first words of Book VII are as follows:

> No — I think, I said I would write two volumes every year, provided the vile cough which then tormented me, and which to this hour I dread worse than the devil, would but give me leave — and in another place — (but where, I can't recollect now) — speaking of my book as a machine, and laying my pen and ruler down cross-wise upon the table, in order to gain the greater credit to it — I swore it should be kept agoing at that rate these forty years, if it pleased but the fountain of life to bless me so long with health and good spirits.
> (Sterne 1903 [1759–67]: 435)

As for proliferation within the internal context of the things and people discussed, this is very common in ordinary everyday gossip, and also in letters, novels and poems as well, where we hear, as it were, the writer's gossipping voice, sometimes approaching a kind of freely meandering stream of consciousness. But what about drama? Aristotle observed that such liberties tended not to be taken by the tradegians he was familiar with, and neoclassical poeticians of the Renaissance positively advised dramatists against them, recommending the so-called unities of time, place and action as far more realistic. When we are sitting in a theatre, we have the impression, not so much of listening to the gossipping voice of the writer, as of watching the *dramatis personae* talk to each other. Also, to see the stage as representing first one setting and then some totally different setting does require somewhat more imaginative effort than to take it for just some single setting throughout. One dramatist who had clearly thought about this was Shakespeare. In *Henry V* and *The Winter's Tale* he includes, respectively, the Chorus and Time as presenters who can be his spokesmen, gossiping with the audience directly, so to speak, sometimes smoothing over spatial and temporal jumps quite explicitly, and not without apologies:

> O, pardon! Since a crooked figure may
> Attest in little place a million;
> And let us, ciphers to this great accompt,
> On your imaginary forces work.
> Suppose within the girdle of these walls
> Are now confin'd *two* mighty monarchies,
> Whose high upreared and abutting fronts
> The perilous narrow ocean parts assunder.
> (Shakespeare 1951 [1600]: 551 [*Henry V*, Prologue ll. 15–22], my italics)
>
> I ...
> Now take upon me, in the name of Time,
> To use my wings. Impute it not a crime
> To me or my swift passage that I slide
> O'er sixteen years, and leave the growth untried
> Of that wide gap ... .
> (Shakespeare 1951 [1623]: 394 [*The Winter's Tale*, IV i 1–7])

In other plays, however, Shakespeare pays no deference to the neo-classical precepts at all, something for which Johnson later forgives him, on the grounds that the audience do have the imaginative power necessary to follow what is happening. In point of fact, and as Johnson also spells out, "the spectators are always in their senses and know, from the first act to the last that the stage is only a stage, and that the players are only players" (Johnson 1960 [1765]: 38). To which we need only add that the spectators also know that the whole thing is no less the result of human mental and discoursal activity than any story they may hear or tell in the theatre bar. Their unspoken presupposition is that if the playwright, producer and actors have been able to get their heads round it, then so can they themselves.

Lastly, and most importantly for the present discussion, with texts that are written or otherwise recorded there will obviously be a proliferation of the real-world junctures at which receiving takes place. This applies even though the implied receiver and the implied receiver's implied context are very often fixed as one particular sort of person in one particular sort of milieu, often a milieu that is fairly close to that in which the recorded words are themselves produced. The seventeenth century Anglo-Welsh poet Henry Vaughan, for instance, wrote devotional poems which would particularly speak to Anglicans during the time of the puritan Commonwealth, when their own religious practices were forbidden by law. Yet although most of those readers have now been dead and buried for three hundred years, some people, probably including a fair number of atheists, still read him.

The context in which a literary work is currently being read is a cognitive environment which varies, infinitely, and quite beyond the writer's control or knowledge. The decisive factor is the matter of who, where and when the particular reader of the moment actually happens to be. This has direct consequences for how any given reading works out. A literary text, like any other kind of utterance, calls on its recipients to perform a number of inferential activities: to disambiguate, assign reference, resolve vagueness or indeterminacy; to recover implicit content and/or attitudes; and to take things ironically, metaphorically, symbolically or literally. It is in the study of several aspects of inferencing that a historical yet non-historicist literary pragmatics will come closest to work in the more behaviouristic tradition of pragmatics, where topics such as presupposition, implicature, and relevance have been so central, and where, indeed, relevance is the main focus of the most influential current theory. One of the most obvious consequences of the disparate sitedness of writing and reading is that, during the reader's processes of inferencing, different cognitive environments can jostle against each other. The problems can extend far beyond questions of meaning a narrow sense, to matters of affect and value.

For some time now, literary pragmatic research has been investigating this. An important pioneer was Marlene Dolitsky (1984), who argued that we draw on our existing knowledge and perceptions in order to project ourselves into the mind-set of other people. She also pointed out what happens when differences of background cut us off from necessary assumptions and conventions of interpretation. To begin with, the interpretation we come up with is quite likely to be nonsense, and in such a case the difference between a writer's and a particular reader's contexts means that the reader's attempts to make sense of the text will be bumpily non-automatic. This awkward kind of inferencing process is discussed by Christine Richards (1985), too, whose development of historical distinctions, in a scholar making references to relevance theory, is somewhat unusual, but suggests that relevance theory is indeed not a-historical in itself. Some of the consequences of the communicational triangle and contextual proliferation are no less clearly stated by Marilyn Randall (1985, 1987, 1996), another scholar who has become interested in relevance theory:

> In the case of literary texts, which are notoriously divorced from the contexts and the intentions which produced them, the presuppositions of the author and those of the readers are ... constitutive of meaning.
> (Randall 1996: 831)

On the one hand, a historical yet non-historicist pragmatics emphasizes that human beings from different life-worlds can have things in common, and are quite good enough at imagining themselves into widely varied scenarios to be able to communicate with each other. Similarly, a text's implied reader in its implied context is a construct with which most readers will probably try to identify themselves, often to considerable effect, in an effort to arrive at a "correct" or "faithful" reading. On the other hand, their success will probably be less than total — how, actually, could it ever be measured, and by whom? — and between the implied reader's implied context and a real reader's own situationality and personal life-experience there may also be a tension, or even a contradiction, which not all readers will be passive enough to repress. Different sitings do have an interpretative and evaluative bearing, and the relationship between them is in principle one of full human parity, which for a literary critic aiming at positive mediation is the fundamental fact of life. It is between the life-worlds of different real-world junctures that mediation will in effect have to take place.

As in linguistics, so in literary scholarship, the great attraction of the unitary context assumption is that it keeps things neat and tidy. Hermeneutically and evaluatively, both forms of it result in a monologic regularity. What it suggests is that any given text can only be taken in just some single way: either according to the putative intention of its author, or according to the understanding of the current commentator. At first, the main consequence of rejecting the assumption may seem to be an altogether more problematic chaos, which would perhaps have to be theorized with a gesture towards poststructuralist deconstruction. If a unitariness of context is not criticism's most fundamental premise, one might think, no interpretation or judgement will be better than any other, so that the general motto could be: "Anything goes!" In practice, it will be as if the reader-biassed form of the assumption has won in any case.

What we have here, though, is once again an interpretative dilemma reminiscent of the West's epistemological dilemma between rationalism and nihilism. Western discourse has always forced us to think of ourselves as either sane or mad, a choice which became especially clear-cut from the time of the Enlightenment. Either we shall accept a norm of monologic reason, which can lead to a progressive, utilitarian morality, and to a technological and instrumental expertism in both public and private life. Or we shall be pessimistically irrationalist, chaotic, and hopelessly imaginative. Against this background, scepticism has often figured as nothing more than a failure to decide one way or the other, since there seems to be no real middle ground. That many of our practices, beliefs and values could somehow be simultaneously reasonable and contingent is apparently out of the question (cf. Hollinger 1985: ix-xx).

Or such, at least, was the situation up until modern times, when a middle ground certainly was opened up, to begin with by Vico and Herder, in their accounts of various civilizations as each having their own coherent but different, or even incompatible perceptions and values. This type of argument has now been tested and further developed by more recent German hermeneuticians and American pragmatists. Heidegger came to see in the monistic rationality of Western philosophy and science a relentless will to power, while Gadamer, though similarly critical of the Enlightenment, could not accept the counter-Enlightenment historical school of Dilthey either, because it perpetuated the objective/subjective dichotomy of scientistic absolutism. William James, John Dewey and Richard Rorty, meanwhile, have sought to base the culture of real life and practice on a Socratic conversation that is very much sited, more or less ethnocentrically. Work in both these traditions seems not only to recognize the finitude and historicity of human life and culture, but also to offer, within particular traditions and social practices, certain kinds of rootedness, knowledge, and morality. In postmodern times, the idea of a single and objective truth has certainly been very strongly challenged. But *what counts* as truth in any given context is still recognized as having a fundamental importance, and any particular community will accordingly have its truth protocols by which to decide the matter (cf. Section 2.1). This means that the spirit of much current epistemological discourse, and, by the analogy I have noted, of much social and cultural critique as well, is neither exactly rationalistic nor exactly irrationalistic.

This kind of *tertium quid* can be seen in recent feminist thought, for instance. Having traditionally challenged the dichotomies of rationalism/

nihilism, sanity/madness, science/imagination as reinforcing a dichotomy of masculine/feminine, feminists are now hesitant simply to reject the culturally prioritized first terms of those binarisms in favour of the second terms, and regard the extremist structuralist or poststructuralist reduction of the self to social or linguistic programming as actually a masculine nihilism, developed at the precise moment when women were beginning to construct an autonomous identity as a necessary step towards liberation. At the same time, many feminists are developing what remains of their liberation narrative with considerable caution, lest too heady an Enlightenment aspiration entail an essentialistic universalization of womanhood, from which the experiential realities of many actual women would be excluded (Waugh 1996).

One of the ironies of the present situation is that Lyotard and other postmodern commentators have supported their protest against the logocentric certainties of the older science by an appeal to what they see as a more indeterminate and symbolistic world-view in the mathematics and physics of the twentieth century. The irony is actually double: first, that they should have wanted their critique of scientific truth to be scientifically truthful;[14] secondly, that they may have fundamentally misunderstood twentieth-century science, which according to many scientists themselves is still based on ontological realism: on the idea of truth as a state of affairs obtaining independently of any observer (Sokal and Bricmont 1998 [1997]).

Yet even if an independent truth is something which contemporary scientists still seek to approximate by rational means, they would hardly deny the far-reaching consequences of viewpoint, or the strong implication of much postmodern commentary that assessments made on the basis of different positionalities can hardly be the same. That this last issue is being so extensively debated may in practice improve the chances of what Habermas calls *reasonable* disagreement. Certainly the task of mediation, whether in literary criticism or in other spheres, becomes a lot easier to conceptualize.

By comparison, the twentieth century's earlier a-historical and de-humanizing paradigm would have been more likely to obscure the possible grounds of contention, so postponing any palliative as well. Modernist literary formalism, for instance, unquestioningly took over the binarism of traditional Western

---

14. A point made in a brilliant paper entitled "The Two Cultures Revisited", delivered by Patricia Waugh at the 1998 Conference of the International Association of University Professors of English in Durham. I understand that Professor Waugh is planning to publish her observations.

thought, assuming a universal truth or reason, to which literature's imaginative fiction was an unusual and irrational alternative, albeit interpretable in only the one "scientific" manner of a-historical de-personalization. Not only did New Critics carry on regardless of the tradition of pragmatist semiotics (cf. Section 2.1). They were just as untouched by philosophical hermeneutics, or by literary scholarship of a more ethical orientation — the cross-purposes exchange between René Wellek (1937) and Leavis (1962 [1952]b: 211–22) was oddly definitive. Nowadays, their conception of the aesthetic heterocosm is sometimes said to have reflected a typically male sense of individuation, as a process of separating-off, in the first instance from the mother, and subsequently from everybody else as well, an ego-ideal to which feminist goals of relationship are diametrically opposed (Waugh 1996). In short, the entire formalist tradition can perhaps be said to have placed a higher value on abstraction than on the facts of situated experience, so that its affinity with the universalizations of structuralist linguistics and generative grammar was close indeed.

Seen in this perspective, the Barthesian wave of structuralist and poststructuralist criticism was sometimes an over-correction, suggesting that the only interpretative alternative to such monolithic regularities was, precisely, a quite ungovernable chaos. Pioneers of approaches such as cultural materialism, cultural studies and postcolonial studies not only emphasized the scope for disagreement arising from different situationalities, but sometimes offered potent cocktails of Foucauldian pessimism and "all-the-way-down" sociohistorical determinism, so leaving little discoursal choice apart from a rhetoric of blame, an insincere political correctness, or a ghettoized dissensus with partitioning walls of silence. Deconstructionists, similarly, not only highlighted the scope for proliferating interpretations in the process of linguistic semiosis itself, but sometimes came so close to solipsism as to undermine the sense of dialogue even within one and the same collective. According to Paul de Man, when the judges sentenced the servant-girl for the crime committed by Rousseau, they were taking the words through which Rousseau accused her to have a stronger purchase on human relationships than language can ever have. For other poststructuralist commentators, a sheer inadequacy intrinsic to human speech *per se* was the very theme and cause of poetry. In Geoffrey H. Hartman's view, for instance, the "Ode — Intimations of Immortality from Recollections of Early Childhood" was straining to say things which may not quite allow themselves to be said, thereby setting up several conflicting lines of association. What, if anything, Hartman asked, can Wordsworth be taken to mean by "a timely utterance", or by "fields of sleep", or by "thoughts that do often lie too deep for tears"? Hartman's "mild deconstruction", having taken "a timely utterance" as his starting point, and having "made many angels dance on it", concluded that Wordsworth was yearning back to the first and most effective words of all, spoken by God: "Let there be..." (Hartman 1996 [1987]: 89). This reading, which paradoxically highlighted something of Wordsworth's own amazing verbal achievement, simultaneously underestimated and overestimated the difficulties of communication in general. It *under*estimated difficulties, in that Hartman's discussion of Wordsworth himself was based on the unitary context assumption. Wordsworth and Hartman were taken as sharing a kind of universal present, which to the extent that it could be pinned down at all sounded rather like the Yale of the mid-1980s. Hartman would never find Wordsworth's mental frameworks seriously difficult or wrong-headed. And Wordsworth would approve of Hartman's interpretation without a second thought. As for *over*estimating difficulties, what Hartman seemed to forget was that any kind of language use prompts receivers to engage in just the same kind of inferencing as he himself successfully applied to Wordsworth's poem. Their success is often just as great as his, even when they are fully aware of the distance between the context of sending and their own context of receiving, and aware of the imaginative empathy this calls for as well.

For a view of communication more promising for the aims of mediating criticism, we can return to Jerome McGann's editorial pragmatics and Ziva Ben-Porat's "two-way" literary pragmatics (McGann 1991a, 1991b; Ben-Porat 1991). Both McGann and Ben-Porat frankly treat the sociocultural history of writings and readings as a matter of contacts between different lifeworlds, and neither of them underemphasizes the problems of understanding, or ever loses faith in its possibility and benefits. As for readers' ways of actually dealing with contextual proliferation, important hints are to be had from linguistic pragmaticists specializing in cultural interfaces, with their clear sense that sender context and receiver context are indeed different (e.g. Gumperz 1982; Blum-Kulka, House and Casper 1989; Wierzbicka 1991; Kasper and Blum-Kulka 1993).

And still more relevant to the present work's emphasis on *pragma* is the tradition of philosophical hermeneutics. Gadamer, especially, in describing the merging of different horizons of expectations, fully recognizes that linguistic communication may really change a differentiated status quo. From his seminal account of how the relative truths of different situationalities can enter into negotiation[15] I have borrowed the view of communication as not simply flowing in just one direction, but as bi-directional within a situation that is basically triangular. As Gadamer sees things, a confrontation with human otherness is not a one-sided affair. Neither is it a matter of the meanings and value judgements attaching to isolated utterances or encounters. Rather, it is a process in which different world views can dynamically interact within the minds of both parties, who thereby become involved in reciprocal interpretation. Gadamer speaks of two equally and simultaneously involved communicants trying to meet each other half-way, so as to arrive, if possible, at a shared view of the third component of the situation: whatever it is they are talking *about*.

In most of Gadamer's work, this third entity is the world, or truth; this is what philosophers have usually assumed that people talk about. But the same kind of set-up applies for the often fictional world of, say, a poet, and by flouting expectations of specific and episodic truth such a fictional world can implicate general or moral truth about the real world. The poem's internal contexts and their denizens "within" the poem can be thought of as suspended in between the poet's context of writing and the current real reader's context of reading, as important matters about which the poet and the reader are in communication. Nor is there any reason why the things talked about should not also include one of the two flesh-and-blood communicants themselves, as in the case of some lyrical, and all confessional poetry. In any event, readers' understanding of what is mentioned "in" the poem is the main issue between them and the poet, and their responses to it stem in no small part from a

---

15. Perhaps the best introduction to philosophical hermeneutics is Kurt Meuller-Vollmer (ed.), *The Hermeneutics Reader: Texts of the German Tradition from the Englightenment to the Present* (1985), which includes helpful commentary and bibliographical assistance for further reading. The English translations of Gadamer's most important writings are: *Philosophical Hermeneutics* 1976 [1962–72]; *Reason in the Age of Science* 1981[1976, 1978, 1979]; *The Relevance of the Beautiful and Other Essays* 1986 [1967, 1977, 1980]; *Truth and Method* 1989 [1960]. Excellent general commentaries on Gadamer are: Georgia Warnke, *Gadamer: Hermeneutics, Tradition and Reason* (1987); and Joel Weinsheimer, *Gadamer's Hermeneutics: A Reading of* Truth and Method (1985). For hermeneutics and literary study see: David Hoy, *The Critical Circle: Literature, History, and Philosophical Hermeneutics* (1978); Judith Perkins, "Literary History: H.-G. Gadamer, T.S. Eliot and Virgil" (1982); Joel Weinsheimer, *Philosophical Hermeneutics and Literary Theory* (1991); and *New Literary History* 10 (Autumn 1978), a special issue on this topic.

negotiation of the different situationalities of the writing and their own reading.

In their efforts to deal with this, readers try, consciously or otherwise, to guess what the language used must have meant for the author in the context of writing. Even though they can never become a "typical" member of some "first" audience (problematic notions at best); even though they will interpret, value and use the text in their own way; even though the process of semiosis in principle never comes to an end: they nevertheless go through this empathetic movement into the context of writing. Their common-sense notion of the author's historical identity remains an ever-returning point of reference, even though it is always open to modification.

To this extent, at least, reading and interpretation are driven by a desire to pin things down, initially as the intention, feelings, experience, or ideas of the historical writer. Semiotic proliferation can continue all the time, but it is also always coming back to a momentary halt at precisely this point. New interpretations and new evaluations are for ever arising, but each new interpretation and evaluation can only result from a temporary freezing of the semiotic process in its tracks, a rigidification which for the time being assumes virtual finality as what the author is thought to be saying. For given readers at given times and places, a text has a range of meanings and values which is to all intents and purposes perfectly determinate, once those readers have "made up their minds", and which stays that way until they "change" their minds once more. In this, literature is again no different from any other type of language use. The relationship between the two halves of the linguistic sign, the signifier and the signified, is always arbitary. But in any given configuration of circumstances there usually come points at which people begin to take the signifier as intended to mean or do something in particular. Readers, of course, are for most of the time guided by what they know of the sign relationships which were conventional within the writer's society, and they will also have other knowledge and presuppositions, on the basis of which to make the most appropriate inferences they can manage. If this were not how all language processing worked, human societies could not use language as a medium. It is only because semiosis is constantly coming to these provisional halts that the normal business of living does not itself seize up. Just as a balance has always had to be struck between the life of contemplation and the life of action, so the interpreting mind is for ever pulsing between deconstruction and reconstruction.

In effect this means that there will be many aspects of text-comprehension which do not much change from one generation or community of readers to another, which is why Iser's sometimes a-historical reader-response criticism, despite, but also because of its limitations, does have its value. To return to Dickens, for instance, there will be particular lines of interpretation, particular connections, particular ways of filling in gaps, to which his readers have always resorted, and always will resort, in their efforts to contextualize his language in the way he might have expected. So much so, that countless readers have been interested in finding out about Dickens as a person. Biography is probably the most widely read branch of Dickens scholarship, and roughly speaking there has been one new life of Dickens for every new decade. There has also been a great deal of popular or semi-popular discussion of sociocultural minutiae connected with Dickens, often channelled through *The Dickensian: A Magazine for Dickens Lovers*, published by the Dickens Fellowship since 1905. Much other Dickens scholarship has seen a need to recreate, not only Dickens's life and Victorian social history, but the Victorian thought-world. Jerome Meckier (1987) highlights intertextualities with the novels of Dickens's contemporaries, while Harry Stone (1979) explores Dickens's use of popular fairytale elements. One of the most important functions of Dickens scholarship is to help present-day readers recreate the Victorian lifeworld and thought-world in order to be able to contextualize Dickens's texts in as Dickensian a way as possible.

Take Miss Havisham in *Great Expectations*. This old lady, having long ago been jilted on her wedding day, dressed for ever since in her decaying bridal finery, scarcely moving from the gloomy room in which the cobwebs descend over the rotting wedding breakfast, fanatically educating Estella to be a *femme fatale* who shall wreak revenge on the opposite sex, finally dies in a spectacular rush of flames, her crinoline having caught in the hearth. Even in its own day, all this was powerfully Gothic. In the twentieth century, we recognize continuities in the films of Hitchcock or the novels of Daphne du Maurier. It turns out, though, that for Victorian readers, Miss Havisham would not have been quite so fiercely singular as perhaps for us now. Scholars have noted that cases of strangely obsessed people were often reported, sometimes by Dickens himself, in the popular press — there was the Woman in White who haunted Berners Street, for instance (Sadrin 1988: 215–41). And crinoline dresses did sometimes lead to just this kind of fatality, which was also widely discussed (Witt 1989). Even such little details can significantly strengthen our sense of Dickens's distinctive mixture of fantasy and realism.

In the tradition of philsophical hermeneutics, the reconstructive kind of scholarship that helps us here finds strong support. For hermeneuticians, writers' putative understanding of their own words has always held a privileged position. For Friedrich Schleiermacher, interpretative understanding was in no small part the sheer avoidance of misunderstanding, by means of historical and philological reconstructions. Wilhelm Dilthey, similarly, argued that interpreters need a firm historical grounding as a safeguard against romantic whim and sceptical subjectivity. Not even Gadamer denies that some interpretations are erroneous, or that a theory and methodology are necessary in order to correct them. Emilio Betti and the American literary hermeneutician E.D. Hirsch have for their part both warned of the danger of actually losing sight of the object.

Yet readers' attempts at empathy do not occur in a vacuum. They read within their own contexts of reading, which means that they have not only their own ignorance of the past or the alien, but their own knowledge and values as well, which the author could not have foreseen. Not least, they may well know something about the author as interpreted in the subsequent cultural tradition. The text will come to them already surrounded with a tissue of different interpretations resulting from different uses, and to this extent the tendency of some Barthesian commentators to assimilate literacy to orality is more understandable. Literature, needless to say, is a form of literacy, making for at least some degree of textual stability, and lending itself to a certain continuity of associated commentary, particularly of commentary that is itself written down and published. But many different interpretations of a text do always circulate, and some of them are always mutually contradictory. There will be conflicting hypotheses available about what it means, and conflicting estimates of its distinctive qualities and ultimate value. Was Fielding, as not only Leavis but also André Gide, Dr Johnson, and Lady Mary Wortley Montagu all complained, insufficiently serious? Would his novels have been better if they had portrayed the deepest soul-searching of characters caught up in excruciating moral dilemmas, like novels in the line from Richardson to Lawrence? Or are they, as Chesterton or Coleridge or Boswell would have said, all the better for *not* being in that line? To each new reader, such differing judgements can become simultaneously and undisconcertingly present, just as the same reader will unproblematically negotiate the crosscurrents of gossip upon countless other, non-literary topics as well. Far from detracting from the text's cultural force, the contradictions of literary gossip are precisely what strengthen it, just as the range of speculation about, say, President Gorbachev towards the end of 1990 — Was he no longer in control? Or was he a new Stalin? — did nothing to undermine his then formidable presence to the international gaze. A literary text, like any well known text, and also like a public figure, is a kind of communal symbol (Engler 1990: 23–41), whose significance and affective power are at once cumulative and polysemous, its semiotic potential never ceasing to unfold. As contexts of reading change, new interpretations and new evaluations are for ever evolving, and older ones can also be recycled (cf. Sell 1994a).

By recognizing these factors as well, the tradition of philosophical hermeneutics has tended to grant interpreters a certain freedom. Even Schleiermacher expected them to engage in something he called divination, and Dilthey's distinction between the human sciences and the explanatory physical sciences was based on the idea that history was understandable by virtue of life's own organic unity, something which as human beings we simply know about. The point was stated in its sharpest form in Heidegger's ontological hermeneutics: for human beings, to be is to interpret. "Thrown" as we are into the world at a particular time and place, we "already" have the knowledge that follows from that positioning. We "already" mysteriously know what, to us at least, things are "for", just as Rudolf Bultmann argued that the Bible is always pre-understood by biblical scholars: they cannot help being subjective even when they wish to see it objectively. Of Dickens, we could similarly say that he continues to be interesting and central to our cultures, not only because of what he himself put into his texts, but also because readers are continuing to read him according to their own lights, in ways that are typical of their own particular "thrownness". To return to Miss Havisham for a moment, she is now a central figure in the discourse of feminist literary critics, who use her fate and her own reactions to it, together with Dickens's actual treatment of her, as a catalyst to their larger understanding of the history and lives of women (Raphael 1994 [1989]).

In one sense, this makes their reading prejudiced. They read Dickens with certain questions in mind, and perhaps even with some foregone conclusions as well. But Gadamer would see this as inevitable. Even if some state of affairs — the "truth" — obtains quite independently of all observers, on his account we inevitably have the prejudice of our own historical and cultural positionality, which he actually thinks is just as well, since prejudice at least helps us to get the processes of understanding started. As his critics complain, this can make him seem rather complacent and culturally conservative, as if the ideas and values we hold at present were always in the right. But at other points he clearly says that current, often traditional wisdom is merely as right as we can get it for the moment, and that prejudice is always to be revised through trial and error. This is where the theory and methodology would come in, to test the prejudice, as it were, so enhancing our attempt to merge our own horizons of expectation with somebody else's. Gadamer is *not* critical of an aspiration to be at least as rational and reasonable as possible, and does *not* encourage interpreters to be knowingly unfaithful to the otherness they seek to understand.

In a historical yet non-historicist literary pragmatics, similarly, readers' negotiation of different assessments in their to-and-fro between the context of writing and their own context of reading is a central theme. This can greatly strengthen the work of mediating critics, helping them to counteract the unitary context assumption by keeping the contexts of sending and receiving in human parity. On the one hand, if the context of reading dominates, an author may be deemed simply irrelevant and not be read at all, or may acquire relevance only by being forced into an inappropriate mould. In such cases, the past and/or the foreign tends to be regarded as a very parochial sort of location, whereas the values of the here and now are taken as universally applicable. If F.R. Leavis yielded to this temptation, he was by no means untypical of the English critical tradition generally, which Julius in this respect continues, in the form of the postmodern rhetoric of blame. On the other hand, if the context of writing takes precedence, the result is an arid historical and/or cultural purism, which may deny the validity of the current reader's own responses altogether, and deny, too, the very possibility of communication across lines of difference. This is what would be happening if insincere political correctness led a critic to say that Anthony Hecht and Ramona Lofton are both excellent poets, but can each be appreciated only by their own community. It may also have been a risk when C.S. Lewis (1992 [1961]: 88), in clear disapproval of Leavis, said that the best kind of reading essentially seeks to "receive" what the writer has written, or when Richard Wollheim (1992 [1980]: 228), similarly reacting against "the tendency to conceive of aesthetics as primarily the study of the spectator and his role", described the critic's task as one of "retrieval". The task, said Wollheim, is

> the reconstruction of the creative process, where the creative process must in turn be thought of as something not stopping short of, but terminating on, the work of art itself. The creative process reconstructed, or retrieval complete, the work is then open to understanding.
> (Wollheim 1992 [1980]: 185)

What Wollheim says here is perfectly true, which is why genre criticism, literary biography, and studies of sources and influences are far more important than twentieth century literary critics and theoreticians have sometimes allowed. At the same time, his words are actually a *half*-truth, if, as it seems, he thinks that "understanding" is somehow separated off from "retrieval" or "reconstruction", as something which comes afterwards — if it comes at all, that is, the work being merely "then *open* to understanding" (my italics). At best, the retrieval from within the original context takes place simultaneously with the understanding within the current context of reception. What happens is a kind of parallel processing or hermeneutic circle, and has an on-going affective and ethical dimension as well. All the time, the person on the receiving end is responding as a human being. Otherwise, the situation does not involve a human parity, and communication is not, strictly speaking, taking place.

Given the appropriate balance, reading is a meeting of two minds, such that readers' grasp of the author's words within the context of writing is constantly affected by their sense of themselves and their own current context of reading, and *vice versa*. Looked at from the here and now, the past and/or the foreign can no longer seem as it did or does to its own denizens. To many twentieth century readers, David Copperfield has seemed to have some incapacitating hang-ups about gentility and sexuality, and at just the points where many Victorian readers would have found him most readily understandable and even admirable. But a present-day reader, having empathized with difference, cannot think of the here and now in quite the same way either. This is why any act of reading at all is, in itself, incipiently a process of mediation. It is also what Gadamer has in mind when, in terms I silently borrowed earlier on, he describes a movement of understanding as one of self-discovery through self-alienation:

> To recognize one's own in the alien, to become at home in it, is the basic movement of spirit, whose being consists only in returning to itself from what is other.
> (Gadamer 1989 [1960]: 14)

As we "read" the mind of David Copperfield, we can let David Copperfield "read" ours, so to speak. We can let him ask us whether, in an age of greater social equality and sexual freedom, we are any happier, for instance. Without wishing to surrender anything we may have gained, we can at least start to wonder whether there might also be something we have lost, something perhaps recoverable with Dickens's help. Or to return to the example of Henry Vaughan, his poetry can still speak to present-day atheists. The human qualities they find in his response to circumstance may positively inspire them in their own very different lives.

4.2. Social individuals and their co-adaptations

Especially for an author seeking to address foreigners or posterity, the disparities between context of writing and context of current reading make the outcome of literary interchanges difficult to predict. For literary scholars, what is even more de-systematizing is the element of human individuality. Both writers and readers can behave in ways which, for their own time and place, are maverick. They are social beings, but they are social *individuals*, and their two modalities can enter into processes of co-adaptation.

Here again, the contrast between a historical yet non-historicist literary pragmatics and many other types of linguistic and literary scholarship is rather marked. Behaviouristic structuralism was by no means the first or last movement in linguistics to give the impression that human beings' observance of various kinds of rules is somewhat robotic. Linguistics necessarily seeks to pin down regularities, and languages would not work without them. But some theories and methodologies, and almost inevitably those with a synchronic orientation, allow little attention to how rules get broken or even changed. As for literary scholarship, even criticism written under liberal humanist auspices was itself a constant proof of the awesome paradox of liberalism which I mentioned *à propos* Rousseau and the Jacobins: that a respect for the individual human being's dignity and freedom can all too easily flip over into repression or exclusion. In point of fact, this applies to criticism of both earlier and later periods as well. With however much token deference to their readers' rights and intelligence, by far the majority of literary critics have tended to write as if an interpretation in any way different from the one being currently advanced would be pretty wrong-headed. In effect they have presented their own interpretation as what Kant (1951 [1790]) would have called a pure judgement of disinterested taste, universally valid, and grounded in common sense. The clear implication has been that readers who disagreed would be revealing themselves as less than human, an implication usually strongly reinforced by the unitary context assumption I have questioned in the previous section: the assumption that the writer of a literary work and all its readers in every time and place are members of a single discourse community.

A historical yet non-historicist literary pragmatics, by contrast, will have more in common with a rather different aspect of Kant's aesthetics, in which he largely agreed with Hume (1757) and was followed by Wittgenstein (1978): his perception that judgements of taste, far from being completely objective and automatic, are somewhat mysterious. More specifically: his twin assumptions that an aesthetic judgement can only flow from a personally felt response, and that it cannot be based on rules. Having little sympathy with Baumgarten's proposal of an objective "science of the beautiful" (also dismissed by Wittgenstein, as "too ridiculous for words"), Kant did not allow his own universalist ideal to blind him to reality, or to the importance of dialogue between the dissident individual and the commonality. In effect, he sometimes seems to have thought of common sense as still under evolution or negotiation.

On the one hand, we cannot now afford to ignore Barthesian commentary. The insistence of structuralist and poststructuralist scholars on the social and linguistic sitedness of writers and readers directly challenges the assumptions about a stably independent self and sovereign free will which ordinary readers bring or used to bring to their reading, and such liberal humanist assumptions are certainly not immune to the de-centering critique. Even the strongest individuals are of a particular time and place and culture. The psychic life of a person living here and now is never the same as that of a person living there and then. A person's own sense of self can even be largely unstable or multiple, shaped afresh in each new interchange, in ways we shall later need to consider.

On the other hand, from such a valuable insight it is all too short a step to seeing the interpersonal relations offered by a literary text as a matter, not of individuals realizing themselves through society or language, which was the liberal humanist oversimplification, but of society or language channelling itself through individuals, which is the historicist oversimplification of David Trotter on Dickens and the bourgeois discourse of modernity. The historicist oversimplification makes talk of real authors and real readers, and talk of characters in literature as if they were imitations of similarly real people, unsustainable, and such extremist de-centering was taken one stage further still in the campaign to deconstruct logocentric realism altogether. Under scrutiny here was any meaning a text might be thought to carry about a state of affairs, and, as in pragmatism and speech-act theory, there was a strong sense of truth as a linguistic construct. This, though, was accompanied by none of pragmatism's hospitality to truths which are provisional, because the relative weightings of iterability and interpersonal contextualization were not Austin's but Derrida's (cf. Section 2.4). In the most radical kind of deconstructive critique, the process of semiosis arising from a text was therefore allowed to run on even faster and more freely than in Hartman's account of Wordsworth, becoming a kind of acid in which any emergent constructs were immediately broken down. This undermined the credibility both of knowing subjects and of known objects. It meant, if anything, that a literary text itself, say, could be featured as a kind of animistic "active object", about which there could be "a multitude of competing meanings, each of which denies the primacy of the others" (Machin and Norris 1987: 3, 7).

Explicitly laying claim to a pedigree in traditional Western nihilism, radical deconstruction presented itself as a tool for the ideology-free analysis of ideologies of all colours. As seen by its critics, however, it served as the cover for a positioned, hyper-reactionary abstinence from ethical concern.[16] At the very least, it could involve a somewhat mechanical opposition to any received opinion, so ignoring the variety and contradictions of received opinions themselves, and relying for much of its effect on a head-on collision between theory and experience. What it systematically denied was that unsophisticated logocentric assumptions about the world, human beings' personal identity, and their power of voluntary interaction do have a pragmatic validity, for life and for reading alike.

In point of fact, these basic notions of reality, self, and moral responsibility function as categories of thought in almost the same way as space and time do. They continue to provide frameworks within which we can get our manifold impressions into some sort of shape. As Gadamer might say, they are

---

16. See Patricia Waugh "Stalemates? Feminists, Postmodernists and Unfinished Issues in Modern Aesthetics" (1996), and Sandy Petrey's remarks on Paul de Man (noted above, p. 50). The recent climate of discussion can be further gauged from John D. Caputo, *Against Ethics: Contributions to a Poetics of Obligation with Constant Reference to Deconstruction* (1993); Jeffrey T. Nealon, *Double Reading: Postmodernism after Deconstruction* (1993); and Michael Payne (ed.) *Working Through Derrida* (1993). Important assessments of a somewhat earlier date include: Gerald Graff, *Literature Against Itself* (1979); Jonathan Culler, *On Deconstruction: Theory and Criticism after Structuralism* (1982); Vincent Leitch, *Deconstructive Criticism* (1983); Howard Felperin, *Beyond Deconstruction: The Uses and Abuses of Literary Theory* (1985); John Ellis, *Against Deconstruction* (1989).

a kind of prejudice which at least helps us to set our adjustment to the world in motion. What then emerges is a provisional truth which, rational for the time being within its own terms, serves as the common sense basis for behaviour and understanding. To say this is not to reject ontological realism, for there could well be states of affairs which are quite independent of any attempt to observe or define them. But neither is it to claim that the current version of common sense has already fulfilled Kant's high aspirations for it. As Gadamer explicitly notes of prejudice, common sense is always a temporary approximation to any existent reality, and is relative to particular circumstances and experiences. It is heuristic, and open to challenge and modification.

In the last analysis, moreover, it is we ourselves who change it. Although we can easily submit to being socially pressurized, brainwashed, or carried away on the flood of semiosis, we are under no biological compulsion to do so, and our mind is at least partially our own. Nothing is more anomalous than proofs of cultural or linguistic determinism advanced by commentators who, as exponents of the society or language under discussion, would *a priori* have to be just as determined as anybody else. Clearly, their own formation must be determined less than totally, since they are scrutinizing common sense from the viewpoint of some other rationality, sometimes going so far as to recommend ideological shifts or social reforms. They are both of, and not of, their society, in other words, and as we saw with Foucault, they may actually have to disguise their own degree of relative individuality in order for their theories to remain intact.

My argument here is valorizing facts of experience which have already been championed by some interesting witnesses. Take the testimony of Frank Kermode, for instance. Looking back over his own life at the age of 75, Kermode is keenly aware of the most radical structuralist and poststructuralist attempts at de-centering, having done much to make them more familiar to English-speaking readers, both during his time at University College London and as editor of the Fontana Modern Masters Series. Nevertheless, he writes as follows:

> ...people will go on asking the question whether there is such a thing as a self; how, if it exists, it is constituted; what it has to do with those clownish, distressed, cheating, honourable, sober, drunken selves that gesticulate at the roadside as one drives smoothly down the highway of memory. According to David Hume, "There is properly no simplicity in [the mind] at one time, nor identity in different [times], whatever natural propensity we may have to imagine that simplicity and identity," and he certainly wasn't the last to

question our natural propensity to imagine that we each have a self, a self that might speak for all those discontinuous states. "A single string speaks for a crowd of voices," as Wallace Stevens raptly if obscurely remarked.

Indeed, it is now commonplace that the self is a recent invention or illusion, that external ideological pressures compel each of us to make one because, as subjects, we are easier to keep in order. But I think it was good of Hume to allow us a *natural* propensity, so that we can at least think we have a certain primordial right to choose to have selves, or possibly only to imagine that we are doing so, rather than simply suffer them to be imposed on us. I have difficulty with the idea that I, or for that matter you, can be understood as merely the site of conflicting discourses, merely the product of practices we have no control over and no direct knowledge of. Frankly, if I could not continue to assume, unphilosophically, that I have a self, I shouldn't be bothering with this [i.e. writing his memoirs]. I do see that my self is not immune, in its formation, to social and ethical prejudice and control, but I cannot feel that these are powerful enough to eliminate a certain continuity. Or anyway, a *natural propensity* to assume it, a modicum of identity in different epochs (to be sought, naturally, under differing appearances); and a natural propensity also to take responsibility for all the selves subsumed under this hypothetical self. Or anyway, to assume a right to speak for them, even in a manner that by trying to make them seem interesting falisifes them, insofar as what does not exist can be falsified.
(Kermode 1996: 157–8)

Some of the twentieth century's most influential intellectual celebrities have routinely rejected the evidence of Kermode's kind of personal testimony, on the grounds, first, that it comes too close to common sense and, secondly, that an individual cannot possibly be conscious of the psychological, social or linguistic processes in which he or she is caught up. The implication has been that the intellectual celebrities themselves, by virtue of their scholarly and scientific achievements, are *not* so caught up, and therefore have enlightening things to say. Paradoxically enough, while their actual theorizing has deliberately obscured the possible difference between the individual and society, they in another sense endorsed it, tacitly laying claim to intellectual superiority over everybody else. Their following, not slow to read between the lines, granted them a kind of clerical privilege, so that a few of them even became cult figures, who in the life of secular intellectuals were able to play a role formerly reserved for gods or their earthly representatives and prophets. Not only within their theories, then, but also within the relationship posited — and sometimes therapeutically or academically institutionalized — between themselves and the lay person, the lay person's own thoughts, experiences and emotions, and in particular the lay person's sense of having a certain moral autonomy and temperamental distinctiveness, were systematically discredited. Even Kermode himself, in a shrewdly co-adaptive move, refers to his own way of thinking as unphilosophical. In challenging the gurus, he professes to defer to the gurus' likely verdict on himself.

Yet for some time now, the gurus' imposture has been on the defensive. The titles of Richard Webster's *Why Freud Was Wrong: Sin, Science and Psychoanalysis* (1995) and Richard Noll's *The Jung Cult: Origins of a Charismatic Movement* (1996) give a fair idea of their contents, and the present section's philosophical underpinning has already been developed in a series of books by Raymond Tallis: *In Defence of Realism* (1988), *Not Saussure: A Critique of Post-Saussurean Literary Theory* (1988) and *Enemies of Hope: A Critique of Contemporary Pessimism, Irrationalism, Anti-Humanism and Counter-Enlightenment* (1997). In a nutshell, the error Tallis exposes is that of ignoring the following words of Saussure himself, one of structuralism's founding fathers:

> Language [*langue*] is not a function of the speaker; it is a product that is passively assimilated by the individual .... Speech [*parole*], on the contrary, is an individual act. It is wilful and intellectual.
> (de Saussure 1978 [1916]: 14)

No matter whether the structured system be that of the psyche, language, society or culture, human beings *operate* it, and are not to be conflated with it. Without wishing to re-instate "the transparent, self-possessed, controlling Cartesian *cogito*", what Tallis objects to is Lévi-Strauss's influential talk of the myths "think[ing] themselves out in the men and without men's knowledge" (Lévis-Strauss 1970 [1964]: 46). His own project is to re-assert

> the centrality of individual consciousness, of undeceived deliberateness, in the daily life of human beings. We are not absolutely transparent to ourselves but we are not utterly opaque either; we are not totally self-present in all our actions but nor are we absent from them; we are not complete masters of our fates, shaping our lives according to our utterly unique and original wishes, but neither are we the empty playthings of historical, political, social, semiological or instinctual forces.
> (Tallis 1997: 228)

So Tallis's sense of the human is as a combination of positioned structuration with the more arbitrarily personal. Nor is my own account of the social individual by any means the first attempt to express something similar within cultural and literary theory, a field in which Tallis himself, indeed, a professor of geriatric medicine, gives further proof of his polymathic competence. Even — perhaps especially — for anthropologists, Lévi-Strauss no longer seems to tell the whole story, and before long my discussion will again be indebted to anthropological linguists. Film critics, too, in forming an impression of a filmmaker's complete *oeuvre*, on the one hand tend to see many features as merely generic — just part of the general production culture of the film industry — but on the other hand can instantly distinguish it from the *oeuvre* of somebody else. Their sense of both the generic and personal dimensions is captured in the way they refer to a film-maker as an *auteur*, a term which Ian A. Bell (1994: 35–44) has therefore borrowed into literary theory, as a compromise between the liberal humanist "author" and Barthesian talk of the author's "death". Similar moves are to be found in some feminist commentary, as when Cheryl Walker (1991) argues that poststructuralist critical discourse, in replacing authorship with the abstract indeterminacy of textuality, went too far. Even though authorship can involve formations that are typical of the culture as a whole, Walker insists that it can also carry the patterns of ideation, voice and sensibility of a particular individual. This duality she proposes to examine by means of "persona criticism", a persona being at once *more* personal — more gendered, for instance — than intertextuality, and *less* personal than an original author as imagined by liberal humanists.

For a growing body of opinion, then, to say that Frank Kermode's type of personal testimony bears the marks of ideological delusion just will not do. The extremist structuralist and poststructuralist de-centerings are now seen for what they were. They were not based on stronger evidence than Kermode's remarks, were not better argued, were at least as much creations of the mind, and were positively contradicted by experience. That is why, as the only way to pre-empt reasoned objections, the impressions of ordinary people had to be rejected as sadly uninformed about ordinary life.

Above all, these fashionable positions were unable to explain how other people's words and deeds can become the object of our admiration or disapproval, or how we come to have a sense of our own personal achievement or failure — Kermode's list of possible selves ("clownish, distressed, cheating, honourable, sober, drunken") is very human in its pathos and its ethical overtones. By attributing everything that happens to the workings of suprahuman animistic abstractions such as the unconscious, culture, society or language, the extremist theoreticians actually renounced human responsibility of any kind, so helping to induce a sense of powerlessness that was more than enough to fuel postmodern paranoia, divisiveness and blame.

Altogether more realistic in the relative autonomy it offers is Emmanuel Levinas's *humanisme de l'autre homme*, involving an "I" that is neither just a de-centred social construction, nor just a centred ego reaching out to know and seize the world (Levinas 1974). The "I" of Levinas is not only an entity which defines itself through relations with an irreducible "not-I", but one for which the ethical dimension of life is genuine. And given this much, we can indeed include, as one aspect of the human being's ethical engagement, an element of temperamental distinctiveness, by which I mean the kind of factor that enabled Karl Jaspers (1954) to speak of the personal relativity of world-views, or Norman Holland (1975 [1963], 1975 [1968]) to discuss readers' responses to literature in terms of personality traits. Sometimes an individual's temperamental disposition — the individual's most characteristic attitudes, responses, frame of mind — will obviously correspond with postures currently in fashion. But in principle, temperament perhaps goes deeper than social formation, and can even be in conflict with it, so serving as a stimulus to social change.

Before I elaborate further, a methodological note may be in order. As at other points in this book, the most decisive evidence for my claims will be, in the nature of the case, introspective. At best, both the objectivity of behaviouristic scientism and the deterministic gurus' contempt for personal testimony had scholarly justifications of their own: the former as a reduction of variables in the interests of heuristic power; the latter as part of certain kinds of philosophical speculation. But even at best, they could not directly facilitate an understanding of the most intimately personal areas of human life and experience. An accumulation of introspective evidence, by contrast, most certainly can. Introspection can be adduced in wholly rational arguments of the form: "Very many people agree that p", where p is some proposition about human life or human nature. To substantiate such an argument, one could offer a list of some of the people who have testified to p, and perhaps back this up with notes on the portrayal of humanity in biography, literature, film and academic psychology as well. But no list would be exhaustive — new people are being born all the time. Nor can we at present know whether such an exhaustive list, if it were indeed feasible, would be longer than an exhaustive list of all the people who would testify to not-p. As for the supplementary notes on biography, literature, film and academic psychology, here, too, exhaustiveness would be impossible in favour of either "p or not-p. It is under these circumstances that I once again appeal my readers' own sense of the matter. To use the Kantian language, my question is: Can the suggestions I am making be regarded as universally valid and grounded in common sense? This question, because it is not merely rhetorical, does not cast doubt on the humanity of any readers who disagree with me. As perhaps in Kant himself no less than in Gadamer, the appeal to universal standards still leaves open the possibility that common sense may be revisable by negotiation. What the question does reject, rather, is the deconstructionists' sometimes knee-jerk opposition to common sense in any form.

One way to understand my proposal, then, is as a slight extension of one put forward by K. Anthony Appiah, who himself draws on Charles Taylor, who in turn draws on Bakhtin. A Bakhtinian framework enables Taylor to describe the process of human individuation as basically dialogic:

> We become full human agents, capable of understanding ourselves, and hence of defining our identity, through our acquisition of rich human languages of expression. For my purposes here, I want to take *language* in a broad sense, covering not only the words we speak, but also other modes of expression whereby we define ourselves, including the "languages" of art, of gesture, of love, and the like. But we learn these modes of expression through exchanges with others. People do not acquire the languages needed for self-definition on their own. Rather, we are introduced to them through interaction with others who matter to us — what George Herbert Mead called "significant others". [In a footnote Taylor attributes this term to Mead 1934.] The genesis of the human mind is in this sense not monological, not something each person accomplishes on his or her own, but dialogical.
> (Taylor 1994: 32)

Taylor's remarks alone represent an important insight. From our own memories of growing up, and from everything else we know about ourselves and other people, it is surely possible to say that the human mind can do exactly what he says it does: can flexibly embrace a number of different positionalities and their concomitant perceptions or opinions, either in series or simultaneously. In the course of experience, mental life surely does seem to pulse in a kind of fluent alternation between a centering systole and a decentering diastole. Our sense of our own identity surely can range from a firm singleness, through a multiplicity, to an ineffable confusion, and our sense of other people is surely similar.

To speak of the interpersonality of literature, in particular, is not to think of writerly and readerly selves as frozen in just some single form. That would underestimate what Berlin calls "the force of imaginative insight", and thereby render both writing and reading, let alone any other sort of communication, impossible, which is precisely the problem with some of the socially and linguistically constructed subjectivities arrived at by structuralist and poststructuralist de-centering: they are simply too rigid a reduction — actually too common-sensical! — and thereby incapable of the empathy required for dialogue. No less sharply defined are those "notions of how a proper person of … [a certain] kind behaves" which Appiah (1994) finds so problematic in the discourse of multicultural politics. Here, too, a kind of overly rigid common sense comes into operation, so that a person categorizable in some certain way is expected to adopt the relevant "modes of behaviour" as almost mandatory.

Appiah himself, voicing just the kind of personal testimony which extremist structuralist and poststructuralist analysis ruled out of court, expresses discontent with the roles apparently scripted for him as a black homosexual American male. Very astutely, in the passage I have chosen as an epigraph he also notes that role models actually change over time, so that nowadays the quality of wit would be a far more *individual* property than it used to be in the England of Addison and Steele. In this particular essay, Appiah is still mainly concentrating on the pressure of what he calls social reproduction. The only idea I am adding is that an individual's *resistance* to that pressure is very much the potential through whose realization the public scripts do get changed, even if the line of *least* resistance is obviously to adopt them wholesale.

Within the framework of a historical pragmatics that is non-historicist along the lines suggested here, it will be possible to inspect the two modalities of the social individual as they come into co-adaptive interplay. Both a writer and a reader, by interacting with prevailing sociocultural circumstances, can do something which may bring about a change in both themselves and in those circumstances, a change which may ultimately be to the wishes of the individual writer or reader. As far as influential readers are concerned, the standard practice of literary critics, in particular, is to write about authors in such a way that we at least recognize them as the authors we already know, yet to propose, at the same time, a different twist. Changes to a community's thought-world are never absolute. The new builds on the old. And as far as writers are concerned, co-adaptation is most readily observable in their rhetoric of persuasion. Especially when trying to influence public opinion very directly, they are wise to make some concessions to it. Isaiah Berlin championed civil liberties through the language of the patriarchy. Frank Kermode challenges fashionable philosophical dogmas while clownishly disclaiming philosophical expertise. Dickens reluctantly conformed to proprieties laid down by Mrs Grundy, but only to get back at her. On balance, he probably tended to convince his readers that Victorian mores involved a lot of humbug and injustice, so cutting the ground from under Mrs Grundy's feet. Even *David Copperfield* could alert its first readers to their own hang-ups about gentility and sexuality, precisely because David was such a good Victorian himself.

Further than this, however, explanations of literary deeds and their reception cannot go. There remains a mystery which defies greater systematization. With luck, we can perhaps speak intelligibly about tensions between one lifeworld and another, and between a particular community and a particular social individual. But beyond a certain point, the social individual's individuality — the ethical initiatives, the features of temperament and personal disposition — seem autotelic, being neither communal nor universal, and apparently capable of taking, quite unpredictably, any form whatever, whether precedented or — for all we know — unique.

In one sense, perhaps, the comparative philologists, structuralist linguists, literary formalists, and extremist cultural structuralists and poststructuralists get the last laugh. Human individuality is the wildest variable of all, and a methodology that leaves it to one side, or a theory in which it is positively devalued, is perhaps more likely to discover at least something than an approach which is ambitious to face humanity more head-on. Quite simply, there may be aspects of human identity and activity which are unamenable to scholarly generalization. In another sense, however, a scholarship which counts human beings *in*, even if it is doomed to imprecision and uncertainty, may in the long run be more interesting: interesting, as the word can only mean, after all, to human beings themselves. Concepts such as individuality, free will, genius and creativity may never be fully rehabilitated, and now definitely call for the kind of historical qualification entailed by *"auteur"* (Bell), "persona" (Walker) and "social individual" (Sell). But critics who once bandied them around more freely were perhaps wiser than those who now scorn them in the name of various reductive determinisms. At the close of the present book there will remain a black hole of human strangeness, and by the same token there will be a crucial role for a mediating criticism in the mode of literary appreciation, a type of commentary which at best would approach the very quick of literary experiences.

Especially by comparison with the paradigm of a-historical de-humanization, an appreciatively mediating criticism with foundations in a historical yet non-historicist pragmatics would be conspicuously interested in the real experiences of human beings. Research conducted within that earlier paradigm had its own aims and assumptions, needless to say, and in the areas actually dealt with made huge advances. The pioneers of the alliances between literary formalism and linguistics would not have minded being described as dehumanizers, since in their view linguistics was a science which offered precise and falsifiable statements based on exact data. To most people, though, all those impressions, intuitions, evaluations and emotions which elude such positivistic criteria do seem important, so that scholars might just as well try to understand them, at least as much as possible. Literary scholars will never be able to exhibit the quick of life completely formulated, sprawling on a pin. But they can certainly aim to cultivate at least *some* sense of human realities.

The quick of life, in our experiences of literature as of anything else, varies not only from person to person but from moment to moment. We can even ask whether it is pre-linguistic and merely waiting to be put into words, or whether, at least to some extent, it might not be language which brings it into being. Not, however, language on its own, as poststructuralist extremists would argue, but language as *used* by social individuals. For Eliot and Leavis, what opened up new perceptions and new experiences was the exploratory-creative use of language by poets, an idea which chimes almost perfectly with the present argument. On the one hand, the language is there in the culture, and its users, including even poets, are empowered by it to say, think and feel certain things. On the other hand, a linguistic determinism of the kind controversially attributed to Benjamin Lee Whorf (cf. O'Halloran 1997) would be out of place. Users not only adapt to language, but can adapt language to themselves, permanently affecting the range of human possibilities. Indeed, the only qualification that needs to be made to Eliot and Leavis's account is that, although by no means as elitist as Ezra Pound's, it did underestimate the extent to which the quick of life can manifest itself in co-adaptive expression by any language-user at all.

The quick of life is also something we discuss, and to no small extent we can understand each other's different experiences of it. Life is something on which we are all experts. To disqualify our own perceptions and judgements at the behest of prestigious *savants* makes very little sense. Although the variety of viewpoints is endless, although rationalities and values vary, we do have the capacity for empathy and comparison, a capacity which can focus on the quick of life as experienced by some other person, or as experienced, or still to be experienced, by ourselves under different circumstances from the present. In effect, our ability to envisage widely differing life-worlds represents a preparedness for communication, and paradoxically enough, Wilson Harris, one of the postcolonial writers most preoccupied with various kinds of sociocultural difference, also speaks of a "psyche of humanity" that is actually "cross-cultural" (Harris 1983, 1989: 137). On even a conservative estimate, human beings share the sameness-that-is-difference of the human condition itself, and are fascinated, for intimately personal reasons, by its manifold sociocultural manifestations. To grasp, in Berlin's words, how some other, very different person "might be a full human being, with whom one could communicate" can have transforming consequences.

So a historical yet non-historicist literary pragmatics is a matter of both the situationalities and the idiosyncrasies of literary experience. It does not pretend that everybody always creates or experiences literature in the same way. It faces up to both the samenesses and the variations, and tries to relate them, as much as possible, to contexts of writing and reading alike. At the same time, it also recognizes from the outset that there may not be a one-to-one correlation between a particular situationality and a particular experience, and that a person and a milieu can reciprocally influence each other.

Because the Western dichotomy of rationalism versus nihilism is still not a thing of the past, some of my own readers may already be accusing this whole approach of obscurantism and weak ambition, while others may be praising it for avoiding scientific pride of intellect. My aim is actually to recognize the difficulty of systematic generalizations, while also pushing them as far as they will go. A historical yet non-historicist literary pragmatics cannot explain the variety of literary experiences away, even though it can explain it to a certain extent.

In this, I submit, it is merely being truthful. But such a theory has another very strong recommendation as well. Its recognition that individual readers are not always bound by the norms of communal readerships is the greatest possible asset as a basis for mediating criticism. Together with the emphasis on readers' empathetic imagination, this is how the theory explains such a criticism's very possibility. Conversely, the implausibility and, from our present point of view, unprofitability of extremist Barthesian commentary lie in a failure to recognize that readers have the psychological and moral predisposition to distinguish themselves from their own community, even to the extent of moving, so to speak, into another one. If readers' minds were really so tightly under communal lock and key, mediating criticism would be a lost cause.

4.3. The protean self and communicative personae

As I suggested in Section 4.1, readers' imaginative mobility between different situationalities is made easier to discuss by the work of philosophical hermeneuticians. Philosophical hermeneuticians do not tell the whole story, however, because — if I may put it this way — they are only philosophers. The types of understanding they themselves discuss usually relate to truth and the general nature of things, and involve what Searle would call assertive speech acts. Their work is all rather cool, calm and collected, and is not concerned to illuminate the interpersonal charge of writing, or the textual means by which that charge is carried across to the current context of reading from a context of writing which may be so very different.

The most important concepts here are those of the implied author and the implied reader, which were developed by formalist poeticians and narratologists. The irony is that the formalists tried to use them as a way of *sealing off* an aesthetic world from the real world, so that works of literature would not really count as communication between real writers and real readers. That the implied author and reader personae of literature have a positively communicative function, and that they have exact formal and functional equivalents in the textualities of other discourse types as well, has often been overlooked by literary scholars and linguists alike.

In any sort of language use at all, such sender and receiver personae are textual constructs serving as communication's necessary slotting-in points, into which real "senders" and "receivers" can fit themselves by an imaginative projection of their relatively malleable selfhood. For the purposes and duration of communication, senders in at least one part of their mind *become* the implied sender, and receivers the implied receiver.

The feasibility of this arrangement depends on the human being's psychological predisposition to it. Given the continuities of moral autonomy and temperamental disposition suggested in my previous section, human malleability can clearly not be total. To a rough and ready common sense, the self can actually seem quite stable. Yet even common sense, the common sense of educationalists or moral counsellors, say, is also able to think of the self as a kind of *tabula rasa*, and a perception of it as potentially variable, as a fairly protean polymorphism which refuses to be pinned down once and for all, has haunted the writers of fictional, confessional and psychoanalytical texts ever since Augustine (Jay 1984). In twentieth century commentary, the self's continuous identity has at times completely disappeared from view, as in Henry Adams's description of the ego as a chaos of "multiplicities", or in Barthes's account of the divided, dispersed and contradictory subject. Elsewhere, as for instance in the personal testimony I have quoted from Frank Kermode, or in remarks to follow later from Salman Rushdie, its stability and instability are caught in trembling balance.

Charles Taylor's account of human individuation is to the same effect. If we accept that individuation is dialogic in the way he suggests, then there is a crucial link between communication and psychological growth. We "learn ... modes of expression through exchanges with others": with the "significant others" who matter for us (Taylor 1994: 32). On the one hand, this must mean that each of us is at least to some extent innately particular. We have a disposition to experience only certain other people as significant to us personally, and communication can in this way result in personal changes, some of which may prove to be personally distinctive. On the other hand, Taylor also clearly stresses that at the outset we are an unwritten page. We do have our own peculiar potentialities, but in the absence of very particular social contacts they may well remain latent, so that we will end up with some other kind of formation.

What can happen in social contacts is that we give free rein to our "force of imaginative insight", as Berlin calls it. We project ourselves into as many of the available role models as we choose, in effect trying them on for size. The way we present ourselves in everyday life can actually be quasi-theatrical (cf. Goffman 1959), and some of our role-play is rather experimental. Partly on the basis of this histrionic sampling, we in due time acknowledge certain models as relevant for us personally, even when this entails some modification of the self as we have mainly presented it hitherto. As Taylor argues in another place (Taylor 1976: 281–7), the self can in fact be shaped through a sort of productive hypocrisy, by which we desire ourselves to become a different kind of desirer. Certain other role models, by contrast, we shall accept more reluctantly, or even positively resist, as inappropriate to the desirer we desire to be. Some of these, as K. Anthony Appiah points out, may be models with a high public prominence. Other people may regard them as almost obligatory for the kind of person they imagine us to be.

In any particular communicative encounter, the possibilities for selfhood and dialogue do temporarily narrow down. As soon as we open our mouths, put pen to paper, or start to read, we begin to negotiate sender and receiver personae, both for ourselves and for our communication partners. In this way we work towards a functional model for the temporary interrelationship, to which most partners will probably agree for the purposes of understanding, but which will be historically conditioned and reductive — and perhaps rather rigidly common-sensical. In face-to-face conversation there is a feedback channel, by which a person can seek to redress the receiver persona being offered: "Hey, wait a minute! You've got me wrong. That's not the way I think." But in reading literature or other forms of written communication, we do not have this opportunity, and one of our main concerns is in any case to negotiate the writer's foregrounded otherness (cf. Section 3.4). To this end, our powers of imaginative projection enable us temporarily to identify even with a receiver persona that is totally unlike our own self-image, so ensuring our participation in communicative activity nevertheless. Although we can always *stop* reading, one of the great unspoken secrets of literature is the readiness with which we do make such allowances. The personae proposed for himself and his readers by a Cervantes will never exactly correspond to communication partners in any other time and place, nor even to Cervantes himself and his first readers as they "really" were. This is something we must have cottoned on to at a fairly early stage in our reading experience. The concessions we make have long since become automated. With however little pleasure, a feminist can quite effortlessly understand a text that is written as from one male chauvinist pig to another.

Pinning down what people "really" are is actually problematic. To say that a "real" author and "real" reader truly *are* more real than implied ones will never quite do, even if the "real" ones apparently have greater permanence, and are privately perceived by the individuals concerned as more accurate. This is one of the points where Wayne C. Booth's account of writer-reader relations seems rather questionable. According to him, the implied author made available as part of the vehicle for the author-reader relationship is a version of the author that is not just virtual or ideal, but positively ideal*ized*.

> Everyone knows that the character implied by the total act of writing any literary work (the implied author) is always (but always) an "improved"

version over the flesh-and-blood creator — not necessarily improved by your standards or mine, but improved by the standards of the author.
(Booth 1988: 254)

Think only of "Jim Joyce", says Booth, "who became a learned man indeed, [but] was not nearly as learned as James Joyce the implied author" (Booth 1988: 276). Booth even imagines himself haranguing an entire pantheon of such august abstractions:

> Unlike "real" people, you are an idealized version of the writer who created you, the disorganized, flawed creature who in a sense discovered you by expunging his or her duller times and weaker moments. To dwell with you is to share the improvements you have managed to make in your "self" by perfecting your narrative world. You lead me first to practice ways of living that are more profound, more sensitive, more intense, and in a curious way more fully generous than I am likely to meet anywhere else in the world. You correct my faults, rebuke my insensitivities ...
> (Booth 1988: 223)

And so on, and so on. Booth's naive didacticism and hero-worship will not be to everyone's taste. Presumably, like Matthew Arnold (1888: 101–3), he would prefer not to have known about Keats's undignified letters to Fanny Brawne. More to the point, though, he also seems to have forgotten his own quotation of Charles Taylor's words on the psychology of productive hypocrisy. On Taylor's argument, any ontological — though not moral — distinction between a real and an idealized self would be considerably weakened, in that they both represent kinds of desirer that we can desire to be. They are both available as possibilities, and the idealized one, even though not at present actualized, is not necessarily less authentic. After all, if we are thinking about the self of a person we know, assessing its authenticity is obviously rather tricky. Although we do sometimes have the feeling that somebody is not being true to themselves, this may only be a matter of their apparently not being the same as hitherto perceived, which would not be so surprising, given that a certain amount of histrionic unauthenticity is actually built into human behaviour, as the main catalyst to both personal growth and communication. As for our view of our own self, this is no simpler. Even if I am of the opinion that, for me personally, some role and mode of expression would be far less authentic than some other, such a judgement can only be provisional. If I successfully desire to be another kind of desirer, things may change. And even granting that some of the models on display will be more significant to me personally than many others, how can I ever be sure that I have responded to *all* the ones of potential significance, let alone to the ones of *greatest* potential? No matter how much I may enjoy my current life-style, no matter how strong my confidence that I have "discovered who I am", there could always be some latency remaining in me, which further dialogue might still trigger. The self, although faithful to an individual autonomy of choice and temperament, and thereby more predisposed to some roles than to others, is nevertheless positionable and chameleonic. Quite unpredictably, some of its possible future changes may turn out to be more permanent than others.

That is why C.S. Lewis's description of his own reading habits slightly strains belief. Having made his point that the best kind of reading seeks to "receive" what the author has written, he then claims that this leads to an

> enormous extension of our being. My own eyes are not enough for me. ... But in reading great literature I become a thousand men and yet remain myself. Like the night sky in the Greek poem, I see with a myriad eyes, but it is still I who see. ... I transcend myself; and am never more myself than when I do.
> (Lewis 1992 (1961): 140–1)

A more stirring account of the self's aptitude for imaginative projection would be hard to find. Yet Lewis also seems to be closing the door to personal change. By seeing himself as always the same underneath, he represents his receptive encounters with literary authors as somewhat reserved, in effect narrowing the gap between himself and the kind of strongly evaluative critics he so deplores. My own point, to spell it out, would be that all reading is in fact both receptive and evaluative, and that the best reading is receptive in the most actively self-projecting way possible, and evaluative in a way which is prepared for self-modification. For the record, I am also happy to bear witness that reading of this kind is precisely what Lewis's own scholarship can encourage. His dislike for what he saw in Leavis as a puritan narrowness has, I think, clouded his view of his own procedures. Not wishing to endorse a judgemental stance, he at first overreacts by disclaiming evaluative concerns altogether, which would be to carry empathy to the point of sympathy. But then his memories of reading interrupt his theorizing, to remind him that this is not quite the way it feels after all. He therefore back-peddles, a bit too vigorously, with the gobbledegook of non-self-transcendent self-transcendence.

The goings-out and comings-in of the protean self are even more radically underestimated in varieties of literary pragmatic theory which flirt with formalist distinctions between literature and "ordinary" communication.

Marcello Pagnini (1987 [1980]) and Richard J. Watts (1981), for instance, speak of the author and reader personae as entirely fictional in scope: as constructions confined to the aesthetic heterocosm, and therefore merely to be contemplated and held at a distance. As for "real" authors, the initial assumption is that they are quite unknowable. But Pagnini and Watts are themselves both excellent readers of literature, whose scholarly integrity is far too complete to disguise that, as in the case of Lewis, a theory is sometimes contradicted by experience. Pagnini ends by saying that we can and do relate implied authors and readers to (what I am writing as) "real" ones. He even grants, just as I shall myself, a legitimate role to biographical and affective criticism. Watts, similarly, having first argued that the "real" reader and "real" author of *Hard Times* are not in communication with each other, goes on to say that, by means of implicature, the "real" reader nevertheless extrapolates the "real" author's intentions from the internal dialogue of the implied personae.

Although anthropological linguists have not themselves made the connection, their work helps us to see that the mechanism of ordinary conversation is actually identical with this very ordinary way of reading literature. They clearly confirm that communication always functions by people's casting themselves and others in roles (Ochs 1986; Ochs and Schieffelin 1986; Haviland 1986; Besnier 1986; Biber and Finegan 1986). Everything we say or write already entails a concept of ourselves, of our communication partners, of the situationalities of communication (Sinclair 1993; Dakubu 1987), and of appropriate frames of emotional, attitudinal and moral response. This is the kind of textualization-cum-contextualization I began to discuss in Section 4.1, and a key role is played by the sender and receiver personae. These are offered as virtual selves for the purposes of the particular interchange, so providing communication's necessary bridge. In literary communication, admittedly, the distance between the proposed writerly-self-within-context and the proposed readerly-self-within-context will usually be far less than that between the "real"-writer-within-context and the "real"-reader-within-context. But when the "real" reader, by an effort of imaginative histrionics, tries to empathize with both of the proposed personae, meaning and affect will in any case start to flow.

One way to discuss the gap to be bridged between "real" writers and readers is in terms of intertextuality, perhaps the most valuable of all the ideas developed by cultural structuralists such as Roland Barthes (1980), Julia Kristeva (1980) and Michel Foucault (1979 [1969]). Intertextuality was part of their emphasis on the human subject's implication in a particular society. Every word, expression or text exists in intertextual relationship with every other word, expression or text within the same culture. The here-and-now occurrence of any particular linguistic item recapitulates and modifies all its previous occurrences, and bears a differential relation to the occurrences of every other expression in the same language culture as well. It is much more than a matter of conscious allusions. Nor can it be reduced to a matter of sources and influences.

Such total, infinitely multifaceted intertextuality is difficult to pin down for analysis, not least because it can never be located within any single mind, let alone within a single consciousness. Although we have all been sufficiently exposed to our culture's intertextuality for language actually to work for us, our exposure is really only the merest sampling, and the processes by which we extrapolate from this in communication are highly automated. Such is the case with heteroglossia, for instance, and a text's sociolectal features will prompt a reader who shares or knows about the world from within which it emanates to infer its writer's and characters' class and ideological position. Bakhtinian critics have even shown that the differences silently registered in this area can set up tensions that are central to a text's entire mode of working (Fowler 1983; Sell 1986; Lodge 1990). Conversely, when readers get the feeling that they are not quite on the writer's wavelength, or when they misread a writer without realizing it, the cause of the trouble can be the heteromorphic intertextualities of the two different life-worlds.

But in proposing writer and reader personae, writers for their part inevitably tend to behave as if their readers shared their world of knowledge and values, and to fill in the necessary details when this cannot really be the case. That is why the more universalizing type of reader-response criticism is by no means totally unwarranted. There *is* only one reader, as one might put it: the virtual reader, whom readers of all the manifold historical kinds are invited, for the time being, to become. This reader's various dimensions are proposed as part of the textualization-cum-contextualization. They belong to the textual replica of the communicative situation.

The linguistic devices involved here are the same as for communication of any kind at all. I have already mentioned that deixis, for instance, is a matter of features by which every utterance "points" to its sender, to its recipient, and to the persons, things and events which it mentions. As the result of this orientation, its recipients make inferences about the relationships pertaining between their virtual selves as conceived by the sender and various other areas of reference. Person deixis assigns first-, second- and third-person roles, while social deixis marks the degrees of respect the sender conceives as being demanded or manifested by various parties. Both these types of denotation help to establish the sender and receiver personae as communicative latching-on points, and they are reinforced by time deixis and place deixis, which offer to set the virtual sender, the virtual reader, and the worlds and people under discussion within temporal and spatial relationships as well.

Speakers and writers include deixis from their opening gambit onwards. It is impossible to use language without doing so, and the first words of a poem, for instance, are absolutely crucial for the interpersonal orientation they propose. In most cases readers do not even think about this. But every once in a while they will read a poem which draws attention to it, by offering interrelationships which are out of the ordinary. One celebrated example, which will indirectly throw light on the less surprising kinds of set-up, is the first line of Donne's "The Canonization":

> For Godsake hold your tongue, and let me love ...
> (Donne 1965 [1633]: 73)

Somewhat unusually, Donne stages the implied sender and implied receiver as co-present and actually in dialogue. Except as a quotation of somebody else's words, "Hold your tongue" is semantically inappropriate in writing, since it indicates disagreement with words which have just been spoken face to face. The line's pronominalizations ("your" and "me"), together with its two imperative verbs ("hold" and "let"), reinforce this impression of actual eye-contact, as does also the colloquial tone. In point of fact, the tone is very much that of a spoken outburst of annoyance, starting as it does with an oath, continuing with a very marked degree of impoliteness *vis à vis* the "you", and at first saying nothing very specific about the love affair which is figured as actually causing the disagreement. Donne's entire strategy at this point is to foreground, not that "third" entity, but the relationship between the two parties figured as discussing it, a relationship which the deixis makes as close as possible in spatial and temporal terms, but very strained in terms of mutual respect. A more conventional opening for written texts would figure the writer and reader as separated by time and space, as nourishing reasonably polite sentiments about each other, and as mainly drawn together by an interest in the real, hypothetical or fictional entity under discussion, which would be more immediately focussed. Donne, however, is unrelenting. As the poem progresses, he does say more about his relationship with his lady. But at the end he is still sharply insistent on his relationship with other people as well. By this time, moreover, the person addressed is being switched to a third person role, and augmented to include the entire human race apart from the two lovers. "You" becomes "all". And the social deixis, far from becoming more accommodating, is even more extreme. Donne and his lady are now saints. "All shall approve/Us canonized". All will reverently beseech assistance as they try to sort out their own love lives.

So much for deixis. Then there are all the presuppositions which senders make about knowledge and value judgements. Many things may of course be clearly stated. But receivers can get an even stronger idea of what kind of world a sender expects them to belong to from modal expressions, and from emotive and evaluative expressions, which do not always draw attention to themselves. In literary texts, such expressions may constitute a very high proportion of the total word-count (Sell 1991c). Like social deixis, they are affective and attitudinal, sometimes involving questions of moral judgement, taste and ideology. As a result, they help to constitute the sender and receiver personae in such a way that these duly instantiate assumptions, values and responses which will operate within a shared world of discourse. Because they work so subliminally, they are probably far more effective than explicit statements in achieving this necessary ethical flow.

Modality is the linguistic means by which senders indicate to recipients some degree of commitment or hesitation as to the truth, probability or desirability of whatever they happen to be talking about. It is carried by a surprisingly wide range of expressions, whose processing is highly automated (Perkins 1983). In addition to the primary modal verbs (in English, *will, shall, can, may, must*), whose fairly unspecific core meaning has to be pragmatically disambiguated by reference to context, there are also:- secondary modal verbs (*could, might, ought to, would, should*); quasi-modal auxiliaries (*have got to*); adverbial, adjectival, participial, and nominal expressions; and modal lexical verbs (*allege, argue*). Sometimes modality is also bound up with tense, conditional clauses, questions, and negatives. As for the way it affects a literary writer's modelling of writer-reader relationship, the opening words of a text can again be crucial, and the choice between a more categorical expression and a more hesitant expression is a lot more than just a question of what the words actually mean. One of the most frequently quoted and analysed passages of English literature is the first sentence of *Pride and Prejudice*:

It is a truth universally acknowledged, that a single man in possession of a good fortune, must be in want of a wife.
(Austen 1932 [1813]:3)

But suppose Jane Austen had written:

*It is not impossible, that a single man in possession of a good fortune, will be in want of a wife.

All the irony disappears at a stroke and, with it, all that delightful coaxing of the reader into the fellowship of the author's not unkind superiority *vis à vis* personages soon to be introduced. In Austen's own version of the sentence, the author's context of writing and a reader's context of reading in any time and place whatever are immediately brought much closer together, by their implied equidistance from the amusing otherness of the text's internal context.

As far as emotive and evaluative expressions go, they can be almost anything — nouns, adjectives, adverbs, verbs or expletives. In a piece of writing such as a user's manual or a physics textbook, the manner of expression will have a certain neutrality of tone. But there are many text-types in which a stronger personal engagement is not frowned upon, and where an emotive and evaluative loading will be spread over very many of the words actually used. Not that a word's exact loading is fixed for all time. As always, receivers have to make inferences by means of pragmatic contextualization. The verb *plod*, if applied by Agatha Christie to a police officer less intelligent that Hercule Poirot, prompts the reader to feel a certain contempt. Applied by John Bunyan to Christian, it might trigger pity for the trials and tribulations of his pilgrimage.

All this means that in language use of any kind at all there will be plenty of features which tend to bridge the gap between the context of sending and the context of current receiving, offering readers of literature, for instance, a sense of who and where and when the writer imagines them to be, and of what they are taken to be thinking and feeling. At the same time, author-reader relations are often further affected by the ways in which problems of inferencing within different worlds become an important part of a text's own *subject-matter*. It is something which can actually get dramatized, when characters within the story are shown as interpreting or misinterpreting some of the things being said or done around them, which can be crucial to their own fortunes and to the entire plot.

One of the most important affective possibilities arising from this is bound up with the phenomenon of dramatic irony. When both the implied writer and the implied reader know something more about the literary characters' situation than they know themselves, this forms a ground of communion between the "real" writer and the current "real" reader, even though their worlds can in other respects be so very different. In detective stories, admittedly, the balance is usually the other way round: the writer and one or more of the characters know something which is for a long time concealed from the readers. Yet as the plot evolves, the reader can gradually be drawn into a commonality of understanding, and new consciousnesses may be imagined as joining in intradiegetically as well: writer, reader and characters all end up in some sort of agreement as to the way things stand. This is so even with the novels of Thomas Hardy, where, under the pitying gaze of Hardy and his readers, the characters at first blunder on so painfully from one misunderstanding, mistake or contretemps to the next.

In the comedy of Jane Austen, the irony, dramatic or otherwise, may at first seem to be at the expense of characters in the novel, only to change direction, as it were, and playfully target the reader and even Austen herself. As a result, the novel's concluding hint of a human commonality can be even stronger. Granted, the Johnsonian certainty of that opening sentence in *Pride and Prejudice* is most immediately attributable to somebody such as Mrs Bennet, a mother of nubile girls, with a sharp interest in their welfare and in keeping up appearances. Insofar as the statement is gently ridiculed as Mrs Bennet's sort of opinion, Jane Austen is inviting every possible reader into an intimate circle of wiser commentators, who would judge that wife-hunting, for wealthy bachelors like Bingley and Darcy, will at least not be an all-consuming concern. By the end of the novel, however, Jane and Elizabeth Bennet have become Mrs Bingley and Mrs Darcy. The opening of the last chapter glances back to that of the first:

> Happy for all her maternal feelings was the day on which Mrs Bennet got rid of her two most deserving daughters. With what delighted pride she afterwards visited Mrs Bingley and talked of Mrs Darcy may be guessed.
> (Austen 1932 [1813]: 385)

Mrs Bennet did not become "a sensible, amiable, well-informed woman for the rest of her life". She was still "occasionally nervous and invariably silly" (*ibid.*). But her maternal feelings, despite the frankness with which the "got rid of" reports them, are now receiving somewhat stronger endorsement, and the plot has confirmed, twice over, a decided willingness in single men of good fortune to contemplate matrimony. Jane Austen, having lulled her readers into a sense of kindly superiority, ends by indirectly taking them down a peg — if they will, to their own amusement — and by amusedly hinting her own ordinariness as well. There are topics on which Johnsonian certainty is actually her preferred manner of expression. As far as she is concerned, certain truths might just as well be universally acknowledged, by writers, characters, readers and all, even though novelistic persuasion will often take the form of indulgently testing fallacies. To wax sentimental at the spectacle of a good match may well be rather silly. But it is also rather human, and makes one kind of sense, directly related to economic realities.

Whether a character in a novel can know something of which both readers *and* the writer are positively ignorant is a nice philosophical point, perhaps too nice. But one part of an active reader's inferencing certainly tends to flesh characters out with more knowledge than they are actually stated to have, and some such "extra" knowledge must doubtless be implied, or would at least not be denied, by the writer. Characters in Rabelais, Swift, Joyce and Doris Lessing are sometimes explicitly conscious of their own bladder, bowels or menstrual cycle. This is not the case in Sir Walter Scott, but nobody has ever supposed that Waverley or Anne of Geierstein are physiological freaks. The fact that, all other differences of life-world notwithstanding, Scott can rely on readers *not* to make such a supposition, and that readers *sense* Scott's confidence in them, again makes for a kind of author-reader bonding across the ever-widening gap by which they are otherwise separated.

A writer actually has no choice but to assume that readers will understand, and a reader no choice but to try, by bringing to bear as encyclopedic as possible a knowledge of languages, peoples and their histories. To achieve one particular kind of reader-writer relationship, however, a writer will sometimes appeal to knowledge more indirectly, which for some readers can make the text more than usually alien. The special effect I have in mind is that extreme intimacy of bonding which results from allusiveness, at points where the writer deliberately seeks to raise an intertextual relationship to consciousness. On the one hand there has to be something in the text which seems to release the semantic supercharge, as one might call it, and readers who are in the know can even distinguish various intensities of allusiveness (Schaar 1991). On the other hand, the potential of a deeply allusive text is latent rather than free; readers must bring with them a certain previous experience of reading if they are to release it, although a helpful editor or anxious poet may also anticipate possible cultural gaps, as when T.S. Eliot points out in a footnote to *The Waste Land* that the lines

> A crowd flowed over London Bridge, so many,
> I had not thought death had undone so many

echo Dante's response to the sight of so many people in Hell. Possessed of this literary precedent, a reader can see the city rush-hour in an unexpected and disturbing light. Without it, the lines may seem slightly odd.

Another kind of inferencing and relational effect can arise from narrative passages cast in the form of free indirect discourse (cf. Sternberg 1991). Uncertainties arise when, as readers, we are not quite sure whether the sentiments expressed are attributable to the virtual writer, to the characters in the story, to our virtual readerly selves, or to some combination of these possibilities. In the following passage from *Dombey and Son*, for instance, whose are the exclamations?

> The Doctor gently brushed the scattered ringlets of the child, aside from the face and mouth of the mother. Alas, how calm they lay there; how little breath there was to stir them!
> (Dickens 1982 [1848]: 9)

For us now, the border-line is blurred between what, at the beginning of the third millennium, we can think of as three discourses: the communication involved in the Doctor's own self-communion; the communication between Dickens and his first readers, in which he offers them a typically Victorian tableau, conveying emotions which the Doctor or any other feeling contemporary would have shared; and the communication between Dickens and us now, for whom the intervening diatribes of the Modernists against Victorian sentimentality have made this type of gentle pathos no longer standardly decorous, and even somewhat disconcerting. Dickens proposes some emotions for his virtual reader; we see what they are; and one part of our mind even has to share them, since we can have no reaction to them at all until we have made them real, so to speak. But then there is another part of our mind, in which we have a sense of looking back to Dickens and his world across a wide distance, not quite sure whether all his feelings and attitudes apply today, probably resisting some of them, yet sometimes wondering, perhaps, whether Dickens's sensibility might still have something to be said for it.

The free indirect speech in this example is actually a marked case of what literary writers are doing all the time. They draw readers into their world, in every way trying to instate a monomorphic intertextuality. This is not to say that an author cannot include irony signals, or a dramatic set-up, which will deliberately accentuate the inevitable lack of correspondence between textually implied personae and "real" text-external people. In addition to the implied author and implied reader, there may also be an internal narrator and narratee, or there may actually be more than one implied reader. Sometimes in children's literature, for instance, the appeal to an implied child listener can be perhaps overheard, so to speak, by an implied adult reader (Wall 1991). Love poems, similarly, may be addressed, not only to the loved-one but, as Martha Woodmansee was perhaps hinting in connection with Elizabeth Barrett Browning, to another readership as well, especially when they are published or otherwise circulated. So although Donne's "The Exstasie", written as it is in the first person plural, at first may seem to involve only Donne himself and his lover, he may also be buttonholing some other person, *of whom his lover is perhaps unaware*. Indeed, he may be stationing some such person, politely, or perhaps with a ripple of irony, as a rather unusual sort of voyeur, high-minded enough to start with, but capable of even of further refinement. While Donne and his lover are lying side by side,

> If any, so by love refin'd,
> That he soules language understood,
> And by good love were growen all minde,
> Within convenient distance stood,
> He (though he knew not which soule spake,
> Because both meant, both spake the same)
> Might thence a new concoction take,
> And part farre purer than he came.
> (Donne 1965 [1633]: 59)

Yet in all such cases, the ambiguity of address, as long as it is actually noticed, will be part of the content in relation to which the "real" writer establishes a discourse with "real" readers. In all other cases, readers have no choice but to take writers as they come across, humanly self-contradictory though this may well be, and they also have to assume that the implied reader, often similarly indeterminate, is the writer's honest conception of likely recipients.

All these possibilities were already established in the pioneering books by Altieri and Lanser. Part of the point is that authors, in stating or implying feelings and opinions about whatever real, hypothetical or fictional entity is under discussion, are often quite obviously *sincere*. To suggest, as twentieth-century formalists so typically did, that there is a sincerity gap — that literary writers never communicate their "real" thoughts and feelings — is to travesty and impoverish literary communication. If readers do not register irony signals or other counter-indications, they take writers at their apparent word, ambiguous though it may perhaps be, unless, having sat at the feet of a New Critical, structuralist or deconstructionist mentor, they have been trained to do otherwise, or unless a writer does seem to be positively insincere. If sincerity is *not* in doubt, readers may still not take a text at face value. But this will be because they register some special set-up, or some particular reason for a depersonalizing reading. Even here, they will still be assuming that they know what the writer really means — or, at least, what the writer really does not mean. This is an assumption which they cannot do away with, since even though it can never be proved or disproved, it is the only way for the receptive process to take place at all.

As for the reader's own identity, in any process of communication at all the specified personae do limit the possibilities for selfhood. Sometimes, the writer and reader personae proposed by literary texts can strike particular readers as very limited indeed, or simply too inaccurate. Although there is normally no feedback channel by which they could seek to redress the persona proposed for them, at least literary critics may publicly register their dissatisfaction, and in ways which throw light on more trouble-free communication as well. Sara Mills, for instance, who speaks as a "female-affiliated reader", dislikes John Fuller's poem "Valentine" (Fuller 1983: 46–8). To her, it seems to imply an ideology of patriarchal, heterosexual romantic love, coupled with an expectation that male readers will identify with the "I" and female readers with the "you". If the expectation proves correct, readers of both descriptions will be gently amused. The female-affiliated reader, however, is *not* amused. She

> cannot take up either of the positions or roles offered by the poem as the dominant reading; that does not mean to say that she is unaffected by them, but that she is more concerned to describe, analyse, and resist the effects of the poem. ...[S]he can arrive at a description of the dominant reading. Once that has been located, ... [it] can be criticized and the reader can move on to developing a position of resistance to those meanings.
> (Mills 1992: 204–5)

In passing, I cannot help wondering whether Mills, in so strongly speaking up for her affiliation, is not boxing herself into to the kind of publicly defined mode of expression which K. Anthony Appiah finds so problematic. But be that as it may, her account does explicitly pinpoint the way we — *all* of us! — most commonly hear or read other people's words. For the purpose of receiving a meaning at all, we register the virtual selves proposed for us and our communication partner, and there is also that sense in which we cannot disagree with something until we have made it real for ourselves by testing it — by trying to agree with it. In addition, and by virtue of a sustained simultaneity of parallel processing, there can also be an element of personal readjustment. As a result of the confrontation, our own original stance is either intensified or altered.

For the reading of literature, the matter is perhaps best put by the middle-aged Eliot. According to him, readers can always learn from self-projection into the human variety offered by literature, but there is a crucial difference between poetic assent and philosophic belief. By assent, he means a more provisional agreement for the duration of the reading experience, whereas belief would remain for a longer time, as something more our own (Eliot 1951 [1929]: 257–8). We assent to the roles and world-view and emotions an author proposes for the immediate purposes of comprehension, but, as Mills so clearly shows, reject them if we cannot permanently endorse them.

Perhaps the only qualification Mills's remark calls for is that literature, during the moment of reading and comprehension, also offers us the interest, and perhaps the pleasure, of becoming something totally different from what we normally are, or would even want to be. I, too, have reservations about Fuller's poem, even if I would not usually pause to say why. To me, it seems fatuously callow in an embarrassingly English way, and I simply want to hurry on to the countless other poems, plays and novels I can find. Yet in letting our rejection happen too instantaneously there is a danger. If we withhold assent (in Eliot's sense of initial assent) from works written by people unlike our present selves, we may end up reading nothing but our own writings. Eliot suggests that readers who spurn an author whom a majority of other readers admire — it is too early to say whether Fuller would count in this connection — perhaps need to examine whether there is some obstacle to appreciation in their own attitudes. Here as elsewhere, the criticism of Eliot's middle and old age, so much less well known than "Tradition and the Individual Talent" or the essay on the Metaphysicals, comes very close to what I understand by positive mediation.

Mills's indignant reaction to Fuller's poem is a reminder that "making sense" and "understanding" are perhaps the least part of reading literature. The philosophical hermeneutician's preoccupation with meaning, so central to many aspects of my present undertaking, needs to be complemented with an awareness of potentialities for more dynamic interaction. Literature, with its starting point in the dramatizable interplay between the vicarious selves proposed as the writer and reader personae, gives rise to valuations, intuitions, feelings, and even real-life change and action. The failure of late-twentieth-century literary theory, and even of speech act theory of literature, to deal with literature's perlocutionary dimension has been perceptively discussed by Keir Elam (1988). The topic is one which earlier theories of poetics, and theories of dramatic literature especially, have taken very seriously, their terminologies ranging from catharsis (Aristotle), through instruction (Horace), improvement of social harmony (J.C. Scaliger), emotional satisfaction (Coleridge), experience of spiritual death and rebirth (Fuchs), the return of society to original chaos (Artaud), to revolutionary praxis (Brecht). Despite New Critical invective against the so-called affective fallacy, perlocution becomes a dimension to any literary text that is activated by reading, by performance, by citation, or in the memory, and as speech act theorists were the first to admit, perlocutionary effect is also the most unsystematic and unpredictable aspect of communication. It is precisely the point at which everything that is most strongly individual about hearers or readers is most likely to override social constraints.

At its most full-blooded, the interpersonality of literature is mysterious and awe-inspiring, partly because perlocutionary effect does not come to an end. A poem written a thousand years ago can still work on us today, which is why Jacob Mey (1987) has described the pragmatics of reading poetry as a matter of "breaking the seal of time". To study this would be to describe and critically investigate the conditions that readers must meet in order to recapture the original experience. Presumably, the first points to be recognized would be that literary writers and their readers do not communicate with each other face-to-face or one-to-one, and that the reading of a text (except by the writer) seldom happens simultaneously with its writing. Even writers who are still alive at the time of the current reader's reading have a slim chance of monitoring that reader's reactions, and stage drama, again, involves actors, directors, producers, designers and so on as an "extra" level of intervention. But even if, for these reasons, literary interactivity cannot be assimilated to "ordinary" conversation, it can feel much more *real*! Nor is it any coincidence that each of the five discourse features just mentioned — non-face-to-face, non-one-to-one, non-contemporaneous, non-monitored, interventional — is also to be found in types of language use which no scholar would hesitate to call interactive. Except when unduly influenced by twentieth-century literary theory, readers themselves are clear enough about literature's interpersonal dimension, not least in their responses to its politeness, another of the topics illuminated by pragmaticists with an anthropological orientation (see Section 5.4 below).

If a literary text's interpersonal charge is to carry from the context of writing to readers' own current context of reading, they only have to do what they do with contextual discrepancies in any other kind of communication. As part of their normal processes of personal development and communicative behaviour, they are all the time engaging in a kind of experimental histrionics: in an imaginative polydirectionality between different role models and contexts, so entering into and exploring many different potentialities for being. Transferred to literature, this enables them provisionally to accept writer and reader personae, together with their contexts, attitudes and emotions as read from the wording. Signs of dramatizing ironization, dual address and so on they will deal with on the standard communicative assumption that they can still make a fair guess at what the other person has in mind.

When readers break the seal of time or, come to that, the seal of a sociocultural difference obtaining in the present, it is thanks to this personal effort of empathetic understanding, this willingness to share in their imagination the relationship proposed between the implied writer and reader personae. In Eliot's meaning of the word, they assent. Without a preparedness to give the other selves and their worlds a try, what takes place would not really be communication at all but something much more small-minded, which a mediating critic may have to warn against.

At the same time, readers' relationship with writers is one of human parity. Their communicative assent does not overrule their critical faculty, and does not necessarily affect their positionality. To stay with Eliot's terms, assent is not at all the same thing as belief. Readers take stock of what they read. Partly or wholly, they may accept the text's proposal: accept the relationship figured between sender and receiver; accept the view developed of the real, hypothetical or fictional entity under discussion. And anything they accept will be co-adaptively integrated into their more long-term thought-world, which will never be the same again. Yet having provisionally assented, they may also, partly or wholly, reject what is on offer. From the very first sentence — from "For Godsake, hold your tongue ...", from "It is a truth universally acknowledged ..." — the proposed communicative relationship is something they move in and out of, not always coolly and disinterestedly.

Chapter 5

Interactive Consequences

5.1. Typology, hermeneutics, affect, ethics

Seen in terms of a historical yet non-historicist pragmatics, literature involves an ongoing interactivity of deed between the sender and the current receiver, who are always to a greater or lesser extent disparately sited, but whose interactivity, though strongly influenced by their situationalities, is not totally determined by them. There can be co-adaptations between the individual and the social norm, and what makes communication possible in the first place is the human being's ability to move between different sociocultural formations through an act of imagination, using textually proposed sender and receiver personae as stepping stones. This basic pragmatic set-up is continuous with the pragmatics of any sort of communication at all. Its consequences for literary communication will in principle be the same as for language use in general.

In turning to these I begin, in Section 5.2, with typological consequences. Senders of any kind of utterance whatever can only avail themselves of the text types available in their context of sending, but can nevertheless enter into co-adaptations with them, which will actually develop the range of available options. Receivers, in their turn, will know about text types available in their current context of receiving, but in order to appreciate the sender's use or development of the text types that were available in the context of sending may have to make something of an autodidactic effort.

This is one aspect of the wider hermeneutic consequences of the pragmatic set-up, which I deal with in Section 5.3. The distance between the context of sending and the context of current receiving always calls from an effort of empathy, which can be greatly facilitated by various kinds of historical knowledge, including literary-historical and even biographical knowledge.

Nor is it only a matter of the more cerebral aspects of understanding. The pragmatics of communication also has affective and ethical consequences, which I discuss in Sections 5.4 and 5.5 respectively. A sender's psychological and moral impact vary as the distance between sending and current receiving increases. For a receiver who does not use what the sender has sent as the occasion for a solipsistic ego-trip, and who genuinely tries to receive it *as* it was sent, its current impact will have a certain bi-dimensionality, involving an interrelationship between the sending-in-its-context-there-and-then and the receiving-in-a-context-here-and-now. It is as a result of negotiating this relationship that the current receiver may actually undergo personal change, which may ultimately contribute towards a wider change in an entire climate of ideas.

To repeat, these consequences of the pragmatic set-up relate to communication of any kind. Here, though, I shall here be concentrating on literary communication, and especially on the insights most relevant to the work of a literary critic seeking to mediate sociocultural difference. Some of my points may at first seem rather old-fashioned, as when I stress the importance of literary history and seek to rehabilitate biographical criticism and studies of influence. Other suggestions may seem rather far-fetched, as when I highlight readers' experiences of writers' politeness, and what I shall be calling beauties from history. Yet underlying the argument at every step will be the historical yet non-historicist view of pragmatics already outlined.

Another point to bear in mind is that a socio-cultural difference is always a sociocultural difference, quite irrespective of whether its axis is synchronic or diachronic. So although most of my examples will continue to be drawn from the literature of the past, this is only because the dust and heat of the current culture wars might otherwise have obscured the central questions of principle. Once these have been firmly grasped, their practical implications for the mediation of contemporary literature will be self-evident, as I shall stress by way of conclusion in Chapter 6.

5.2. Generic co-adaptations through time

For a mediating critic, the most important typological question has to do with the reception of a literary work within a cultural milieu which is not the same as the one within which it was written. More particularly, how do readers whose sociocultural siting is significantly different from the author's perceive the author's co-adaptations with generic norms? Since those norms were the norms of a particular context, can a text produced in symbiosis with them even work at all when read in some other context?

Although precisely the same question would apply to uses of other, non-literary text types as well, for many earlier literary theoreticians and critics this would have seemed an anomalous sort of worry. From classical antiquity onwards, there was a widespread assumption that a literary work has essential properties whose appreciation is quite unaffected by differences between one milieu and another. Aristotle spoke as if tragic catharsis, for instance, would always happen in exactly the same way everywhere. And although *The Poetics* itself was not well known in the West until the fifteenth century, the idea that the various genres of literature unproblematically convey knowledge or experience that is universally valuable remained very common. One type of argument descended from Horace's suggestion that literature offers both the *dulce* and the *utile*, an idea which still underlay the mediaeval account of allegory. Later on, Renaissance and Neo-Classical poeticians regularly spoke as if the European vernacular literatures of their own time could emulate the classical genres with no basic change. Nor have such assumptions ever been permanently rooted out. Although Thomas Warton ushered in a phase of historical criticism which lasted on through the nineteenth century, the Modernist period saw new accounts of literature's timelessness, in practical criticism *à la* I.A. Richards and the American New Criticism.

The New Critical line was strongly urged in René Wellek and Austin Warren's *Theory of Literature* of 1949, which relegated history to "the extrinsic study of literature". Wellek and Warren did consider making an exception for a "purist" literary history, which in tracing the development of literature as an autonomous art form would presumably have given genre history a central place. In W.W. Greg's *Pastoral Poetry and Pastoral Drama* (1906) this type of study was already under way, and Wellek and Warren's plea for an exclusively aesthetic history of literature was even more clearly anticipated by the Russian Formalists, for example in their accounts of the short story (Eichenbaum 1978 [1925]), and in their distinctions between verse and prose (Tynyanov 1978 [1924]). Many Modernist critics, however, and not only those most clearly in the Romantic-Aesthete-Symbolist tradition, continued to write as if each genuinely new work were a kind of one-off with a *raison d'être* of its own. Even if Leavis (1964 [1936]: 17) could see that there were "respectable figures" who "serve ... to set up a critically useful background" to a writer such as Donne, a truly great work of literature could often divert attention from the contemporary norms above which it raised itself, and explanations of literature's universality continued to be in ready supply. Paul van Tieghem (1938) proposed that literary genres stem from a general human psychology, such that each emotional taste, and each social or religious need, is at the root of some particular genre, causing it to blossom either more or less happily. André Jolles (1956 [1930]), similarly, spoke of simple forms: forms such as the myth, the joke or the riddle, which are as broadly dispersed as human language itself. According to Jolles, they are intimately connected with the way we actually use language to organize the world, and underpin even the most sophisticated literary works.

All these ancient and modern ideas are at least partly in key with the non-historicist side of the pragmatic theory presented here. I have argued, for one thing, that communication between widely varying sociocultural situationalities is both possible and valuable. Human beings have the necessary power of imaginative empathy, and the sameness-that-is-difference of the human condition itself provides quite enough interest and motivation. For another thing, I have also commended those aspects of Hume, Kant and Wittgenstein's aesthetic thought which capture the more mysterious side of art. Especially important are the twin assumptions that an aesthetic judgement can only flow from a personal experience, and that it cannot be based on some kind of rules of taste. There is actually a question of critical tact here. Even readers not unwilling to be faithful to an author will in any case read in their own way, in no small part influenced by the milieu in which they happen to live their own lives. A critic who supplies them with huge amounts of historical information or formal analysis may even hold their literary appreciation back. To suggest that the acquisition of literary taste is a very arduous process would be rather misleading, and certainly counterproductive.

On the other hand, an uninformed, impressionistic subjectivism does lay itself open to sceptical critique. It can all too easily suggest that perceptions and judgements in artistic matters do not lend themselves to rational argument. In point of fact, the three philosophers just mentioned, albeit each in his own way, do strongly uphold the logical discussability of subjective aesthetic impressions, a claim for which there is empirical evidence as well. People do conduct such discussions without much difficulty, agreeing and disagreeing with each other in a spirit of satisfactory reasonableness. Many of a literary work's formal features will in any case have a thoroughly objective reality, and its author may well have expected some of them to strike readers as innovatory in ways that are relevant to its overall meaning. Readers' sensitivity to this kind of effect will clearly depend on their grasp of typological history. Unless they perceive the unexciting contemporary norms above which a great work of literature towers, its own rare magnificence will not be fully perceptible either. The two perceptions are interdependent.

It is this kind of consideration which underlies the work of Alastair Fowler (1982, 1987), whose aesthetic history of literature involves a sense of genres as a pragmatic resource, both for a writer in composition and for a reader in interpretation. No less suggestive is Heather Dubrow (1982), with her emphasis on the ideological dimension of genre. Nor are Fowler and Dubrow the first scholars to have described genres as very culture-specific indeed. Take, for instance, the form-historical school of German protestant theology. Theologians such as Bultmann and Gunkel stressed that each of the various genres to be found in the Bible stemmed from a very definite function or locus in life — a typical situation or mode of behaviour in the life of a particular community (see Jauss 1982: 100–3). Similar arguments have also figured in Marxist literary criticism, and even in the treatises of Renaissance poeticians. According to George Puttenham's *The Arte of English Poesie* (1589), the beginning of an epithalamium was sung

> at the first parte of the night, when the spouse and her husband were brought to their bed, & at the very chamber dore, where in a large vtter roome vsed to be (besides the musitiens) good store of ladies or gentlewomen of their kinsefolkes, & others who came to honor the marriage; & the tunes of the songs were very loude and shrill, to the intent there might no noise be hard out of the bed chamber by the skreeking and outcry of the young damosell feeling the first forces of her stiffe & rigorous young man, she being, as all virgins, tender & weake, and vnexpert in those maner of affaires. ... The tenour of that part of the song was to congratulate the first acquaintance and meeting of the young couple, allowing of their parents good discretions in making the match, then afterward to sound cherfully to the onset and first encounters of that amorous battaile, to declare the comfort of children, & encrease of love by that meane cheifly caused: the bride shewing her self euery waies well disposed, and still supplying occasions of new lustes and loue to her husband by her obedience and amorous embracings and all other allurements.
> (Puttenham 1904 [1589]: 53–4)

Seen from this angle, the historical circumstances of writing are so vital to an understanding of the ways in which any particular instantiation of a genre really works that a separation of the extrinsic from the intrinsic study of literature seems artificial. A "pure" literary history, or an a-historical poetics, might even be challenged as a kind of ideological deception. Aristotle, for instance, in valuing tragedy for its purgation of pity and fear, and in seeing the human psyche as everywhere and eternally of a single formation, could perhaps be accused of implying that the only things to be pitied and feared come from the gods, or as the result of a human being's own personal flaws of character. If so, this would overlook man's inhumanity to man in precisely the way entailed by Aristotle's own particular class allegiance as, among other things, a person eligible to teach the future conqueror of the then known world — pity and fear, needless to say, being highly detrimental to military discipline. The socially explicit discriminations his poetic theory does make are mainly in the area of literature's subject-matter. Comedy contains low characters, tragedy high characters, and the only connection between this and his theory of tragic function is the claim that *all* spectators will feel pity and fear at the sufferings of a great man, a claim whose ideological effectiveness proved to be long-lived. Two thousand years further on, and with great men still in the saddle, this same inclusion of social discriminations under internal content still recurred in the so-called Wheel of Virgil, a classification of genres which was very influential during the later middle ages, and even closer to our own time, in the ingenious map of literature devised by Thomas Hobbes (Fowler 1982: 240–1). True, the ancient distinction between the three styles, the high, the middle and the low, did have clear social implications, and continued to be held up as a principle of decorum for would-be writers well into the nineteenth century. But this had never brought with it much detailed discussion of the positionalities of either writers themselves, the people they were writing about, or the people they were writing for. Even the Preface to the *Lyrical Ballads* was not a complete revolution, in some respects merely substituting one kind of universalism with another. If Wordsworth challenged traditional proprieties by rejecting genres and rules, and by setting out to write "high" poetry about "low" people in a more or less "middle" language, the organic form of each unique lyrical ballad was nevertheless to be taken as a quintessence of poetry in general, and the poet himself as a kind of superman addressing the entire human race. On the one hand, the interrogation of neoclassical precepts begun by Warton had now reached the point at which Aristotle, in his own sphere of influence, could be seen as a tyrant scarcely less harmful than the world's unjust rulers in theirs. On the other hand, an extension of the Enlightenment-Romantic ideal of liberty *beyond* the literary sphere is not strongly evident from the poetry of either Wordsworth himself or even Shelley. On the contrary, poetry written on the principle of their new universalism would still have been so totally inaccessible to the poor and suffering people who were sometimes its subject-matter that Wordsworth's claim to adopt their language had to include some parenthetical fudging:

> The language, too, of these [simple countryside] men has been adopted (purified indeed from what appear to be its real defects, from all lasting and rational causes of dislike or disgust) because such men hourly communicate with the best objects from which the best part of language is originally derived ....
> Wordsworth 1950 [1802]: 735

Any more historical perspective on literary genres will be at least partly in key with the historical side of the pragmatic theory I am proposing here, just as the universalizing perspectives are partly in key with its non-historicist side. But this is not the whole story, since these two types of perspective may sometimes come all too close to the two different forms of the unitary context assumption, from which my theory sharply distances itself. Universalizing genre theories may tend to grant a high degree of interpretative grounding to the current reader's here-and-now context of reading. After all, in both their classical, neo-classical and Romantic versions such theories represent the whole of literature as something which readers of any time and place will be fully able to appreciate. As for historical genre theories, in resisting such a suggestion they correspondingly tend to prioritize the writer's original context of writing, so leaning towards forms of historical and/or cultural purism. A pragmatics that is historical yet non-historicist, by contrast, must fully recognize the inevitable effect of *both* contexts — both the context of writing and the current context of reading — for any communication that is actually taking place. Literature is seen as at once timeless and not timeless.

This paradoxical view is not altogether original. In a way it was anticipated by Wordsworth, with his plan for a universal poetry about late-eighteenth-century Lakeland shepherds. Precisely from the Romantic period onwards, various genres have been described as representing the general human needs of a particular people in a certain time and place. For Hegel (1975 [1820–1]:1045), the epic genre reflected "the child-like consciousness of a people [who as yet feel] no separation between freedom and will." For Nietzsche (1872), Greek tragedy arose when the austere harmony and comforting radiance of

Apollonian culture was challenged by the darker knowledge and musical life-spirit of the Dionysiac. Brunetière (1890), in an exercise in literary Darwinism, linked the development of satire to the rise of the bourgeois spirit. For Malinowski (1938 [1923]), the oral stories told by Trobriand Islanders enhanced the solidarity of the group, for instance by reminding them of the need for unity in face of famine. And Walter Ong (1982: 161), as we have seen, said that the performance of an oral epic can "serve ... simultaneously as an act of celebration, as *paideia* or education for youth, as strengthener of group identity, as a way of keeping alive all sorts of lore — historical, biological, zoological, sociological, venatic, nautical, religious — and much else".

Some genres' combination of historicity and universality is a matter of simple observation. While a genre such as the Elizabethan epithalamium can seem very firmly tied to its original locus in life, tragedy and the epic travel much more easily. Hundreds and thousands of years after their original locus in life has disappeared, old instantiations can continue to be read, though inevitably in new ways, and new instantiations can also continue to arise, though inevitably re-shaping the genres themselves. So on the one hand, we still value *The Iliad*. On the other hand, *The Aeneid* was already composed in very different circumstances from those of *The Iliad*, and *Orlando Furioso* or *Paradise Lost* in very different circumstances again, each successive example opening up whole new possibilities for the epic genre. Even literary sociologists of a Marxist persuasion might have confirmed this. Although they accounted for literary forms by the interdependence of social infrastructure and ideological superstructure, they also said that genres, after the moment of their social formation, can outlast their historical hour of fate, in a kind of anachronistic afterlife (cf. Jauss 1982: 91).

Aristotle, too, was aware that genres are subject to historical change. But rather than detailing changes in function, he spoke in terms of a formal entelechy. As the result of many transformations, Greek tragedy, in particular, had finally blossomed into its true and complete perfection. This was why Renaissance and Neo-Classical rhetoricians recommended the Aristotelian typology to vernacular writers aspiring to emulate ancient glories. Some of the writers following such advice allowed themselves so little room for individuality and innovation that they come across as cold and lifeless. Yet a restrictive preoccupation with typology re-surfaced even in the twentieth century. From the neo-Aristotelian critics of Chicago (in Crane 1952), it is possible to get the impression that a poet's sole reason for choosing a particular genre is in order to write a poem in that genre. By the sound of it, the be-all and end-all is to meet the genre's formal requirements, so that if a particular epithalamium seemed to be joyful, this would have nothing to do with the poet's having experienced a joy which called for expression. Joy was merely the emotion which had to be mustered up in order to write an epithalamium.

The Chicagoan excesses were a reaction against the excesses of the Romantic-Aesthete-Symbolist-Modernist tradition, which in its own turn had started as a response to Aristotelianism in the form of neo-classical rules. In 1759, four years after the first edition of Warton's sympathetic account of the *Fairy Queen*, Edward Young's *Conjectures on Original Composition* made some of the same points of general principle:

> All eminence and distinction lies out of the beaten road; excursion and deviation are necessary to find it; and the more remote your path from the highway, the more reputable .... [R]ules, like crutches, are a needful aid to the lame, though an impediment to the strong.
> (Young 1918 [1759]: 11–12. 14)

In 1783 Hugh Blair's *Lectures on Rhetoric and Belles Lettres* put entelechy into reverse: the most highly developed forms of genres may represent a falling-off in sheer power —

> In the rude and artless strain of the first poetry of all nations, we ... often find somewhat that captivates and transports the mind.
> (Blair 1965 [1783]: 322–3)

In the thought of Coleridge and Wordsworth this becomes entirely a matter of course. A poem's sole justification is quite simply its poetry, understood as supreme powers of creative expression. Compared with this, the question of what particular form of writing an author chooses is a mere irrelevance. As Wordsworth put it:

> Why trouble yourself about the species till you have previously decided upon the genus? Why take pains to prove that an ape is not a Newton, when it is self-evident that he is not a man?
> (Wordsworth 1952 [1802]: 741)

Such anti-genre views flowed naturally into the traditions of Aestheticism and Symbolism, and have been fundamental in some Modernist theories as well. For Benedetto Croce (1992 [1902]), every true work broke generic laws, and a preoccupation with formal classifications was positively unbeneficial: it represented a blindness to the artist's all-important intuitive knowledge. For

New Critics such as Cleanth Brooks (1968 [1947]), the main desiderata were the tensions, paradoxes and ironies by which truly imaginative works reconcile, in Coleridge's phrase, opposite and discordant qualities. For Northrop Frye (1957), literary taxonomizing was certainly possible, but only in terms of intuited mythical structures, which permeated many different kinds of writing throughout the ages. Generally speaking, post-Kantian aesthetics saw literature as fundamentally independent of social conventions. This was reflected no less in a strongly individualistic attitude to genres than in the talk of imaginative worlds which were alternative to the ones explored by the logics of science and ethics.

From the work of literary historians, the clash between the Aristotelian and Romantic legacies is already familiar enough. My own point here is once again that a historical yet non-historicist literary pragmatics can resolve a long-standing controversy, this time by viewing genres as the site of co-adaptation between the social and the individual. Aristotelianism could be as over-solicitous for the social as Romanticism for the individual.

Here, too, the compromise has some noteworthy precedents. On the one hand, Longinus (1965 [? 1st c. A.D.]), after exploring the nature and origins of the Sublime — that quality in a text which overwhelms us with the feeling that here is "the real thing" — , concluded that a great writer can infringe rules of writing with impunity, whereas a writer who merely obeys them can seem to lack sincerity and emotional conviction. After Boileau had in 1647 translated Longinus into French, such sentiments were repeated in the many accounts of Shakespeare as an untaught genius, and in Pope's *Essay on Criticism* of 1711. On the other hand, Longinus had also said that the Sublime comes and goes as suddenly as a flash of lightening; for the most part a writer relies on existing conventions as a sustaining prop; so the conventions do deserve to be carefully catalogued and taught. For Pope, sublime originality and inherited norms were actually in symbiosis. And if Croce forgot that a true work cannot break generic laws unless there are generic laws to be broken, this consideration was well understood by the Russian Formalists when, as in Shklovsky's famous essay on *Tristram Shandy* (1965 [1921]), they extended their concept of artistic defamiliarization from language to genre.

More recently, Richard Wollheim (1992 [1980]) has suggested that art, *pace* George Dickie (1974), is not merely a matter of institutionalization. Although a society's art-world can be well established and influential; although new arts are promoted by analogies with old ones; although individual works are understood by both artists and their public as falling within particular traditions; and although one therefore certainly can speak of a kind of art institution: this still does not rule out the possibility that the institution's human representatives *have a reason* for endorsing certain works, a reason, that is to say, connected with the works themselves. In this way, Wollheim at once recognizes the power of the art institution as such, and sets a limit to it. That his idea is basically of the social and the individual in a kind of co-adaptation becomes even clearer from his own account of what art actually is. In a move reminiscent of Wittgenstein, he sees art as a form of life that is analogous to language. This can only mean that, on the one hand, artists are surrounded by culturally pre-existent possibilities, while on the other hand, we can never be quite sure how they will use them, or even change them.

More recently still, Peter Swirski (1996) argues to similar effect, but in the fascinatingly different terminology of game-theory mathematics. Games like chess or poker are semantically so impoverished that their rules can generate all the conceivable configurations of play. The number of permutations is astronomical, yet mathematically normalizable and finite. Literary works, by contrast, lead to interpretative moves which are non-normalizable and non-finite. The relationship between the reader and writer is as of players in a mathematically free-form game, since "some, and in some cases even most, rules of the game are made up as the game progresses." The pragmatics of literature leaves "plenty of room for vagueness, imprecision, ambiguity, or even radical misinterpretation," since "social and literary games tend to be environmentally rich, necessitating an extensive discussion of their social settings". So unlike a "standard matrix-type game", literature calls for "a greater amount of attention to the context, to grasp the full character of the play", and literary rules are usually open to modification or even abolition. Literary works which do have normalizable rules are "structurally and/or semantically depleted". They are "generic fossils, bereft of ingenuity and individuality".

So to move now from aesthetic and mathematical theory to an actual literary example, when Yeats wanted to mark the death of a group of people inspired to bravery by a common cause, he was not starting from scratch. For one thing, whatever he wrote would be bound to enter into intertextual relationships with Tennyson's "The Charge of the Light Brigade" of 1854, the poem printed and discussed on pp. 110–113 above, and still very much a favourite with Mr Ramsay in *To the Lighthouse*. Without thinking about it, Mr

Ramsay and his contemporaries would probably have assumed that, give or take a few variations and optional features, Tennyson had given this particular genre its definitive form. Most typically, such a poem would be either in a higher style reminiscent of epic, or in a lower style reminiscent of a ballad, except that Tennyson had already gone in for a kind of mixture of the two. It could either be fairly long or, like Tennyson's, fairly short. And the heroic action could either be particularized to the deeds of individuals or, as in Tennyson, treated in a more general way as the behaviour of an entire group of characters. As for the *sine qua non*, the heroic action itself would surely have to be clearly narrated, presumably as in Tennyson in the third person, and there would be little doubt about the heroism's value, which, after all, was such a poem's *raison d'être*. Any moral judgements would be likely to be straightforward in themselves and plainly stated, though not unemotionally.

But what did Yeats write?

> Easter 1916
>
> I have met them at close of day
> Coming with vivid faces
> From counter or desk among grey
> Eighteenth century houses.
> I have passed with a nod of the head
> Or polite meaningless words,
> Or have lingered awhile and said
> Polite meaningless words,
> And thought before I had done
> Of a mocking tale or a gibe
> To please a companion
> Around the fire at the club,
> Being certain that they and I
> But lived where motley is worn:
> All changed, changed utterly:
> A terrible beauty is born.
>
> That woman's days were spent
> In ignorant good-will,
> Her nights in argument
> Until her voice grew shrill.
> What voice more sweet than hers
> When, young and beautiful,
> She rode to harriers?
> This man had kept a school
> And rode our wingèd horse;

This other his helper and friend
Was coming into his force;
He might have won fame in the end,
So sensitive his nature seemed,
So daring and sweet his thought.
This other man I had dreamed
A drunken, vainglorious lout.
He had done most bitter wrong
To some who are near my heart,
Yet I number him in the song;
He, too, has been changed in his turn,
Transformed utterly:
A terrible beauty is born.

Hearts with one purpose alone
Through summer and winter seem
Enchanted to a stone
To trouble the living stream.
The horse that comes from the road,
The rider, the birds that range
From cloud to tumbling cloud,
Minute by minute they change;
A shadow of cloud on the stream
Changes minute by minute;
A horse-hoof slides on the brim,
And a horse plashes within it;
The long-legged moor-cocks dive,
And hens to moor-cocks call;
Minute by minute they live:
The stone's in the midst of all.

Too long a sacrifice
Can make a stone of the heart.
O when may it suffice?
That is Heaven's part, our part
To murmur name upon name,
As a mother names her child
When sleep at last has come
On limbs that had run wild.
What is it but nightfall?
No, no, not night but death;
Was it needless death after all?
For England may keep faith
For all that is done and said.
We know their dream; enough
To know they dreamed and are dead;

> And what if excess of love
> Bewildered them till they died?
> I write it out in a verse —
> MacDonagh and MacBride
> And Connolly and Pearse
> Now and in time to be,
> Wherever green is worn,
> Are changed, changed utterly:
> A terrible beauty is born.
> (Yeats 1996 [1916]: 287–9)

This is not much longer than Tennyson's poem. But even stylistically, there is a marked difference, since it is still more varied than Tennyson's mixture of ballad and epic. The first ten lines or so are certainly low key, and even realistic — *Dubliners* is not far away —, while the last ten lines or so do rise to a bardic chant. But the intervening lines about the stone in the midst of the stream apparently belong to a third, Symbolist mode. A still bigger surprise, however, is in the matter of narration. Not only are both the generalizing and individualizing alternatives rejected. There is actually no narration of the heroic action at all. A putatively obligatory feature is quite missing. The opening lines may seem like the beginning of a story, and the closing lines may seem like a retrospective comment on a story, but there is no explicit narrative middle. All we are given is the series of epitaphs, which are puzzling enough in themselves, being a good deal less than flattering. Not only that, but the narrative gap also connects with certain other innovations. Not least, the pronouns of the story-like beginning and end include the first person singular and plural: the strategy throughout is to foreground *responses* to events rather than the events themselves. For, and this was the positively disconcerting novelty, Yeats's own response is troubled and ambivalent. The value of the heroism is questioned. The beauty is "terrible". So complex, in fact, are the feelings expressed that in the central passage of Symbolism even plain statement is set aside.

In Swirski's terminology, "Easter 1916" invited the reader to play a mathematically free-form game. In my own language, the poem represented Yeats's co-adaptation with the genre. He could not have written it without the genre's pre-existence. But once it was written, the genre was no longer the same, and his generic modulation was inextricably tied up with what he was actually saying. Far from making for communicative difficulties, the maverick a-systematicity of original writing was the strongest way to make his point. As the Russian Formalists so clearly saw, the wildness of unpredictability makes far more impact than slavish conventionality. In the technical sense of the term, it is more informative.

To return to this section's starting point, then, how do readers reading in a milieu very different from Yeats's own actually go about it? Well, for one thing they will probably put his writing to some new use of their own. With the passing of time, new significances will in any case accrue to a genre's particular instantiations. As I was writing an earlier draft of this chapter at Easter 1998, I could not think about "Easter 1916" except in relation to the Irish question in that later, no less critical but more hopeful phase. As I send the typescript press in early February 2000, Yeats's question "Was it needless death after all?" may be about to assume a gloomier resonance than ever.

Then again, we have our intimately personal fascination in the sameness-that-is-difference of the human condition itself. Un-annotated, Yeats's thumbnail epitaphs on Constance Markiewicz, Patrick Pearse, Thomas MacDonagh and John MacBride would become more and more cryptic with every passing year. Editors do provide helpful annotations. But in our own way we should probably manage in any case, the poem becoming less and less about the particular martyrs with their own precise motives, and more and more about fanatical martyrdom in general. With the uncanny eye to immortality of a great artist, and especially in the Symbolist passage, Yeats actually anticipated this trend. As a result, what is in one sense an occasional poem could turn out to be functional not only for an age but for all time, while what in another sense is a Symbolist poem was able to have a forceful topicality at that original moment in time. The two text types have entered into a maverick merger.

Nowadays, appreciation of that merger is likely to be at least somewhat acquired. "Easter 1916" has itself become familiar. We are rather less likely to experience it in relationship to "The Charge of the Light Brigade" than to think of it on its own, so to speak. Yet something so much a part of Yeats's world as the pre-existent genre, and something so directly connected with his writing, is something which later or foreign readers do well to assent to (in Eliot's sense of provisional assent), even when this calls for a considerable mental effort. Alien intertextualities can be baffling at first, and in one part of our mind the (to us) alien genre convention which an author has modulated may even continue to be alien. Alongside our attempt to empathize with the authorial co-adaptation, there may still be our own situated response to its textual manifestation, resulting in an a-systematic match between the way the writer originally expected readers to take it and the way this part of our own mind actually does take it today. If, in 1916, Yeats was having the same doubts about heroic self-sacrifice as some of the poets who were themselves being killed in the trenches of France, then for us now, his poem falls into place beside Owen's "Dulce et Decorum Est", and both of them thereby seem a tiny bit more normal and less shocking. In our own world of reference, they have "always" had a central place. More abnormal now is "The Charge of the Light Brigade", though it is only a mediating critic such as Jerome J. McGann who can help us see how abnormal it was for *its own* time.

Such differences of perspective, however, are not an insuperable barrier, but a challenge and potential enrichment. Even within the here-and-now of everyday life, we are endlessly coming up against unfamiliar intertextualities, and we have long since developed a knack of making them our own. With luck, our assenting empathy will be sufficiently well-informed to pick up even the maverick messages of generic innovation, without which Yeats's poem would lose much of its force. The shocking surprises it once sprang can be imaginatively re-enacted.

As will be clear, the poem's function for us in the new millennium can never be simply the same as for its first readers. As McGann's commentary on Tennyson so well illustrates, in order to appreciate the first workings of a piece of writing, and especially of an occasional poem, we shall probably need the help of historians. By Easter 1916, the First World War had already been under way for nearly one and a half years. By then, too, the cause of Irish nationalism had its own long roll of martyrs — Fitzgerald, Emmet, Wolfe Tone, Parnell, O'Leary — but had also borne fruit in the Home Rule Bill of 1913. Yeats's feelings about Ireland were somewhat ambivalent. He was personally impressed by O'Leary, he admired Lady Gregory and other great landowners for patronizing the arts, and he saw the peasantry as a rich source of imagination and mythology. What dismayed him was the money-grubbing small-mindedness of the Irish middle class. When Sir Hugh Lane had offered Dublin a collection of Impressionist paintings, for instance, the city fathers refused to build an art gallery to house it, so provoking Yeats's scorn in "September 1913". With the outbreak of the First World War, implementation of Home Rule was shelved, and rumours started to circulate that England would not keep faith. Then, while the battle of the Somme was still dragging on, came the Easter Rising, in which a group of Irish patriots, with German support, tried to take control of Dublin. They were forcefully repressed by

England, so that the cause gained new martyrs, at which point Yeats added a note to "September 1913" to the effect that the poem now seemed out of date. All this is information which, together with kind of comparisons and contrasts I have drawn with Tennyson, helps us imagine the original writing and impact of "Easter 1916". Nowadays, many readers will not have it at their fingertips unless they have read some helpful editorial introduction or footnotes.

Editors do do their job, however, historians do write history, both literary and general, and readers certainly can make the effort of historical imagination. Although they belong to their own time and place, their most remarkable endowment is their versatility, not least their power of *mental* self-projection into manifold mind-sets and scenarios. In one part of their mind they can try to re-stage a literary work's debut, and to imagine its generic conformity and nonconformity as having the original effect. Simultaneously they will always read in the other ways as well, so that genres break free, as I have put it, from their original locus in life. But not to respond to a writer's generic co-adaptation at all is, once again, not really to read what has been written. To mediating critics, this will always seem a most serious shortcoming, quite irrespective of whether the writer is alive or dead. It is something which, by drawing on relevant information and perspectives, they will seek to prevent.

5.3. Re-living biography and influence

The typological issue is merely one aspect of a larger problem, which must be central to pragmatic research into any kind of communication at all: the problem of how a receiver makes the empathetic leap from the current context of receiving to the context of sending. Approaches to pragmatics with an intracultural and synchronic orientation have tended to endorse the unitary context assumption: the assumption that senders and receivers share one and the same life-world. Yet this, I have argued, never quite corresponds to reality. Contemporaries belonging to one and the same culture will always have differences of memory and awareness, however slight, which can be the occasion to communication in the first place, and which can also be reduced by it, in what is a historically linear process. As for communication between one culture or one period and another, the different situationalities are obvious, and their consequences are being explored in much valuable research into intercultural and historical pragmatics. This is likely to bring about a certain rapprochement between general pragmatics and a more traditional philology (Sell 1994b, 1999). Pragmaticists interested in literature, similarly, are bound to see the value of traditional literary biography and literary history.

The precondition for any worthwhile response people may have to a piece of language is that they have tried to make it real for themselves: that they have tried to live their way into its sender's inferential world, including both the range of available typological possibilities and much else as well. At the same time, any language use, though dependent on the intertextualities of the sender's own culture, can involve a co-adaptation with these. So in the previous section I was suggesting that we cannot, today, really read Yeats's "Easter 1916" or Owen's "Dulce et Decorum Est" unless we de-naturalize them. We have to see them *in relief* against earlier writing, and in particular against Tennyson's "The Charge of the Light Brigade". Otherwise, we shall not recover the shockingness which represented their strongest originality and the crux of what they were saying.

True, the relationships with other writers entailed by a co-adaptation are not always particularized and fully conscious. The affinity between Tennyson's

> Some one had blundered:
> Their's not to make reply,
> Their's not to reason why,
> Their's but to do and die:

and Yeats's

> O when may it suffice?
> That is Heaven's part, our part
> To murmur name upon name ...
> Was it needless death after all?

is hardly a matter of allusion or source. Both extracts discuss, in trimeter, an obligation to unquestioning acceptance, though in the first this belongs to the dead heroes, in the second to the surviving mourners, for whom, in line with Yeats's general drift, it is more difficult. This twentieth-century dissonance, however, can differentiate itself from harmonious Victorian certitudes of which a reader's instant recall may be rather vague and general. Since intertextual inferencing is so highly automated, "The Charge of the Light Brigade", arguably the most relevant precedent here, need not actually come to mind. Although Tennyson was Yeats's own favourite poet, there can be no knowing whether even he had thought about it at precisely this point. In such a case, to speak of a definite influence on the wording is just not possible.

Yet genuine readers, for reasons of human parity already partly touched on, will be interested in Yeats as Yeats. What did he consciously think and try to do in his writing? Where exactly was he coming from? What was distinctive about him? And how can one attune oneself to it? "Easter 1916" reflected that important change in his assessment of the Irish situation, and the feelings expressed in the poem are easier to catch if we have some knowledge of both the immediate occasion and Yeats's own earlier views. Readers who do not make an effort of mental self-projection into Yeats's situation and attitudes tend to respond with a simple universalization — "a poem about fanatical martyrdom" — or with misreadings along lines suggested by intertextualities and frames of value obtaining within their own sociocultural milieu.

To talk about influences on Yeats, similarly, is in fact quite possible (see e.g. Kermode 1957), and one can just as easily speak of Yeats's own influence on, say, Larkin, or debate, as I did earlier, the possible influence of Eliot's anti-Semitism on later writers. The author who influences can hardly be held *responsible* for the author influenced, and when the latter is a major creative force, a slavish derivativeness is in any case ruled out. The differences can be at least as striking as the similarities. But for writers themselves, the influences upon them do have a profound psychological reality, sometimes generating strong feelings, described by Harold Bloom (1973) in terms of Freudian anxiety. As for readers, a clear grasp of a writer's relationship with a significant predecessor or contemporary can make it easier to perceive that writer's own quiddity.

Seen in a pragmatic perspective, then, both biographical criticism and studies of sources and influences may well be interpretatively crucial. Both these types of commentary can help a reader in the empathetic attempt to relive, as much as possible, the writer's precise situation in writing. Put another way, such approaches can be a major resource for a mediating critic.

That they long ago went out of fashion was partly thanks to the Aesthete-Symbolist-Modernist reaction against the crasser forms of nineteenth-century historical scholarship. The Russian Formalists and American New Critics both perpetuated the Romantic stress on the autonomy of literature, but with none of the Romantic fascination with the genesis of literature in the life and mind of the poet. That was no longer part of what Wellek and Warren recommended for the intrinsic study of literature. The tendency to regard literary works as more autogenous than they can ever really be, and to ignore historical considerations as a support to understanding and appreciation, had already emerged during the Victorian period, sometimes in critics who in other respects had worked hard to broaden readers' horizons. To Arnold, for instance, biographical information had sometimes been unwelcome. Fearing for the dignity of literature, he opined that Keats's letters to Fanny Brawne have "something underbred and ignoble" in their "relaxed self-abandonment", like the love-letter "of a surgeon's apprentice which one might hear read out in a breach of promise case, or in the Divorce Court" (Arnold 1888: 101–3).

Even today, the more prurient forms of gossip can seriously interfere with appreciation of a person's public achievements. Yet Arnold's hauteur carried its own class prejudice, and his comments on Keats's actual poetry are the better for leaving it behind. Indeed, the insight he has reluctantly acquired from the letters clearly heightens his sense of the poetry's nobility. This, basically, represents a structure of argument which can be applied to many other writers as well. To take a twentieth century example, the unpublished plays of Robert Frost are autobiographical in the bad sense that they reveal serious personal problems which he has failed to get on top of. This can help us to see that some of his best work is distinctive precisely in its artistic grip on those very same problems (Sell 1980: 51–91, 1985a).

Here again, and in the face of literary criticism and theory of several different kinds, I am basically trying to de-mystify authorship. The pragmatic reasons for doing so were already clear from Jacques Barzun's protest against New Criticism (Barzun 1975). A more recent champion of the obvious has been Stanley Fish: "it makes no sense to urge a return to biography, since biography is not something from which we can swerve". To refrain from reading biographically is to refrain from construing meaning — to refrain

> from regarding the marks before ... [us] as manifestations of intentional behaviour. ... [C]riticism can only proceed ... when notions of agency, personhood, cause, and effect are already assumed and are already governing the readings we produce.
> (Fish 1991: 14–15)

Lovers of literature are in any case not so easily fooled (cf. Sell 1994a). The twentieth century has seen many truly magnificent literary biographies, which have sold much better than most literary theory and criticism, and may well have done far more to promote an appreciation of poems, novels and plays.

This applies not only to lyric or confessional poetry which openly expresses the poet's own feelings, but to all the other genres which the Aesthete-Symbolist-Modernist tradition of criticism unduly de-personalized, and not least to the novel. In Britain and the United States, Modernist novel criticism was profoundly affected by the essays and prefaces of Henry James, with their synthesis of nineteenth century Realism and Aestheticism. James's ideas were systematized in Percy Lubbock's *The Craft of Fiction*, first published in 1921, a year before *The Waste Land* and the complete *Ulysses,* and from Lubbock onwards one of the main Modernist desiderata for novels was dramatic presentation or "showing", as opposed to "telling". The blatant personalities of intrusively omniscient authors went somewhat out of fashion, not to be rehabilitated until forty years later by Wayne C. Booth's *The Rhetoric of Fiction* (1961). The sharp discrimination between allegedly modern "showing" and allegedly old-fashioned "telling" was typical of a certain simple-mindedness in much twentieth-century criticism, which vastly underestimated the mental flexibility of readers, and ignored the variety and sophistication of writers of many periods.

What is actually going on, then, in a novel written on the allegedly Modernist model, and including, to boot, a well-known version of the relevant credo?

> The personality of the artist, at first a cry or a cadence or a mood and then a fluid and lambent narrative, finally refines itself out of existence, impersonalizes itself, so to speak. The esthetic image in the dramatic form is life purified in and re-projected from the human imagination. The mystery of esthetic, like that of material creation, is accomplished. The artist, like the God of creation, remains within or behind or beyond or above his handiwork, invisible, refined out of existence, indifferent, paring his fingernails.
> (Joyce 1960 [1916]: 214–5)

Stephen Dedalus's words are themselves dramatized. Lynch, his companion, even asks him whether the artist's fingernails are refined out of existence as well, and it is hard to believe that Joyce himself did not find Stephen amusingly precious. Yet how often have not Stephen's words been remembered as Joyce's own? As Richard J. Watts noticed, a writer can use dramatized characters to "filter in" personal views. This applied to Modernist writers at least as much as to writers of any other period, and most readers would not think twice about taking Stephen as, to some degree, Joyce's spokesman, or the spokesman, at least, for an earlier phase of Joyce's life, which he here remembers with wry affection. Experienced readers will be unable to assimilate the wording of this passage without recognizing, not just an intertextuality, but a positive coming-to-terms with those two major influences, Pater and Wilde. In theory, the Modernist novelist was supposed to be "objective", forcing readers to make up their own minds about the characters and events in the story. In reality, objectivity was a chimera, since the details "shown" could not select themselves, and neither could the words in which they were described, one word always working differently from another. What happens here is surely that Joyce filters in a point of view which has had a special relevance for his own personal development, well knowing that some readers will catch the authorial negotiation with Pater and Wilde, and at the same time allowing Stephen's hyperbole and Lynch's comment to cast an ironical reflection on Stephen and himself alike.

In this complexity of tone the writing is, we might say, pure Joyce. For a lover of literature, a piece of dramatizing "impersonal" fiction by one of the great Modernists is not only personal, but can never be mistaken for the work of some other writer. *A Portrait of the Artist as a Young Man* is not written by the author of *The Waves* and never could have been, and *vice versa*. This is quite simply an experiential fact, and any discussion of it which does not speak of different writerly personalities runs the risk of seeming trivial. Esteemed novels do come to us with the novelist's hallmark on them. The personal hallmark is one of the most important things which, consciously or not, we look for in an effort to make sense of a text. Sometimes it is most clearly to be seen when writers distinguish themselves, more or less deliberately, from the other maverick writers who have influenced them most.

Both writing and reading are dialogic. A literary work is not just washed up from a sea of anonymous intertextuality. Writers tend positively to engage with some of their predecessors and contemporaries. A reading, similarly, has to be a reading *of* a writer. It cannot really take place at all, unless the writer is allowed to speak as freely and distinctively as possible, which requires in the reader a sensitivity to the context of writing embracing not only the inferential worlds, intertextualities and generic possibilities of the writer's culture at large, but the writer's more particular relationships with other writers.

One catalyst to reader-writer dialogism is therefore literary history, because it sees particular writers in relation to other writers, such relationships between "this one" and "that one" being nothing less than central. At best, what literary historians undertake is itself a process of mediation, between the context of a literary writer's writing and the context of the historian's own scholarly labours. We who read the historian are likely to be somewhat more inward to the historian's context than to the writer's. But the historian's task is to supply us with a historical perspective on our experience of the writer, a perspective which will eventually infiltrate that experience, as we strive to move inside the context of writing. In always reminding or informing us of particular other writers as well as the particular writer under consideration, the literary historian is sensitizing us to that writer's own most positive engagement with tradition, and so assisting our own pragmatic processing.

Considerations of influence and biography were not exactly re-legitimated by Barthesian commentators. Literary criticism and theory of a structuralist and poststructuralist turn can be seen as a reaction, not only against formalist de-historicization, but against a very powerful academic and pedagogical tradition in France: the *explication de texte*, which had some of its roots in nineteenth century historical preoccupations of the more personalizing varieties. So for Barthes it was, so to speak, the society, the culture, the language which wrote and got themselves read so variously, and from this followed his objection to much biographical criticism:

> The image of literature to be found in ordinary culture is tyrannically centred on the author, his person, his life, his tastes, his passions, while criticism still consists for the most part in saying that Baudelaire's work is the failure of Baudelaire the man, Van Gogh's his madness, Tchaikovsky's his vice. The *explanation* of a work is always sought in the man or woman who produced it, as if it were always in the end, through the more of less transparent allegory of the fiction, the voice of a single person, the *author* confiding in us.
> (Barthes 1977 [1968]: 143)

Barthes astutely puts his finger on the social dimension of our make-up. Many uses of language are not strongly coloured by the personality of the user, and even literary writers are of their own time. Their personalities, like anybody else's, are to no small extent composite constructions which draw on the potentialities for subjectivity available within their culture as a whole, something which is of a piece with their participation in current intertextualities. No less timely was Barthes's poststructuralist insistence on the reader's exposure to manifold interpretative options. And needless to say, there are rich potentialities for literary, art- and music criticism which have nothing at all to do with allegorizing the artist's personal life.

But the individual dimension of our make-up cannot be shrugged aside, and the facts of experience remain. In getting to grips with literary texts, readers develop a sense of some writers as significantly different from other writers, quite regardless of whether the text is written according to an aesthetics of impersonality or, at the opposite end of the generic spectrum, as a piece of self-revealing lyricism or confessionalism — possibilities which Barthes's animadversions on biographical criticism somewhat overlooked. In every case, readers' impressions of the author can be central to the total effect, and knowledge about influences and biography can assist their effort to move from their own context of reading into the author's context of writing in the way that the text seems to invite.

This means that the concept of intertextuality needs to be supplemented with ideas of a different ancestry. Intertextuality has a strong grounding in theory; is of great analytical value in the exploration of inferential worlds and literary genres; and is completely adequate to the analysis of an anonymous oral tradition. But for written texts, not least for literary ones, there are other factors as well. Since men and women are not just social beings but social individuals, their handling of the common language can sometimes be rather personal. A literate culture, in which authors' works descend to posterity with their own names on the title-page, preserves such individualities as personal hallmarks. One particular writer's open dialogue with, or adaptations of other particular writers can give rise to some of literature's most typical pleasures. Readers' interest extends well beyond a text's general participation in the culture at large. They also develop a sense of the writer's own characteristics, and often of specific relationships with other writers to whom a personal response is being offered. Since the concept of intertextuality was introduced as part of the strategy for de-centering the self, the ideological work cut out for it was precisely to purge critical vocabulary of terms such as "influence", "source", and "allusion", the terms so characteristic of nineteenth century comparativist approaches, because they were now felt to give particular authors an unacceptably sharp profile. In the attempt to assimilate literacy to a more folksy orality, "intertextuality" worked in much the same de-personalizing way as "echo", "parallel", "similarity", "tradition" and "convention", the last two of which had been central to the aesthetics of Modernist formalism. On the strength of a historical yet non-historicist literary pragmatics, by contrast, the mediating critic can once more draw on the older, comparativist terminology, which allows us to see writers as individuals who react to each other in very distinctive ways: as individuals who do have a social being within history, but without being swamped by history.

No less than the Modernist attitudes, the attitudes to biography and influences prevailing in much Barthesian commentary make for pragmatic breakdowns, resulting from an interest in history that is rather uncatholic. Readers will be that much more likely to find themselves in situations where, to use Marlene Dolitsky's terminology, their comprehension is awkwardly non-automatic, because their feel for the context of writing is simply too insecure. As for the particular form of the Barthians' limitation here, their account of history very much prioritizes the social at the expense of the individual. History, far from being peopled by human beings who are recognizable as themselves, has become the battlefield for sweepingly impersonal general forces. In cultural critique as practised by John Drakakis, for instance, a lack of concern for the historical individual is valorized as the precondition for a postmodern challenge to traditional legitimacies.

According to Drakakis, it was once perfectly acceptable to appeal to an authority like Shakespeare as a source of straightforward adages and archetypes by which to interpret the history of one's own time. Now, he continues, this is no longer so, and we are even getting beyond the stage when the establishment's fund of monologic wisdom is dialogically challenged by carnivalistic parody and burlesque. The establishment itself, he claims, is crumbling or diversifying. Shakespeare is no longer the exclusive property of some particular grouping, so that possession of him is not in itself a guarantee of cultural supremacy. Instead, his plays have become the medium through which the ideologies of several different groupings engage each other in contest. As a result, says Drakakis, Shakespeare is now "primarily a collage of familiar quotations, fragments whose relation to any coherent aesthetic principle is both problematical and irremediably ironical". And with Shakespearian quotations thus drawn into the culture wars of postmodern multicultural societies, Shakespeare himself, like other cultural icons, is in Drakakis's view a kind of fetish, paradoxically used in *resistance* to fetishization. History itself, similarly, far from being straightforwardly knowable, is described in Drakakis's climactic final sentence as a mere

> pluralist, multiform trace of discontinuous, conflicting practices in which the variable demands of power cohere, disperse and are reconstituted.
> (Drakakis 1997: 170)

In effect, what Drakakis catches is the difference between a literate and an oral way of relating to the past. As described by him, the postmodern manner of quoting Shakespeare has all the egocentricity and wayward unpredictability of people engaged in gossip, plus gossip's often rather lukewarm concern for historical accuracy — for the certainties and near-certainties of carefully weighed historical evidence as to what particular individuals did, said or thought. His claim is really that an uncoercively polysemous orality is now gaining ground at the expense of literate forms and historical knowledge. This development he relates to a wide-spread levelling of distinctions between high and low culture, and to a still more general breaking down of an older hegemony. Anything which undermines meanings purporting to be definitively verifiable as those of a named person is experienced by Drakakis as democratic.

Whether the oral is more conducive than the literate to democracy, however, is a moot point, thoughtfully debated by Eisenstein (1979), Goody (1968, 1977, 1986, 1987), Halverson (1992), and Havelock (1982, 1986, 1989). In an evolutionary perspective, the five-thousand-year history of literacy is very short. Yet written culture, especially print culture, has already been enormously important for the spread of knowledge, which as we say is power, and has also made possible the accurate keeping of enduring records, which are crucial to justice. Nor is it as if writing and reading were still the exclusive prerogative of the powerful, or as if oral cultures were necessarily non-hierarchical utopias.

Especially problematic is Drakakis's analysis of the very latest phase of culture. On the one hand, throughout the history of literacy, and even when writing and reading skills came closest, in the West, to being universal, there has been a continuing and important oral dimension to society and culture all along. On the other hand, despite an adult illiteracy that is fairly widespread, and despite the new, technologically enhanced accesses of orality, literacy is still a very major feature of our culture even today. In particular, the writings of Shakespeare are still the work of a named author in a tradition of literature. Not that their author has ever had a monopolistic control over the way his words are interpreted and used. Shakespeare, despite and precisely because of his cultural centrality, has actually turned out to have far *less* control than most other language users. His own intentions have entered into relationship with those of countless publishers, editors, critics, scholars, teachers, translators, producers, directors and actors, to say the very least. Yet even so, we still experience his words as coming down to us as his. Culturally speaking, they are a very different thing from the orally transmitted, cumulative products of an anonymous folk (cf. Sell 1999).

In denying this, Drakakis draws support from Terence Hawkes:

> A text is surely better served if it is perceived not as the embodiment of some frozen significance, but as a kind of intersection or confluence which is continually traversed, a no-man's land, an arena, in which different and

opposed readings, urged from different and opposed positions, compete in history for ideological power.
(Hawkes 1986: 7–8)

Hawkes is a very lively and amusing critic, whose writings must have done very great deal to open up Shakespeare to younger generations. Nor is what he says here completely incompatible with the theory advanced in the present book. A stance of historical purism certainly must break down, so that a text's significance will never be freezable. But in arguing this, Hawkes and Drakakis are in effect speaking up for *readers*, who, necessarily and by right, develop their own interpretations. What we have in Hawkes's professed desire to serve *the text* is an extremist form of the cultural structuralist or poststructuralist's conferral of sense and sensibility upon the inanimate and abstract, a move which also neglects an obligation towards the *author,* who after all wrote the text, and had a right to think that it meant something. Even in postmodern times, the business of reading starts by trying to respect this and to enter into dialogue. The process Hawkes imagines readers as engaging in is not actually a process of reading another person's words. It could never be at all enriching — could never really serve readers — , but would merely be a form of solipsism, having much in common with the feats of a ventriloquist.

Seen in this light, Hawkes's decision to label his approach, not literary pragmatics, but "literary pragma*tism*" (Hawkes 1986: 6, my italics) is rather appropriate. The American pragmatists he invokes (William James, John Dewey, Richard Rorty) were philosophers preoccupied with epistemological questions to do with the truth or falsity of our ideas about the world. And admittedly, the business of constructing what we hope will be true ideas about the world does involve processes of inferencing within context which resemble the processes studied within pragma*tics* — the inferencing we get involved in when trying to work out other people's meanings from the words they use. The cardinal difference is that in interpreting meanings, at least two subjectivities are in relationship. We are negotiating the otherness of the other person. In truth-making, by contrast, only our single subjectivity is involved, unless, of course, we are religious enough to read the world of nature as the *liber dei.* For Hawkes, Shakespeare's words are merely like stones in an atheist's universe, from which all and sundry can derive their own sermons.

As for Drakakis, his argument is thrown in doubt by his own formulations. Take, for instance, those remarks on the irremediably ironic relation of the postmodern Shakespearean collage to any coherent aesthetic principle.

The question arising here is: How can the oral incoherence Drakakis is valorizing define itself except by contradistinction from a continuing potential for the certainties of literate coherence? Similarly, although Drakakis's peroration represents history as gossip-like in its "pluralist, multiform trace of discontinuous, conflicting practices", his perceptive analysis of Peregrine Worsthorne's journalistic appropriation of Shakespeare for a current political mythology is couched in very different terms:

> Worsthorne's grasp of history ... [is no] more controlled than his grasp of Shakespeare.
> (Drakakis 1997: 158)

There speaks a historian and philologian. This is the thought-pattern of a literate culture. And at such points at any rate, Drakakis acknowledges that this is also a thought-pattern which can still be brought to bear on Shakespeare.

Literacy makes possible the careful compilation of philological and historical knowledge, and enables us to discuss authorial intention according to agreed protocols of reason and truth. This form of discussion often leads to a comparative certainty, in which readers representing many different sociocultural groupings can acquiesce, and which can run alongside the postmodern challenges to traditional legitimacies. To say this is not to propose a return to nineteenth century positivism, or to nineteenth century bardolatry, or to nineteenth century humanism's suppression of difference. It is simply to point out that Shakespeare, for instance, though not an author in the old humanist sense of a self-sufficient monad, is certainly still knowable as a social individual, and can be read as such, his individuality very easily distinguishable within the culture with which he entered into co-adaptation. Partly thanks to the invention of writing, both Shakespeare and all his readers have enjoyed a somewhat larger autonomy than Drakakis allows. To echo Stephen Greenblatt (1996 [1990]), Shakespeare's works can combine the historically resonant and the uniquely wonderful, while readers, for their part, can admire and not admire him, agree and disagree, in either case significantly empowered by the labours of philologians and historians.

Drakakis's marginalization of historical knowledge and literacy is in clear descent from certain traits already noted in Barthes. But not even Barthes placed an absolute veto on biography. Whereas his professed lack of interest in Baudelaire the man, van Gogh's madness or Tschaikovsky's vice may overstate his point for the sake of emphasis, his own *Sade/Fourier/Loyola* itself concludes with a sequence of mini-lives. His main wish would presumably be to stress their fragmentariness. Infallibly sensitive to nuance, Barthes — if anyone! — would always pick up a personal vibration in a writer's work. What would probably trouble him are, first, the attempts of would-be omniscient biographers to force human experience into too inflexible a mould, and secondly, the *reduction* of writing to a writer's life as so distorted, especially since it could then most certainly be manipulated, perhaps coercively and unbeneficially.

Barthes's caution here is no less than reasonable. Nay more, it shows a due ethical seriousness. Considerations of biography and influence must never be allowed to *override* a literary work, for that, too, would be to disrespect its author. This is what would happen if *A Portrait of the Artist as a Young Man* were described as Paterian or Wildean *tout court*, or if a third-person narrative were interpreted as if it were straightforwardly lyrical and autobiographical. Here considerations of genre can once again be crucial. Biographical knowledge about T.S. Eliot or Robert Frost may well sensitize us to a personal vibration in *The Waste Land* or "The Subverted Flower". Yet for a reader to feel that a poem is "for real", that it was not just the doodling of an idle hour, is not at all the same thing as to read it as self-revealing, as is an appropriate mode for some of Andrew Young's best poetry, for instance. Too much attention to influences and biography can be just as distorting as too little. The most important aids in our approach to writers are sensitivity and good judgement, just as in all our other human intercourse.

Even in the case of Andrew Young, there is not a single poem or sequence of poems which actually amounts to an *autobiography*. Readers could never mistake the difference between that genre and Young's "An Old Road", for instance:

An Old Road

None ever walks this road
That used to lie open and broad
And ran along the oakshaw edge;
The road itself is now become the hedge.

Whatever brambles say
I often try to force a way,
Wading in withered leaves that spread
Over dead lovers' tracks a sighing bed.

> Is it the thought of one
> That I must meet when most alone
> That makes me probe a place like this,
> Where gossamer now gives the only kiss?
>
> I shall see no one there
> Though I had eyes to see the air,
> But at the waving of a bough
> Shall think I see the way she went but now.
> (Young 1998 [1933]: 14)

Such poems include autobiographical *elements* or *moments* — most often a single feeling or *aperçu*. But they do not of themselves compose an entire and coherent life-story. If readers want to, there is nothing to stop them from putting the autobiographical bits and pieces together, nor from making intelligent guesses as to things left unsaid. An author entering the public arena in Young's way can only expect to promote such speculation, which, thanks to readers' ability to read in several modes at once, can hardly damage the poems as poems, and will probably generate a lot less pleasurable prurience than kindly fellow-feeling. Yet readers are under no compulsion to read this way, and those who refrain from constructing a life-story for Young will still be able to grasp his poetry. Indeed, they will be reading it as Young himself has written it, as long as they fulfil the one condition that really is essential: as long as they take the implied or lyrical "I" of the writing as an aspect of Young himself. As argued earlier, to say that an implied author is less authentic than a "real" one is problematic at the best of times. Nor, with Wordsworth, Hardy and Edward Thomas as important influences, did Young himself expect such formalist sophistry.

The pragmatic value of knowing something about major influences within the tradition in which a writer is writing and expecting to be read is precisely that it sharpens our sense of the personal vibration and its sincerity. And even if one does not read the literary works *for* the life-story, the same value attaches to knowledge of certain basic details of an author's life and circumstances. I have already said as much *à propos* Yeats and Dickens. No less enrichment and confirmation is to be had from knowing something about the creator of Stephen Dedalus.

Once again, there is no difference in principle between the reading of historical literary works and of contemporary ones. So within literary culture as we know it, considerable responsibility rests on reviewers. In their efforts to help other readers situate new texts, they need a fair amount of knowledge and good judgement, dashed with luck. The publisher of a new book is not obliged to provide either an author profile or a certificate of literary pedigree. Every publication stands in intertextual relation with every publication of earlier date, so that the possibilities for comparison are endless, and not all of them significant. Reviewers' descriptions and evaluations are bound to be hit and miss, relying on whatever happens to be the current style of literary discussion. Sometimes writers themselves are directly or indirectly responsible for the treatment they receive. Consciously or unconsciously, they may put words into reviewers' mouths.

Nor does the pragmatics of historical knowledge — of influence studies, biography, literary history, cultural history, sociopolitical history — rule out another, no less powerful pragmatic factor. In this and the previous section I have been mainly concerned with only one dimension of pragmatics: the receiver's empathetic movement into the context of sending. But as always, I am not making a plea for historical or cultural purism. Readers' empathetic impulse can never result in a total identification, either with the writer or with any member of some first audience. The writer's intention and original impact can only be a matter of informed guesses. There is much that readers can never know about the past or the alien, and their perceptions, responses and evaluations are inevitably shaped by their own situationality. This is the other dimension of literary pragmatics, which I must now bring in more fully. The task of a mediating critic is to alternate in a balanced and self-conscious way between the two.

5.4. Changes in politeness

The other dimension of literary pragmatics has to do with the current reader's own historicity. Readers reading a work in contexts different, as always, from the context of writing may try very hard to enter into the writer's life-world. But inevitably, they still belong to their own. To use Eliot's terminology, a reader who empathetically grants *assent*, will not necessarily end up *believing* in some more permanent and fundamental way. Given the reader's own circumstances, belief will usually involve some reservations, and may even seem quite impossible or inappropriate.

At the same time, the impact of literature is neither entirely cerebral nor entirely conventional. The current reader's emotions are just as central to the interpersonality of literary communication as the writer's, and although they are just as specifically situated, they can also be just as individual. So individual, in fact, that not even the response to a work by its first audience can be readily generalized. Although readers will probably try to identify with a text's implied reader, their interpretative activity cannot be seen in terms of a behaviourist systematicity. A poem is not a stimulus mechanically producing a single and ever-repeatable response in a reader-automaton. Readers come to poems with psychological baggage of their own (cf. Holland 1975 [1973]). They are under no obligation to ditch this, and even the most situationally unrepresentative of responses may one day become more fashionable.

For a historical view of a full-bloodedly affective pragmatics, I turn to the question of politeness. Politeness is already a familiar subject within general pragmatics, even if (with exceptions such as Sell 1992 and 1994b) it has not generally been dealt with in a way that is historical without being historicist. In terms of literary theory, a concern with politeness is more unusual, and will require some lengthy exposition, in the face of a rather obvious objection. To speak of the politeness of *The Rape of the Lock* may seem natural enough. Pope belonged to what we still call the *age* of politeness. But in other phases of cultural history, politeness has not been valorized in anything like the Augustan manner. So what about *The Waste Land*, for instance? For many of its first readers, politeness considerations were certainly raised, in that they found it profoundly shocking and even insulting. But is that one of the more important things to say about it? Surely such readers were simply unprepared and unappreciative?

That, I submit, would be an oversimplification, partly arising from deceptive appearances. Just as for any other type of human behaviour, so for any kind of language use and its interpretation, politeness considerations have always been absolutely central. Like oxygen, politeness had been around for a very long time before anyone identified and named it. And even though it is now less talked about than it used to be, it is still with us, at the very heart of literary activity as much as anywhere else. Consciously or unconsciously, a reader will always have an immediate gut response to the degree of politeness experienced in the author's address, and an author, willy nilly, knows this, and takes it into account while writing. To study politeness will therefore be a natural continuation of the present work's stress on literature's interpersonal *pragma*. Indeed, it is in the politeness of literature that this dynamism is realised most primitively. Politeness is the respect in which literature is least of all the impersonal heterocosm described by Modernist orthodoxy, and least of all the anonymously communal voice sometimes described by Barthesian commentators.

Granted, the interpersonality of writing was something that earlier scholars had their doubts about. Even today, some linguists, including some pragmaticists, do not fully recognize that writing does have a politeness dimension. The fullest pragmatic study of politeness is by Penelope Brown and Stephen Levinson (1987 [1978], but all their examples are drawn from face-to-face spoken interchange. And Geoffrey Leech, even though he theorizes a politeness principle, and even though he sees communication as a far more dynamic process than the speech act theorists do, discerns a category of collaborative illocutionary functions where the illocutionary goal is indifferent to what he calls the social goal, and where politeness is "largely irrelevant". This a-polite language activity includes asserting, reporting, announcing, and instructing, and according to Leech, "most written discourse comes into this category" as well (Leech 1983a: 104–5). On this view, writing is definitely less politeness-oriented than speech.

In its own way, Leech's account makes sense, and can describe important aspects of linguistic activity. On the other hand, it is typical of Western linguists' phonocentric prioritization of presence, and another view is also tenable, deriving from the arguments advanced above for the interactivity of writing in general. Seen this way, politeness is of the essence, precisely because writing involves such a heavy burden of soloistic boldness and unmitigated finality. When we are writing, we cannot instantaneously monitor the effect of our words on any recipients they may happen to reach, and we are much less certain than when speaking of how to win and retain attention. In order to forestall the dreaded reaction "So what?", there are various strategies we can resort to. Sometimes we include overt or covert evaluations of our subject matter, while at other times we nervously hedge: we use inverted commas, indirect speech acts, phrases such as "so to speak" and "as it were", or mitigating modal expressions, sprinkling our text with "perhapses" and "may's". Another tactic is to be extremely cohesive, pointing up our argument with metatextual comments, summaries, headlines, and structural parallelisms or antitheses, and we can also choose between stylistic embellishment and unostentatious plainness as more likely to carry the day. When the worst comes to the worst, we may even try to break out of our authorial loneliness, by means of an imploring or coercive use of the first person plural — as in this and the previous few sentences! These are only the most obvious symptoms, a full account of which would have to mention the strategic usefulness of *im*politeness. Every word we write is an interactive shot in the dark.

That we more readily speak of Pope in connection with politeness than of T.S. Eliot is partly because, for the Augustans, poetry was straightforwardly interpersonal, whereas in one corner of our consciousness now there is Eliot's own claim that poetry is *im*personal. No less to the point, though, ideas about politeness itself have changed, which is one reason why research into pragmatics needs to be, in the most obvious sense of the word, historical. Politeness, unlike oxygen, is a human phenomenon of which it would be possible to write a social history. Different types of behaviour, linguistic and otherwise, have seemed polite or impolite in different times and places.

In considering Yeats's "Easter 1916", I was already hinting that a work of literature is always written and first read within one particular environment of politeness. Read in some different environment, its interpersonal effect will be only partly, if at all the same. One of the complements a mediating critic needs to the tradition of hermeneutic thought is therefore a powerfully interactive orientation, such as to be found in pragmatic scholarship with a more anthropological slant. To study the history of readings of *The Waste Land* would be to trace the merging of different *horizons of politeness expectations*. It would be to watch a Modernist poem, originally experienced by many readers as very *im*polite, itself become historical, as it gradually begins to be associated with a new range of affect. A poem whose author professed to aim at an impersonality beyond time, a poem which was described by some of its first readers as impersonal, and by others as just downright rude, is no longer experienced in either of these ways exclusively.

Changes in politeness are no easier to periodize than many other sociocultural changes. The basic problem in scholarly periodizations of history is that horizons of expectations are always already merged. Because, as K. Anthony Appiah reminds us, an individual's temperament and general disposition are not just a matter of social formation, people can have deep-seated feelings and intuitions that are out of key with their own time's most fashionable attitudes. In point of fact, a period never has just some single emphasis. The more we understand it, the more it will remind us of other periods as well, so that although its notions of politeness will be connected with its sense of human nature in general, this will never be a simple matter. On the one hand, even periods not usually noted for widespread misanthropy have left room for cynicism — and many human beings have always been quite adequately depraved to justify it. On the other hand, even more gloomy, disillusioned periods have still allowed some hope to spring eternal — thanks partly, no doubt, to striking exemplars of human nobility. In most periods, there has probably been considerable confusion, both about human nature in general and about politeness in particular.

As in all philosophy, so in moral philosophy, the disagreements can be traced through competing, but not always explicit definitions of central terms. Take, for a moment, an example that has nothing at all to do with politeness. What did "prudence" mean in eighteenth-century England? Did it mean a narrow calculation of personal advantage, associated if necessary with hypocritical dissimulation? Or did it mean a wise foresight, a conscientious husbandry of God's vineyard? Well, Sister Western, in Fielding's *Tom Jones*, lives up — or rather, down — to the first of these definitions, accommodating the virtue in question to her own innate pride, guile and suspiciousness. For Squire Allworthy, on the other hand, and in the same novel, the second definition would ring more true, even though this does not prevent the good-hearted gentleman from making several sorry misjudgements of fellow mortals. In Sophia, meanwhile, Fielding conceptualizes a prudence that gets the best of both worlds: as "wise as serpents, and harmless as doves" (*Matthew* 10: 16).

What literary writers sometimes show us is that a term associated with a high view of human nature in one age, in subsequent ages is taken up by people who have a decidedly lower view. So the term itself narrows in reference — perhaps inconspicuously at first —, and can even become ironized. In that case, the disputants rally each other in terms of a binarism of old-fashioned/new-fangled.

This is what happened with a number of words whose more lofty meanings have at some stage been close to that of "politeness". In early-seventeenth-century England, "gentle", "courtier" and "chivalry" no longer meant everything they had meant for Chaucer or the translator of Castiglione. The middle-class was now buying etiquette books in order to teach themselves a gentlemanliness which, obviously not their birthright, and far from an autotelic moral good, would be a means to the realization of social ambition. Those described as courtiers in *Hamlet* ranged from the sententiously foolish, to the popinjay, to the timeserver, while the chivalrous don, in an English translation well nigh simultaneous with the Spanish original, was quaintly tilting at his windmills. In our own day, we have sometimes heard "chivalrous" on the lips of militant feminists, a smearword connoting antediluvian patriarchal subterfuge.

"Politeness", too, has for three centuries been involved in similar processes. In the eighteenth century it could have, like "prudence", both loftier and baser connotations. Since then, the loftier connotations have faded a good deal, so that the term has sometimes been ironized like "chivalry". It is its baser connotations that have largely come to dominate, at least in what people think about it consciously.

At the zenith of its lofty meaning, politeness was the quintessentially Augustan aspiration, involving a confidence in the blessings of civilization and rational intellectuality. Philosophically underpinned by Shaftesburian benevolism, ameliorism and moral sensibility, politeness was associated with the metropolitan aristocracy, in sharp contrast with the conservative provinciality of the countryside. It meant a high degree of mental cultivation and elegant refinement, polished manners, and neo-classical good taste. Such qualities were said to be their own reward, and they were epitomized in a polite conversation that was well-informed and pleasurable — easy, free, natural, pliant, open-ended, humorous. They were also reflected in what was called polite literature. The politeness of literature *was* these qualities.

When used by students of English literature, the term is still almost invariably applied to eighteenth century writers, and has much the same connotations as it had for the Augustans themselves. It is along these lines that Thomas Woodman (1983), for example, discusses Parnell. Parnell started by trying to write a protestant sublime in the tradition of Du Bartas, but he was no Smart or Blake, and his true forte emerged only under the influence of *The Spectator* and the Scriblerus Club, to be posthumously hailed by Pope as entirely *comme il faut* — "With softest Manners, gentlest Arts, adorn'd" (Pope 1747: A2). The features noted by Woodman include: old-fashioned *sprezzatura*; impersonality, polish, brevity, sureness of tone; archness, raillery, irony; burlesque of the classics; urbane laughter at the expense of moral philosophy; and a distrust of protestant enthusiasm and false sublime. Whereas a standard view of Parnell's "The Hermit" and "Night Piece" is that they anticipate pre-Romantic emotionalism and Gothicism, Woodman emphasizes their superordinate witty elegance. They present nature as surveyed by a gentlemanly connoisseur, with decorum duly observed, and pure diction. Their piety is not actually tepid, but does involve a strong appeal to logic, with a connection intimated between the orderly symmetry of the poetry and the deity's ordered universe.

For Woodman, politeness does not quite correlate with either a deadened conscience or a heart closed to God. Despite Parnell's acquired distaste for plodding didacticism and religious ecstasies, moral pointers of a more oblique kind were still permitted, along with the rational admiration of a rational creator. With many of his contemporaries, Parnell believed it was quite possible to cultivate polite manners and remain a decent Christian, and there were also those who suggested that well-bred manners, if thought of as a matter of mere elegant surfaces, were sadly misunderstood. For them, polite behaviour involved good-heartedness and kind consideration. As Fielding put it in his "Essay on Conversation":

> Good-breeding ... , or the *Art of pleasing in Conversation*, ... may be reduced to that concise, comprehensive rule in Scripture: *Do unto all men as you would they should do unto you.*
> (Fielding 1903 [1743]: 249–50; cf. Rawson 1972: 3–34)

But Fielding would hardly have written this if the lofty sense of "politeness" had reigned unchallenged. The more cynical understanding was hinted by *The English Theophrastus: or, the Manners of the Age* of 1702:

> *Politeness* may be defined a dextrous management of our Words and Actions, whereby we make other people have a better Opinion of us and themselves.
> (Anon.1702: 108)

That politeness could be a facade for something far removed from Christianity was pointed out by Bishop Berkeley, who, though effortlessly polite himself, and actually valuing Christianity because it "visibly softened, polished, and embellished our manners" (Berkeley 1979: 108), was nevertheless worried about that Shaftesburian style of philosophy which made it the polite pursuit of a gentleman. In his dialogue *Alciphron* (1734), he hinted that the gentlemanly manner, with its distaste for pedantry, could brush aside serious discussion, thereby becoming a kind of *im*politeness: a way of not treating other people's views with due consideration. He also saw it as the natural medium of free-thinkers and atheists, whom *Alciphron* was mainly designed to attack. According to other writers, the frame of mind masked by politeness went beyond inconsiderateness and irreligion to positive selfishness, malevolence and evil, a perception which had earlier been given an entertaining twist in Restoration comedy, with its standard contrast between refined exterior and underlying lusts, a convention which Fielding's plays quite happily prolonged. Fielding's *Amelia*, however, his last novel, was far less jovial. What if the human psyche were *only* a Hobbesian mechanism? In that case polite manners would connote, not a refinement in feeling, but only the most sinister refinement in lying, which was the explicit assumption of Chesterfield's letters on etiquette: "[at court,] if enemies did not embrace, they would stab. .... The guile of the serpent simulates the gentleness of the dove" (Stanhope 1817 [1749]). This earned for the letters Johnson's remark, "They teach the morals of a whore, and the manners of a dancing master". They clearly bore out Johnson's experience of the noble lord's own politeness, which had taught him that a patron was "one who looks with unconcern on a man struggling for life in the water, and, when he has reached ground, encumbers him with help" (Boswell 1906 [1791]: I 156–9).

As this example perhaps reminds us, the less edifying operations of politeness were not only an affair between individuals but had something to do with class tensions as well. From having been an ideological strategy for marginalizing the Tories and maintaining the Whig supremacy, politeness became, after the French Revolution, an establishment specific against radicalism and unrest (Smith 1984). By now, though, there were no Parnells. No representative nineteenth century writer embraced politeness as a standard worthy of unqualified respect. In nineteenth-century novels, in particular, countless observations on the interweaving of politeness with class and power endorsed the Johnsonian type of assessment, often spiced with ironical sneers at the old-fashionedness of politeness.

In *Emma*, Mr Knightley's dislike of Frank Churchill's facility in writing "a fine flourishing letter, full of professions and falsehoods" (Austen 1933 [1816]: 148–9) is not to be explained simply by his jealousy of an apparent rival for Emma's love. It is also a matter of the kind of man Churchill is, human kind being still partly defined in terms of a morally loaded urbane/rustic binarism. Churchill, who at one point says that he returned to town merely to have his hair cut, remains a shallow sort of person even when it turns out that his trip had other purposes as well. Indeed, he is placed as one who allowed that deception — and deceptions far more grievous — to gain ground in the first place, thereby revealing his sheer failure of consideration for the woman — not Emma herself — he finally professes to love.

In *Little Dorrit*, William Dorrit, socially insecure after all his years in the Marshalsea debtors' prison, employs Mrs General — though pecuniary arrangements must never be mentioned by their real name — to Augustanize his daughter. The instructress's understanding of her commission leads her to chastize even the slightest sign of that New Testament sentiment which makes Amy such a good child, and Dickens's ventriloqiuistic dramatization of vicious but outdated propriety is in a spirit of exuberant ridicule:

> "If Miss Amy Dorrit will direct her own attention to, and will accept of my poor assistance in, the formation of a surface, Mr. Dorrit will have no further cause of anxiety. May I take this opportunity of remarking, as an instance in point, that it is scarcely delicate to look at vagrants with the attention which I have seen bestowed upon them, by a very dear young friend of mine? They should not be looked at. Nothing disagreeable should ever be looked at. Apart from such a habit standing in the way of that graceful equanimity of surface which is so expressive of good breeding, it hardly seems compatible with refinement of mind. A truly refined mind will seem to be ignorant of the existence of anything that is not perfectly proper, placid, and pleasant."
> (Dickens 1979 [1857]: 462–3)

In *Dombey and Son*, the third generation head of the family firm vaguely hopes to cash in on the ideal of polite civilization, and in time begins to aspire to a connection with the aristocracy. But the school in which little Paul is to be veneered, though over-full of the letter of high Augustanism, is lugubriously devoid of the spirit. One of Dickens's implicit messages is that Dombey, rather than allying himself with the effete Cousin Felix, would do better to pal up with some brash new man — a railway magnate, say.

Since the time of Dickens, much has happened to undermine the prestige of the high Augustan ideal still further. The industrial and urban society which upset the old balance between town and country is itself giving way to post-industrialism and the global village. Two world wars have seriously challenged the Enlightenment assumption of human rationality, and the associated processes of social levelling, or the advances of democracy, real and apparent, may have put Shaftesbury and his illustrious colleagues far from our mind. If we do remember them, if we spurn the allegation that they were simply rapacious, over-privileged elitists, if we admire wide cultivation and polite manners springing from an underlying moral decency, if we exemplify such qualities ourselves, in the world of today we shall probably have little clout. Any suggestion that politeness ought to arouse as much excitement as it still did in the breasts of Mr Dombey, William Dorrit, or Mr Knightley's more skittish neighbours in Highbury would now be greeted with incredulity, while the idea of a politeness deeply rooted in fine cultivation would be still more alien. *The Waste Land*, insofar as it is *about* politeness, was already dyspeptically elegiac to just this effect — think only of the

> young man carbuncular ...
> A small house agent's clerk, with one bold stare,
> One of the low on whom assurance sits
> As a silk hat on a Bradford millionaire.
> (Eliot 1969 [1921: 68])

Much the same goes for Pound's *Hugh Selwyn Mauberley*, or for Yeats's poems written in the aura of Lady Gregory. All this was merely of a piece with Modernist disillusionment at human nature in general, a disillusionment which was to be long-lived. Al Alvarez praised the shamelessly confessional poets of the early 1960s at the expense of the Movement, a handful of English poets who were also university teachers, librarians, and civil servants, and who yearned, according to Alvarez, for a gentility that was pre-Modernist and escapist.

> Gentility is a belief that life is always more or less orderly, people always more or less polite, their emotions and habits more or less decent and more or less controllable; that God, in short, is more or less good.
> (Alvarez 1962: 25)

So how, if at all, do people think about politeness today? Perhaps as the velvet glove to hide an iron fist. Or as a social lubricant, cheaper and less nocuous than alcohol, but, like free booze, still useful to the *corps diplomatique*.

Although "polite" is no longer a buzzword in ordinary conversation, however, new styles and fashions can still involve an element of effrontery. In practice this can only be described by at least implicit reference to a current horizon of politeness expectations. No less to the point, scholarly insights into politeness continue to be offered by sociologists and anthropological linguists, whose conclusions tend to perpetuate the modernistically cynical view of it. Erving Goffman's *The Presentation of the Self in Everyday Life* (1959) develops the idea already noted from *The English Theophrastus* of 1702, in that Goffman sees social life as a kind of theatre in which people behave like actors, projecting for each other an image of self which quite undermines distinctions between truth and falsehood. And Penelope Brown and Stephen Levinson (1987 [1978]), on the basis of empirical work in three widely separated cultures, describe politeness as a set of strategies, linguistically realized, by which human beings seek to maintain and consolidate their position.

More specifically, Brown and Levinson posit a model person with two endowments: a practical reason, which enables him (*sic*) to work out what means can be used to achieve his given ends; and face. Face has both a negative aspect, in the desire to be left alone and free to do as he wants, and a positive aspect, in the desire that other people actually approve of him and include him in their circle. In the calculations of his practical reason, the model person also assumes that other people are endowed with positive and negative face as well, and that his own goals are more likely to be achieved if he takes this into account. In fact the politeness options arise only when the model person wishes to do or say something which somehow threatens another person's face — to commit a face-threatening act (an FTA). The most polite strategy is to commit the FTA in a way that is "off record", with the threat veiled in metaphor, irony, understatement, hints and so on, so that the actual meaning is to some extent negotiable and the other person not openly forced to recognize it. For example: "Damn! I'm out of cash. I forgot to go to the bank." Less polite, though still polite to some extent, are two "on record" strategies involving redressive action: negative politeness and positive politeness, by which the model person, though now performing the FTA explicitly, nevertheless pays deference to, respectively, the other person's negative and positive face. For example: "Excuse me, could you possibly lend me five pounds?" and "Lend me a fiver, old boy?" Lastly there is a bald on record strategy, in which the FTA is performed with no polite redress at all: "Lend me five pounds".

It is perhaps as well to supplement Brown and Levinson with Goffman, as a reminder that politeness is more than a matter of strategies which are realized linguistically. But even as just a matter of language use, it can be thought of rather broadly. The value of Brown and Levinson's analysis is in their sharp concentration on instances involving an FTA. But politeness considerations must obviously enter into communication at every point, even though a scholarly mapping of each new utterance onto an underlying interaction will remain problematic.

One way to conceive of politeness is as a communally sustained spectrum of evaluation which, calibrated from extreme offensiveness to extreme obsequiousness, also has a central range that is more or less neutral. To express it in a deterministic manner which I shall soon have to qualify, all actions and all speech will necessarily register themselves at some point or other on the politeness spectrum; in a given type of situation in a given culture, a given behaviour or type of expression will be experienced as either to some or other degree impolite, or as to some or other degree polite, or as more or less neutral as to politeness; and a behaviour or type of expression which will not register somewhere on the spectrum is impossible.

One scholar who examines politeness from this point of view is Richard J. Watts (1989, 1992). What I am calling impolite behaviour Watts labels as impolitic behaviour, and what I call polite behaviour he calls explicit politeness. Under this heading he groups ritualized, formulaic behaviour, indirect speech strategies, conventionalized linguistic strategies for saving and maintaining face, address formulae, indirectness, the minimizing of imposition, hedging, the conferral of in-group status, and feigned modesty. All such explicit politeness Watts sees as a conventionally interpretable and marked subset of "politic behaviour", politic behaviour being "socioculturally determined behaviour directed towards the goal of establishing and/or maintaining in a state of equilibrium the personal relationships between the individuals of a social group ... during the ongoing process of interaction" (Watts 1989: 5). The behaviour which I am describing as in the spectrum's neutral middle region, finally, Watts calls unmarked politic behaviour. In behaviour which seems neither deferential nor rude, he carefully traces ongoing strategic considerations.

Politeness considerations can also be thought of as coming into play at a rather *earlier* stage than the one which interests Brown and Levinson. Their analysis begins at the point when a speaker has already opted for an FTA. The prior stage is a decision, conscious or otherwise, as to whether or not to commit the FTA in the first place, where the politer course is obviously *not* to commit it. Some of the eighteenth century writers on politeness were very particular about this, at least when their view of human nature was most sanguine. To the creator of Blifil in *Tom Jones,* Brown and Levinson's typically twentieth century account of the sinister model person who is always manoeuvring to promote his own ends would have been perfectly comprehensible. Yet the statement from the same author's "Essay on Conversation" is worth repeating: "*Good-breeding,* ... or the *Art of pleasing in Conversation,* ... may be reduced to that concise, comprehensive rule in Scripture: *Do unto all men as you would they should do unto you*".

Politeness can also enter the picture much *later.* It is quite possible to perform an act which is not in itself an FTA in such a way that it is nevertheless perceived as both face-threatening and impolite. Or to put this the other way round, despite the cynical things which lay-persons and anthropological linguists nowadays actually say about politeness, it can still be experienced as an overall style of behaviour that is decidedly acceptable. In the postmodern age, politeness may actually have become less sinister again. Political correctness, at least, is already expected of everybody, almost as if Augustan attitudes were being strangely rehabilitated under the banners of a pluralistic democracy. Although people are not prepared to let either an individual or a whole class gain sway over them merely by cultivated behaviour; although they are under no illusion that they themselves, by maintaining or acquiring cultivated behaviour, could hold sway over others; and although they therefore feel that politeness is, on the whole, neither here nor there: they nevertheless react as if a manner bespeaking civilized and genuine consideration for other people really did have a value.

Much polite behaviour is actually harmless and non-coercive, then, and we should usually find it difficult to predict what politeness will actually achieve. Especially in situations where polite phrases or gestures are as routinely conventional as subject-verb syntactical concord, to omit them would be almost unthinkable, and to include them brings no particular rewards. Omission is perhaps the only way to provoke any reaction at all here, and there may also be cases where deliberate impoliteness actually helps people to get what they want. Although the politeness spectrum will always have a powerful pragmatic reality, a historical understanding of this should stop well short of a historicist determinism. As always in pragmatics research, there needs to be a complementary humanizing emphasis. Speakers are not unfailingly deferential, yet may exert a hold on our attention all the same. Although a careful handling of politeness certainly can increase the likelihood of our granting them the floor, some crucial pragmatic paradoxes must also be noted. Few listeners would stop listening simply as a response to impoliteness. We are just as likely to do so in face of flattery. And even though well-bred and pleasing conversationalists of the kind admired by Fielding can often strike lucky in the treatment they receive, a degree of impoliteness is a risk which speakers are sometimes prepared to take. An act performed by one person is received as impolite, whereas, performed under the same circumstances by somebody else, the same act is received as polite. As in human interaction generally, in other words, the felicity conditions for illocution can be very tricky to pin down, and the gap between illocution and perlocution is often wide indeed, quite simply because human beings have not only a social side to their make-up but an individual side as well, making them somewhat unpredictable. The people who handle politeness most skilfully strike us as having uncanny intuition, and if they also happen to be literary authors, this is presumably one aspect of their — old-fashioned word! — genius. What operates here is once again a co-adaptability of cultural context and individual language user, as a result of which the context, including the norms of politeness itself, can be *changed*.

As I say, most earlier sociological and linguistic accounts of politeness have been synchronic and somewhat ethnocentric in their empirical focus, and structuralistically determinist in their theoretical orientation. One thing that needs to be stressed, therefore, is that perceptions of politeness do vary from one time to another and from one culture to another. The variations achieve a fair degree of social explicitness in so-called generation gaps, and also in the behaviour of people experienced as alien. In short, there is nothing more "rude" than a young foreigner, which is precisely how, in 1922, some outraged English readers perceived the author of *The Waste Land*. The other thing to stress is what I have just hinted: that a particular individual's perfectly voluntary and self-conscious rudeness can be quite unpredictably successful in moving the history of politeness on into a new phase. Because politeness works through a process of co-adaptation, its rules can be most honoured in a breach which introduces *new* rules, as did *The Waste Land* (Sell 1992, 1993).

So turning now from politeness in general, how can we talk about the politeness of literature in more detail? Perhaps the first thing to underline here is the preposition "of": the politeness *of* literature. As we have seen, for linguists such as Leech politeness is largely irrelevant as an aspect of writing. Likewise, a formalist stylistics of the Leech and Short variety maintains that a literary message does not "take effect" in the real world because there is "a sincerity gap". Possibly influenced by such warnings, some of the scholars interested in literature and politeness have confined themselves to the politeness of characters *in* poems, novels, and plays (Wadman 1983; Simpson 1989; Hardy 1991; Leech 1992; Haverkate 1994). In other words, their research belongs to the formalist wing of literary pragmatics. As far as it goes, it can be very illuminating, even if it retains a concentration on FTAs, and even if it sometimes fails to make clear whether literary authors are being praised for providing new insights into how politeness works, or for confirming the insights already arrived at by professional sociologists or linguists. Either way, such studies do not regard literature itself as a form of communication, whereas the politeness relevant to the present argument is not the politeness represented intradiegetically, but the politeness experienced by real readers in the way they feel themselves to be addressed by real writers. This is the politeness *of* literature.[17] It has an affective impact which can change over distances of time and culture, and like the politeness of any other kind of communication, can be discussed as partly a matter of selection and partly a matter of presentation.

Selectional politeness is more or less an anthropological notion. It has to do with the choice of things to say, and of words to say them with, choices which relate to questions of taboo and fashion. One linguistic area where the consequences are generally recognized is the choice of speech-act. In particular, an indirect speech act (e.g. "Could you close the window?") is experienced as more polite than the direct command ("Close the window!"). Similar points apply within the pragmatics of narrative. For instance, a mitigating indirection can be introduced into an act of narration by a framework-and-tales structure. Chaucer, in his tongue-in-cheek way, even comments on this, when giving his Miller and Reeve stories which are blasphemous, bawdy and scatological:

> The Millere is a cherl, ye knowe wel this;
> So was the Reve eek and other mo,
> And harlotrie they tolden bothe two.
> Avyseth yow, and put me out of blame.....
> (Chaucer 1957 [? c. 1390]:48)

As for lexicalization, it soon becomes obvious whether a spade is being called a spade. To stay with Chaucer, the narrating Miller is his excuse for *swyved*, *ers*, and *queynte*, which the twentieth-century editor of the text just quoted squeamishly glosses with "lie with", "buttocks" and "pudendum".

As for *presentational* politeness, this is a psycholinguistic notion and has to do with the manner of presenting the subject-matter. Is the sender being helpful towards recipients? Is it easy for them to see what the point is, what is happening, what the general bearings are? More particularly, to what extent is

---

17. The present chapter draws on my previous attempts to develop this line of enquiry, for instance in: "Tellability and Politeness in 'The Miller's Tale': First steps in Literary Pragmatics"(1985); "Politeness in Chaucer: Suggestions towards a Methodology for Pragmatic Stylistics" (1985): "The Politeness of Literary Texts" (1991); "Literary Texts and Diachronic Aspects of Politeness" (1992); "The Difficult Style of *The Waste Land*" (1993); and "Postdisciplinary Philology: Culturally Relativistic Pragmatics" (1994). For reasons which appear in this present paragraph, if I were re-publishing the second of these items today, I should change its title from "Politeness in Chaucer ..." to "The Politeness of Chaucer ...". No alterations would be necessary to its content, however. Its orientation is not literary formalist.

the sender observing Grice's maxims for cooperative communication? Here the frame of reference must again differ from that of Leech, who in his interpersonal rhetoric does include a politeness principle, but quite separately from the cooperative principle, which for him has no politeness dimension at all. The early work on politeness by Robin Lakoff (1973), by contrast, saw conversational rules of cooperative clarity as a subset of the first of her three politeness rules: "Don't impose!". An approach to the politeness considerations at work in literary presentation can be in the same spirit. In particular, it can examine infringements of Grice's maxims in the light of research by text-linguists, discourse analysts and psycholinguists. Relevant concepts include salience and foregrounding, frame/scenario/schema, and macro-structure/sectional boundary. But perhaps the easiest way to illustrate the kind of features emerging into view is with examples of communicative dynamism and discourse deixis.[18]

Communicative dynamism has a lot to do with the way in which "old" information is related to "new" information by the structure of individual sentences, and by the textual interrelations of sentences in sequence (Brown and Yule 1983: 183, Linde 1979; Prince 1981). In English of all periods, the most usual arrangement has been to put old information towards the beginning of a sentence and new information, or old information which has not been used for some time, towards the end:

> The cat [the cat already mentioned] came into the kitchen [an action which is news]. It [still the same old cat] walked across to its milk bowl [more news].

At a crucial point in a narrative, however, a writer may reverse this practice, deliberately causing readers a temporary bafflement. In the sentence position where they expect to find mention of something currently familiar, they instead find words whose reference they cannot at once pin down, as in the final turning point of "The Miller's Tale":

---

18. As for salience and foregrounding, this is a matter of the formal linguistic means by which texts keeps certain things mentioned more prominent than others (Hopper 1979; Longacre1981, Wallace 1982, Osgood 1980, Levinson 1983: 225). Frames, scenarios, and schemas are mental representations of the world and of human beaviour, which recipients either simply have, or construct from scratch, and to which they refer the on-going text as the only means of assimilating it to their world view (Brown and Yule 1983: 236–71; de Beaugrande and Dressler 1981: 90–1). Macro-structure and sectional boundaries have to do with the linguistically marked coherence between different parts of a text in terms of space, time, characters, events and worlds (Longacre 1979; Chafe 1994). See Sell 1985b.

"Help! water! water! help, for Goddes herte!"
This carpenter out of his slomber sterte
And herde oon crien "water" as he were wood [= mad].
(Chaucer 1957[c. 1390]: 54)[19]

The carpenter has not been mentioned for 169 lines, and since then the action has been very fast and complicated. So readers' immediate reaction on moving from Nicholas's scream for help in the form of water may well be, "Which carpenter?!". A more normal ordering would have been something like (Mod. Eng.) "All this woke up the carpenter." Chaucer, it would seem, has been presentationally impolite.

But then there are the co-adaptive parodoxes and uncanninesses of politeness, the interactive gambles. Absolute politeness, of either kind, will not do. Too much selectional politeness is merely obsequious, too little is off-putting. Fielding knows that he can call his reader a blockhead, and he knows just how often as well, just as Donne knows that he can begin a poem with the words "For Godsake hold your tongue ...". As for presentational politeness, too much of it, as in the more notorious of Wordsworth's lyrical ballads, gives the recipients too little to work out for themselves, so risking bathos. Too little, as in some of Pound's Cantos, is merely baffling. Chaucer's slight presentational unhelpfulness at the climax of "The Miller's Tale" seems much better judged, and can only increase readers' involvement and curiosity. Goaded into remembering something about the carpenter, they probably begin to half-anticipate how the earlier part of the story is going to slot in with the most recent part to form the comic climax. The young student Nicholas has cuckolded the carpenter by convincing him that a second Noah's flood was on its way, and that his best hope of surviving it would be by stationing himself in a tub up in the attic. When the flood waters rose, he would be able to cut the ropes suspending the tub and float out through the roof. Since the point at which the carpenter, having accepted this advice, fell asleep in the tub, much has happened. Nicholas and Alisoun, the carpenter's wife, have indulged their sexual appetites in the carpenter's more usual bed. Absolon, another of Alisoun's admirers, has stood in the street beneath the bedroom window and implored her for a kiss. Alisoun has projected her naked backside out of the window and allowed him to kiss that. The incensed Absolon has been to fetch a white-hot iron from the blacksmith's, and implored a second kiss. Upon

---

19. For a fuller discussion of communicative dynamism and this example, see Sell 1985b.

which, Nicholas has stuck his own naked backside out of the window, only to be targeted by the iron. This amply explains his cry: "Help! water! water! help, for Goddes herte!" From which point onwards, there is almost a sense in which Chaucer helps readers complete the climax for themselves. Because of the presentational impoliteness, the switch back to the carpenter is very abrupt and difficult to process. But as text-linguists point out, there are inevitable trade-offs between efficiency — the help a writer gives the reader in making the text understandable — and effectiveness — the impact made on the reader (de Beaugrande and Dressler 1981: 65, 69, 75). Once readers have remembered who the carpenter is, where he is, why he is there, and the great dread which has been obsessing his mind, they will begin to foresee the finale — his thinking "Allas, now comth Nowelis [*sic!*] flood!", cutting the ropes, and crashing down in his tub through the intervening floors to ground level — just about as fast as the Miller can tell it. The Miller's narration will at once stimulate and confirm readers' own powers of imagination, to which the presentational impoliteness has served as the trigger. For Chaucer as a writer, the impoliteness will have paid off. His audience will be well pleased, having themselves participated in the narrative sport.

Now although a writer's degree of politeness is not necessarily stable or predictable, for both presentational and selectional politeness it is possible, at least to some extent, to talk about styles of politeness. In other words, some of the relevant features can be counted. In turn, certain politeness styles correlate with certain roles, certain periods and genres, certain target recipients, certain senders.

This is where some of the most obvious examples are a matter of discourse deixis. Discourse deixis is different from the kinds of deixis mentioned earlier — person, temporal, spatial and social deixis — , in that discourse deixis is metatextual. It has to do with a text's way of "pointing to" itself, so as to help its recipients keep track on where it is going (Levinson 1983: 85, Stubbs 1983: 48–57). In the slow-paced courtly romance narrated by Chaucer's Knight, the discourse deixis is very prominent. There is a large number of metatextual signposts, which deferentially assist readers or hearers in getting from one part of the story to the next. One verse paragraph will end by saying that Palamon has made up his mind either to lose his life

> Or wynnen Emelye unto his wyf.
> This is th' effect and his entente pleyn.

Then the next verse paragraph, though it begins with the second line of the same couplet, will clearly mark the transition back to Arcite:

> Now wol I turne to Arcite ageyn.
> (Chaucer 1957 (c. 1390): 31)

In the climactic couplet of "The Miller's Tale", by contrast, the far more abrupt transition from Nicholas's cry for water back to the carpenter in his tub is no less typical of this fabliau's brute directness. To be more precise, metatextual signposting takes place in the first couplet of only 3 of the 63 verse paragraphs making up "The Miller's Tale", as against no fewer than 35 of the 113 verse paragraphs making up "The Knight's Tale" (Sell 1985c).

Then again, many politeness phenomena cannot be counted as features of the surface text in this way, but depend on pragmatic processing, on reading between the lines, and even on a kind of primitive gut reaction, which may still underlie a fully-fledged critical argument of considerable sophistication. For F.R. Leavis, certain rhythms often seemed to go together with a mixture of selectional affront and presentational boringness, and clear signs of this remained in his published commentaries:

> [In *The Plumed Serpent*] it is by a kind of incantation, a hypnotic effect figured in the endless pulsing of drums playing so large a part in Don Ramón's campaign, that Lawrence tries to generate conviction, and he produces boredom and a good deal of distaste.
> (Leavis 1964 [1955]: 71)

> In the end we find ourselves protesting — protesting against the routine gesture, the heavy fall, of the verse, flinching from the foreseen thud that comes so inevitably, and, at last, irresistibly; for reading *Paradise Lost* is a matter of resisting, ... and ... we surrender at last to the inescapable monotony of the ritual.
> (Leavis 1964 [1936]: 43)

If our sense of a text's politeness or otherwise can be so strong, then, what is the relationship between this and the disparate sitedness of literary pragmatics? In order to facilitate my own presentation, I have so far spoken as if all readers of Chaucer's texts have always responded, and always will respond, in one way and one way only. Hermeneutically and pragmatically this is nonsense, and I hope I have been guilty of it only when dealing with those linguistic items whose interpretation is least likely to vary with variations in the sociocultural context of reading. Particularly, but not only when speaking of selectional politeness, it is essential that discussion should be culture-specific and historical. Writers can write as they will, and readers of any period can try their best to empathize. But it is the readers, reading in their own situation, who finally decide exactly how a text is currently taken. What was polite or impolite in one milieu may at first glance seem very different to readers reading in some other milieu.

Take Tennyson as read by Eliot, for instance. Eliot argues that *In Memoriam* is Tennyson's greatest work, not least because the extended lyric mode is what suits Tennyson best. In pressing home this judgement, Eliot suggests the following frank contrast with "The Princess":

> We can swallow the most antipathetic doctrines if we are given an exciting narrative. But for narrative Tennyson had no gift at all.

As far as Eliot was concerned, the doctrines of "The Princess" remained obstinately impolite selectionally, while its narrative failed to negotiate a successful presentational bargain, remaining simply dull. As for the content of "In Memoriam", Eliot was much impressed by "the quality of its doubt". "Its faith is a poor thing, but its doubt is a very intense experience". To conventionally pious Victorians this was presumably not all that welcome, and Eliot accordingly pointed up his judgement here with an allegation of overdone selectional politeness in some of Tennyson's other poems. In these, he was "the surface flatterer of his own time" (Eliot 1951 [1936]: 331, 336, 338). Here, as so often with Modernist critics, immediate gut response clearly weighs a good deal heavier than historical perspective. It is hardly surprising that the author of *The Waste Land* should admire another poet for the quality of his doubt. Although the Tennyson essay was published some six years after *Ash Wednesday*, Eliot's Christian faith was no more facile than his admired Pascal's, and a fair amount of Modernist gloom about the human condition remained instinctive with him, a matter less of social formation than of personal temperament. So much so, however, that he unhistorically lambasts Tennyson's more confident affirmations for deferring too much to his Victorian contemporaries, almost as if Tennyson had not himself been a Victorian writer, albeit a writer in whom the Victorian and Modernist horizons of expectations can be thought of as always already merged.

Further anachronistic comments on politeness are to be found in Pat Rogers's otherwise excellent book on Pope. Rogers writes with great insight into the interactive gambles of politeness, Pope being both the polite Augustan writer *par excellence* and a devastating critic of his age. Rogers shows how

Pope made his readers feel that they and Pope were almost the only people of true judgement and morality, while at the same time exposing the deepest flaws of ... those very same readers. But then, so keen is Rogers to help university students of the 1970s enjoy Pope, that he suddenly extends Pope's aims and strategies to embrace them as well:

> Shock tactics are a common feature in modern literature. But Pope needs first to enlist our [*sic!*] sympathy. He makes writing seem a civilized business, a polite form of communication as unthreatening as (to take extreme examples) a wine list or a bus timetable [*sic!*].
> (Rogers 1975: 16–17)

Lionel Trilling, on the other hand, in discussing those very shock tactics of modern literature —

> No literature has ever been so shockingly personal as that of our own time — it asks every question that is forbidden in polite society.
> (Trilling 1967: 23)

— has a much stronger sense of changing horizons. Trilling goes on to note that Modernist texts, which began by seeming electrifyingly impolite, within a few decades became the staple of routinely dull university lectures.

It is this firm historical sense that we shall need if we are successfully to mediate politenesses from one period to another, from one culture to another, or between co-existent sub-cultures of one and the same culture, including even the age of high politeness itself. Pope may have been duly courteous about the refined verses of the dear departed Thomas Parnell. But in the last analysis, Parnell had not belonged to the innermost circle of wits. An instructive exercise is to compare his and Pope's re-writings of some of Donne's satires. Parnell smooths and tames, just as if he himself were Pope's soft dean who "never mentions hell to ears polite". Where Donne's compressed syntax and procrastinating word-order only makes a frank expression come with greater force —

> ... And shall thy father's spirit
> Meete blinde Philosophers in heaven, whose merit
> Of strict life may be' imputed faith, and heare
> Thee, whom he taught so easie ways and neare
> To follow, damn'd?
> (Donne 1967 [1633]: 11)

the verbiage of Parnell's more pedestrian constructions merely beats about the bush:

> And shall thy father's spirit meet the sight
> Of heathen sages cloath'd in heavenly light,
> Whose merit of strict life, severly suited
> To Reason's dictates, may be faith imputed,
> Whilst thou, to whom he taught the nearer road,
> Art ever banished from the blest abode.
> (Parnell 1779: 99)

Pope's interactive gamble is altogether bolder, apparently rendering Donne less uncouth, yet remaining still savagely colloquial. Donne's second satire opens:

> Sir, though (I thanke God for it) I do hate
> Perfectly all this towne, yet there's one state
> In all ill things so excellently best,
> That hate, towards them, breeds pitty towards the rest.
> (Donne 1967 [1633]: 7)

Here Pope actually *introduces* a mention of hell, and of other indelicate matters, too:

> Yes; thank my stars! As early as I knew
> This Town, I had the sense to hate it too:
> Yet here, as ev'n in Hell, there must be still
> One Giant-Vice, so excellently ill,
> That all beside one pities, not abhors;
> As who knows Sapho, smiles at other whores.
> (Pope 1963 [1735]: 676)

Rogers skilfully suggests that the secret of Pope's extraordinary dynamism as a writer is that he is never entirely of his own time, even when he is most Augustan. As I hinted in Chapter 1, in a line such as

> This Nymph, to the Destruction of Mankind,

one knows not where one has him. Is he specially laughing at his time's male establishment, or is he not? In Pope's kind of work, both aspects of the social individual are so strongly in evidence that they are very sharply each other's foil, as also with Tennyson, or Yeats, or any other major writer. Wordsworth, by purifying his rustic characters' language "from what appear to be its real defects, from all lasting and rational causes of dislike or disgust", was indirectly acquiescing in the establishment's discoursal marginalization of radicalism and unrest (cf. Smith 1984). Yet this apparent concession to polite neo-classical taste was actually co-adaptive: a strategy likely win over readers to his lyrical ballads' rejection of "high" genres and "high" characters. Even the Eliot of *The Waste Land*, similarly, was not just a brash young American Modernist. In his public persona there were also elements of the late-Victorian gentleman and pillar of society, and the same applied to the writing itself. The poet of

> –Yet when we came back, late, from the hyacinth garden,
> Your arms full, and your hair wet, I could not
> Speak, and my eyes failed, I was neither
> Living nor dead, and I knew nothing,
> Looking into the heart of the light, the silence.
> (Eliot 1969: 62)

could have met Pre-Raphaelite admirers of Dante half-way, and was closer to Tennyson than he usually wanted to admit (cf. Christ 1981, 1984; Tobin 1985; Plasa 1991). His later description of Tennyson as the surface flatterer of his own time was rather rich. Tennyson may more conspicuously have pleased, and Eliot, at least in his earlier poetry, more conspicuously have challenged. But like all great writers, both of them pleased and challenged, flattered and affronted, at the same time. That, at bottom, is how co-adaptation works.

A hermeneutically oriented account of politeness pragmatics can help to substantiate this, while at the same time further rehabilitating literary history. Writers, no matter how individual they may be, necessarily belong to particular times and places, and take full advantage of the openings for co-adaptation, even to the extent of re-fashioning the proprieties. As a result of that re-fashioning itself, the gut responses of readers coming to their work fifty years after its publication can be entirely different from those of their first readers, even though, as part of the empathetic dimension of reading, new readers are well advised to try to re-live those older responses as well. No reader today can spontaneously experience the intense sense of outrage that overwhelmed many of Eliot's readers in 1922. Eliot himself has been dead and buried for three decades, and his first major poem is now as distant in time as was *In Memoriam* from his own first readers. *The Waste Land*, still partly Victorian from the start, and borne up by the train of mitigating commentary following upon Eliot's own criticism, gradually created its own audience and became a classic. Yet to read it only as a classic is to universalize away its unique historical identity, which in turn is to miss the extraordinary vigour of Eliot's engagement with the culture of his time, a vigour which so typically led to an at first unwelcome violence. This is a loss we can ill afford. At precisely the moment when both his personal life and human civilization in general seemed to have fallen to pieces, Eliot summoned up the gusto of co-adaptive creativity to make old forms and readers anew, with consequences that were not only painful and shocking, but ultimately joyful, as his offensiveness can gradually come to be re-apprehended as an ecstatic ebullience of style. If our historical sense of his transforming energies is only strong enough, their inspiration will carry, in ways quite unpredictable by Eliot himself, into our very different but no less demanding world today.

The negotiation of different affective patterns is one of the most crucial, albeit least discussed aspects of the entire reading experience. And since a sociocultural difference is always a sociocultural difference, the affective disparities need not always be between different historical periods. They can just as well be between two cultures or sub-cultures in a state of coexistence. This is already clear from a comparison of Pope and Parnell. Here, too, is where we might recall Pat Buchanan's reaction to reports of Ramona Lofton's "Wild Thing"(cf. Section 3.5 above). What this showed beyond all question was that the different groupings of postmodern society can find each other's literature deeply offensive. In such cases, one opening move for mediation is precisely through an appeal to readers' heuristic capacity for a simultaneity of contradictory responses. Here critics will be strengthened by the knowledge that a text which a readership begins by decrying for its shocking outlandishness can sometimes, like *The Waste Land*, even come to be admired for it. Understanding the kind of accommodation involved, critics will try to accelerate it by supplying relevant information and perspectives, but without for that reason detracting from the inherent and invaluable challenge of its otherness. Especially in comparison with certain forms of political correctness, the mediating strategy opened up by a historical yet non-historicist literary pragmatics is constructive and honest.

5.5. Bi-dimensional beauties from history

To think about the politeness of literary writing is very much to grasp it as an interpersonal deed. By the same token, such a line of examination begins to reveal a type of beauty not normally catered for by aesthetic theory, a beauty inseparable from interactional relationships between deeds of writing and historical circumstances. At the centre of most nineteenth-century and some more recent aesthetics, by contrast, has been the idea of symbolic form, an idea which can be traced back to Kant, who encouraged a sense of the aesthetic as a *tertium quid* that was quite distinct from the realms of reality and ethics. For Modernists such as the New Critics, then, the literary work was in the nature of a timelessly well-wrought urn, the measure of whose beauty was not to be taken until it had been exhumed from the distracting rubble of history, and every last speck of obfuscating interpersonality and social attachment meticulously removed.

Some readers now fear that the strong reaction against New Criticism — in particular, the work of post-Marxist, feminist, new historicist, cultural materialist, gay and lesbian, postcolonial, and ethnic critics — may have deprived literary works of a due autonomy. But as the philosopher Peter Winch has sought to reassure them, "[t]o exhibit a text's *internal* relation to elements in its surroundings is not to submerge it in something extraneous; on the contrary, it is a contribution towards showing what it *is*"(Winch 1987: 26).

To this we can add, I think, that certain aspects of certain communicative acts can be seen as beautiful in ways pertaining to Kant's realm of ethics. Even in pragmatics, admittedly, the behaviourist legacy is still so deeply entrenched that the relationship between language use and ethics is not always seen as an appropriate scholarly concern. But common idiom itself shows the way here, as when we describe something somebody has said as "a beautiful gesture". A pragmatics that is historical yet non-historicist can readily articulate the two key points. First, linguistically harnessed beauty of this kind derives from a person's exercise of relative moral autonomy, in processes of co-adaptation with history by which both aspects of the social individual are brought into play. Secondly, as the distance between sending and receiving increases, so the interpretation of such ethically beautiful language use becomes more complicated, as its interpersonal valency changes as well. The bi-dimensionality which my previous section identified with regard to politeness applies here, too. Words which were a beautiful gesture in the there-and-then can only be a beautiful gesture in the here-and-now by working somewhat differently.

Warton's *Observations on the Fairy Queen of Spenser*, with its thoughtful comparisons and contrasts between the mediaeval taste for romance and the neo-classical taste which paid deference to Homer and Aristotle, was far more likely to encourage an ethical bi-dimensionality than the Augustan scholarship he was throwing into question. Augustan literary history had sometimes shown a very weak sense of original contexts and interpersonal valencies, relying less on the careful sort of archival and philological enquiry that we associate with a literate culture than on a rather erratic kind of hearsay. Giles Jacob (1720: 4–5), for instance, described Sir John Beaumont as "an excellent Poet who liv'd during the reign of King *Richard* the Third" (d. 1485). In point of fact, Beaumont lived from c. 1582 to 1627. Jacob was confused because Beaumont's most famous poem is "Bosworth Field", a mini-epic about the battle in which Henry, Earl of Richmond defeated Richard III, so ending the Wars of the Roses and inaugurating the Tudor royal dynasty. Not knowing its author's dates, Jacob would also have missed the poem's tribute to James I, whose legitimacy as King of England involved a somewhat controversial claim to descent from Richmond (Sell 1974: 20, 32–3, 35–6, 66–83, 217–31). For partly the same reason, Jacob is very struck by the "*Phœbean* Fire" of Beaumont's verse. As an anticipation of Denham, Waller, Dryden and Pope, the heroic couplets he quotes from "Bosworth Field" were very remarkable even for the 1620s. For the 1480s, they would have been nothing short of miraculous.

As for Warton's immediate successors, they were seldom as vague as Jacob. In the nineteenth century both literary history and literary biography could be decidedly positivistic. In reaction to this, though, the Kantian strand in Romantic, Aesthete, Symbolist and Modernist formalism was greatly strengthened.

As always in dealing with literary formalism, it is as well not to throw out the baby with the bathwater. That the Modernist critical heritage tended to suppress ethics, making it more difficult to speak of the beauty or ugliness of a literary deed, was extremely unfortunate. But formal beauties are no less real than ethical ones. To deny them would be an absurd refusal of pleasure, and a very rewarding balance has been struck by Geoffrey Hill. Style, he says,

> is a seamless texture of energy and order which, time after time, the effete and the crass somehow contrive to divide between them; either paying tremulous lip-service to the "incomparable" and the "incommunicable" or else toadying to some current notion of the demotic.
> (Hill 1991: 81)

On the one hand, the tradition of Aesthete-Symbolist-Modernist aesthetics certainly can seem effete: in its claims for an untranslatable artistic uniqueness; in its Wildean contention that there are no good books and evil books but only books that are well and badly written; and in its New Critical view of implied writer and reader personae as hermetic seals between the literary realm and life. Even though literary works written on the Kantian assumptions deserve to be read with those assumptions in mind as a belief that is relevant to their pragmatics, formal beauty is not actually the manifestation of a timeless aesthetic heterocosm, but is in some of its aspects unmysteriously objective, and even in its more subjective elements has a marked historical dimension, being differently perceived from one cultural milieu to another. Indeed, for a critic such as Anthony Hecht (1995: 164–8), artistic qualities are quite inseparable from qualities of moral sensibility in the world of action. That is why he insists that the hatred, bigotry and malice expressed by the poetry of Pound are a grotesque blemish.

On the other hand, a reduction of literary effect to history and ethics certainly will result in crass oversimplications. An evil deed of writing can be carried out with great craftsmanship and imaginative energy. These qualities, however reluctant we may be to say so, are wonderful and inspiring in their own right. When Helen Vendler told John Ashbery that "only Fascists like Pound" (Vendler 1992), she was being somewhat disingenuous. There is nothing the least bit Fascistic about Donald Davie's chapter on the pleasures of rhythm in *The Cantos* (Davie 1975: 75–98), and those pleasures are there for all who have ears to hear, neither cancelling, nor cancelled by, the hideous moral deformities noted by Hecht. Pound's formal beauty may not represent the highest of all values. But it should certainly be clearly recognized and distinguished, both as something to be enjoyed, and as something to be wary of, lest it soften our hearts to the evil.

But even during the high Modernist era, certain scholars were in effect resisting Kantian aesthetics by going to the opposite extreme. They declined to recognize formal beauty *per se*. The seminal idea was rather I.A. Richards's emotivism, which had much in common with A.J.Ayer's logical positivism. According to Richards, impressions of a literary work's beauty arose, not by virtue of a quality of beauty inherent in the work itself, but because the work produced a certain kind of emotional effect: it promoted in the mind of its audience an optimal psychological balance between impulses more usually in conflict (Richards 1924). For Richards's pupil Empson, a valuable literary work could in addition stimulate a rich simultaneity of different understandings (Empson 1930). And still more relevant here is Leavis, the third member of this Cambridge triumvirate, because, for him, literary quality was also so much a matter of ethical sensitivity. Jane Austen, George Eliot, Henry James and Conrad were remarkable for the "human awareness they promote". They were "all distinguished by a vital capacity for experience, a kind of reverent openness before life, and a marked moral intensity" (Leavis 1962 [1948]: 10, 17). Leavis's mission was accordingly to place literary study at the centre of the university, so as to relate it to all the big issues, both eternal and more topical.

Leavis's unflagging sense of human relevance represents a type of commitment which literary scholars shirk at their peril. In his Augustan-like insistence that the great writer, even if historical, is experientially always present, in his empathizing sense of livingness, he is perhaps the most striking exemplar of that inwardness to literature, that readiness to participate in it as a form of human interaction, without which there is nothing for a literary scholar to be scholarly *about*.

The only risk was of the unitary context assumption: the risk that his powerful responses to literature's immediacy would ignore its simultaneous pastness and/or foreignness, and so become ethically one-dimensional, rather like the postmodern rhetoric of blame. Hecht's verdict on the moral ugliness of Pound steers clear of this, being in full accordance with pragmatic theory as developed in the present work. Pound continued in his evil ways long after there was even less excuse for not knowing better. Unlike Julius in his commentary on the no less indisputable anti-Semitism of Eliot, Hecht does not lapse into anachronism or uncircumstantiality. On the contrary, the blame attaching to Pound springs not from the critic's disregard for contextual disparities but from his sensitivity to them. So what about Leavis, then? When it came to it, was he actually capable of distinguishing the here-and-now from the there-and-then? Or was his mental voyaging a running on the spot?

In one respect not at all. Although he pours scorn on aesthetic argumentation as a mere Bloomsburian distraction, his own criticism derives from an intense sensitivity to language, and in practice does register features of formal beauty, if not under that particular label, then certainly as instances of writing which in and of itself promotes crucial ethical qualities. In speaking of such features in their *least* ethical aspect, moreover, his perceptions can be delicately relativistic, and the bi-dimensionality of literary pragmatics has seldom been more succinctly hinted than in some of his comments on Donne. In the opening chapter of *Revaluation* (1936), he tells how it could feel to come across Donne in the recently published *Oxford Book of Seventeenth Century Verse*. "After ninety pages of ... respectable figures" we are suddenly confronted, he says, with something different. He then quotes the first stanza of "The Good-Morrow", and makes some remarks which have become very well known:

> At this we cease reading as students, or as connoisseurs of anthology pieces, and read on as we read the living. The extraordinary force of originality that made Donne so potent an influence in the seventeenth century makes him now at once for us, without his being the less felt as of his period, contemporary — obviously a living poet in the most important sense.
> (Leavis 1964 [1936]: 18)

Donne, here, is experienced as unquestionably a major writer, a writer still "living ... in the most important sense", and this is the type of emphasis which most readers will carry away from *Revaluation* as a whole. But although the book suggests that the writers it praises are universally valuable and relevant, and although Leavis takes upon himself all the authority needed in order to pronounce on this scale, his actual wording connects his massive statement to a historical perspective. Even today (i.e. even in 1936), it is still the force of Donne's originality *in the seventeenth century*, still his potency of influence *then*, that "makes him at once for us ... contemporary" and "living" *now* (in 1936). Note, too, that originality, Donne's great force, is itself said to be in the first instance a historical matter, and that Donne's contemporaneity for Leavis is apparently undiminished by his "being ... felt ... as of his period", and is even partly constituted by it. "Respectable figures" such as Greville, Chapman and Drayton "serve at any rate to set up a critically useful background" (*ibid.*). Their historical respectability is described as a foil to qualities in Donne which, original at the time, are still there to be freshly appreciated by any modern reader who takes the trouble to recreate those earliest intertextualities.

As for Leavis's more directly ethical concerns, he first deserves to be defended against youngish critics who think of him as a crude moralizer. According to a pleonastically emphatic account by J. Storey (1995: 256), for instance, the literary text "is for Leavis a treasury of timeless moral truths, and thus a source of moral order. In short, the achievement of great writers is to give literary form to timeless moral truths." In point of fact, it is rather difficult to glean wise saws from Leavis's writings, since what he values most are qualities of living responsiveness, openness to experience, and intelligent responsibility, whose workings will of their very nature be *ad hoc*.

That said, however, it is also quite true that Leavis does arrogate to himself that formidable legitimacy. Most characteristically, ethical relativism is conspicuous by its absence. There is little sense of writers as writing within certain contexts, and none at all of the critic as reading within a different one. Leavis's own pronouncements are often even more absolutist in tone than those of other critics contemporary with him, which in turn can make his dialogues with such colleagues rather perfunctory. Granted, he calls one of his books *The Common Pursuit*, a phrase requisitioned from Eliot, who professed that

> the critic, ... if he is to justify his existence, should endeavour to discipline his personal prejudices and cranks — tares to which we are all subject — and compose his differences with as many of his fellows as possible, in the common pursuit of true judgement.
> (Eliot 1951[1923]: 25)

But Leavis, though he quotes this passage in full (Leavis 1962 [1952]a: v), does little to justify his existence in the way recommended, and a habit of positive mediation would be quite foreign to him. His style speaks less of self-discipline than of immense self-confidence — of a conviction that he is weeding out the personal prejudices and cranks of his fellows. Truth in literary judgement, we are given to understand, is actually unequivocal, and Leavis himself discovered it long ago, any challenge to his authority being quite unthinkable.

It is not to Leavis that we turn, then, for examples of patience. What is all too likely to stick in the memory is the tone of his remarks on C.P. Snow (Leavis 1962). Snow's own novels were not like the ones praised in *The Great Tradition*, and Leavis, having urged so strongly the case for English literature as the central university discipline, had no desire to understand the community of scientists, technologists and administrators from within which Snow was writing. Even less could he accept Snow's generalizations about the snobbish superciliousness of English literary intellectuals, or warm to Snow's vision of a society in which neither poets nor engineers would be pariahs (Snow 1959). Indeed, he did his hysterical best to make a pariah out of Snow. Their quarrel about the two cultures was a sad anticipation of our own time's culture wars, with, on Leavis's side, a quite prodigious rhetoric of blame, to which Snow's response (1993 [1963]) was a good deal more dignified and reasonable.

In mitigation it has to be said that Leavis's absolutism, at times so damagingly intemperate and unconstructive, was part and parcel of a frankness which can nowadays seem foreclosed. Under no temptation to veil himself in an insincere political correctness, Leavis said what he thought, and made no apology for hoping that other people would think the same. He honestly believed they would be the better for it. If, sixty years further on, we disapprove, this may be partly because lack of forthrightness can now do service as a virtue. As yet, there is no widespread practice of positive mediation, in which frankness and conciliatoriness would go hand in hand.

Nor would it be fair to say that Leavis's absolutism gave rise to a fanatical cult. He did have followers, who were sometimes fanatical, but for whom he cannot be held responsible. He himself did anticipate postmodern paranoia, but maybe not without all provocation. If he was preoccupied with the role of a truly cultured and humane minority in the age of mass civilization, this showed a certain realism. We do not have to know much about human history, not least the history of the early and mid-twentieth century, to feel that Snow's vision of a single, re-united culture, for all its foretaste of the positive mediation I am advocating here, was a touch on the blithe side, as may also be the case with Raymond Tallis's attempt to supplant our own time's cultural pessimism (Tallis 1997). Leavis certainly longed for a clan of kindred spirits. But in principle there was no limit on the clan's size except his own sense of the probabilities involved. If he was elitist, he could well claim that this was by historical accident rather than personal choice. It certainly did not stop him from becoming enormously influential as an educator.

Even so, his absolutism was sometimes not unlike that of a rather blinkered non-scholarly reader. The considerations he deemed external to the actual experience of literature included sociological and religious questions, and he could also brush aside history. Even though the interdisciplinary study of history and literature was one of the things he campaigned for, in practice he was no less likely to de-contextualize writing and reading than I.A. Richards or Wellek and Warren.

Especially weak, though not exceptionally weak for the period, was his sense of his own historicity. His intense confrontation with literature was so un-self-conscious that he seldom, if ever, got outside of it. In setting up his great tradition of the English novel, he did foresee the charge of narrowness, but thought it would attach to the smallness of the group of writers he was dealing with, in which connection he remarked, quite reasonably enough, that one has to be selective and assert the highest standards if one is ever actually to *say* something about literature. What he never seems to have grasped is just how obviously every sentence he wrote was a sentence from the pen of F.R. Leavis. Every judgement passed or hinted was the judgement of that highly individual reader, who at a certain juncture of English history eventually came to regard

D.H. Lawrence as almost a saviour. Seemingly unaware that his canon might be experienced as the canon of just one critic during just one period, he indulged in what many more historically minded scholars, and not a few non-scholarly readers as well, could only see as a belligerently paraded glibness, praising Austen, George Eliot, James and Conrad for not being Fielding, Dickens and Thackeray, who in their turn were damned, with never a word of analysis, for not being Austen, George Eliot, James and Conrad. The anticipation of some postmodern exercises in canon-formation is rather striking.

Leavis's most influential work was published more than half a century ago. But during the past fifteen years or so, Michael Bell (1997) and a number of other literary scholars have once again turned to ethical considerations, some of them, like Geoffrey Galt Harpman, promisingly convinced that ethics "is ... the point at which literature intersects with theory, the point at which literature becomes conceptually interesting and theory becomes humanized" (Harpman 1995: 401; see also Harpman 1992). Dominic Rainsford, for instance, has drawn attention to the care with which the responsibility of authorship is handled by Blake, Dickens and Joyce. These writers "earn a special credibility for the role of the literary text as a vehicle for productive ethical debate through linking an implicit scrutiny of themselves, as author and as human agents, to their analysis of the world around them" (Rainsford 1997: 3).

Certain other critics, however, though claiming to study the entire ethics of fiction, have tended to prioritize the current reader's act of reading. Some of them simply fail to historicize authors' deeds of writing, taking too little account of their circumstances, aims and interests, and consequently misreading them. Other critics, even though showing more respect for an author's historical autonomy, are nevertheless just as willing as Leavis to arrogate to their own world-view an unassailable legitimacy. Either way, the disparate sitedness of writing and reading, and the corresponding bi-dimensionality of literature's ethical uglinesses and beauties, escape notice.

John Hillis Miller, it is true, does describe the ethics of reading as twofold: there are the acts which a reading might lead somebody to perform, as when a literature teacher talks about a book to a class; and there is a sense of responsibility towards the text, such that one cannot interpret it simply as one pleases, not even if, like Miller himself, one has been a champion of deconstruction. This second dimension of reading ethics sounds reassuring, until Miller launches an attack on "the attempt to explain works of literature by their political, social, and historical contexts" (Miller 1987: 5), an attempt which certainly must be made, I have argued, in order to be faithful them, and which does not necessarily connote a reductive historical purism. Perhaps Miller's attitude here is of a piece with his enthusiasm for a university of dissensus. If he really believes that difference is "all the way down", if he simply cannot envisage a dialogue across lines of sociohistorical division at all, then his reluctance to work for it is perfectly understandable. His own criticism, I need hardly say, is never less than thought-provoking, and in practice often belies his theory by its well informed sensitivity to the contexts in which authors have written. Like anybody else, however, he does not have the whole of history at his fingertips. So given that his theory does not goad him into doing his historical homework, his interpretations are occasionally rather improbable, revealing less about the historical authors ostensibly under inspection than about the twentieth century milieu within which Miller is reading them.

In the case of Trollope, for instance, he falls into a vulgar Freudianism reminiscent of the 1930s. Trollope, he says, experienced the act of writing as decidedly sexual. For him, it was a matter of impregnating himself with characters by means of a pen, described by Miller as "a cylindrical object from which a liquid flows". Trollope, within himself, played "the role of both male and female, going it alone, as they say" (Miller 1987: 94–5).

Having read Miller's comments here, it may be difficult to forget them while reading the passage adduced from Trollope. But there are two problems. First, Miller's reading is rather obviously his own imposition. In Trollope's text, the pen actually figures in between two metaphors, to the first of which Miller has chosen to annex it:

> I have been impregnated with my own creations till it has been my only excitement to sit with the pen in my hand, and drive my team before me at as quick a pace as I could make them travel.

Although Miller could just as easily have linked the pen to the second metaphor, as a kind of whip, he could also have taken it as simply a pen, and could have read the juxtaposition of metaphors as an infelicity not deserving comment. Secondly, the reading Miller does go in for is almost certainly anachronistic, and in the simplest sense. In a footnote, he quotes from the following passage in Freud's 1926 paper on "Inhibitions, Symptoms and Anxiety", which has influenced him:

> As soon as writing, which entails making a liquid flow out of a tube on to a piece of white paper, assumes the significance of copulation, or as soon as walking becomes a symbolic substitute for treading on mother earth, both writing and walking are stopped because they represent the performance of a forbidden sexual act.
> (Freud 1979 [1926]: 240)

But presumably the writerly inhibition did not become at all common until after 1884, when Lewis Edson Waterman perfected the technology of the fountain pen, the implement clearly at issue in both Freud and Miller. For Trollope, who wrote the passage Miller quotes in 1875–6, a pen was probably either a quill, a steel pen, or a slip pen, whose structure and mode of operation were even less penis-like than a fountain pen's. Even though Trollope could indeed have been thinking of a rudimentary fountain pen, the chance of this was small enough to make Miller, if he had looked into it, at least think twice about his speculation here.

Wayne C. Booth (1988: 9–10) complains that Miller's a-historicism makes him ultimately insensitive to literature's sheer variety of ethical impact. According to Booth's own ethics of fiction, every literary text offers its own particular kind of confrontation, and authors are genuinely our companions, whom we choose for their distinctive qualities. This view of the matter is consistently endorsed by Booth's detailed critical commentaries, in which his author-companions are allowed to speak with their own voice, and from within their own time and place. The only problems arise from Booth's own response to them, which takes the form of a judgement on their morals, as viewed by a person of Booth's own situationality and temperament.

The less serious issue here is a matter of tone. Booth quotes C.S. Lewis to the effect that, for F.R. Leavis, literary works were "so many lamp-posts for a dog" (Booth 1988: 50). Booth's attempts to seem less promiscuously incontinent of censure are somewhat comical. He chastises his author-companions more in sorrow than in anger, tut-tutting in the most affable tones, and demonstratively awarding brownie points wherever possible.

The deeper problem is that some of his verdicts, which not even his extreme deference can disguise, actually seem irrelevant. Discussing Rabelais from a feminist point of view, for instance, he unsurprisingly detects signs of what we now call sexism, which occasions one of his gentle rebukes (Booth 1988: 383–418). But why any rebuke at all? Obviously it is important to see Rabelais for what he was. But we can hardly reform him now, any more than Rabelais can now corrupt alertly intelligent new readers. A companion as sexist as Rabelais could not escape censure today. But how shall we ourselves be judged five hundred years from now? However much Booth tries to rein in his judgementalism, he is sometimes simply unprepared to let his authors be themselves. In such cases, what he finds hardest to accept is their flesh-and-blood refusal to transform themselves into implied authors deserving homage and veneration. What he would really like is for them to be at least as holy as himself, and preferably more so. Hermeneutically, his reprimands can only result in an imbalance. The dialogicality of true reading breaks down, because the one question he never asks is: "How would Rabelais and these other gifted delinquents take to *me*?"

For a firmer grasp of the bi-dimensionality of artistic ethics we can go back to one of the most passionate and explicit protests against the grip of Kantian aesthetics: John Dewey's *Art and Experience* (1934). This is a high-minded and energetic contribution to that tradition of American pragmatism of which New Critics took so little notice. Richard Shusterman (1992: 3–6) has pointed out its corresponding neglect by the period's analytic philosophers, whose aesthetics also tended to fall within the then dominant paradigm of a-historical de-humanization.

Dewey begins with what he sees as the aesthetically integrated society of ancient Greece, in which good acts were unhesitatingly described as beautiful (*kalon-agathon*), and in which the arts were so integrally a part of the ethos and institutions of the community that the idea of art for art's sake would have been incomprehensible. The art critics of later times, he complains, have come to focus too much on the perfection of the work of art in itself, so isolating it from "the human conditions under which it was brought into being and from the human consequences it engenders in actual life-experience". Criticism has thus built a wall around artworks which "renders almost opaque their general significance" (Dewey 1934: 3). This is not to say that the human relevance of the arts can be captured by preachy moralizing. That would be to ignore "the collective civilization that is the context in which works of art are produced and enjoyed" (Dewey 1934: 346). Art positively resists dogma, by keeping alive the sense of "purposes that outrun evidence and of meanings that transcend indurated habit" (Dewey 1934: 348). With a nod towards Shelley's "The Defence of Poetry", Dewey continues:

> The first intimations of wide and large redirections of desire and purpose are necessarily imaginative. Art is a mode of prediction not found in charts and statistics, and it insinuates possibilities of human relations not to be found in

> rule and precept, admonition and administration.
> (Dewey 1934: 349)

In order to take account of this, the philosophy of the fine arts ought to

> restore continuity between the refined and intensified forms of experience that are works of art and the everyday events, doings, and sufferings that are universally recognized to constitute experience.
> (Dewey 1934: 3)

In Dewey's view, this need arises for macro-economic reasons: art museums, the means by which art is separated from ordinary life, are a result of capitalism; and the international market now cuts art off from roots in local patronage. But these harmful separations also have their ideological defences, the seminal text being Kant's exposition of aesthetics in his *Critique of Judgement*. Dewey does not mince words:

> Kant was a past-master in first drawing distinctions and then erecting them into compartmental divisions. The effect upon subsequent theory was to give the separation of the esthetic from other modes of experience an alleged scientific basis in the constitution of human nature. Kant had referred knowledge to one division of our nature, the faculty of understanding working in conjunction with sense-materials. He had referred ordinary conduct, as prudential, to desire which has pleasure for its object, and moral conduct to the Pure Reason operating as a demand upon Pure Will*.

The asterisk cues in a pungently chauvinistic footnote: "The effect upon German thought of Capitalization [*sic*] has hardly received proper attention". The main-text diatribe then continues:

> Having disposed of Truth and the Good, it remained [for Kant] to find a niche for Beauty, the remaining term in the classic trio. Pure Feeling remained, being "pure" in the sense of being isolated and self-enclosed; feeling free from any taint of desire; feeling that strictly speaking is non-empirical. So he bethought himself of a faculty of Judgment which is not reflective but intuitive and yet not concerned with objects of Pure Reason. This faculty is exercised in Contemplation, and the distinctively esthetic element is the pleasure which attends such Contemplation. Thus the psychological road was opened leading to the ivory tower of "Beauty" remote from all desire, action, emotion.

What Dewey most dislikes about this doctrine is that it overlooks

> the doing and making involved in the production of a work of art (and the corresponding active elements in the appreciative response).

It reduces perception to a mere act of recognition: a "thoroughly anaemic conception of art" which excludes most architecture, drama and the novel (Dewey 1934: 252–4).

In marked contrast with the present-centred ethical aesthetics of Leavis, Miller and Booth, Dewey has a strong sense of artistic activity as a dynamic interaction with its own time and place. Several of his formulations — for instance, "the human conditions under which ... [art] was brought into being and ... the human consequences it engenders in actual life-experience" — represent the work of art as a kind of gesture or product which at one and the same time arises out of particular circumstances and, in and of itself, actually alters that status quo. In effect he sees a co-adaptivity of art and context which does much to undermine the distinction between them.

In this he anticipates more recent anthropological pragmaticists, whose discussion of artistic speech and narrative is another explicit rejection of the Kantian paradigm (Briggs 1988). Such scholars have shown how a wide range of genres — myths, folktales, epics, trickster tales, exhortations, Supreme Court opinions, and the narratives of litigants and legal professionals — are not only styled and structured according to their particular context of use, but also negotiate and even change that context. Whereas a sociologist such as Pierre Bourdieu thinks in terms of a deterministic structuralism, so tending to presuppose relatively fixed relationships between social configurations and language use, anthropologists now often see language use, and especially story-telling, as placing social reality under scrutiny. The narrative involved in processes of litigation, for instance, reconstructs reality in the courtroom (Bennett and Feldman 1981).

Geoffrey Hill, too, though by no means blind to formal beauty, in effect lays stress on interactional co-adaptation. As he sees things, authors can never be totally disconnected from the world they live in, and they can certainly do their bit to re-shape it, even if this can only be assessed from a later point in time. The writers he discusses were, if not entirely *of* the world, at least very self-consciously *in* it. They were for ever battling to retain their integrity, but sharply aware that positive offensiveness would reduce their impact. The group is mainly seventeenth-century — Donne, Hobbes, Wotton, Walton, and above all Dryden — , and Hill's account of their predicament often draws on seventeenth-century phraseology:

> Good writing is a contributor to "Civil Conversation", yet at the same time it is not; it "travails through the Enemy's country" along the paths of civil

conversation and "the common Track of Business, which is not always clean".
(Hill 1991 :80)

Essentially, though, Hill sees "Enemy's country" as the terrain of all true writers, whose force is parried by strategems which vary little from one century to another. So one poem which, for Hill, plays into enemy hands is "Envoi (1919)". Weighed down by lyrical cliché, Pound's integrity here dwindles to a sincerity that is ephemeral and solipsistic.

Resisting, as always, extreme formalist theory, Hill sees poetry as a type of communication between real people in real circumstances. Here he can draw on a specialist historian's knowledge of the precise compromises by which each of his chosen writers was tempted, and the author of *Mercian Hymns* and *Tenebrae* also has a sense, not only of the power of particular words to lead us astray in particular ways under particular circumstances, but of the control by which they can nevertheless be mastered. This holding-back from linguistic determinism, of great interest in view of some of the theoretical controversies I have touched on, is in line with American pragmatist semiotics, and with the emphasis on co-adaptivity and creative originality in recent anthropological pragmatics. Hill's analyses of poems in their historical contexts apprehend the field of voluntaristic human interaction with unflagging intensity. The splendid climax of his book, for instance, is an unravelling of friendly generosity and proud reservation in the text and circumstances of Dryden's "To the Memory of Mr Oldham".

One kind of beauty from history, then, involves an interplay between frank integrity and well judged politeness. It combines honest intelligence with tact and decorum. That an artistic elegance can communicate such a genuinely ethical vibration is something of which Dewey, too, is fully aware, even if Richard Shusterman's otherwise excellent commentary somewhat overlooks this. Shusterman, having argued that traditional rationalist aesthetics have tended to privilege firm external art-forms, finally claims that the great value of Dewey's treatise is in helping us to see the "dynamic and experiential in *bodily* aesthetics" (my italics). Better balanced breathing and good posture; greater kinesthetic harmony; increased somatic consciousness: all this, says Shusterman, can enhance our awareness of felt experience. Yet the connection he suggests with the ethical is hardly very direct: bodily aesthetics helps "transform the self emotionally, cognitively, and ethically by instilling greater psychological balance, perceptual receptivity, and open, patient tolerance" (Shusterman 1992: 261). As Shusterman himself so disarmingly says, his idea can actually seem a bit New Age. Or as Raymond Tallis (1997) might complain, it bears all the marks of an academic culture which, by bracketing off consciousness, intellectuality and responsibility, reduces the human to the animal. To Henry Fielding, similarly, bodily aesthetics would have sounded like a job description for gentlemen dancing-masters, who taught a graceful ease of bearing which, though he himself found its absence unattractive, could all too readily conceal a moral foulness. Though doubtless to Shusterman's own regret, his remarks might easily become the justification of readers who, without even noticing the anti-Semitism, surrender to *The Cantos* for their rhythm. Hill, by contrast, is writing in the same tradition of commentary as Donald Davie (1967 [1952]), with his sense of pure diction as an appropriateness to circumstances that is both stylistic and moral. And although, like Leavis, both Hill and Davie speak of form and ethics as interwoven with each other, *un*like Leavis they are consistently aware of literary writing as historically situated action. Correspondingly, their assessment of its ethical beauty is more concrete, and much more modest in its own claims to legitimacy. The original context of writing and the current context of reading are in communicative parity.

Hill and Davie's type of demonstration is still a necessary corrective to Modernist aesthetics. Most of the literary criticism and theory produced since the heyday of New Criticism has not been interested in beauty at all, let alone in a beauty from history. Myth criticism and psychoanalytic criticism dealt with timeless universalities, and so, in various ways, did Jakobsonian structuralist poetics and narratology. Deconstruction would have dwelt on the element of nominalism in beauty. Anything so much in the eye of the beholder will always be partly a matter of wording. As for Marxist structuralism, feminist sociological criticism, cultural materialism, gay and lesbian criticism, postcolonial criticism and ethnic criticism, these movements, though all concerned with history, would tend to reject talk of beauty as one or another kind of ideological imposition. To some extent the same applies for new historicism as well. Although Stephen Greenblatt has a sense of both historical resonance and aesthetic wonder, some of his colleagues would accuse him of liberal self-deception.

Now on Hill's account, the communal and the exceptional enter into a creative tension. Literature's beauties from history come across as co-adaptations in which both aspects of the social individual respond to each other. Seen this way, literary works can exemplify the potentiality for change: change within the self, and change to society at large. Even a profoundly disturbing text may also be inspiring and eclectically life-affirming, thanks to its writer's having made an impressive effort of co-adaptation in the first place.

But such exemplary force would never carry across to readers unless writers had faith: the sheer faith to write; faith in their own co-adaptive grapplings with circumstance; faith in readers; faith in the final outcome of the communication. Here as always, literary pragmatics is continuous with communicative pragmatics in general. The kind of faith involved is the same as for interchanges of many other kinds. To use a rhyme-pair in which English poets once found a pregnant antithesis, words are far better than swords. As long as people go on exchanging words, there is still a chance that problems will be solved. Even a bitter pessimist, by going public, may be challenging others to steel themselves to endurance, or perhaps even to turn over a new leaf. At the very least, and irrespective of any conscious intention, a publishing pessimist is inviting the kind of qualification I have already offered to Foucault's account of social discourse and to John Hillis Miller's proposal for a university of dissensus. The pessimism which still makes itself heard is simply not pessimism of the darkest dye imaginable. And as if to corroborate this, in even the grimmest of literary texts the tragedy is seldom unrelieved. However fitfully, however much against the odds, literature, like human intercourse in general, pulses with a hope of joy. Even when it shows human life and human nature in the bleakest possible light, it entails an assumption that life would definitely be better if joy were possible. In this way it endorses attempts to see the world as humanly meaningful, so forging a bond between people of even widely differing backgrounds and experience. As a matter of fact, then, there is a sense in which literature has already tried to do the mediating critic's job. Or rather, and to put things in their true perspective, in a society free of impediments to communicative interchange, a mediating criticism would not be needed. Without any special persuasion, readers would do themselves the favour of responding to writers' faith in them. Their approach to the spiritual meeting-place afforded by the sameness-that-is-difference of the human condition would be eager and hopeful.

Literature is not a collection of simple moral truths. But in order to give a clearer idea of writers' communicative faith and powers of inspiration, I can hardly avoid a kind of shorthand here. In a work of mediating criticism in action, the set of thumb-nail assessments I am about to offer would have to be fully substantiated, and advanced without the slightest trace of dogmatism. Leavis's "This is so, is it not?" would itself set the wrong tone: insufficiently courteous to other judges, and pre-emptive of literature's communicative reach. From a mediating critic, the invitation would be more along the lines of: "This is what I think for the moment. What do you think?" If other readers were to find the chosen authors inspiring in some other way, or to find some other choice of authors far *more* inspiring, so much the better. Writers, themselves writing in hope of a fully human response, cannot force readers into one particular human mode, but are a source of insight, energy and resilience whose implications may be wonderfully varied. This is what some of them have had a sense of when claiming to write for posterity.

A work's beauty in the here-and-now can never be exactly the same as its beauty in the there-and-then. The disparity between the context of writing and the current context of reading gets greater all the time, and one of the mediating critic's two main interests is to help new readers grasp the exemplary force of a literary deed in something approaching its historical valency. In the poetry of Eliot, we can come to see afresh the creative breaches of decorum, the bold rhetorical compromises between Modernist and Victorian (Sell 1992, 1993). Henry Vaughan and Dickens, similarly, even if some of their gestures were more uniformly respectable, can be re-apprehended as anything but tame. Vaughan's most distinctive beauty went with a certain slight unseemliness, amounting to a discoursal instability that was quietly defiant (Sell 1987), while in Dickens, a colourlessly homogenizing middle-class decorum was threatened by a garish kaleidoscope of heteroglossic difference (Sell 1986). What many critics seem to have missed is the sheer force of such interactional unexpectedness, and the creative charge of its impoliteness. As for the idea of co-opting it, as a kind of ur-Modernism of the make-it-new, this seems never to have struck them.

Nor was it as if the dynamism they were overlooking was merely internal to particular authors' own spiritual development. Far more significant was the inspiration it offered to readers, whether as a living example of sheer energy, as a wellspring of resistance or change, or as a clue to very survival as a social being. The social, indeed, was the dimension of literature which many Modernist critics disregarded most systematically, and not least in writers who were their own contemporaries. What they failed to note in Robert Frost, for instance, was a concern with class formation which was so radical as to suggest that human integrity will never be more than a kind of theatricality

(Sell 1980: 79–91). The histrionics of human individuation was something Frost understood very well. In one sense, what his poems open up to readers is a series of life-experiments.

In a historical yet non-historicist literary pragmatics, this kind of interaction between real authors and real readers is fundamental. The depersonalization entailed by extremist versions of Modernist and Barthesian commentary, by contrast, shifts agency and enunciation from flesh-and-blood authors to something quite inhuman. In literary formalism, there was the animation of texts, as if they lived lives outside of human heads. In the various literary structuralisms, the animation tended to be of that great abstraction, society, while in literary poststructuralism, even language in general seemed to become animate, as if speech had a mode of being quite separate from its users. To read exclusively in one of these modes is ethically questionable. Not to put too fine a point on it, what they all tend to condone or anticipate is the work of the grim reaper. It is less a question of the death of the author, than of the author's murder. And as for the other side of the coin, readers, too, have their privileges. They are entitled to far more freedom than was acknowledged by either literary formalism or the more recent determinisms. Rightly and inevitably, authors' intentions do become interwoven with those of the other people who read them. Nor can a reverence for authors dead and buried be allowed to legitimate a present injustice.

The siting of the current reader is increasingly distant from that of the author. So far I have been sketching the quality of writerly deeds by Eliot, Vaughan, Dickens and Frost within their own immediate worlds. That is the line a mediating critic will take in helping readers with their humanly obligatory effort of empathy. Then there is the other dimension of reading: the moral force of an author as it continues to radiate down through time, and/or across space, into our own, ever more different world. Present-centred critics such as Leavis or Miller or Booth can often do something to illuminate this. But ideally, what we seek to contemplate within our own context of reading will be a text's historically reconstructed interpersonality and co-adaptivity: the author's original deed as far as we can grasp it, and directed towards the original audience as far as we can understand it, as represented by the implied reader. The beauties pertain to qualities of action perceived as having had a value in the there-and-then, but with a continuing, albeit necessarily quite distinct applicability in the here-and-now as well. Applicability in the here-and-now is in fact the mediating critic's other main interest, developed in the knowledge that a water-tight historical or cultural purism is a hermeneutic impossibility.

Confronted as we are today, then, by the postmodern tensions between the centripetal and the centrifugal, between social fragmentation and globalization, what is it that we can take to heart from the work of earlier writers? To relapse into shorthand, in Eliot there is that unbending urge, when civilization and personal life have both fallen apart, to change things, even with disconcerting vigour, and so break through to joy. In Vaughan, we can find an astonishing and very accessible instance of a persecuted, marginalized identity which resists, recoups, and endures by making new. In Dickens, there is the diplomatic yet resolute clash between a bourgeois identity that is more narrowly centred and something more excitingly manifold: a striking example of the readiness for compromise and coexistence, in conjunction with a restless and prodigious creativity. In Frost, there is the human ability to hang on tight, to achieve identity by accepting that all identities have shifting foundations, to create an anomalous autonomy out of an endlessly flexible nonentity, embraced as infinitely preferable to death.

As a reader reads literature of this calibre, the moral charge is so powerful that the situational disparity between the writing and the current reading can take on a special significance. The hermeneutic alignment of self and other, the movement from context of reading to context of writing and back, can alter perceptions of other and self alike. This is how the reader may undergo a kind of self-discovery through self-alienation. And as long as questions of meaning are also clearly seen as inextricably intertwined with questions of affect and ethics, this process can be described in Gadamerian terms as a merging of different horizons.

Another metaphor for human interaction, and this, too, sometimes used by Gadamer and Gadamerians, is the metaphor of ... metaphor (Weinsheimer 1991: 64–86). After all, the semantic movement between a metaphor's vehicle and tenor is not as unidirectional as often assumed. Take, for instance, the sentence,

> George is a lone wolf.

As Max Black (1962: 232) points out,

> [i]f to call a man a wolf is to put him in a special light, we must not forget that the metaphor makes the wolf seem more human than he otherwise would.

Examples can be multiplied. If a man gives his IBM Thinkpad the nickname

"Judy", it suggests a special kind of affection for it. But if his wife's name is also Judy, how will *she* feel? In Shakespeare's sonnet "Shall I compare thee to a summer's day?" such undesirable back-pressure from the vehicle onto the tenor is deliberately raised to consciousness. It is all very well to compare somebody you love to the month of May. But "[r]ough winds do shake the darling buds of May". On the one hand, Shakespeare's argument is that his loved-one is unique, and therefore beyond compare. On the other hand, this claim would never have stood up, unless the metaphor he rejects had been at least plausible. According to psycholinguists, without the help of metaphors we should never be able to organize our experience at all (Lakoff and Johnson 1980; Lakoff 1987; Lakoff and Turner 1989). Nor was Robert Frost (1949) the only poet to have intuited that metaphors are our only way of saying something new. In the end, obviously, a metaphor always breaks down, quite simply because x is never y. The loved-one always *is* unique! Yet when x and y are metaphorically juxtaposed, they certainly can become mutually illuminating. Judy's husband, poring over his laptop-Judy, may one day start to question his priorities, precisely by thinking about the name he has given it. Or in valuing our loved-one as May-like, we may suddenly be alerted to something rather rough and wind-like from his or her quarter, and — who knows? — perhaps to something rather vulnerably bud-like in ourselves. No less readily, a metaphor chosen for its derogative charge can easily flip over into a positive implication. A person whose presence "puts a damper on things" can sometimes be the right person in the right place at the right time. Other metaphors, again, will always hover between polite and impolite. Is a lone wolf resourcefully independent, or hatefully dangerous, or both?

In short, when metaphors bring x and y together, they raise possibilities, open up new perceptions, generate enquiry. One human being's encounter with another, likewise, can be experienced as placing both parties under review, and literary encounters are no exception. It is at least as much the author who reads the reader, so to speak, as the reader who reads the author. Or to switch to Frostian metaphors, readers venture forth into the unknown, the better to build soil on the home patch. What serious readers of an old or foreign text can never fail to be affected by is the continuing potentiality it will suggest for their own psychic formation. It can only make them more fully aware of all the richness and poverty of their own milieu and moment. What it offers may be the significant other.

This type of reading can also be a preparation for dealing with cultural interfaces in everyday life, and is the reading style which will be especially encouraged by mediating critics. The alternatives have little to recommend them. If readers do what so many scholars and critics have seemed to expect, if they see literature as either totally unhistorical, or as historically totally determined, they will not only forego the indescribable pleasure of interacting with literary authors. They will also be that much more likely to react in a dull, sub-human way in life at large: more likely to resist empathy, to silence dialogue, to avoid responsibility. In the final analysis, the ethical enormity will consist in their de-humanization, not only of authors but of themselves. Refusing to expand their own horizons, they will abrogate their capacity for genuinely two-way interaction. What they miss in literature will be the challenge of an abundant semiotic, affective, and ethical potential for their own future lives, and possibly a stimulus to fruitful change. If anything, by a feat of violent ventriloquism they will project the sensibility and values made fashionable by their own grouping's intelligentsia onto some quite other grouping, past or present. What results from this can only be a spiritual degradation, extending, as in cases of rape or colonization, to victims and perpetrators alike. Readers will be violating old or alien authors' words, and with nothing but impoverishment to themselves and their own community.

A historical yet non-historicist literary pragmatics offers the best foundations for mediating criticism. It promotes the most positive and explicit assessment of the action at both the writer's end and the current reader's end. It also sees the disparate contexts as ultimately bridgeable, and can envisage personal and social change as a real possibility. Such change can take place by virtue of human beings' power of imagination, their capacity for co-adaptation, and the reciprocal trust which underlies all real attempts at communication.

One last point. Although this chapter's examples have tended to work on the diachronic axis, to have a particular past is to have a particular present, and *vice versa*. When critics put together their historical canons, they are expressing a sense of their own community's difference now. But if they appreciate the beauties of literary deeds belonging to the more distant phases of their own tradition, then their response to other communities in the present is more likely to be in a spirit of positive mediation. Already appreciating the inspiration that can flow from otherness, they will be that much less distracted by dissensus, pessimism and blame, yet without slipping into the more disingenuous forms of political correctness. All these postmodern stalemates involve a life-impairing blindness to beauty from history, because their ethics is too one-dimensional.

Chapter 6

Mediating Criticism

6.1. The theory for the practice

Given the need in postmodern societies for a mediating criticism, I have been trying to supply the necessary theoretical foundations. These I have sought in a historical yet non-historicist literary pragmatics that is continuous with the pragmatics of communication in general. The argument has not been entirely straightforward, since the field of general communicative pragmatics is itself still being explored. Some of the most important claims I have advanced are:

that a communicative situation is basically triangular;

that in both literary and non-literary communication, the things or people under discussion can just as easily be hypothetical or fictional as real;

that fictionality makes communication no less genuinely interactive, not least because specific or episodic *non*-truth can implicate general or moral *truth*;

that when communication is indeed taking place, a human parity obtains between the sender and the current receiver, even when the sender is absent or actually dead;

that this is especially so in a tradition of literate communication, with its back-up in the form of reasonably reliable historical and philological knowledge;

that except in connection with an oral tradition, to speak of an impersonal use of language is problematic;

that there is inevitably a disparity between the contexts which different communicants bring to bear, even when they are co-present members of a single community;

that human beings are paradoxically social individuals, partly determined by their own situationality, but also imaginatively, intellectually, emotionally, morally and temperamentally capable of distancing themselves from it, and capable of co-adaptations between the social and the individual;

that communicative behaviour is therefore never totally predictable;

that the slotting-in points for communicants' assays of empathetic self-projection are discoursally constructed communicative personae, which are part of a larger textualization-cum-contextualization;

that communicants' mental alternation between their own and other contexts has major hermeneutic, affective and ethical consequences;

that there is actually a direct connection between communication, personal individuation and social change;

that any real attempt to participate in the give and take of communication builds on good faith and the hope of fellowship;

and that even from the outset, communication therefore tends to make the world a better place.

When developed along these lines, a communicative pragmatics does seem to redress what, for a mediating critic, are the most serious shortcomings in earlier and current theories of a more specifically literary orientation.

The considerable merits of formalist and formalist-behaviouristic theories of literature, for instance, did not include a sense of its interpersonal valency, nor of its rootedness in all the sociocultural differences of history. Even speech act theoreticians of literature, and even some literary pragmaticists, have spoken as if literature was not really of this world, and as if all its writers and all its readers were of exactly the same formation, a universalization also evident in several other kinds of approach, ranging from myth criticism and Freudian criticism to more straightforwardly evaluative criticism. So long as literature is viewed in this way, the need for a criticism which would mediate between different communal groupings can never be even recognized.

The theory proposed here, by contrast, is in descent from the de-essentializing poetics of Reichart and others in the late 1970s and early 1980s, and from the pragmaticists who are developing explicitly historical and anthropological interests. It firmly stresses not only literature's interpersonal valency across time and space, but the full implications of that disparity between the context of writing and a context of current reading. In other words, it can envisage that the need for mediation between different groupings may indeed arise.

In point of fact, history has already been brought back into literary studies through the efforts of Barthesian commentators, in work which valuably suggests the human being's malleable involvement in the intertextualities of society, culture and language. The difficulty, though, is that there have been versions of post-Marxist, new historicist, cultural materialist, feminist, gay and lesbian, postcolonial, and ethnic criticism which actually *over*-correct liberal humanist assumptions about personal autonomy, so ending up as a pessimistic determinism. This tends to suggest that difference is all the way down, such that people of dissimilar situationalities cannot communicate at all, or can engage only in recriminatory slanging matches. According to some scholars, the interpretation of literary authors is a kind of free-for-all in which the decisive factor is the current reader's own political self-interest, and in which considerations of historical and philological accuracy have as little scope as within purely oral cultures. Other commentators, while believing no less strongly in the insuperability of sociohistorical divisions, try to minimize cultural conflicts, by way of an insincere political correctness which prevents any real give and take at all. To very many present-day commentators, then, a frank yet conciliatory mediating criticism would seem either theoretically impossible or socially inadvisable.

Once again, the contribution of a historical yet non-historicist literary pragmatics is distinctive. It does *not* confine writers or readers to some single communal formation. Human beings, though far more implicated in their cultures and societies than recognized in extreme versions of liberal humanism, are nevertheless individuals, endowed with at least a relative autonomy of choice and temperament, and with that amazing versatility of empathetic imagination. This means that communication between different situationalities is most certainly possible. Given, too, that a reader's self-projection into the communicative relationships proposed by a literary text involves the same mental effort as is required for any other kind of communication, and given that such heuristic dialogicality is indistinguishable from the very process of human individuation, the experience of literature can even result in significant self-reassessment and self-development, which may ultimately entail a change to society as well.

On such a view, and especially when full account is taken of its typological, hermeneutic, affective and ethical consequences, mediating critics stand a real chance of bringing different readerships into reasonable negotiation and new relationships. For the reasons mentioned by Heraclitus and Stuart Hampshire, a complete consensus is neither possible nor desirable. But mediating criticism's openness of interpretative exploration will be of immense value, and so will its endorsement of agreements to disagree. Even cases of downright offensiveness can be openly discussed, in the knowledge that impressions of the politeness of literary texts in any case change over time, and in ways which can perhaps be understood and speeded up.

As the theory makes very clear, what critics specially need to draw on are all those kinds of philological, literary-historical, general-historical, and even biographical information which can serve to bridge the gap between the current context of reading and the context of writing. Another aim must be to awake a sensitivity to writers' communicative faith in their readers' human receptivity, a faith which in a more perfect world would itself be enough to bring readers of different backgrounds so powerfully together as to make mediating criticism redundant. Above all, perhaps, there needs to be a sense of literature's bi-dimensional ethics: of its moral force both in the there-and-then and in the here-and-now. This will allow us to speak of a work's historical beauty or ugliness, and of its continuing though necessarily changing power of inspiration. The ratio between its potential stimulus to the current reader and the sociocultural distance from the context of writing to the current context of reading is directly proportional. In plainer language, a writer very like ourselves can be surprisingly boring! A mediating criticism based on a historical yet non-historicist pragmatics, by bringing this kind of thing home to us, can prepare us for what may be a very radical challenge.

So much for theory. As I explained at the outset, extended examples of mediating criticism in practice will be found in another book I am hoping to complete. All that remains here is to speculate on the circumstances under which future mediating critics will have to be operating, and to clarify one or two points about general strategies, with particular reference to the postmodern crisis with which I began in the Introduction.

6.2. Trajectories of mediation

Mediating critics will in no small part be helping readers to empathize with writings experienced as in some way distant and "other". In this they will basically be practising a sort of ethnography. When ethnographers report on the fieldwork they have carried out within an exotic culture, they are making it easier for members of their own culture to understand it.

Yet to assume that writers and readers are thoroughly representative of their own particular communities at a particular time, and that the need for mediation arises only between one such community and another, would be to oversimplify. A historical yet non-historicist pragmatics stresses, rather, that human identity is a paradoxical blend of the social and the individual, such that the two dimensions can enter into co-adaptations with each other. Such a co-adaptation may itself be seen as an instance of mediation that is not so much inter-communal as *intra*-communal. Although communities are partly definable by their differences from other communities, they have differences within themselves as well. Hence K. Anthony Appiah's slight discomfort at being grouped as a gay black. "If I had to choose between the world of the closet and the world of gay liberation, or between the world of *Uncle Tom's Cabin* and Black Power, I would, of course, choose in each case the latter. But I would like not to have to choose" (Appiah 1994: 163). Appiah is not complaining about being on collision course with an American stereotype of white heterosexuality. He is hinting that even "deviant" groupings are sometimes limiting, and further decomposable.

This means that, in addition to ethnographical commentary, a mediating critic may also have another kind of task: to deal with relationships between a community, or even a sub-community, and its own members, especially those of them who are unusual. By way of mnemonics, we could perhaps compare this to the job of a talent scout. The critic seeks to identify individuals who are in some way out of the ordinary, and to promote appreciation of them.

In principle, then, we could say that mediating criticism has three possible trajectories. When critics write about a community's contemporary texts for the benefit of readers belonging to that same community, they will clearly be more talent scout than ethnographer. The aim is to help the community recognize the growth points of valuable co-adaptations with its current norms. As regards the community's canon of historical texts, secondly, a rather different aim arises. Here there are the different phases of the cultural tradition to be negotiated, which commits the critic to an ethnographical role, in order to help the community relate to its own alien past. This diachronic kind of axis has applied to most of the literary examples discussed in the previous chapters. Finally, there is ethnographic mediation between the different cultures and sub-cultures co-existing within a single present. The need for this in the postmodern societies of our own time was this book's starting point. For many critics, it is likely to seem the most urgent task of all.

In practice, however, such demarcations may be rather too tidy. The distinction between synchronic inter- and diachronic intra-cultural approaches cannot be drawn very sharply, since two communities will never fully understand each other unless they grasp their own and each other's history. As for ethnography *versus* talent-scouting, here, too, there can be a complementarity. Those members of a community who are unusual are the ones most likely to contribute to its understanding of other communities. Conversely, when a community comes to a better understanding of other communities, it can more easily understand its own more unusual members. It is the dual concern to mediate both the social and the individual which makes mediating critics so alert to creative co-adaptations between the two.

6.3. Inside and outside

Regardless of their more particular trajectory, what mediating critics will seek to cultivate is readers' ordinary flexibility of mental projection: in particular, an oscillation between situationally differentiated ways of seeing one and the same thing. Every kind of scholarly and critical perspective on literature, including literary history, can be thought of as an intellectual activity taking place "outside" of readers' spontaneous "inside" experience of literature within their current context of reading. A mediating commentary, by simultaneously enlarging on both a work's context of writing and the context in which it is currently being read, will seek to heighten readers' self-consciousness as to whatever kind of spontaneity is for the moment coming most naturally to them. In so doing, it may also help them to see how their understanding can be broadened, so that their future spontaneities will perhaps be better informed and more complex.

The interrelation of various situationalities involves some curious paradoxes. A scholarly perspective from the "outside" has to *know* a reader's spontaneous "inside" experience, simply in order to target it for educational efforts in the first place. An "inside", in turn, though it can only be known from the inside, cannot become self-conscious except in opposition to something it is not: to an "outside". Then as I say, the whole point of the exercise is that the scholar's "outside" should become part of the human world within which literature is experienced spontaneously, so that the orbits of knowledgeable "outside" and experiential "inside" come closer together.

As in any field of interest whatever, a scholarly way of seeing things can indeed become an ordinary way of seeing things. Scholarly terminology can catch on in common speech — a phenomenon discussed by Richard Rorty and Thomas Kuhn, both of them in scholarly terminologies of their own, which are already becoming common speech. To take a literary example, we nowadays feel in our bones that Wordsworth and Keats are Romantic poets, even though that literary historical label was not yet available to Wordsworth and Keats themselves or to their first readers. In the course of time, not only can a scholarly "outside" and a readerly "inside" become one and the same like this. They can even swop places, as when some of the common feelings and perceptions of people who lived during an earlier period, for instance the ways of reading engaged in by Wordsworth and Keats or their first readers, are knowable to us only through scholarly reconstruction.

Yet the relationship between "inside" spontaneous experience and "outside" scholarly perspective can also go awry. What it requires of the critic is a certain psychological realism. Particularly in the twentieth century, the difference between real reading and what is sometimes called a *critical reading* has often been considerable. Between published commentaries on literature and non-scholarly readers' actual experience of it there have even been radical discontinuities. Not that criticism could ever become the same thing as an instant off-the-cuff response. When presented for discussion in the public domain, criticism is of a piece with serious thought on any other important or interesting topic. It is part of a larger effort to describe stabilities and changes within the worlds of nature and society, and to frame human ways of relating to it all. In the form of literary criticism, however, such thought has often ended up as descriptions, explications, and evaluations of literature which are somewhat too scholastic. Especially within institutions of learning and education, critical activity has taken place under the pressure of some very firmly established genre expectations, which critics have sometimes satisfied too unresistingly and one-track-mindedly.

Twentieth-century criticism's devaluation of literature's human dimension was actually twofold. In addition to the de-personalizing dogmas and reading habits promoted within both behaviouristic-formalist and some Barthesian commentary, there was this element of rationalization under certain very specific institutional and professional circumstances. As a result, critical writing became a form of pseudo-communication, produced in vast quantities, and actually read by very few people indeed.

More literary criticism was produced during the twentieth century than ever before, as practical criticism became a central pedagogical technique in secondary and higher education, with thousands and thousands of teachers having to qualify for tenure and promotion by writing more and more of the same. In terms of quality, the results were predictable. In the mid-1990s I compiled a Macmillan New Casebook on *Great Expectations*, re-printing criticism published in the previous two or three decades. My view of the ocean of critical articles and books — hundreds and hundreds of them — into which I was casting my net became occupationally jaundiced. Still, if I were to say there is little worth reading on Dickens since Edmund Wilson's "Dickens: the Two Scrooges" (1941), the spirit, if not the letter of my exaggeration would probably be widely understood. In its institutionalized form, literary criticism was simply unable to guarantee fidelity to the facts of real reading, and "critical readings" and "interpretations" were churned out as a matter of rote. Not that run-of-the-mill literary criticism was anything new *per se*. There had long been a place for it, since it is only through the repetition of familiar mental motions that ideological involvements can actually be expressed and sustained. The trouble was that literary critical observances became as widespread, officially organized and routine as political or religious ones, at the risk of becoming just as impersonal and uncompelling. Forgiveably, therefore, would-be star performers began to strive for originality at all costs, some of them, as we have seen, by coming up with new, improved explanations of why newness is impossible, some of them, indeed, by seeing literature as the humble egg to Theory's (*sic*) glorious chicken. These and various other concerns provided a welcome and increasingly fashionable relief from the ever more uninspiring discussion of actual literary texts. But with academic criticism veering in this way from the utterly boring to mere self-display or pure abstraction; with access to higher education becoming wider and wider still; with Western culture entering a new (or returning to an ancient) mode of orality and visuality, in which literary pursuits have lost some of their interest and prestige: with all this, by the late 1970s literary criticism no longer seemed nearly as important an activity as it had done during the age of Leavis's *Scrutiny*. A decade or so further on, Bernard Bergonzi (1990), himself a very fine critic, was expecting it to disappear from universities almost completely, its place being taken by cultural studies. By the year 2010, the genre could well be back where it was in the nineteenth century: written and read, in much more modest amounts, by people with no particular involvement in education.

The future of literary criticism is bound up with the future of literature itself, a topic which I must soon discuss. But much also depends on whether critics can maintain an appropriate balance of outside and inside.

On the one hand, they do have a responsibility to extend the reader's mental horizons by means of "outside" scholarly perspectives. That literary critics have often had ideas about literature which would not have occurred to most other readers while actually reading is as it should be. If literary scholarship aspires to be continuous with other important and interesting thought, it has to talk about literature from some point of view in order to perceive the larger bearings, thereby frankly placing itself outside of conventional literary experience. Senior critics such as Frank Kermode (1990 [1989]) and Harold Bloom (1995 [1994]) have reprimanded recent trends in literary scholarship for introducing concerns which are actually irrelevant to literature as literature. Their complaints have much force and, as cannot be repeated too often, a literary scholar who has no inside experience of literature is incapable of constituting it as a topic for discussion in the first place. All the same, not even Kermode and Bloom themselves have written from within a view of literature as already generally experienced. On the contrary, some of the outside perspectives they have brought to bear at first seemed pretty odd to other readers. Can those of us who were alive and reading at the time even remember our first reaction to concepts such as "the sense of an ending" or "the anxiety of influence"? Thanks to the work of these two great scholars, new outside perspectives have gradually become part of the thought-world within which readers deal with writers *prima vista*. The conclusion to be drawn is clear enough: no new perspective can be rejected without fair trial.

On the other hand, a reader's spontaneous "inside" experience of literature can be self-contradictory and untidy, and critics need to bear this in mind. There is no point in their aiming at a definitive interpretation, since any such single-mindedness is only one phase in the real processing of a text, as also in subsequent memories and re-processing. Thanks to the arbitrary and ultimately unstable relationship between the linguistic sign's signified and signifier, a definitive reading is a contradiction in terms, which is why the list of them gets longer all the time. More particularly, a historically or culturally puristic fidelity to an author's intention, though it could understandably be thought of as an essential aim in reading, is in reality never possible. Pragmatics, we have seen, is always bi-dimensional, with the empathetic movement into the context of sending inevitably complemented by the accommodation to the current context of receiving. More generally, any sort of rigid explication soon breaks down. The undogmatic way people actually assimilate literature into their lives; the pulsing alternation between reconstruction and deconstruction; the things a reader actually values in a text, which sometimes will lend themselves to complex formal analysis but sometimes will not; the way the emphasis falls differently in different times, places, and communities: all this matters profoundly.

For any particular reader, the inside will correspond to norms and reading habits which are culturally familiar, the outside to those which are more alien. For a critic hoping to mediate between the adjacent cultures or sub-cultures of postmodern societies, this inside-outside duality will be the thing to work on. Much can be learnt from the finest criticism of the past. Some of the great exemplars, though totally opposed to each other in terms of ideological commitment, have shared the appropriate antitheticality of mind-style. The later Eliot argued for a return to a Christian society, Theodor Adorno for a secular socialism. But the later Eliot carefully distinguished between being "taken in" by a novel and a more critical reading which sees it as the production of a particular mind, just as Adorno explained that "those who have only an inside view of art do not understand it, whereas those who see art only from the outside tend to falsify for lack of affinity with it" (Eliot 1936: 104–5, Adorno 1984: 479; cf. Shusterman 1990). Adorno's formulation also recalls Eliot's distinction between a reader's poetic assent and philosophical belief, a point to which he returned in his essay on Goethe: in reading a great poem of belief, one not only identifies with the position of a believer, but detaches oneself and regards the poem from outside of belief. Identification will be the more conscious of the two processes if the belief is alien, detachment if it is familiar (Eliot 1957: 225; cf. Srivastava 1988).

Eliot's later criticism is very unlike his earlier a-historical exercises in Modernist trend-setting. It comes much closer to the mode of Warton's *Observations on the Fairy Queen of Spenser*. What he now offers is in effect a kind of mediation in the ethnographical mode, an ethnographer being somebody who, having been born and bred within culture A, attempts to go native within culture B, but then returns to culture A in order to explain culture B in such a way that it can be understood in culture A's terms.[20] This back-and-forth between empathetic immersion and objectifying distance is what a literary critic can seek to emulate, zooming in and out between perspectiveless impressionism, which is all from the inside with no outside bearings, and disengagement, which is all from the outside with no feel for the inside.

This is not to say that judgement never comes to rest. Like ordinary reading, a critical attempt at positive mediation is not the same thing as an uncritical acceptance of anything and everything. Our mental flexibility may well have limits. Mediation certainly can take a stand, and mediating criticism *is* criticism. It scrutinizes the available interpretations and evaluations, and is concerned with problems of legitimation which, though as old as human history, have become especially urgent as part of the postmodern dilemma. Claims to authority enforced by a tacit appeal to a power base are seen for what they are. So are claims whose only justification is that they are oppositional. The mediating critic's assumption is merely that human beings *can* be in more than one state of mind at a time, not that they always *must be*, which would itself be a very single-minded claim.

Equally, though, a judgement can always be reconsidered. Not even mediating criticism itself represents some absolute standard, since it does not exist in the abstract. It is a type of discussion carried out by particular human beings with particular complexes of cultural allegiance, about which they will try to be *self*-critical, imagining themselves as others see them from the outside. Though certainly prepared to weigh everything up and state an opinion, they have no Johnsonian compulsion to talk for victory. Believing that "perpetual conflicts between rival impulses and ideals" are important to "life, and liveliness, within the soul and within society" (Hampshire 1992

---

20. As Michael Moerman (1992: 23–4) says, the ethnographer lives "among some other people in order to learn their way of life, and then return to his ... own people and ... [tries] to communicate that understanding". The main goal is "to find out how the events he observes and experiences in the alien world make sense to the aliens, how their way of life coheres and has meaning for those who live it. The ethnographer's other goal is to use theory so as to understand what he has observed as an instance of a general type (such as peasant society), phenomenon (such as ritual), or process (such as modernization). But these concerns may not be the natives' concerns." Moerman also roundly mentions the danger of the ethnographer's two goals coming into conflict. Theory can get so far away from native experience that it distorts and demeans it.

[1989]: 189), they will not regard their inability to coax others into a consensus as a failure. They are much more likely to sit down and have another think. Or better still, another chat.

Having reached this far, we can perhaps return to the contrast between a strongly evaluative critic such as F.R. Leavis and a scholar such as C.S. Lewis, whose *An Experiment in Criticism* (1992 [1961]) so sharply expresses the apparent opposition between them. Huge amounts of literary theory, criticism and scholarship have been produced since the time of Leavis and Lewis, without, however, progressing beyond this tension. In reconsidering it, I have related it to issues which have emerged within the philosophical tradition represented by Gadamer. One of the most important insights arising from such an approach is rather simple: that there will *always* be a tension between, on the one hand, value judgements and, on the other hand, knowledge of society, culture and tradition, and that this tension is part of what makes for a fruitful symbiosis of the inside view with the outside. In pragmatic terms, it is a matter of that inevitable interrelationship between a somewhat self-centred contextualization in the here-and-now and an empathetic contextualization in the there-and-then. Paradoxically, the universalizing claim entailed by many critics' value judgements results from a limited perspective that is internal to a particular reading community, whereas a scholarship which minutely registers historical qualifications may represent an aspiration to a perspective that is less exclusive and far broader.

This raises the delicate question of whether a value judgement can ever actually be right, and the no less delicate question of whether historical knowledge can really ever mean anything more than *comprendre, c'est tout pardonner*. The answer suggested by the foregoing chapters would be that a value judgement is always right for the people actually making the judgement at the particular time and place, but that through the two-way process of positive mediation this same judgement can always be informed by a historical and/or cross-cultural understanding, which modifies the judges' sense of their own time, place and identity. In the light of increased understanding of both self and other, assessments can always self-adjust. Even a writer who seemed profoundly offensive can later be perceived as profoundly inspiring. This is one of the countless ways in which outside and inside can swop places.

6.4. What medium for mediation?

So mediating criticism is fundamentally a dialogue between outside and inside, a dialogue in which a last word never needs to be spoken. All its judgements, no matter how much time and thought goes into their making, are offered as provisional. Like any other sort of judgement, they may well seem either too sympathetic or too harsh, so offering a stimulus to the next round of discussion. To the critic who puts them forward, their instability is expected. Mediating criticism is not authoritarian and oracular.

We might well conclude that to cultivate the to and fro of the mediating critic's dual perspective is to turn the clock back: that it is to adopt a style of humanism a good bit older than the universalizing pronouncements of the nineteenth century, and closer to the spirit of Sir Thomas More, with his delight in the ironies and loose ends of a convivial conversation which can always be re-opened:

> ... I was not sure he could take contradiction in these matters, particularly when I recalled what he had said about certain counsellors who were afraid they might not appear knowing enough unless they found something to criticise in other men's ideas. So with praise for the Utopian way of life and his account of it, I took him by the hand and led him in to supper. But first I said that we would find some other time for thinking of these matters more deeply, and for talking them over in more detail. And I still hope such an opportunity will present itself some day.
> (More 1989 [1516]:110)

Could it be, then, that mediation, in order to be credible and profitable, will have to be conducted in a medium through which dialogicality is positively enhanced? More particularly, does open-ended dialogicality stand a better chance within the new (or new-old) orality and visuality of postmodern culture than within a culture that is more exclusively literate? One reason for the rhetoric of blame so characteristic of the present-day culture wars could perhaps be that critics still too willingly allow their bile to coagulate on the printed page. Subjected to the sanity-inducing warmth of more informal and ephemeral interchanges, it might evaporate. Scholars based in universities have always had opportunities to discuss their ideas face to face with students and colleagues. But nowadays they can also use the Internet to transmit written work in a more provisional form than that of traditional publication, and to a vast number of potential dialogue partners all over the world. As a seedbed for mediating criticism, this surely has a lot to be said for it.

Yet to dispense with printed books would probably be unwise, even though to write one can be a lonely task, carried out in the silence of scholarly libraries, and in front of a personal computer in non-interactive mode. Such circumstances are in themselves decidedly unconducive to positive mediation, and the critic's inevitable failures of balance between outside and inside, between context of writing and context of reading, will seem all the more glaring because of the book format itself, with its suggestion of definitiveness. But even Barthes, Hawkes and Drakakis, scholars whose personal brand of utopianism tends to privilege orality as the solvent in which elitist privilege would decompose, are very distinctively writers, whose published advocacy of their arguments enormously facilitates a reasonable discussion of them. And since power and hate do arm themselves with print, print, as Barthes, especially, has also shown, is a very good weapon to use in reply.

Quite simply, published books continue to attract a particular kind of attention. Not only do they refuse to go away. The response they invite is very much in accordance with the most widely acceptable protocols for rational argument. For a message of change, especially in areas where patterns of power are most deeply ingrained, they are arguably the best bet.

6.5. Dealing with conflict

A mediating critic does sees power everywhere, and also power's anomalies. Contemplating the postmodern tension of centrifugal and centripetal, we do not need to be as paranoiac as Foucault to sense that it is for real. Given the economic, political and technological clout of certain countries, of the United States especially, and given the globalization of communications, there was always going to be a likelihood of some sort of cultural imperialism. At the same time, we might also wonder whether the country now most likely to be culturally imperialistic is not also the one most self-consciously taken up with cultural fragmentation. "American literature", for instance, is one of the categories now under strongest challenge in American universities (Jay 1997). America, it begins to seem, may rule the world, but does not rule America. In any holistic sense, America does not exist, and American diversity, together with *theories* of American diversity, are steadily becoming a staple cultural export.

Sometimes the centripetal and the centrifugal may seem to be in balance, with things running along quite nicely. Perhaps Salman Rushdie has had this impression, for what he detects, at both the personal micro- and the national macro-level, is a kind of manifold oneness:

> In the modern age, we have come to understand our own selves as composites, often contradictory, even internally incompatible. We have understood that each of us is many different people. Our younger selves differ from our older selves; we can be bold in the company of our lovers and timorous before our employers, principled when we instruct our children and corrupt when offered some secret temptation; we are serious and frivolous, loud and quiet, aggressive and easily abashed. The nineteenth-century concept of the integrated self has been replaced by this jostling crowd of I's. And yet, unless we are damaged, or deranged, we usually have a relatively clear sense of who we are. I agree with my many selves to call all of them "me".
> This is the best way to grasp the idea of India. The country has taken the modern view of the self and enlarged it to encompass almost one billion souls. The selfhood of India is so capacious, so elastic, that it accommodates one billion kinds of difference. It agrees with its billion selves to call all of them "Indian". This is a notion far more original than the old pluralist ideas of a melting pot or a cultural mosaic. It works because the individual sees his own nature writ large in the nature of the state. This is why Indians feel so comfortable about the strength of the national idea, why it's so easy to "belong" to it ...
> (Rushdie 1997)

So be it. And by never actually giving a full response to people from a cultural grouping different from our own, we can at least muddle along without too much open conflict. Gerald Graff (1992) has noted that in American university English departments, for instance, several different literary canons are taught in parallel, and taken to be simply incommensurate. The working assumption is that everything will be just fine, as long as none of them gets a disproportionate share of classroom hours or funding. Students can form their own opinions, if they really must.

Or are things quite so simple? The situation Graff describes is actually an institutionalization of insincere political correctness. It represses the normal workings of interpersonal pragmatics, with the risk that, when conflicts do emerge into the open, there will be no well-cultivated habit of mediation to fall back on. The more natural thing will be to fall to blows.

That conflicts erupt should not surprise us. Rushdie's optimism, for which we are eternally in his debt, is the more admirable for his own, his family's and his country's sufferings: his own life has been seriously threatened because his secularism proved offensive to a religious grouping; his family was split by Partition; and India as a whole has still not recovered from that colossal tragedy, caused by, and further fuelling, religious conflict. Gerald Graff, for his part, is by no means as *laissez-faire* as the departmental practices he comments on. He refuses to pretend that latent conflicts just dissolve. Conflicts have to be taught.

Graff's plea for understanding is close to what I mean by positive mediation. One of my own suggestions has been that a teacher's first step can be to draw on conflicts lying very close at hand. For Henry Adams, even the individual human being alone was a chaos of multiplicities, and Robert Frost, I have hinted, was deeply divided, his self-division clearly internalizing the cultural conflicts extant in American society at large. For Frank Kermode and Rushdie, again, a continuing personal identity at least has to be sought under many different appearances. And what I am presenting here is not a quartet of oddballs. Or if they are, then most of us are oddballs. Either way, teachers who have dialogized their own inner differences are more likely to help their students in dialogizing difference in an outer world as well.

The issues, now so topical, do have a pre-history. In their early- and mid-twentieth century form they were discussed by Eliot, whose later prose writings did offer those valuable clues for positive mediation, even though his youthful criticism was so seminal for the de-historicizing and de-humanizing paradigm. Granted, there were moments when the chaos of conflicting cultural voices was too much for him, so that in *After Strange Gods* (1934), especially, he tried to force through a consensus by means of an overbearing rhetoric of judgementalism. Later, he acknowledged the dangerous irresponsibility of this, and embraced an ideal of unity with diversity, allowing for a much greater degree of subjectivity, not unlike Hilary Putnam's "pluralist ideal" of "human flourishing" (Putnam 1981: 148). In defining literature, similarly, he was certainly on the look-out for a unifying essence or tradition, but was on balance faithful to his strongly historical feel for sheer diversity. He gradually moved well away from his early notion of a text's meaning as single and uninterpretable in any but its own wording, towards a sense of tradition as simultaneously comprehensive and open-ended. "Full understanding", as he once put it, merely counts "within a limited field of discourse" (Eliot 1951 [1929]: 270). When he finally re-conceptualized tradition as culture, he expressed an even fuller sense of variety, now seeing cultural frictions as positively creative. Increasingly, his idea was that a culture, though supportive and even formative, does not totally limit the individual, and is actually open to dialogue with other cultures, which may result in change. His own personal failures to maintain dialogue, and the failures of his culture to do so, shamed him. Underlying much of his work was a desire for fairness.[21]

As Stuart Hampshire says, it would be wishful thinking to imagine that cultural conflicts could disappear altogether, and as both Hampshire and Eliot say, the tensions can actually spur creativity. But without fairness, a fairness which a historical yet non-historicist pragmatics will strengthen through its firm reminders of circumstances and contextual disparities, literary conflicts will continue to overheat. The reception history of *The Satanic Verses* illustrates not only that literature is for real, but just how vitally important it would be to have a habit of well-intentioned cross-cultural dialogue to fall back on. There simply is no substitute for a fully articulated response from all parties, fully discussed in a spirit of positive mediation. Spelt out like this, the point may seem obvious enough. Yet our world would greatly benefit from its being taken seriously.

In addition to commentators of Eliot's calibre, other sources of inspiration could include the creative work of our own time, and especially that of postcolonial writers, for whom the issues are very central. For some of them, an inside-outside oscillation is so habitual that, to the consternation of postcolonial literature's more deterministic theoreticians, they supplement their strong sense of cultural and ethnic difference with a strong sense of correspondences or samenesses (Maes-Jelinek 1991). Rushdie himself is a case in point, and the passage already quoted typical enough. Another example would be Wole Soyinka, who argues for a genuinely eclectic understanding of creativity, with no historical or geographical limits; for an awareness, in fact, of a "universal catalogue of metaphors of art" (Soyinka 1988: 65, 71, 77). Wilson Harris even speaks of a kind of "cross-cultural psyche of humanity, a cross-cultural psyche that bristles with the tone and fabric of encounters between so-called savage cultures and so-called civilized cultures" (Harris 1989: 137).

Or take the Guyanese writer Fred D'Aguiar, now resident in London. D'Aguiar's television programme, *Sweet Thames*, moves in and out of the language of West Indian immigrants to Britain, in and out of the language of a white, male English immigration officer, and for much of the time is also

---

21. In my sense of Eliot's continuing significance I am indebted to Richard Shusterman's *T.S. Eliot and the Philosophy of Criticism* (1988).

pitched in a poetic lyricism belonging to no particular sociocultural grouping. This last is a case of English as a *lingua franca* expressing a psyche that is consciously cross-cultural. Something similar is also to be heard in D'Aguiar's wonderful first novel, *The Longest Memory* (1994), set on a Virginian plantation in 1810. The writing here implies a firm grasp of social and ethnic difference, yet its representational convention is totally unrealistic. Each and every character is created through a stream of consciousness that is unfailingly beautiful but socioculturally unspecific, and there is an absolute minimum of direct speech. As a result, the facts of heteroglossia never actually surface, even though they are always an urgent presupposition. The novel has only 137 pages, and the convention could probably not have been sustained much longer. There would always have been a danger of its becoming just as euphemistic as the middle-class decorum of the longueurs in Dickens. As it stands, though, the writing idealizes or demonizes neither the slave owner, Mr Whitechapel, who is not a mere whited sepulchre, nor the old slave, Whitechapel, named after his master, who is as dignified as his master but no more so. Difference here is not quite so "all the way down" as John Hillis Miller believes, and definitely not a matter of better or worse. In a way which might appeal to K. Anthony Appiah, D'Aguiar is even gently questioning the roles and modes of expression towards which so much public discourse tends to force us. The tension between the individual and the social dimensions of human identity is finely caught.

Texts such as this could perhaps be central for a whole wave of mediating criticism, judicious yet tolerant, always ready to change its mind. As I say, mediating critics' salutation to their readers is not so much Leavis's "This is so, is it not?" as "This is what I think for the moment. What do you think?" Here, too, is where the excitement would come in, an excitement tinged, not with the vindictiveness of sectarian criticism, but with the hope of a multifarious creativity, a creativity which, though inevitably conflictual, might also warm our hearts. As Caryll Emerson (1996) reminds us, Bakhtin, so often seen as the patron saint of difference, also envisaged a dialogue of love. For what, after all, is the alternative? If — as would happen in a university of dissensus, for example — fragmentation were finally to get the better of globalization, what would the total withdrawal from grand narratives and universalizing visions mean in practice? At least on David Harvey's assessment, it would not only leave us with a duller sense of justice. It would also cut us off from important sources of renewal (Harvey 1989: 116).

Hopefulness need not be starry-eyed. Mediating criticism will scrutinize the arguments of all parties, fully embracing the postmodern concern with legitimation. Not even mediating critics themselves can boast of special exemptions or privileged powers of judgement, since they are "thrown", just like everyone else, into a particular situationality. The future they envisage will have nothing to do with cultural homogenization, and their criteria, not bound by the old Western dichotomy of reason versus unreason, will result in neither nihilism nor hectoring judgementalism. Through reasonable discussion, they will strive towards clarity on even the most difficult issues of all, hoping for a sharing of views which will entail nobody's subjugation, and which will have obvious practical benefits, albeit necessarily provisional. Though their watchwords will be rationality and justice, they will immediately acknowledge that rationality and justice have been the pretexts for history's most appalling evils. Precisely because rationality and justice are not timeless absolutes, the risk of their being violently hijacked or nihilistically surrendered is the spur to constant vigilance, in literary negotiations as much as any other.

6.6. A future for literature?

Amid the noisy contestation of different literary canons, a mediating criticism could have consequences for human life at large. Nowadays the issues are so highly politicized that many scholars are tending to see literature in a predominantly sociocultural perspective. Although plenty of books are still published *as* literature, there is a fairly widespread feeling that the category "literature" should perhaps be dropped or fundamentally re-thought, so that literary studies and literary criticism could once and for all come under the aegis of social and cultural studies. In many forms of scholarly organization and activity, from university departments to academic journals, associations and conferences, this has happened already.

Seen within some such framework, literature can apparently dissolve. So-called literary texts follow no single prescription as regards features of style or content, and judgements of literary merit are not always made according to standards that are readily ascertainable and universally acceptable. Nowadays literature is often defined on the basis of a nominalistic institutionalism: it is said to consist of the texts to which the cultural institutions of some interest grouping award the literary cachet, such acts of labelling being a bid to consolidate the interest grouping's own power within society as a whole. Adjudication in literary matters, then, is seen as relative to who is pronouncing on whom. Insofar as literature is a category which is being filled in different ways by different groupings, and is frequently merging with other categories such as film and music, it makes good sense, the argument concludes, to assimilate the concept of literature to those of culture and society in general.

Then there is another argument. Many present-day literary scholars still fear that centripetal forces are hegemonic. More specifically, they fear that the category of literature can be operated in such a way as to ramify forms of social injustice. By re-classifying literature as cultural production they hope to counteract this. Leftist critics, in particular, have often explicitly rejected the traditional distinction between high culture and low culture, sometimes by appealing to Gramsci's notion of a "national-popular", as an ideological rallying point for various different interest groupings against a common rightist enemy (Forgacs 1993 [1984]). What some groupings find especially vicious is traditional literature as allegedly conceived by the West's white middle-class heterosexual males. But even within English-language cultures, there can be other antagonisms, too, as when black feminists were saying that accounts of women's literature had been monopolized by feminists representing the white middle class. Within the emergent sociocultural paradigm of literary scholarship, a keenness to detect and neutralize political threats is often a central concern.

Senior white male critics tend to reply that literature is always literature and has nothing to do with politics. They accuse the new approaches of distorting literature by reading it in the service of an ideology. Harold Bloom writes that "we are destroying all intellectual and aesthetic standards in the humanities and social sciences, in the name of social justice" (Bloom 1995 [1994]: 35). Bloom would not really include himself in the "we" of his sentence here, and neither would Frank Kermode, who has expressed similar misgivings (Kermode 1990 [1989]: 1–46). Bernard Bergonzi (1990) proposes, reluctantly but very firmly, that English departments might just as well give up the pretence of literary criticism once and for all. Instead, they could devote themselves more or less entirely to cultural studies, except that there could also be a new, quite separate degree programme for the few students really interested in poetry as an art form. He seems to resign himself to a future in which the discipline of English "explodes" into many enquiries having nothing fundamentally to do with literature, plus the one very small and specialized rump which would know poetry from the inside.

These eminent commentators have a point. Their basic claim, that scholarly discussion of literature is worthless if it is not based on sensitive reading, is irrefutable. On the other hand, insensitive reading is nothing new, and even within the most fashionable of current scholarly approaches there are some truly excellent readers. Take Chris Fitter (1992), for instance, and the wonderful fidelity to language in his cultural-materialist analysis of landscapes of war and devastation in the poetry of Vaughan. It is worth adding, too, that the interpretative and critical skills required to handle the new high-tec media of visuality and orality could in the end, not so much replace our traditional-yet-not-so-ancient skills of literacy and literary criticism, as complement and extend them.

The opposition between literate and non-literate cultural forms was never completely hard and fast, and may actually be breaking down still further. Not only are literate and non-literate modes actually quoting each other, and even positively integrating. The opposition has also lost much of its underpinning in social reality. Certainly in the West, class distinctions have been considerably reduced by half a century of increasing material prosperity, of increasingly post-industrial types of production, of increasing polyculturality, and of increasing access to higher education.[22] To put it very concretely, there must already be thousands and thousands of people from many different backgrounds, and the oldest of them already well into middle age, who take pleasure, not only in Ted Hughes's *Tales from Ovid*, A.S. Byatt's *Possession* or Britten's *Peter Grimes*, but in pop videos, the Internet or Manchester United.

Unsurprisingly, then, the distinction challenged by Gramsci, between elitist high culture and the low culture of the masses, has continued to be targeted within the postmodern critique of traditional legitimations. Partly as a result, the nineteenth century conception of literature can sometimes seem quite distant, a development not foreseen even by Eliot. For him, poetry, at least, would always be special, not because it was art, but because it was so close to religious experience. The point is, though, that "literature" in any such Arnoldian sense no longer covers many of the things that people set store by, and is often perceived as snobbish. How could it be otherwise, when so many

---

22. Discontented with remaining imperfections and new afflictions, we may forget the very substantial improvements which have taken place since the Second World War. Useful reminders are offered by Eric Hobsbawm (1994), a historian not noted for right-wing bias.

twentieth-century critics and teachers have given the impression that reading novels, poems and plays is an esoteric form of masochism: very much an acquired taste, involving no real human interest and no straightforward pleasure? (Cf. Carey 1992.) Many of those same critics have also portrayed mass culture as crudely immediate in its hedonism. But according to Richard Shusterman (1992), allegations of popular art's spuriousness, passivity, superficiality, and lack of creativity by no means always stick. Shusterman himself has precisely the credentials needed to make this kind of point, for his interests are, very emphatically, both up- and down-market. His is one of the finest intellects at present devoting itself to literary and cultural theory, yet his advocacy of a bodily aesthetics almost intellectualizes intellect away. When he writes about a popular art form such as rap, it is as if the two halves of his personality achieve a reconciliation, a kind of mind-body synthesis which many of his contemporaries would probably endorse.

With such defences of the popular becoming more widespread, nominalistic accounts of literature will presumably gain still more force, and the disappearance of both high-brows and low-brows continue apace. To imply, in the manner of the earlier debates, that an individual will always and only enjoy just one form of cultural production would simply be inaccurate. It would be to underestimate, not only the human flexibility of mind, but the pluralistic freedom with which that flexibility is now being exercized.

Whether the term "literature" will actually survive with new, non-nineteenth century connotations remains to be seen. Its meaning could well expand to cover a wide range of cultural activities in various media, so becoming even broader than the notion of literature before its nineteenth century specialization. Alternatively, the word could gradually disappear altogether, in which case "culture" could replace it as a hold-all term, denoting the province of "cultural critics". Whatever happens, we shall probably continue to speak of the novel and its critics, poetry and poetry critics, drama and drama critics, television and television critics, film and film critics, jazz and jazz critics, and so on. Any linkage perceived between particular cultural products and particular social formations will probably continue to weaken, and the range of cultural production of all kinds continue to widen, with crossings of many different sorts between written language, spoken language, and many other media: television, theatre, performance, film, photography, music, dance, electronic genres. The sites or stagings of cultural production are likely to become even more diversified, with new popular genres gaining in esteem, just as they always have, at the expense of those already established. No less likely is a continuing development of separate literary canons (if "literary" is still the word), some of them representing cultural constituencies making their voices heard for the first time.

As a result of all this, a wider range of cultural texts could also be expected to graduate from particular canons to the status of classic. Put another way: whatever else happens, people in general, and scholars in particular, will go on making value judgements. Despite the fears of Bloom, Kermode and Bergonzi, a sociocultural turn in literary scholarship and criticism cannot in the long run entail a nihilistic vacuum. In the words of Steven Connor (1992: 8–33), evaluation is an unavoidable imperative. Human life is simply too short to do without it. Surrounded by countless opportunities, we often have to formulate preferences.

By the same token, nominalistically institutional theories of the arts will never quite wash. Or more precisely, their nominalism will wash, but not their institutionalism. This is because of something partly hinted by Richard Wollheim. As we saw earlier, Wollheim notes that a powerful art institution's representatives might actually have some *good reason* for approving a certain work, a reason which has something to do with the work itself. Here he might possibly be thinking in terms of the kind of essentialism suggested by Socrates' question to Euthyphro: Is piety pious because it is loved by the gods, or do the gods love piety because it is pious? In the same way one might ask: Is literature literary because the cultural institution says so, or does the cultural institution say that literature is literary because it *is* literary? In view of Wollheim's lively awareness of Wittgenstein, however, he is likely to be conceiving of a good reason in some more relativistic sense. And if so, he would perhaps say that the type of work endorsed by the one society's art institution might also be endorsed by that of some other society, but in a different language, spoken from the different motivations that are of weight in the different context.[23]

---

23. As I indicate, I am not exactly sure what Wollheim thinks here. If I am not mistaken, it was not part of his intention that I should be. As noted earlier, he is writing in opposition to "the tendency to conceive of aesthetics as primarily the study of the spectator and his role." For this reason, the first edition of his essay (1969) has nothing to say on evaluation at all. To the second edition (1980) he appended an essay entitled "Art and Evaluation", but this still does not take up what he calls "the substantive values of art", and although he does discuss the question of "how aesthetic value is justified", enumerating what he calls four plausible answers (the realist, the objectivist, the relativist, and the subjectivist), he does not, I think, seek to express a clear preference. (Wollheim 1992 [1980]: 227–40, esp. 228–30.)

At least such a view would be in line with my argument here. On the one hand, it is far too late in the day to relapse into an unqualified universalism, and we can easily recognize that powerful cultural institutions do have a central role in changes of taste. Literary works which are not at present in fashion can also be re-valued, and there can be cross-cultural mergings of horizons by which values themselves will not remain unchanged. On the other hand, some literature does *seem* to be universal, even though it is impossible to say in any single language what its universality consists of. If anything, it represents a universality that is integrally made up of difference, a phenomenon whose forces are both centripetal and centrifugal.

This, in effect, is what literature has always been. Readers have traditionally read books by all sorts of different people, and from many different times and places. One of the main changes in the polycultural societies of postmodernity is merely that difference is no longer thought of as outside the city walls. It has come in from the cold, so to speak, and its voice is augmented by the new-found voice of the difference which was on the inside all along.

So assuming that the trend continues, what "good reason" will the readers of various formations have for valuing some texts more than others? As in the past, there may be no single answer. Sometimes it may be a matter of objective formal features; sometimes, of perceptions of beauty that are more subjective; sometimes, of both. The desirability of some kind of non-Kantian aesthetics is something I have hinted from the outset, and what I have in mind would be very much in addition to the ethical aesthetics I proposed in Section 5.5. Other criteria, though, certainly will be ethical. Value will be found in texts and genres which seem humanly accessible and widely relevant, even if their relevance varies from readership to readership. Classic texts will go on satisfying a huge range of predilections, including some that are politically and ideologically motivated. So however much their readers try to empathize their way into the contexts of writing, and into the intradiegetic contexts, a wide range of interpretation will also persist. Insofar as the human potentialities read into the classics are indeed manifold, these texts' universality will remain non-essentialist and acquired. The only common denominators will be the sameness-that-is-difference of the human condition itself, plus writers' underlying and catholic faith in readers. Responding to that faith, readers themselves may increasingly have the sense of being drawn together around a concentration of semiotic, affective and ethical potential that is globally accessible. At the same time, they may become increasingly aware of that potential's simultaneous yet different take-up within the many widely different contexts of reading. If so, what will again be brought into play is the human mind's extraordinary flexibility. Readers will be reading classic texts in their own way, yet in complete comprehension of the fact that other readers will be reading them in somewhat different ways.

Human beings are indeed separated by their cultures, and separated by the subdivisions within their cultures. But they still find that they can understand each other, as they are increasingly obliged to do by trends in population, technology, trade and political structure. Difference does not necessarily connote bigotry and war, and the communicative hope of literary writers can be polymorphically vindicated. There is no question of some single human norm, by which the majority of human beings would be marginalized. At issue here is rather the human being's natural predisposition to positive mediation. Even as common a thing as speaking a foreign language involves moving into a framework of perceptions and values that is different from a more habitual one. To say this is not to accept the deterministic notion that particular languages place particular limits on what can be thought or said. The point is simply that languages' signified-signifier relationships are most typically contextualized and interpreted in terms of particular societies and their formations. Human beings do have sociocultural formations of their own, plus their own continuities of moral autonomy and temperament. Yet their relatively protean selves can empathetically self-project into formations and individualities that are very different. So arises that heuristic histrionics which is integral to communication of any kind at all, and integral, as well, to the process of human individuation itself, a process which can therefore be advanced by the reading of literature.

6.7. Scholarship and culture in symbiosis

Whether or not "literature" survives as a term, in postcolonial writing we are beginning to see a practice which, neither under- nor over-emphasizing the central fact of sociocultural difference, itself improves the chances of positive mediation between opposed communal groupings. Academic literary studies of a sociocultural turn could enter into symbiosis with this development and actively extend it. Scholars have already refined many of the analytical tools needed, and are often motivated by their loyalty to some particular cultural constituency whose values and political rights they wish to promote. In this they can hardly go wrong, providing they take their cue from the positive mediation between inside and outside already evidenced by the best criticism of the past: by critics who have resisted the various professional, institutional, political and generic pressures towards oversimplification. Above all, what must never be simplified away is the element of fair-mindedness. This, as an adequately historical pragmatics makes very clear, depends on a dialogue which fully articulates all the different situationalities, something for which an insincere political correctness is a dangerously counterproductive substitute. As an obvious first step, those critics who at present confine their commentary to the literature of just some single constituency could perhaps broaden their range.

Seen in this particular crystal ball, the study of literature would be part of a larger trend. Throughout this book, I have taken for granted that literary scholars can benefit from a firm grounding in communicative pragmatics, a field in which there is actually at least as much for them to give as to get. They need to be involved in the widest possible discussion of how communication actually works between people, and within and across social groupings. I have also noted the further tendency of literary studies to open up to cultural studies, as the concept of literature is itself challenged.

Such interdisciplinary reasoning gains special impetus from a case such as D'Aguiar's. Although he is probably still best known for his poetry, the study of his poetry is greatly enriched by a consideration of his work for the stage and for television, while the sound track of *Sweet Thames* contains not only the linguistic dialogism, including the poetry, but a musical dialogism as well, plus the sophisticated handling of visual images, both moving and still. The film is all this at once, and it also presupposes, and will further contribute to, a diversified understanding of history. D'Aguiar's work, like many of our time's most vital creations, can only be discussed within the most synergetic frame of reference. Among other things, this will unite literary scholars' traditional concerns with evaluation and history, and will draw on linguistic, sociological, film-studies- and media-studies types of expertise as well. If all these kinds of consideration were to feed into a positive mediation based on a historical yet non-historicist pragmatics, the resultant commentary would be more than a match for the discourses of postmodern stalemate.

So to repeat and come full circle: a soporific consensus is neither desirable nor possible. But given a flourishing mediating criticism, there is a real chance that literature, transformed but — like any living tradition — still continuous with itself, would become the centrifugal-centripetal phenomenon *par excellence*. The textualized difference of all sorts and conditions of people would in that case be universally enjoyed. Different groupings would better understand each other and their different forms of life, because readers would be availing themselves, more than ever, of what Berlin calls "the force of imaginative insight". The conflicts of which Heraclitus and Stuart Hampshire so eloquently speak would still erupt. But in literature, there would be at least one extra, and emotionally very powerful force, over and above the cool rationality of Hampshire's procedural justice, to keep conflicts at least as fruitful and as amiable as possible.

The traditional concept and social character of literature are already changing. But this would be no great loss. The symbiosis of literature with a mediating criticism based on a historical yet non-historicist pragmatics would help to promote a climate of far more reasonable discussion. On the one hand, critics would still be able to propose and discuss criteria, and the intelligence, learning and sensitivity of a Bloom, Kermode or Bergonzi would always be recognized as simply indispensable. On the other hand, no second Leavis would ever rise up to arrogate an unassailable legitimacy, and the educational inequalities stemming from new-liberal economic and social policies would be less likely to revive strong class divisions and a class-linked aesthetics. Instead, the postmodern levelling would continue with more robust self-consciousness, and without impeding the emergence of new classics. They would be classics of many different kinds, and even, by today's standards, of unaccustomed and very mixed kinds. But in terms of both variety and quality, the ultimate gain would never be in doubt, for such co-adaptations really are a culture's growth points. Once upon a time, Johnson had to re-assure civilized readers about even Shakespeare's rule-breaking. And twenty-five years earlier, Fielding had been pleading for a mongrel he could only explain as a comic epic poem in prose.

Glossary

NOTE
The glossary offers linguists and literary scholars some basic information about each others' fields of expertise. Certain other branches of scholarship are also included. And there are notes on the present work's own terminology and framework of ideas.

Barthesian
An adjective formed from the name of Roland Barthes. Barthes was a leading representative of structuralist and poststructuralist thinking in cultural and literary analysis. Such approaches, having originated in France during the 1950s and 1960s, soon spread to influence many different schools of thought throughout the world. (See *new historicism, cultural materialism, cultural studies, feminist criticism, gay and lesbian criticism, postcolonial criticism, ethnic criticism*.) In the present work, "Barthesian" is sometimes used as a collective label for these developments.

The *structuralist* phase reflected the influence of Claude Lévi-Strauss, who adapted the ideas and methods of *structuralist linguistics* to the field of cultural anthropology. For scholars such as Michel Foucault, Julia Kristeva, Jacques Lacan, and Barthes himself, a main interest was in the extent to which the human psyche and forms of literary and other cultural production were the result of social structuration. There was sometimes a direct link with the Marxist analysis of history, and in extreme forms the conclusions drawn involved *the historicist assumption*.

In the later, *poststructuralist* phase, as represented by Barthes, Lacan and Jacques Derrida, a main focus was on the relationship between our sense of reality and the process of *semiosis*; more particularly, on the paradox that language allows meanings to arise about the world yet is in itself a system of *differentialities* with no positive terms. (See *structuralist linguistics*.) In the form of Derridean *deconstruction*, such analysis tended to undermine common-sense *logocentric* assumptions about the real world, including the assumptions about social reality which had still been made during the structuralist phase. So the "post" in "poststructuralism" to some extent does indicate an adversarial relationship, and not merely a chronological sequence. Even in poststructuralism, however, *the historicist assumption* sometimes operated, insofar as the thought- and life-world of human beings was in effect viewed as dependent on the workings of linguistic semiosis within a particular cultural epoch.

behaviourism
Behaviourism was a major twentieth-century school of psychology, deriving from the work of John W. Watson. The main ideas were that emotions and feelings were the result of

conditioning, and that human behaviour in general was best seen as responding to specific stimuli. Human nature was a question of the biology and physiology of a physical body. The soul and mind, to the extent that they existed at all, were bodily functions. Psychology itself was to be a precise science, describing and measuring human beings' activity with no less detachment than if they were animals. Researchers were to leave introspection and contemplation firmly to one side.

In the present work, an affinity is discerned between behaviouristic psychology and *structuralist linguistics*, in that the latter was more interested in the surface form of language than in how human beings used and experienced it interpersonally. Some linguists, and especially applied linguists in the field of foreign language learning, embraced behaviourism in a strong form. They believed that language behaviour could be trained by drilling responses to particular stimuli, for instance in a language laboratory. Other linguists were behaviouristic in the weaker sense that they simply did not raise questions of meaning, intention and experience.

centrifugal, the
See *postmodernity*

centripetal, the
See *postmodernity*

co-adaptation, co-adaptive, co-adaptability
The human being, as a *social individual*, is bound to adapt to prevailing social conventions, yet by doing so can also adapt the conventions themselves to his or her more individual perceptions, desires and goals. This is what the present work means by the term *co-adaptation*, and by saying that the social and the individual exist in a state of *co-adaptability*.

Communicative co-adaptation can occur in several different dimensions. It can be a matter of knowledge or opinion, i.e. of simultaneously saying something old and something new. It can be a matter of text-type expectations, i.e. of both following and breaking with generic conventions. Or it can be a matter of *politeness*, i.e. of a risky interactive gamble between a normal and an abnormal level of respect.

In every case, the co-adaptation between the social expectation and the individual intervention is a matter of the communicator's meeting other people half-way, in order to win them over and bring about change. All effective rhetoric is *co-adaptive* in this sense.

cognitive environment
See *context*.

communication
In the present work, communication is taken to be a semiotic process whereby different parties negotiate, ideally speaking in order to arrive at a shared view, and to bring about some kind of change. Prototypically, the *communicative situation* consists of two parties in communication about some third entity. This third entity can actually include one or both of the communicative parties themselves. But it can also be something unconnected with them,

or something not so much real as hypothetical or fictional, as in most literary communication.

Literature is one of the many forms of written communication, and one in which the initiator is not only not co-present with the other participant, but not necessarily even contemporary. If communication is really taking place, a human parity prevails even after the initiator's death, and also in any other circumstances which rule out explicit feed-back and dialogue.

At the same time, parity *is* parity. The drawback of binarisms such as *initiator/non-initiator, sender/receiver, speaker/hearer, writer/reader* and *narrator/narratee* is that they may tend to privilege their first terms. Communication will not actually happen unless the party represented by their second terms is actively engaged in mental processing and response.

communicative dynamism
A textual principle that has been analysed by Jan Firbas and other members of the Prague Linguistic Circle. It mainly has to do with the way in which "old" information is related to "new" information by the structure of individual sentences, and by the textual interrelations of sentences in sequence. An English sentence, for instance, tends to move from old to new, so that its last words seem to be the most important.

communicative personae
It is impossible to use language without conveying some impression of oneself and of the other person or persons one is communicating with. As part of the ***textualization-cum-contextualization***, communicants consciously or unconsciously shape such impressions into personae, which have the function of modelling, and thereby facilitating, the interpersonal relationship between them. In literary scholarship, these personae are often referred to as the *implied writer* or *implied author* and the *implied reader*. In connection with other types of communication, frequently used terms are *implied sender* and *implied receiver*. For the potential drawback of such binarisms, see ***communication***.

communicative situation
See ***communication***.

comparative philology
The main nineteenth century approach to the study of language, and strongly historical in its orientation. In a spirit of scientific positivism, comparative philologists set out to explain the facts that languages change, and that different languages are related to each other. The main concepts included "language families", together with ideas deriving from Darwin's evolutionary theory. Much of the evidence adduced had to do with word-borrowings and sound changes. The so-called *Junggrammatiker* claimed that there were laws of sound change as regular as those of the natural sciences.

constative
See ***speech act theory***.

context
Colloquially speaking, a context is the set of circumstances under which something happens, is done, or is said. This is sometimes the sense intended in the present work. But in certain clearly marked cases, the term is understood more strictly, as a *cognitive environment* or mental condition. What it then refers to is everything which a person can recall or is aware of, either consciously or in a more automated manner, while speaking, writing, reading, hearing or remembering a particular utterance.

Much of this contextual knowledge will be intimately bound up with beliefs and value judgements, many of which will be widely shared within the person's sociocultural grouping. But in sharp opposition to *the mutual knowledge hypothesis* and *the unitary context assumption*, the present work always draws a distinction between the contexts of different participants in a communicative process, even when their circumstances and backgrounds are apparently very similar.

The distinction is made in terms of the context of sending/speaking/writing and the context of receiving/listening/reading. Here, though, the first terms in such binarisms must not be prioritized as somehow more essential to communication, and care must also be taken to define the communication-internal context of the third entity: i.e. the context of the real, hypothetical or fictional people, events, circumstances and possibilities under discussion (cf. *communication*).

In the case of abstractions, inanimate objects, and hypothetical or fictional human beings, this third, internal context can obtain only in the minds of the people in communication. It does not correspond to a context which really exists for a really existing mind. And even when the third entity is some other person who really exists or has existed, his or her context can still be nothing more than that context as reconstructed by the participants in the current process of communication.

conversational implicature
See *the cooperative principle*.

conversational maxims
See *the cooperative principle*.

conversation analysis
A type of linguistic study which developed simultaneously with *text linguistics* and *discourse analysis*, and, like them, examines whole sequences of sentences. It is specially concerned with naturally occurring speech situations, and with phenomena such as the interpersonal dynamics of turn-taking. One pioneer is Stephen Levinson.

cooperative principle, the
A pragmatic principle, first proposed in 1967 by H.P. Grice, who was partly developing *speech act theory*: "Make your contribution such as is required, at the stage at which it occurs, by the accepted purpose or direction of the talk exchange in which you are engaged". This leads to four *conversational maxims*, also defined by Grice. *The maxim of quantity* tells us to make our contribution as informative as is required. *The maxim of quality* forbids us to say what we believe to be false, or to say that for which we lack adequate

evidence. *The maxim of relation* tells us to be relevant. And *the maxim of manner* tells us to avoid obscurity, ambiguity, unnecessary prolixity, and disorderliness. Somebody who flouts a maxim may be taken as doing so in order to make some kind of *conversational implicature*, and as therefore still observing the cooperative principle after all. Metaphors, for instance, implicate important meanings by flouting the maxim of quality. They say things which are not literally true. The present work suggests that fictional narratives, similarly, can reject *episodic* or *specific truth* as a way of implicating *general* or *moral truth*.

corpus linguistics
The computer-assisted linguistic analysis of large bodies of real-life language production, oral or written.

critical discourse analysis
See *discourse analysis*.

cultural materialism
This is a term popularized by the British Marxist critic Raymond Williams. His idea was that cultures and cultural products, including literature, are structured by economic forces and modes of production. Like other *Barthesian* approaches, cultural materialism sometimes seems to make *the historicist assumption*. But elsewhere, Williams and his followers have seen literary texts as performing a subversive role, not only in their own time but later on as well, when they can become the sites of new contestations of power. The approach is itself aimed at transforming the existing sociopolitical order.

cultural purism
The assumption that the significance of an instance of language use or cultural production is to be defined by, and confined to, the exact cultural circumstances under which it took place. Communication between different positionalities is thereby taken to be impossible and/or undesirable. Compare *historical purism*.

cultural structuralism
A collective term for any approach to the analysis of culture along structuralist lines. (Cf. *Barthesian*.)

cultural studies
Critical approaches to literature and other forms of cultural production. Raymond Williams's *cultural materialism* was an important influence, and the earliest developments took place at Birmingham University's Centre for Contemporary Cultural Studies, founded by Stuart Hall and Richard Hoggart in 1964. Typically *postmodern* in challenging elitist definitions of culture, such approaches sometimes developed in close association with film studies and media studies. They have now become firmly established in university departments of language and literature, whose linguistic work has increasingly emphasized sociocultural and pragmatic dimensions, and whose older notion of a central literary canon is often said to have been politically suspect.

culture wars, the
See *postmodernity*.

deconstruction
See *Barthesian*.

deixis (person, social, time, place, discourse)
Deixis is part of a written or spoken text's inevitable *textualization-cum-contextualization*. It is a matter of features by which every use of language "points to" its sender, to its recipients, to the persons, things and events which it mentions, and to itself. As the result of this orientation, its recipients make inferences about the relationships pertaining between themselves as represented in the *implied receiver* and various other areas of reference. *Person deixis* assigns first-, second- and third-person roles, while *social deixis* marks the degrees of respect the sender conceives as being demanded or manifested by various parties. Both these types of denotation help to establish the sender and receiver personae as communicative latching-on points, and they are reinforced by *time deixis* and *place deixis*, which offer to set the *implied sender*, the *implied receiver* and the worlds and people under discussion within temporal and spatial relationships as well. *Discourse deixis*, finally, is a text's metatextual pointing to itself, mainly so as to help recipients with transitions from one part of it to another.

differentiality
See *structuralist linguistics*.

discourse analysis
A further development of *text-linguistics*. Briefly: text-linguistics plus *pragmatics*. The textual properties of sentences in sequence are related to the sociocultural context and interpersonal interchange within which they occur. Important contributions have been by Willis Edmondson and Malcolm Coulthard. In *critical discourse analysis*, for instance as developed by Norman Fairclough, "discourse" carries Foucauldian implications. Language as used within society is seen as involving rules and conventions which are intimately bound up with power relations. Linguistics becomes a tool of socio-ideological critique.

dramatic irony
The situation which arises when readers, listeners or spectators know more about the situation in a story or play than one or more of the characters in it.

emic
See *structuralist linguistics*.

emotive and evaluative expressions
This term covers any kind of word which, in a particular textual context, seems to carry an emotional charge or a value judgement. Such expressions are important for *textualization-cum-contextualization*.

episodic truth
The kind of truth attributable to reports of an event which actually happened as described (as opposed to accounts of a hypothetical or fictional event). Such reports do not necessarily partake of *general truth* or *moral truth*.

ethnographic mediation
See *mediation*

ethnic criticism
One of the *Barthesian* approaches to literature most clearly representative of *postmodernity*. Its focus is on the literature of ethnic "minorities", e.g. Chicano/a writing and African American writing. One of the main theorists of the latter is Henry Louis Gates..

face-threatening act (FTA)
See *politeness*.

felicity conditions
See *speech act theory*.

feminist criticism
A wide variety of *Barthesian* approaches to literature have emphasized questions relating to the representation, position and power of women within culture and society. Typically *postmodern* in their challenge to traditional legitimations, many such feminist approaches focus on patriarchal (male-dominated) and phallocentric (male centred) institutions and practices, often making a distinction between (biological) sex and (cultural) gender. Feminist critics have often drawn on the concepts and methods of *deconstruction, new historicism,* psychoanalysis, and Marxism. But whereas Europeans such as Hélène Cixous, Luce Irigaray and Julia Kristeva pay special attention to language and to the mother-child relationship, Anglo-Americans such as Elaine Showalter tend to focus on women's own representation of experience, in both fiction and autobiography.

functional linguistics
A type of linguistics paying special attention to the way a language has been shaped by millennia of use so as to perform vital functions in human life. M.A.K. Halliday organizes all such functions under two meta-functions: an ideational meta-function, which covers all the help language gives us in reflecting on and relating to the world; and an interpersonal meta-function, embracing our ways of relating linguistically to other people. There is also a textual meta-function, which has to do with the properties whereby language hangs together and makes meaning. But textuality is obviously merely instrumental for ideation and interpersonality. In other words, this kind of approach, like developments in *pragmatics, discourse analysis,* and *conversation analysis,* reacts against the earlier *structuralist linguistics* by not prioritizing *langue* over *parole*. Its interest in *the historically human* is typical of late-twentieth-century research in the humanities in general.

gay and lesbian criticism
These types of criticism, partly inspired by *feminist criticism*, focus on textual representations of, and readings responsive to issues of, homosexuality. As with other *Barthesian* approaches, the analysis of attitudes, gendering and power is typically *postmodern* as a scrutiny of traditional norms and certainties. Among the pioneers in the 1980s was Eve Kosofsky Sedgwick.

generative grammar
Generative grammar, sometimes called transformational grammar, is the approach to language inaugurated by Noam Chomsky in 1957. The basic idea is that grammar is not learned but innate. Different languages are said to result in the same deep structures, our apprehension of which "grows" in the mind, just as teeth grow in the mouth. Although this concern with deep structure was presented as a mentalistic move away from the *behaviourism* or quasi-behaviourism of *structuralist linguistics*, Chomsky's critics have complained that generative grammar still reduces the human being to a kind of mechanism.

general truth
The kind of truth attributable to statements or narrations which convey an impression of what the world and human life are most typically like, quite irrespective of whether the events, things and people mentioned are fictional or non-fictional. Contrast *episodic truth* and *specific truth*. Compare *moral truth*.

heteroglossia
Mikhail Bakhtin's term for the "different-tonguedness" of social discourse. It refers to the multiplicity of social voices and speech types with which each new use of language must enter into relation.

historically human, the
A collective term used by the present work to refer to approaches to the humanities which, during the second half of the twentieth century, distanced themselves from the earlier paradigm of *a-historical de-humanization*. Among other developments, this includes: in philosophy, the later Wittgenstein's work on language in use; in linguistics, sociolinguistics, *functional linguistics, discourse analysis, conversation analysis, pragmatics*; in literary scholarship, John Reichart's critique of *literary formalism*, *Barthesian* approaches, and the moves towards a historical *literary pragmatics*.

historical purism
The assumption that the significance of an instance of language use or cultural production is to be defined by, and confined to, the exact historical circumstances under which it took place. Communication between different positionalities is thereby taken to be impossible and/or undesirable. Compare *historical purism*.

historicist assumption, the
For convenience, the present work gives this name to the assumption that human beings are so fully determined by sociocultural factors that they lack any real personal autonomy. It is

important to note that many scholars describing their work as historicist would reject such a strongly determinist view.

illocution, illocutionary act
See *speech act theory*.

implied sender/writer/author/speaker
See *communicative personae*.

implied receiver/reader/listener
See *communicative personae*.

indirect speech act
See *speech act theory*.

intertextuality
This term was introduced by literary and cultural structuralists such as Barthes, Kristeva and Foucault (see *Barthesian*). Intertextuality was part of their emphasis on the human subject's implication in a particular society. Every word, expression or text exists in intertextual relationship with every other word, expression or text within the same culture. The here-and-now occurrence of any particular linguistic item recapitulates and modifies all its previous occurrences, and bears a differential relation to the occurrences of every other expression in the same language culture as well. Intertextuality is much more than a matter of conscious allusions. Nor can it be reduced to a matter of sources and influences.

The present work strongly emphasizes the importance of intertextuality in language use of every kind. But since men and women are seen as not just social beings but *social individuals*, it also stresses that language can at the same time be handled in a sometimes very personal way. Unlike a tradition of anonymously oral transmission, a literate culture, in which authors' works descend to posterity with their own names on the title-page, preserves such individualities as personal hallmarks. Also, one particular writer's open allusions to, or adaptations of another are one of literature's main pleasures.

Junggrammatiker
See *comparative philology*.

liberal humanist
This label is often applied to any of the nineteenth-century and more recent approaches to literature which grant a large autonomy to individual human beings, and especially to authors. In extreme forms, such approaches virtually overlook the importance of socio-cultural formation altogether, speaking of a human nature that is timelessly universal. This tendency was therefore much criticized by Marxist critics, and all the *Barthesian* approaches are in one way or another a direct reaction against it.

literary formalism
This is a collective term for the views of literature espoused by the Symbolists, the

Aesthetes, many Modernists, the **Russian Formalists** and the **New Critics**. In their view, literature was a type of artistic production that was non-mimetic and non-expressive. Instead, it created an impersonal aesthetic universe, on which the reasoning of science and ethics had no bearing. The philosophical background here was the aesthetic theory of Immanuel Kant.

literary pragmatics
Pragmatics as it applies to literary communication. Or the study of literature with this as the main focus. Many approaches to literary pragmatics have been close to the spirit of ***structuralist linguistics, generative grammar*** and ***literary formalism***. The present work, by contrast, places a strong emphasis on literature as a form of interpersonal activity, and is also strongly historical, though stopping well short of ***the historicist assumption***. In this way it seeks to offer a theoretical grounding for ***mediating criticism***.

literature
In contrast to ***literary formalism***, the present work avoids essentialistic descriptions of literature in terms of some exclusive properties or function. Rather, literature is seen as one form of communication among many others, with which it has much in common. Within a society the literary cachet is awarded to texts that are highly valued, but the criteria involved can vary from one cultural grouping or epoch to another, even though some features can be described quite objectively. In ***postmodern*** times, the distinction between a highbrow literature and low- or middle-brow types of writing may actually be breaking down, in parallel with similar developments in the other arts, and as one aspect of the larger process of social levelling, with its challenge to traditional legitimacies. Yet even if the term "literature" falls into disuse, value judgements will continue to be made. Since not even the quickest reader can read everything, grounds for choice will always be necessary.

locution, locutionary act
See ***speech act theory***.

logical atomism
This was an attempt, initiated by Bertrand Russell and the early Wittgenstein, to develop a philosophy based on an ideal language. Such a language, they held, would be in a one-to-one ratio with the facts of observation. It would therefore consist of linguistic atoms comparable to the atoms of physics, so actually reflecting the structure of the world. By reducing ideas to these lowest logical components, it would solve some of the central problems of philosophy.

logical positivism
Logical positivism was a mid-twentieth-century movement in philosophy deriving from the work of Moritz Schlick, Rudolf Carnap and other members of the Vienna Circle, and represented in Britain by A.J. Ayer. The main claim was that an utterance, in order to be meaningful, must be verifiable, either by sense experience, or by scrutiny of the conventions governing its use of terms. Moral and religious affirmations which do not meet these tests were said to be not literally significant. At best, they were mere expressions of feeling.

logocentrism
This is the name Derrida gave to the common sense assumption that a text is underwritten by some world that it is "about". (Cf. *Barthesian*.) *Logos*, the Greek word for "word", "speech", and "reason", has in Western philosophy come to mean something like "law", "truth" and even "Truth" with a capital "T". What Derrida threw into question was the idea of some kind of presence which serves as the origin or rationale for language — a legitimating *logos* with which particular linguistic utterances can be compared for accuracy. Derrida's most celebrated aphorism was to the effect that there is nothing outside of the text. As far as he was concerned, our ideas about what may be real and true are very much a linguistic product.

manner, the maxim of
See *the cooperative principle*.

mediating criticism
See *mediation*

mediation
The present work follows common speech in using "mediation" as the term to describe a communicative intervention which seeks to help different parties better understand each other. *Positive mediation* is mediation that is self-conscious, deliberately fair-minded and purposefully future-oriented. *Mediating criticism* is literary criticism which aims at positive mediation between authors and readers and between different readerships. *Talent-scouting* mediation helps readers to understand new or unusual writers belonging to their own culture and period. *Ethnographic* mediation helps readers understand literature produced within cultures or periods other than their own. Sometimes the ethnographical and talent-scouting functions can complement each other.

modality
Modality is the linguistic means by which senders indicate to recipients some degree of commitment or hesitation as to the truth, probability or desirability of whatever they happen to be talking about. It is therefore very important for *textualization-cum-contextualization*. As for its textual realization, it is carried by a surprisingly wide range of expressions, whose processing is highly automated. In addition to the primary modal verbs (in English, *will, shall, can, may, must*), context, there are also: secondary modal verbs (*could, might, ought to, would, should*); quasi-modal auxiliaries (*have got to*); adverbial, adjectival, participial, and nominal expressions; and modal lexical verbs (*allege, argue*). Sometimes modality is also bound up with tense, conditional clauses, questions, and negatives.

moral truth
The kind of truth attributable to statements or narratives which convey an impression of what human life ought or ought not to be like, quite irrespective of whether the things, persons and events mentioned are fictional or non-fictional. Contrast *episodic truth* and *specific truth*. Compare *general truth*.

mutual knowledge hypothesis, the
This is the hypothesis which is presupposed in the *unitary context assumption*, and which underlies accounts of communication as a kind of code system: the hypothesis that users of a language can decode meanings because they share exactly the same knowledge. It is strongly challenged by *relevance theory* and by the present work.

narratology
An approach to narrative which, by analogy with *structuralist linguistics*, and originally strongly influenced by *Russian formalism*, sees every particular telling of a story as a *parole*-like instantiation of a *langue*-like structure of possibilities. Early narratologists such as Vladimir Propp analysed folk tales as linear sequences representing certain *syntagmatic* relationships between their constituent parts, which could be filled by a variety of *paradigmatic* realizations. Mid-century French scholars paid special attention to the ways in which stories can involve the *differentiality* of binary oppositions at the thematic level, an approach closely similar to cultural anthropology as conducted by Claude Lévi-Strauss. Somewhat later, Gerard Genette and others developed a sophisticated terminology for discussing a narrator's handling of a story's time dimension and point of view. Seymour Chatman is one of the pioneers of the narratology of film.

New Criticism
The New Criticism was the title of a book published by John Crowe Ransom in 1941. This gave its name to the type of *literary formalism* which became the dominant American approach to literary study for the next three decades. Treating the work of literary art as a self-contained, self-referential object, New Critics ignored authorial intentions and reader responses as a matter of principle, and had only a limited interest in history. Their energy was mainly devoted to exploring literary textualities in terms of images, symbols, and rhythms, and to charting larger structures in terms of irony, paradox, ambgiuity and tension, a line of interest going back to Coleridge's account of the creative imagination's reconciliation of opposite and discordant qualities.

new historicism
During the 1980s, American scholars such as Louis Montrose, Stephen Greenblatt and Fredric Jameson reacted against *New Criticism* by re-directing attention to historical considerations. As for their historicism's newness, they explored both literary and non-literary discourse simultaneously, were aware of recent developments in Marxist, feminist and other cultural criticism, and were very self-conscious about the bias of their own historical vantage point. An important influence was Foucault's analyses of the discourses of power (cf. *Barthesian*).

objective correlative
A term coined by T.S. Eliot in his essay on *Hamlet* (1919), and central to Modernist *literary formalism*'s account of literature's impersonality. "The only way of expressing emotion in the form of art is by finding an 'objective correlative'; in other words, a set of objects, a situation, a chain of events which shall be the formula of that *particular* emotion; such that when the external facts, which must terminate in sensory experience, are given, the emotion is immediately invoked."

GLOSSARY 293

paradigm of a-historical de-humanization, the
This is the label used by the present work to describe a major trend in humanistic scholarship in the first half of the twentieth century. The types of research carried out under the auspices of *literary formalism, structuralist linguistics, generative grammar, behaviourism, logical positivism* and *logical atomism* all tended to marginalize the personal experience in history of actual human beings. In some cases this was a matter of excluding what is obviously a problematic variable in the interests of heuristic power. It did not prevent a vast extension to the scope of human knowledge.

paradigmatic
See *structuralist linguistics*.

performative
See *speech act theory*.

perlocution, perlocutionary act
See *speech act theory*

philosophical hermeneutics
A mainly German tradition of philosophy devoted to the nature of interpretation. In the seventeenth century it was still a branch of theology, concerned mainly with biblical interpretation. Under the influence of Friedrich D.E. Schleiermacher and Wilhelm Dilthey it became broader and more secular. In more recent times, Martin Heidegger, Hans-Georg Gadamer and Jürgen Habermas have drawn special attention to the relationship between interpretations and the circumstances under which they are made. This is linked to a major ontological question: Is Being itself ever possible or even conceivable except in some historical manifestation? A related line of enquiry has to do with understandings between people whose positionalities are not identical. This, especially as developed by Gadamer, is of central importance to the communicative pragmatics here offered as a basis for *mediating criticism*.

phonocentrism
A phonocentric type of argument or methodology is one which assumes that the spoken word has more presence, and therefore more authenticity and importance, than the written. Derrida, who coined the term, saw phonocentrism as very deeply rooted in Western thought. It was a main aspect of *logocentrism*'s appeal to a legitimizing presence outside of language itself.

politeness
Politeness has become one of the key research topics in *pragmatics*, partly thanks to the work of Penelope Brown and Stephen Levinson, for whom politeness has the function of mitigating *face-threatening acts* (*FTAs*). In the present work, it is seen as involving a communally sustained spectrum of evaluation, on which can be registered any kind of action or speech at all. Calibrated from extreme offensiveness to extreme obsequiousness, the politeness spectrum also has a central range that is more or less neutral.

At the same time, the human being is a *social individual*, so that conventional notions of politeness may not be entirely binding, and communication, including literary communication, can involve a kind of interactive gamble. Here the present work differs sharply from the *phonocentric* linguistics which regards the politeness of writing as somehow unreal. It is also very different from *formalistic literary pragmatics,* which restricts discussion of politeness and literary texts to the behaviour of characters "within the story".

An author's politeness gamble can be analysed in terms of *selectional politeness* and *presentational politeness.* Selectional politeness is more or less an anthropological notion. It has to do with the choice of things to say, and of words to say them with, choices which relate to questions of taboo and fashion. Presentational politeness is a psycholinguistic notion, having to do with the manner of presenting the subject-matter. Is the sender being helpful towards recipients? Is it easy for them to see what the point is, what is happening, what the general bearings are? To what extent are *the conversational maxims* being observed?

political correctness
In its sincere and beneficial form, political correctness is a matter of treating all sorts and conditions of human being with due sensitivity and respect. The need for this has been especially felt under conditions of *postmodernity*. In its insincere and dangerous form, it involves a form of communication which is merely superficial. Sensitivity and respect are ostensibly extended to the person who is "other", yet without really recognizing the person's otherness as a human possibility which can enter into relationships of genuine give and take. Prejudices and antagonisms continue to be nourished beneath an appearance of good neighbourliness, and in times of stress can still break out as violence or abuse.

positive mediation
See *mediation*

poststructuralism
See *Barthesian*.

postcolonial criticism
Representatively *postmodern* in its analysis of traditional legitimations, postcolonial criticism deals with literary texts written within cultures that underwent European colonization. Alternatively, it discusses texts written about a colonized culture by writers representing the culture which colonized it. Issues of gender, race and class are often central, and one important background influence is Marx. Another is Franz Fanon, of Martinique, who attacked pan-nationalism, and argued for the establishment of postcolonial nation states. Further ideas derive from Foucault's analyses of power (cf. *Barthesian*).

postmodernity, postmodern
In the present work, the terms "postmodernity" and "postmodern" have a much broader meaning that the terms "postmodernism" and "postmodernist". These last two terms refer to certain late-twentieth-century trends in the arts: trends which are in continuing dialogue with the challenge to traditional styles and genres first offered by early-twentieth-century

modernism. Postmodernity, by contrast, is a condition diagnosed by Jean-François Lyotard as a crisis of culture, knowledge, and politics which is very far-reaching. Certain manifestations of artistic postmodernism are merely one kind of example.

The "modernity" to which "postmodernity" is the response was basically the modernity of the Enlightenment, with its ideals of rational knowledge, universal brotherhood and freedom. Postmodernity involves a scepticism as to the grand narratives of scientific explanation and political teleology, and raises fundamental problems of identity and legitimation.

These are especially acute in multicultural urban societies, where many new kinds of community and interest grouping are for the first time finding their voice. Hence the so-called *culture wars*, in which artistic and other forms of cultural production become a site for the contestation of communal differences. So much so, that many analysts speak of social and cultural fragmentation or even disintegration. The present work refers to this as postmodernity's *centrifugal* force.

Yet at the same time, powerful trends in economics, international politics, communications technology and environmental concern are bringing about a globalization of human life that is quite unprecedented. What is more, commentators such as Jürgen Habermas and Raymond Tallis are to some extent rehabilitating Enlightenment ideals of scientific expertise, commonality, responsibility and cooperation. So postmodernity has a *centripetal* force as well. The centripetal and the centrifugal co-exist in tension.

practical criticism
This was the title of a book published in 1929 by I.A. Richards, at that time a Cambridge don. Dissatisfied with critical commentary which was vague and impressionistic, or which reduced literature to history and author biography, Richards recommended the habit of detailed close reading. His pupils William Empson and F.R. Leavis put this into effect in their own published work, and practical criticism became a central pedagogical tool, first in Cambridge, and gradually in secondary and tertiary education throughout the English-speaking world.

Especially in the beginning, practical criticism was often underpinned by Richards's theory of value. This was a kind of mixture of *logical positivism* and pyschology, and it also harked back to Coleridge's account of the creative imagination's reconciliation of opposite and discordant qualities. According Richards, a literary work did not have inherent qualities such beauty. Rather, a reader's favourable response stemmed from the fact that a reading of it brought about a mental balance between impulses which were more usually in conflict. This meant that a valuable work could be rather difficult to take. Its complex psychological organization was a real challenge to comfortable stock responses.

pragma
See *pragmatics*.

pragmatics
In early *semiotic theory* or *semiotics* as developed by Charles Sanders Peirce and Charles Morris, *semantics* was said to deal with the meaning of signs, *syntactics* with the way signs can be linked together, and pragmatics with the way signs are used. As for the study of

specifically linguistic signs, both *structuralist linguistics* and *generative grammar* placed the main emphasis on syntactics and, to a lesser extent, on semantics. It is only during the past three of four decades that linguistic pragmatics has come into its own.

The focus on the way language is used in actual communication is central. Particular attention is paid to the relationships between language form and *context*, with context being conceived in varying degrees of magnitude. At one extreme, it is simply a matter of the most immediate circumstances of use, together with the co-text (the text which directly precedes and follows the particular expression under examination). At the opposite extreme, context is discussed in terms of sociocultural epoch, power relations and ideology.

The language-context relation can be explored in various ways. For one thing, there is the matter of *textualization-cum-contextualization*, where *deixis* and *communicative personae* call for special attention. Then there is the workings of *signifier-signified* pairings within particular *cognitive environments*, where important topics include presuppositions, inferencing and *relevance*. Then again, analysis can be in terms of a precisely situated interpersonal activity. In this case "pragmatics" carries a strong echo of the Greek root *pragma (= "act, deed")*, and attention is paid to considerations of power, rhetoric, and *politeness*.

Up until fairly recently, linguistic pragmatics was no less synchronic in its approach than mainstream *structuralist linguistics* had been. The present work is one example of a more historical approach.

pragmatism
An American tradition of philosophy initiated by Charles Sanders Peirce and William James. Their main argument was that an idea can be said to be true if it has a "cash value": i.e. if it seems to work in practice. In more recent times, Richard Rorty has pointed out that our ideas about life and the world are very closely linked with the actual language we use in our descriptions. For Rorty, the ability to generate new descriptions in response to new needs and perceptions is a crucial aspect of human wisdom. Final certainties are unlikely. Ideas work for a time, and then get changed or replaced.

presentational politeness
See *politeness*.

quality, the maxim of
See *the cooperative principle*.

quantity, the maxim of
See *the cooperative principle*.

relation, the maxim of
See *the cooperative principle*.

reception theory, reception aesthetics
A type of *reader-response criticism* pioneered by Hans Robert Jauss. It pays special attention to the history of a literary work's reception through different periods.

reader-response criticism
Various types of criticism which pay particular attention to the role of readers. Even in the mid-twentieth century, Louise M. Rosenblatt was already challenging the *New Critical* orthodoxy that a poem is a self-sufficient verbal icon. For her, a poem was whatever a reader lived through under guidance of the text and experienced as relevant to it. Other scholars were more cautious. When Wolfgang Iser explored the "gaps" a reader has to fill in during the process of making sense of a text, he was thinking of real readers only insofar as they correspond to the *implied reader*, which suggested that all readers could read in the same way. A more complexly psychological account was offered by Norman Holland, who spoke of a role played in reading by readers' own personal "identity themes". And Stanley Fish, by emphasizing sociocultural differences between one community of readers and another, finally opened the way for alliances of between reader-response criticism and the *cultural materialist, feminist, gay and lesbian, postcolonial, ethnic* and *culture studies* approaches so closely involved with the polyculturality of *postmodernity*.

relevance theory, the principle of relevance
Relevance theory takes its starting point from Grice's idea that the interpretation of utterances must work according to a principle of inference that is broad and general. But whereas Grice's *cooperative principle* resulted in maxims of quality, quantity, manner and relation, Dan Sperber and Deirdre Wilson subsume all four types of factor under *relation*, so arriving at the master principle of relevance. The idea is that, when we are interpreting an utterance, the principle of relevance tells us to choose those contextual assumptions, and to recover those implicatures, which for the particular utterance and its circumstances have the greatest number of consequences, and which involve the least amount of processing effort.

Russian Formalism
A Russian manifestation of *literary formalism* which was at its height during the 1920s, in both Moscow and Leningrad. It anticipated (though it did not influence) *New Criticism* in its lack of interest in authors and readers. But scholars such as Victor Shklovsky, Boris Eichenbaum, Boris Tomashevsky and Yuri Tynyanov were much more interested than the New Critics in developing an overall theory or science of literature. Here they borrowed the principle of *differentiality* as expounded in *structuralist linguistics*, and saw literary language in particular as differentiating itself from other language. Further ideas had to do with the way art defamiliarizes the familiar, and with the relationship between a narrative's underlying story (or *fabula*) and its handling by the plot (or *sjužet*). This last point was seminal for *narratology*.

sameness-that-is-difference of the human condition, the
A term used in the present work to suggest that all human beings share certain existential basics (e.g. birth, death, primary and secondary needs, social bonding), but that these are experienced in different ways within different cultures.

selectional politeness
See *politeness*.

semantics
See *pragmatics*.

semiology, semiotic theory, semiotics
See *pragmatics* and *structuralist linguistics*.

semiosis
The process by which meanings arise from signs. Investigated by *semiology, semiotic theory,* and *semiotics*, particularly in terms of *the signified/signifier relationship* and *differentiality*.

signified/signifier
The two halves of a sign as described by Ferdinand de Saussure. See *structuralist linguistics*.

social individual
The present work's synonym for "human being". The human being is seen as in no small part socially conditioned, yet as nevertheless having a certain mental, imaginative, ethical and temperamental individuality and autonomy. This position can be regarded as a kind of compromise between *the historicist assumption* and extreme *liberal humanism*.

specific truth
The kind of truth attributable to statements about a really existing thing or person (as opposed to fictional things or persons). Such statements do not necessarily partake of *general truth* or *moral truth*.

speech act theory
Speech act theory was first proposed in 1962, by the Oxford philosopher J.L. Austin, who was influenced by American *pragmatism* and the language philosophy of the later Wittgenstein. It was an attempt to theorize the relationship between words and deeds, so as to answer the question: How do people actually *do* things with words?

Austin described speech activity under three different aspects: as a *locutionary act*, i.e. speech as the act of producing a recognizably grammatical utterance; as an *illocutionary act* in the real world, i.e. speech as the asking or answering of a question, the giving of information, assurances or warnings, the announcing of a verdict or intention, etc.; and as a *perlocutionary act* in the real world, i.e. speech as something which has an effect on the hearer. Within this general set-up, his first step was to distinguish between two types of illocution: the *constative* and the *performative*. Whereas constatives purport to be a true representation of a state of affairs, performatives perform an action.

In order to work properly, a performative requires a certain context within a community which recognizes it for what it is. This, though, has nothing to do with truth. A performative is felicitous only by actually doing something in the world. Its illocutionary force cannot necessarily be read off from its locutionary form, but is nevertheless partly conventional within the life of the community. That is why people will sometimes even allow an apparent question to function as a request or an order, a phenomenon described by the theory as an *indirect speech act*.

Having set up the binarism between language as saying and language as doing, Austin then deconstructed it. Even constatives are performatives, and faulty constatives fail because they do not fulfil communally recognized conditions. This pragmatist account of truth as a social construct was subsequently sharpened by John Searle, who distinguished between brute facts and institutional or discoursal facts, and firmly attacked the so-called descriptive fallacy: the idea that language simply describes reality. Searle also formalized illocutionary acts into assertives, directives, commissives, expressives, and declaratives, and he greatly refined upon the *felicity conditions* for each type, i.e. the contextual circumstances which have to obtain in order for the act to have the particular illocutionary force.

A related development was Grice's *cooperative principle*, with its four **conversational maxims**.

structuralist linguistics
The main development in twentieth century linguistic theory and research well into the 1960s. To some extent it was a reaction against the historical interests of nineteenth-century *comparative philology*. A seminally systematic account was offered by the American linguist Leonard Bloomfield in 1933. But the key concepts and methods were proposed by the Swiss scholar Ferdinand de Saussure, himself a comparative philologist by training, whose lecture notes were posthumously compiled and published by his students in 1915.

Saussure became interested in the possibility of a general *semiology* or science of signs, and saw language as one example of a sign system. His first step was to define a sign itself as a merely arbitrary and conventional relationship between the thing *signified* and the *signifier* by which the signification is made. There is no particular reason why the word "dog" should signify a canine quadruped. There is simply a kind of communal agreement that it shall do so, at least until further notice. Another of his suggestions was that a switch from nineteenth-century diachronic approaches to a synchronic approach would enable linguists to illuminate the workings of a language's signs as an entire, coherently structured system.

This overarching system, to which he gave the name *langue*, would be entirely based on *differentiality*. Items at all levels of language structure acquire their form, meaning and function from being in contrast with other items. When stringing words one after another into a *syntagmatic* chain, for instance, we pay attention to differences between nouns, adjectives, verbs and so on. In its turn, every word chosen to fill one of these positions stands in *paradigmatic* differentiality with all the other words which would also have been grammatically viable there. Words belonging to the same paradigm are distinguishable from each other by the small units of meaning and surface form of which they are made up. The English nouns "bat" and "cat", for example, are differentiated from each other by their initial phoneme. Whereas a "phone" is just a sound, a phon*eme* is a sound which, within the structure of the particular language, carries meanings thanks to its contrastive relationships with other sounds. Differentiality as a whole is sometimes said to be an *emic* force or principle.

Structuralist methodology was strongly influenced by Saussure's distinction between *langue* and *parole*. *Parole* is any particular instantiation of *langue* as a real-life utterance in a specific context of human interaction. The actual language it uses will be subject to regional, social and situational variation, and may well display non-standard grammar or general looseness as well. The structuralist linguist's task was to examine it only insofar as it offered access to *langue*.

Because the "imperfections" of *parole* therefore had to be refined away, hardly any attention could be paid to contexts of use or to users' intentions and responses. Hence the affinity between structuralist linguistics and *behaviourism*.

stylistics
The study of styles, or manners of expression. Language is used in different ways in different kinds of context, by different individual users, and in different periods. But many scholars still restrict stylistics the discussion of literature, which they furthermore tend to view in terms of *literary formalism*. Sometimes stylistics involves descriptions of style which are openly impressionistic. But especially from the 1960s onwards, some scholars have hoped to achieve a more precise kind of description, by drawing on linguistic terminology, sometimes coupled with statistics. *Russian Formalism* was an important early influence, channelled to the West through the work of Roman Jakobson.

syntactics
See *pragmatics*.

syntagmatic
See *structuralist linguistics*.

talent-scouting mediation
See *mediation*

text-linguistics
An approach to language which, from the mid-1970s onwards, went beyond both *structuralist linguistics* and *transformational grammar*; more specifically, beyond both the description of minimal units and the syntactical analysis of single sentences. The aim was rather to study the properties of the texts made up from sentences in sequence. Pioneers included Robert de Beaugrande and Nils Erik Enkvist.

textualization-cum-contextualization
People who are communicating by means of language have to give a textual representation, not only of the "third" entity which is under negotiation (see *communication*), but of themselves and their own contexts. This is a way of modelling the communicative relationship for the purposes of empathetic understanding. To a large extent it is done by means of *communicative personae, deixis, emotive and evaluative expressions,* and *modality*.

unitary context assumption, the
The assumption that a *context*, even at the outset of communication, can be identical for the two or more people involved. According to the present work, it is fallacious. (Cf. *the mutual knowledge hypothesis*.) Communication is seen instead as a historically linear process by which different contexts become somewhat more homomorphic for the time being.

written-language bias, the
The preference of early-twentieth-century linguists' preference for illustrative examples which were more well-formed and articulate than much real language production. The term is Per Linell's.

Bibliography

Adams, Jon-K.
    1985   *Pragmatics and Fiction*. Amsterdam: Benjamins.
Adorno, Theodor
    1984   *Aesthetic Theory*. London: Routledge.
Altieri, Charles
    1981   *Act and Quality: a Theory of Meaning and Humanistic Understanding*. Amherst: University Press of Massachusetts.
Alvarez. A. (ed.)
    1962   *The New Poetry*. Harmondsworth: Penguin.
Anon. [= Abel Boyer, compiler]
    1702   *The English Theophrastus: or, The Manners of the Age. Being the Modern Characters of the Court, the Town, and the City*. London: Turner, Bassett and Chantry.
Appiah, K. Anthony
    1994   "Identity, Authenticity, Survival: Multicultural Societies and Social Reproduction". In Gutman 1994: 149–63.
Arnold, Matthew
    1888   *Essays in Criticism: Second Series*. London: Macmillan.
Austen, Jane
    1932 [1813]   *Pride and Prejudice* [The Novels of Jane Austen, 5 vols, vol. 2, 3rd ed.], R.W. Chapman (ed.). London: Oxford University Press.
Austen, Jane
    1933 [1816]   *Emma* [The Novels of Jane Austen, 5 vols, vol. 4, 3rd ed.], R.W. Chapman (ed.). London: Oxford University Press.
Austin, J.L.
    1975   *How to Do Things with Words* [2nd ed.. 1st ed. 1962]. Oxford: Oxford University Press.
Banfield, Ann
    1982   *Unspeakable Sentences: Narration and Representation in the Language of Fiction*. London: Routledge & Kegan Paul.
Banfield, Ann
    1992   "Literary Pragmatics". In *International Encyclopedia of Linguistics*, William Bright (ed.), 353–57. Oxford: Oxford University Press.
Barthes, Roland
    1977 [1968]   "The Death of the Author". In his *Image-Music-Text: Essays Selected and Translated by Stephen Heath*, 142–8. Glasgow: Fontana.

Barthes, Roland
1980 "Theory of the Text". In *Untying the Text: A Post-structuralist Reader*, Robert Young (ed.), 31–47. London: Routledge.
Barzun, Jacques
1975 "Biography and Criticism — A Misalliance Disputed". *Critical Inquiry* 1: 479–96.
Bate, Jonathan
1997 "Writ by Shakespeare: The Intrinsic Power of the Countess Scenes in *Edward III*". *Times Literary Supplement*, 17th January: 3–4.
Bell, Ian A.
1994 *Henry Fielding: Authorship and Authority*. London: Longman.
Bell, Michael
1997 *Literature, Modernism and Myth: Belief and Responsibility in the Twentieth Century*. Cambridge: Cambridge University Press.
Ben-Porat, Ziva
1991 "Two-Way Pragmatics: From World to Text and Back". In Sell 1991a: 143–63.
Ben-Porat, Ziva
1996 "Cognitive Poetics and the Experimental Study of Literature in Literary Pragmatics". In de Faria 1996: 818–29.
Bennett, W. Lance and Feldman, Martha S.
1981 *Reconstructing Reality in the Courtroom: Justice and Judgement in American Culture*. London: Tavistock.
Bentley, Bentley, Slater, Michael and Burgess, Nina
1990 *The Dickens Index*. Oxford: Oxford University Press.
Benveniste, Emile
1971 "Analytical philosophy and language". In his *Problems of General Linguistics, vol. I*, 231–8. Coral Gables: University of Miami Press.
Bergonzi, Bernard
1978 [1972] *T.S. Eliot*. Basingstoke: Macmillan.
Bergonzi, Bernard
1990 *Exploding English: Criticism, Theory, Culture*. Oxford: Clarendon Press.
Bergonzi, Bernard
1996 Letter. *London Review of Books*. 4th July: 4.
Berkeley, George
1979 *The Works of George Berkeley, Bishop of Cloyne: Vol. 3*, A.A. Luce and T.E. Jessop (eds). Liechtenstein: Kraus Reprint.
Berlin, Isaiah
1997 "The Pursuit of the Ideal". In his *The Proper Study of Mankind: An Anthology of Essays*, 1–16. London: Chatto & Windus.
Bernstein, Cynthia Goldin
1990 "'My Last Duchess': A Pragmatic Approach to the Dramatic Monologue", *The SECOL Review* 14:127–42.
Besnier, Niko
1986 "Literacy and feelings: the encoding of affect in Nukulaelae letters". In Ochs 1986: 69–91.

Bex, A.R.
    1992   "Genre as Context", *Journal of Literary Semantics* 21: 1–16.
Bex, Tony
    1994   "The Relevance of Genre". In Sell and Verdonk 1994: 107–29.
Biber, Douglas and Finegan, Edward
    1986   "Styles of stance in English: lexical and grammatical marking of evidentiality and affect". In Ochs: 93–124.
Black, Max
    1962   "Metaphor". In *Philosophy Looks at the Arts: Contemporary Readings in Aesthetics*, Joseph Margolis (ed.), 216–35. New York: Scribner's.
Blair, Hugh
    1965 [1783]   *Lectures on Rhetoric and Belles Lettres*, Harold F. Harding (ed.) Carbondale: Southern Illinois University Press.
Bloom, Harold
    1973   *The Anxiety of Influence: A Theory of Poetry*. New York: Oxford University Press.
Bloom, Harold
    1995 [1994]   *The Western Canon: The Books and the School of the Ages*. Basingstoke: Macmillan.
Blum-Kulka, S., House, J. and Casper, G. (eds)
    1989   *Cross-cultural Pragmatics: Requests and Apologies*. Norwood: Ablex.
Boasson, Charles
    1991   *In Search of Peace Research*. Basingstoke: Macmillan.
Booth, Wayne C.
    1961   *The Rhetoric of Fiction*. Chicago: University of Chicago Press.
Booth, Wayne C.
    1988   *The Company We Keep: An Ethics of Fiction*. Berkeley: University of California Press.
Boswell, James
    1906 [1791]   *The Life of Samuel Johnson, LL.D.*. London: Dent.
Briggs, Charles L. (ed.)
    1988   *Narrative Resources for the Creation and Mediation of Conflict*. Anthropological Linguistics 30: nos. 3 and 4.
Brooks, Cleanth
    1968 [1947]   *The Well Wrought Urn: Studies in the Structure of Poetry*. London: Methuen.
Brown, Gillian and Yule, George
    1983   *Discourse Analysis*. Cambridge: Cambridge University Press.
Brown, Penelope and Levinson, Stephen C.
    1987 [1978]   *Politeness: Some Universals in Language Usage*. Cambridge: Cambridge University Press.
Brunetière, Ferdinand
    1890   *L'évolution des genres dans l'histoire de la littérature*. Paris: Hachette.
Caputo, John D.
    1993   *Against Ethics: Contributions to a Poetics of Obligation with Constant Reference to Deconstruction*. Bloomington: Indiana University Press.

Caraher, Brian
 1991 *Wordsworth's "Slumber" and the Problematics of Reading* . University Park: Pennsylvania State University Press.
Carey, John
 1992 *The Intellectuals and The Masses: Pride and Prejudice among the Literary Intelligentsia, 1880–1939* . London: Faber.
Carlson, Lauri
 1983 *Dialogue Games: An Approach to Discourse Analysis* Dordrecht: Reidel.
Carver, Raymond
 1981 "Popular Mechanics" [subsequently re-entitled "Little Things"]. In his *What We Talk About When We Talk About Love*, 123–25. New York: Alfred A. Knopf.
Cassirer, Ernst
 1923–29 *Philosophie der symbolischen Formen* [3 vols]. Berlin: Bruno Cassirer.
Chafe, Wallace L.
 1982 "Integration and Involvement in Speaking, Writing, and Oral Literature". In Tannen 1982: 35–53.
Chafe, W.L.
 1994 *Discourse, Consciousness and Time: Flow and Displacement of Conscious Experience in Speaking and Writing*. Chicago: Chicago University Press.
Chatman, Seymour
 1978 *Story and Discourse: Narrative Structure in Fiction and Film*. Ithaca: Cornell University Press.
Chaucer, Geoffrey
 1957 [? c. 1390] "The Knight's Tale" and "The Miller's Tale". In *The Works of Geoffrey Chaucer*, F.N. Robinson (ed.). London: Oxford University Press.
Chomsky, Noam
 1957 *Syntactic Structures*. The Hague: Mouton.
Christ, Carol C.
 1981 "T.S. Eliot and the Victorians". *Modern Philology* 79:157–65.
Christ, Carol C.
 1984 "Self-Concealment and Self-Expression in Eliot's and Pound's Dramatic Monologues". *Victorian Poetry* 22: 217–26.
Clark, Billy
 1996 "Stylistic Analysis and Relevance Theory". *Language and Linguistics* 5:163–78.
Clark, Ian
 1997 *Globalization and Fragmentation: International Relations in the Twentieth Century*. Oxford: Oxford University Press.
Čmejrková, Světla, Daneš, František and Havlová, Eva (eds.)
 1994 *Writing vs. Speaking: Language, Text, Discourse, Communication*. Tübingen: Gunter Narr.
Cole, Peter (ed.)
 1981 *Radical Pragmatics*. New York: Academic Press.

Coleridge, Samuel Taylor
    1956 [1817] *Biographia Literaria: or Biographical Sketches of my Literary Life and Opinions*, George Watson (ed.). London: Dent.
Connor, Steven
    1991 *Postmodernist Culture* Oxford: Blackwell.
Connor, Steven
    1992 *Theory and Cultural Value* . Oxford: Blackwell.
Cook, Guy
    1994 "Contradictory Voices: A Dialogue between Russian and Western European Linguistics". In Sell and Verdonk 1994: 151–61.
Cooper, Marilyn M.
    1982 "Context as Vehicle: Implicatures in Writing". In Nystrand 1982: 105–28.
Cortright, David (ed.)
    1997 *The Price of Peace: Incentives and International Conflict Prevention.* Lanham: Rowman and Littlefield.
Cox, Geoff
    1986 "Literary Pragmatics: A New Discipline: The Example of Fitzgerald's *Great Gatsby*". *Literature and History* 12: 79–96.
Crane, R. S. (ed.)
    1952 *Critics and Criticism, Ancient and Modern.* Chicago: Chicago University Press.
Croce, Benedetto
    1992 [1902] *The Aesthetic as the Science of Expression and of the Linguistic.* Cambridge: Cambridge University Press.
Culler, Jonathan
    1982 *On Deconstruction: Theory and Criticism after Structuralism.* Ithaca: Cornell University Press.
Cunico, Sonia
    1992 Review of Sell 1991a. *Language and Literature* 2:141–3.
D'Aguiar, Fred,
    1994 *The Longest Memory* . London: Chatto and Windus.
Dakubu, M.E. Kropp
    1987 "Creating Unity: The Context of Speaking Prose and Poetry in Ga". *Anthropos* 82: 507–27.
Davie, Donald
    1967[1952] *Purity of Diction in English Verse*. London: Routledge and Kegan Paul.
Davie, Donald
    1975 *Ezra Pound.* Harmondsworth: Penguin.
de Beaugrande, Robert
    1980 *Text, Discourse, Process.* Norwood: Ablex.
de Beaugrande, Robert
    1982 "Psychology and Compositions: Past, Present and Future". In Nystrand 1982: 211–67.
de Beaugrande, Robert and Dressler, Wolgang Ulrich
    1981 *Introduction to Text Linguistics.* London: Longman.

de Faria, Neide (ed.)
  1996   *Language and Literature Today: Proceedings of the XIXth Triennial Congress of the International Federation for Modern Languages and Literatures* [3 vols]. Brasilia, Universidade de Brasilia.
de Geest, Dirk
  1995   "Literary Pragmatics". In *Handbook of Pragmatics*, Jef Verschueren, Jan-Ola Östman and Jan Blommart (eds.), 351–7. Amsterdam: Benjamins.
de Man, Paul
  1979   *Allegories of Reading: Figural Language in Rousseau, Nietzsche, Rilke and Proust*. New Haven: Yale University Press.
de Saussure, Ferdinand
  1978 [1916]   *Course in General Linguistics*. London: Fontana.
Derrida, Jacques
  1974 [1967]   *Of Grammatology*. Baltimore: Johns Hopkins University Press.
Dewey, John
  1931   *Philosophy and Civilization*. New York: Minson, Balch & Co.
Dewey, John
  1934   *Art and Experience*. London: George, Allen and Unwin.
Dickens, Charles
  1982 [1848]   *Dombey and Son*, Alan Horsman (ed.). Oxford: Oxford University Press.
Dickens, Charles
  1979 [1857]   *Little Dorrit*, Harvey Peter Sucksmith (ed.). Oxford: Clarendon Press.
Dickie, George
  1974   *Art and the Aesthetic*. Ithaca: Cornell University Press.
Diller, Hans-Jürgen
  1991   "Theatrical Pragmatics: The Actor-Audience Relationship from the Mystery Cycles to the Early Tudor Comedies". In *Drama in the Middle Ages: Comparative and Critical Essays*, Clifford Davidson and John J. Stroupe (eds), 321–30. New York: AMS Press.
Dolitsky, Marlene
  1984   *Under the Tumtum Tree: From Nonsense to Sense: A Study in Nonautomatic Comprehension*. Amsterdam: Benjamins.
Donne, John
  1965   *John Donne: The Elegies and the Songs and Sonnets*, Helen Gardner (ed.). Oxford: Clarendon Press.
Donne, John
  1965 [1633]   "The Canonization". In Donne 1964: 73–5.
Donne, John
  1965 [1633]   "The Exstasie". In Donne 1965: 59–61.
Donne, John
  1967 [1633]   "Satyres". In *John Donne: The Satires, Epigrams and Verse Letters*, W. Milgate (ed.), 1–49. Oxford: Clarendon Press.

Doty, Leilani Kathleen
    1984   "Fiction into Drama: A Pragmatic Analysis of Dramatic Dialogues in Adaptations". Diss. University of Washington, 1984.
Doyle, Michael W.
    1997   *Ways of War and Peace: Realism, Liberalism, and Socialism*. New York: Norton.
Drakakis, John
    1997   "Shakespeare in Quotations". In *Studying British Cultures: An Introduction*, Susan Bassnett (ed.), 152–72. London: Routledge.
Dubrow, Heather
    1982   *Genre*. London: Methuen.
Dworkin, Ronald
    1978   "Liberalism". In *Public and Private Morality*, Stuart Hampshire (ed.), 113–43. Cambridge: Cambridge University Press.
Edmondson, Willis
    1981   *Spoken Discourse: a Model for Analysis*. London: Longman.
Eichenbaum, Boris
    1978 [1925]   "O. Henry and the theory of the short story". In Matejka and Pomorska 1978: 227–70.
Eisenstein, Elizabeth
    1979   *The Printing Press as an Agent of Change*. Cambridge: Cambridge University Press.
Elam, Keir
    1988   "Much Ado About Doing Things With Words (and Other Means): Some Problems in the Pragmatics of Theatre and Drama". In *Performing Texts*, Michael Issacharoff and Robin J. Jones (eds), 39–58. Philadelphia: University of Pennsylvania Press.
Eliot, T.S.
    1934   *After Strange Gods: A Primer of Modern Heresy*. London: Faber.
Eliot, T.S.
    1936   *Essays Ancient and Modern* . New York: Harcourt Brace, New York.
Eliot, T.S.
    1951   *Selected Essays* [3rd ed.]. London: Faber.
Eliot, T.S.
    1951 [1919](a)   "*Hamlet*". In Eliot 1951: 141–6.
Eliot, T.S.
    1951 [1919](b)   "Tradition and the Individual Talent". In Eliot 1951: 13–22.
Eliot, T.S.
    1951 [1921]   "The Metaphysical Poets". In Eliot 1951: 281–91.
Eliot, T.S.
    1951 [1923]   "The Function of Criticism". In Eliot 1951: 23–34.
Eliot, T.S.
    1951 [1929]   "Dante". In Eliot 1951: 237–77.
Eliot, T.S.
    1951 [1936]   "'In Memoriam'". In Eliot 1951: 328–38.

Eliot, T.S.
    1957   "Goethe as the Sage". In his *On Poetry and Poets*, 207–27. London: Faber.
Eliot, T.S.
    1969   *The Complete Poems and Plays of T.S. Eliot,* London: Faber.
Eliot, T.S.
    1969 [1920]   "Gerontion". In Eliot 1969: 37–7.
Eliot, T.S.
    1969 [1921]   *The Waste Land.* In Eliot 1969: 59–80.
Eliot, T.S.
    1971   *T.S. Eliot: The Waste Land: A Facsimile and Transcript of the Original Drafts: Including the Annotations of Ezra Pound,* Valerie Eliot (ed.). New York: Harcourt Brace Jovanovich.
Ellis, John
    1989   *Against Deconstruction.* Princeton: Princeton University Press.
Emerson, Caryll
    1996   "Keeping the Self Intact during the Culture Wars: A Centennial Essay for Mikhail Bakhtin". *New Literary History* 27:107–26.
Empson, William
    1930   *Seven Types of Ambiguity.* London: Chatto and Windus.
Engelstone, Robert
    1997   *Ethical Criticism: Reading after Levinas.* Edinburgh: Edinburgh University Press.
Engler, Balz
    1987   "Deixis and the Status of Poetic Texts". In *The Structure of Texts*, Udo Fries (ed.), 65–73. Tübingen: Gunter Narr.
Engler, Balz
    1990   *Poetry and Community.* Tübingen: Stauffenberg Verlag.
Epstein, William (ed.)
    1991   *Contesting the Subject: Essays in the Postmodern Theory and Practice of Biography and Biographical Criticism.* West Lafayette: Purdue University Press.
Fairclough, Norman
    1995   *Critical Discourse Analysis: the Critical Study of Language.* London: Longman.
Faure, Guy Olivier and Rubin, Jeffrey Z.(eds.)
    1993   *Culture and Negotiation: The Resolution of Water Disputes.* Newbury Park: Sage.
Felperin, Howard
    1985   *Beyond Deconstruction: The Uses and Abuses of Literary Theory.* Oxford: Clarendon Press.
Fielding, Henry
    1903 [1743]   "Essay on Conversation". In *The Writings of Henry Fielding: Vol. 14*, William Ernest Henley (ed.), 245–77. London: Heinemann.
Fish, Stanley
    1980   *Is There a Text in This Class? The Authority of Interpretative Communities.* Cambridge Mass.: Harvard University Press.

Fish, Stanley
 1991 "Biography and Intention". In Epstein 1991: 9–16.
Fitter, Chris
 1992 "Henry Vaughan's Landscapes of Military Occupation". *Essays in Criticism* 42:123–47.
Fludernik, Monica
 1993 "Narratology in Context". *Poetics Today* 14: 729–59.
Fludernik, Monika
 1993 *The Fictions of Language and the Languages of Fiction.* London: Routledge.
Forgacs, David
 1993 [1984] "National-popular: genealogy of a concept". In *The Cultural Studies Reader*, Simon During (ed.), 177–90. London: Routledge.
Foster, Hal (ed.)
 1985 *Postmodern Culture.* London: Pluto Press.
Foucault, Michel
 1979 [1969] "What is an Author?" In *Textual Strategies: Perspectives in Post-Structuralist Criticism,* Josué V. Harrari (ed.), 141–60. London: Methuen.
Foucault, Michel
 1990 [1971] "The Order of Discourse". In Rice and Ward 1996: 239–51.
Fowler, Alastair
 1982 *Kinds of Literature: An Introduction to the Theory of Genres and Modes.* Oxford: Oxford University Press.
Fowler, Alastair
 1987 *A History of English Literature.* Oxford: Blackwell.
Fowler, Alastair
 1998 Review of Helen Vendler, *The Art of Shakespeare's Sonnets. London Review of Books.* 2nd January: 11–12.
Fowler, Roger
 1981 *Literature as Social Discourse: the Practice of Linguistic Criticism.* London: Batsford.
Fowler, Roger
 1983 "Polyphony and Problematic in *Hard Times*". In *The Changing World of Charles Dickens,* Robert Giddings (ed.), 91–108. London: Barnes and Noble.
Fowler, Roger
 1993 Review of Sell 1991a. *Journal of Pragmatics* 20: 377–9.
Freud, Sigmund
 1979 [1926] "Inhibitions, Symptoms and Anxiety". In *On Psychopathology: Inhibitions, Symptoms and Anxiety and Other Works* [The Penguin Freud Library, vol. 10], 235–315. Harmondsworth: Penguin.
Frost, Frost
 1949 "Education by Poetry". In *Selected Prose of Robert Frost,* Hyde Cox and Edward Connery Lathem (eds), 33–46. New York: Holt, Rinehart and Winston.

Frost, Robert
  1972 [1928] "Spring Pools". In *The Poetry of Robert Frost*, Edward Connery Lathem (ed.), 245. London: Jonathan Cape.
Frye, Northrop
  1957 *Anatomy of Criticism: Four Essays*. Princeton: Princeton University Press.
Fuller, John
  1983 *The Beautiful Inventions*. London: Secker & Warburg.
Gadamer, Hans-Georg
  1976 [1962–72] *Philosophical Hermeneutics*. Berkeley: University of California Press.
Gadamer, Hans-Georg
  1981[1976, 1978, 1979] *Reason in the Age of Science*. Cambridge, Mass.: MIT Press.
Gadamer, Hans-Georg
  1986 [1967, 1977, 1980] *The Relevance of the Beautiful and Other Essays*. Cambridge: Cambridge University Press.
Gadamer, Hans-Georg
  1989 [1960] *Truth and Method*. New York: Seabury Press.
Gelley, Alexander
  1987 *Narrative Crossings: Theory and Pragmatics of Prose Fiction* . Baltimore: Johns Hopkins University Press.
Givón, T. (ed.)
  1979 *Syntax and Semantics, vol. 12: Discourse and Syntax*. New York: Academic Press.
Goffman, Ervin
  1959 *The Presentation of the Self in Everyday Life*. New York: Doubleday.
Goodman, Nelson
  1978 *Ways of Worldmaking*. Indianapolis: Hackett.
Goodwin, Charles Goodwin and Duranti, Alessandro (eds)
  1992 *Rethinking Context: Language as an Interactive Phenomenon*. Cambridge: Cambridge University Press.
Goody, J. (ed.)
  1968 *Literacy in Traditional Societies*. Cambridge: Cambridge University Press.
Goody, J.
  1977 *The Domestication of the Savage Mind*. Cambridge: Cambridge University Press.
Goody, J.
  1986 *The Logic of Writing and the Organization of Society*. Cambridge: Cambridge University Press.
Goody, J.
  1987 *The Interface between the Written and the Oral*. Cambridge: Cambridge University Press.
Graff, Gerald
  1979 *Literature Against Itself*. Chicago: Chicago University Press.

Graff, Gerald
    1992   *Beyond the Culture Wars: How Teaching the Conflicts Can Revitalize American Education.* New York: Norton.
Gray, Bennison.
    1977   *The Grammatical Foundations of Rhetoric: Discourse Analysis.* The Hague: Mouton.
Gray, Bennison
    1978   Review of van Dijk 1976. *Journal of Pragmatics* 2:189–94.
Green, Keith (ed.)
    1955   *New Essays in Deixis: Discourse, Narrative, Literature.* Amsterdam: Rodopi.
Greenblatt, Stephen
    1996 [1990]   "Resonance and Wonder". In Rice and Ward 1996: 268–88.
Greg, W.W.
    1906   *Pastoral Poetry and Pastoral Drama: A Literary Enquiry, with Special Reference to the Pre-Restoration Stage in England.* London: A.H. Bullen.
Grice, H.P.
    1991 [1967]   "Logic and Conversation". In *Pragmatics: A Reader*, Steven Davis (ed.), 305–15. New York: Oxford University Press.
Grübel, Rainer
    1987   "The Personal Pragmatic Institutions of Poetic Discourse". In *Approaches to Discourse, Poetics and Psychiatry*, Iris M. Zavala, Teun A. van Dijk and Myriam Díaz-Diocaretz (eds.), 147–70. Amsterdam: Benjamins.
Gumperez, John
    1982   *Discourse Strategies.* Cambridge: Cambridge University Press.
Gutman, Amy (ed.)
    1994   *Multiculturalism: Examining the Politics of Recognition.* Princeton: Princeton University Press.
Habermas, Jürgen
    1993   *Justification and Application: Remarks on Discourse Ethics.* Cambridge, Mass.: MIT Press.
Habermas, Jürgen
    1994   "Struggles for Recognition in the Democratic Constitutional State". In Gutman 1994: 107–148.
Halliday. M.A.K.
    1985   *An Introduction to Functional Grammar.* London: Arnold, London.
Halverson, J.
    1992   "Havelock on Greek Orality and Literacy". *Journal of the History of Ideas* 53: 148–63.
Hampshire, Stuart
    1992 [1989]   *Innocence and Experience.* Harmondsworth: Penguin.
Hancher, Michael
    1980   "Understanding Poetic Speech Acts". In *Linguistic Perspectives on Literature*, Murvin K.L. Ching, Michael C. Haley and Ronald F. Lunsford (eds), 295–304. London: Routledge & Kegan Paul.

Hardy, Donald E.
 1991 "Strategic Politeness in Hemingway's 'The Short Happy Life of Francis Macomber'". *Poetics* 20: 343–62.
Harpman, Geoffrey Galt
 1992 *Getting it Right: Language, Literature, and Ethics*. Chicago: Chicago University Press.
Harpman, Geoffrey Galt
 1995 "Ethics". In *Critical Terms for Literary Study* [2nd ed.], Frank Lentricchia and Thomas McLaughlin (eds.), 387–405. Chicago: Chicago University Press.
Harris, Roy
 1987 *The Language Machine*. London: Duckworth.
Harris, Wilson
 1983 *The Womb of Space: The Cross-Cultural Imagination*. Westport, Conn.: Greenwood.
Harris, Wilson
 1989 "Comedy and Modern Allegory: A Personal View". In *A Shaping of Connections: Commonwealth Literature Studies — Then and Now*, Hena Maes-Jelinek, Kirsten Holst Petersen and Anna Rutherford (eds.), 127–40. Aarhus: Dangaroo Press.
Hartman, Geoffrey, H.
 1996 [1987] "'Timely Utterance' Once More". In *A Practical Reader in Contemporary Literary Theory*, Peter Brooker and Peter Widdowson (eds.), 80–90. London: Prentice Hall/Harvester Wheatsheaf.
Harvey, David
 1989 *The Condition of Postmodernity: An Inquiry into the Origins of Cultural Change*. Oxford: Blackwell.
Havelock, E.
 1982 *The Literate Revolution in Greece and its Cultural Consequences*. Princeton: Princeton University Press.
Havelock, E.
 1986 *The Muse Learns to Write*. New Haven: Yale University Press.
Havelock, E.
 1989 "Orality and Literacy, an Overview". *Language and Communication* 9: 87–98.
Haverkate, Henk
 1994 "The dialogues of Don Quixote de la Mancha: A pragmalinguistic analysis within the framework of Gricean maxims, speech act theory, and politeness theory". *Poetics* 22: 219–41.
Haviland, John B.
 1986 "'Sure, sure': evidence and affect". In Ochs 1986: 27–68.
Hawkes, Terence
 1986 *That Shakespeherian Rag: Essays on a Critical Process*. London: Methuen.
Hecht, Anthony
 1995 *On the Laws of the Poetic Art* [= Bollingen Series 35: 41]. Princeton: Princeton University Press.

Hegel, G.W.F.
　　1975 [1820–1]　*Aesthetics: Lectures on Fine Art: Vol. 2.* Oxford: Clarendon Press.
Hildyard, Angela and Olson, David R.
　　1982　"On the Comprehension and Memory of Oral vs. Written Discourse". In Tannen 1982: 19–33.
Hill, Geoffrey
　　1991　*The Enemy's Country: Words, Contexture, and Other Circumstances.* Oxford: Clarendon Press.
Hine, Robert A. and Parry, Donald A. (eds.)
　　1989　*Education for Peace.* Nottingham: Spokesman.
Hirsch, E.D.
　　1988　"The contents of English literature". *Times Literary Supplement*, 10th December, 1359.
Hobsbawm, Eric
　　1994　*Age of Extremes: The Short History of the Twentieth Century: 1914–1991.* London: Michael Joseph.
Holland, Norman
　　1975 [1968]　*The Dynamics of Literary Response.* New York: Norton.
Holland, Norman
　　1975 [1973]　*Poems in Persons: An Introduction to the Psychoanalysis of Literature.* New York: Norton.
Hollinger, Robert (ed.)
　　1985　*Hermeneutics and Praxis.* Notre Dame: University of Notre Dame Press.
Holsti, Kalevi, J.
　　1991　*Peace and War: Armed Conflicts and International Order.* Cambridge: Cambridge University Press, Cambridge.
Hopper, Paul J.
　　1979　"Aspect and foregrounding in discourse". In Givón 1979: 213–41.
Hopper, Paul J. (ed.)
　　1982　*Tense-Aspect: Between Semantics and Pragmatics.* Amsterdam: Benjamins.
Hoy, David
　　1978　*The Critical Circle: Literature, History, and Philosophical Hermeneutics.* Berkeley: University of California Press.
Hume, David
　　1757　*Four Dissertations: I. The Natural History of Religion. II. Of the Passions. III. Of Tragedy. IV. Of the Standard of Taste.* London: A. Millar.
Iser, Wolfgang
　　1974　*The Implied Reader: Patterns of Communication in Prose Fiction from Bunyan to Beckett.* Baltimore: Johns Hopkins University Press.
Jacob, Giles
　　1720　*An Historical Account of the Lives and Writings of Our most Considerable ENGLISH Poets, whether Epick, Lyrick, Elegiack, Epigramatists, &c.* London: E. Curll.

James, Allan R.
　　1983　"Compromisers in English: a crossdisciplinary approach to their interpersonal significance" *Journal of Pragmatics* 7:191–206.
Jameson, Fredric
　　1991　*Postmodernism or the Logic of Late Capitalism*. London: Verso.
Jaspers, Karl
　　1954　*Die Psychologie der Weltanschauungen* [4th ed.. 1st ed.1919]. Heidelberg: Springer.
Jauss, Hans Robert
　　1982　*Towards an Aesthetic of Reception*. Brighton: Harvester.
Jay, Gregory S.
　　1997　*American Literature and the Culture Wars*. Ithaca: Cornell University Press.
Jay, Paul
　　1984　*Being in the Text: Self-Representation from Wordsworth to Roland Barthes*. Ithaca: Cornell University Press.
Johnson, Samuel
　　1960 [1765]　Preface to his *The Plays of William Shakespeare*. In *Samuel Johnson on Shakespeare*, W.K. Wimsatt (ed), 23–69. London: Macgibbon & Kee.
Jolles, André
　　1956 [1930]　*Einfache Formen: Legende, Sage, Mythe, Rätsel, Spruch, Kasus, Memorabile, Märchen, Witz*. Halle: M. Niemeyer.
Joyce, Joyce
　　1960 [1916]　*A Portrait of the Artist as a Young Man*. Harmondsworth: Penguin.
Jucker, Andreas H.
　　1995　Review of Sell 1991a. *Multilingua: Journal of Cross-Cultural and Interlanguage Communication* 14: 95–8.
Julius, Anthony
　　1995　*T. S. Eliot, Anti-Semitism, and Literary Form*. Cambridge: Cambridge University Press.
Kant, Immanuel
　　1998 [1785]　*Groundwork of the Metaphysics of Morals*. Trans. and ed. Mary Gregor, introd. Christine M. Korsgaard . Cambridge: Cambridge University Press.
Kant, Immanuel
　　1951 [1790]　"The Critique of Aesthetic Judgement" [= Part 1 of his *Critique of Judgement*]. New York: Hafner.
Karpenko, Tatyana
　　1993　"Pragmatic Aspects of Literary Communication". Occasional Papers no. 3; PALA: The Poetics and Linguistics Association [Available from Peter Verdonk, English Department, University of Amsterdam].
Kasper, Gabriele and Blum-Kulka, Shoshana (eds)
　　1993　*Interlanguage Pragmatics*. Oxford: Oxford University Press.
Katz, Jerrold
　　1977　*Propositional Structure and Illocutionary Force*. Brighton: Harvester.

Keats, John
    1954 [1817]   Letter to George and Thomas Keats (22 December). In *Letters of John Keats*, Frederick Page (ed.), 51–4. London: Oxford University Press.
Kermode, Frank
    1957   *Romantic Image*. London: Routledge and Kegan Paul.
Kermode, Frank
    1990 [1989]   *An Appetite for Poetry: Essays in Literary Appreciation*. Glasgow: Fontana.
Kermode, Frank
    1996   *Not Entitled: A Memoir*. London: Harper Collins.
Kristeva, Julia
    1980   *Desire in Language: A Semiotic Approach to Literature and Art*. Oxford: Blackwell.
Krysinsky, Wladimir
    1984   "The Pragmatics of Dialogue in the Theatre of St.I. Witkiewicz", *Modern Drama* 27: 64–79.
Labov, William and Waletzky, Joshua
    1967   "Narrative Analysis: Oral Versions of Personal Experience". *Essays on the Verbal and Visual Arts: Proceedings of the 1966 Annual Spring Meeting of the American Ethnologic Society*, 12–45. Seattle: University of Washington Press.
Labov, William
    1981   "Speech actions and reactions". In Tannen 1981: 219–47.
Lakoff, George and Johnson, Mark
    1980   *Metaphors we Live By*. Chicago: University of Chicago Press.
Lakoff, George
    1987   *Women, Fire, and Dangerous Things: What Categories Reveal about the Mind*. Chicago: University of Chicago Press.
Lakoff, George and Turner, Mark
    1989   *More Cool than Reason: A Field Guide to Poetic Metaphor*. Chicago: University of Chicago Press.
Lakoff, Robin
    1973   "The logic of politeness: or, minding your p's and q's". In *Papers from the Ninth Regional Meeting of the Chicago Linguistic Society*, 292–305. Chicago: Chicago Linguistic Society.
Lakoff, Robin Tomach
    1982   "Some of my Favourite Writers are Literate: the Mingling of Oral and Literate Strategies in Communication". In Tannen 1982: 239–60.
Langer, Susanne K.
    1953   *Feeling and Form: A Theory of Art developed from Philosophy in a New Key*. New York: Charles Scribner's Sons.
Lanser, Susan Sniader
    1981   *The Narrative Act: Point of View in Prose Fiction*. Princeton: Princeton University Press.

Leavis, F.R.
 1962 [1948] *The Great Tradition: George Eliot, Henry James, Joseph Conrad*. Harmondsworth: Penguin.
Leavis, F.R.
 1962 [1952]a *The Common Pursuit*. Harmondsworth: Penguin.
Leavis, F.R.
 1962 [1952]b "Literary Criticism and Philosophy". In Leavis 1962 [1952]a: 211–222.
Leavis, F.R.
 1962 *The Two Cultures? The Significance of C.P. Snow*. London: Chatto and Windus.
Leavis, F.R.
 1964 [1936] *Revaluation: Tradition and Development in English Poetry*. Harmondsworth: Penguin.
Leavis, F.R.
 1964 [1955] *D.H. Lawrence: Novelist*. Harmondsworth: Penguin.
Leech, G. N.
 1983a *Principles of Pragmatics*. London: Longman.
Leech, G.N.
 1983b "Pragmatics, Discourse Analysis, Stylistics and 'The Celebrated Letter'". *Prose Studies* 6:142–57.
Leech, Geoffrey
 1992 "Pragmatic Principles in Shaw's *You Never Can Tell*". In Toolan 1992: 259–78.
Leech, Geoffrey N. and Short, Michael H.
 1983 *A Linguistic Guide to English Fictional Prose*. London: Longman.
Leech, Geoffrey and Thomas, Jenny
 1988 "Language, Meaning and Context: Pragmatics". In *Encyclopaedia of Language*, N.E. Collinge (ed.), 173–206. London: Routledge.
Leitch, Thomas M.
 1983 "To What is Fiction Committed?" *Prose Studies* 6: 159–75.
Leitch, Vincent
 1983 *Deconstructive Criticism*. New York: Columbia University Press.
Lemon, Lee T. and Reis, Marion J.(eds)
 1965 *Russian Formalist Criticism: Four Essays* . Lincoln: University of Nebraska Press.
Levin, Samuel R.
 1976 "Concerning What Kind of Speech Act a Poem Is". In van Dijk 1976: 141–60.
Levinas, Emmanuel
 1974 *Humanisme de l'autre homme*. Montpellier: Fata Morgana.
Levinson, Stephen C.
 1983 *Pragmatics*. Cambridge: Cambridge University Press.
Lévi-Strauss, Claude
 1970 [1964] "Overture to *Le Cru et le Cuit*". In *Structuralism*, Jacques Ehrmann (ed.), 31–55. Garden City: Anchor-Doubleday.

Lewis, C.S.
    1992 [1961]   *An Experiment in Criticism*. Cambridge: Cambridge University Press.
Linde, Charlotte
    1979   "Forms of Attention and the Choice of Pronouns in Discourse". In Givón 1979: 337–54.
Linell, Per
    1982   *The Written-Language Bias of Linguistics* [= Studies in Communication 2]. Linköping: University of Linköping.
Lodge, David
    1990   *After Bakhtin: Essays on Fiction and Criticism*. London: Routledge.
Lofton, Ramona (= Sapphire)
    1992   "Wild Thing". *The Portable Lower East Side*, "Queer City" issue.
Longacre, R.E.
    1979   "The paragraph as a grammatical unit". In Givón 1979: 115–54.
Longacre, R.E.
    1981   "A Spectrum and Profile Approach to Discourse Analysis". *Text* 1: 337–61.
Longinus
    1965 [? 1st c. A.D.] *On the Sublime*. In *Classical Literary Criticism: Aristotle: On the Art of Poetry; Horace: On the Art of Poetry; Longinus: On the Sublime*, T.S. Dorsch (trans. and introd.), 99–158. Harmondsworth: Penguin.
Lubbock, Percy
    1921   *The Craft of Fiction*. London: Jonathan Cape.
Lyotard, Jean-François
    1984 [1979]   *The Postmodern Condition: A Report on Knowledge*. Manchester: Manchester University Press.
Machin, Richard and Norris, Christopher (eds)
    1987   *Post-Structuralist Readings of English Poetry*. Cambridge: Cambridge University Press.
Macleod, Norman
    1992   "Lexicogrammar and the Reader: Three Examples from Dickens". In *Language, Text and Context: Essays in Stylistics*, Michael Toolan (ed.), 138–57. London: Routledge.
Maes-Jelinek, Hena
    1991   "Seeking the Mystery of the 'Universal Imagination'". In *International Literature in English: Essays on the Major Writers*, Robert L. Ross (ed.), 447–59. New York: Garland.
Maingueneau, Dominique
    1990   *Pragmatique pour le discours littéraire*. Paris: Bordas.
Malinowski, B.
    1938 [1923]   "The Problem of Meaning in Primitive Languages". In, *The Meaning of Meaning*, C.K. Ogden and I.A. Richards (eds), 296–336. London: Trench, Truber & Co.
Marshall, Peter
    1997   *Positive Diplomacy*. Basingstoke: Macmillan.

Martlew, Margaret (ed.)
   1983   *The Psychology of Written Language: Developmental and Educational Perspectives*. Chichester: Wiley.
Matejka, Ladislav and Pomorska, Krystyna (eds.)
   1978   *Readings in Russian Poetics*. Ann Arbor: University of Michican Press, Ann Arbor.
McGann, Jerome J.
   1985   *The Beauty of Inflections: Investigations in Historical Method and Theory*. Oxford: Clarendon Press.
McGann, Jerome J.
   1991(a)   "Literary Pragmatics and the Editorial Horizon". In *Devils and Angels: Textual Editing and Literary Theory*, Philip Cohen (ed.), 1–21. Charlottesville: University Press of Virginia.
McGann, Jerome, J.
   1991(b)   "What Difference do the Circumstances of Publication make to the Interpretation of a Literary Work?". In Sell 1991a: 190–207.
McGrath, F.C.
   1982   "*Ulysses* and the Pragmatic Semiotics of Modernism". *Comparative Literature Studies* 19:164–74.
McPherson, David
   1997   Review of A.W. Johnson, *Ben Jonson: Poetry and Architecture*. *Renaissance Quarterly* 50: 890–1.
Mead, George Herbert
   1934   *Mind, Self, and Society*. Chicago: University of Chicago Press.
Meckier, Jerome
   1987   *Hidden Rivalries in Victorian Fiction: Dickens, Realism, and Revaluation*. Lexington: University Press of Kentucky.
Merquior, J.C.
   1986   *From Prague to Paris: A Critique of Stucturalist and Post-Structuralist Thought*. London: Verso.
Meuller-Vollmer, Kurt (ed.)
   1985   *The Hermeneutics Reader: Texts of the German Tradition from the Englightenment to the Present*. Oxford: Blackwell.
Mey, Jacob L.
   1987   "'Breaking the Seal of Time': the pragmatics of poetics". In *Language Topics: Essays in Honour of Michael Halliday: Vol. 1*, Ross Steele and Terry Threadgold (eds). 281–91. Amsterdam: Benjamins.
Mey, Jacob L.
   1993   *Pragmatics: An Introduction*. Oxford: Blackwell.
Mey, Jacob L. and Talbot, M.M.
   1988   "Computation and the soul" [review article of Sperber and Wilson 1986]. *Semiotica* 72: 291–339.
Miller, J. and Kintsch, W.
   1980   "Readability and Recall of Short Passages: a Theoretical Analysis". *Journal of Experimental Pyschology: Human Learning and Memory* 6: 335–58.

Miller, John Hillis
    1985   *The Ethics of Reading: Kant, de Man, Eliot, Trollope, James, and Benjamin*. New York: Columbia University Press.
Miller, John Hillis
    1995   "The University of Dissensus". *The Oxford Literary Review* 17:121–43.
Mills, Sara
    1992   "Knowing Your Place: a Marxist Feminist Stylistic Analysis". In Toolan 1992: 182–205.
Milton, John
    1925 [1644]   *Areopagitica: A Speech of Mr John Milton For the Liberty of Unlicensed Printing to the Parliament of England*. In *Milton's Prose*, Malcolm W. Wallace (ed.), 275–324. London: Oxford University Press.
Moerman, Michael
    1992   "Life After C.A.: An Ethnographer's Autobiography" In *Text in Context: Contributions to Ethnomethodology*, Graham Watson and Robert M. Seiler (eds), 20–34. Newbury Park: Sage.
More, Thomas,
    1989 [1516]   *Utopia*, G.M. Logan and R.M. Adams (trans.). Cambridge: Cambridge University Press.
Morris, Charles
    1946   *Signs, Language and Behavior*. New York: Prentice-Hall.
Morris, Charles
    1971   *Writings on the General Theory of Signs*. The Hague: Mouton.
Morris, Charles
    1971 [1938]   *Foundations of the Theory of Signs*. In Morris 1971: 14–77. [First published as *International Encyclopedia of Unified Science*, vol. 1, no. 2. Chicago: University of Chicago Press.].
Morris, Charles
    1971 [1939]   "Esthetics and the Theory of Signs". In Morris 1971: 415–33.
Mukařovský, Jan
    1970 [1936]   *Aesthetic Function, Norm and Value as Social Facts*. Ann Arbor: University of Michigan Press.
Nealon, Jeffrey T.
    1993   *Double Reading: Postmodernism after Deconstruction*. Ithaca: Cornell University Press.
[Cohen, Ralph (ed.)]
    1978   Special issue on literary hermeneutics. *New Literary History* vol.10 no. 1(autumn).
Nietzsche, Friedrich Wilhelm
    1872   *Die Geburt der Tragödie aus dem Geiste der Musik*. Leipzig: Fritzsche.
Noll, Richard
    1996   *The Jung Cult: Origins of a Carismatic Movement*. London: HarperCollins.
Nunberg, Geoffrey
    1981   "Validating pragmatic explanations".In Cole 1981: 198–222.

Nystrand, Martin (ed.)
　1982　*What Writers Know: The Language, Process, and Structure of Written Discourse.* New York: Academic Press.
O'Halloran, Kieran
　1997　"Why Whorf has been misconstrued in stylistics and critical linguistics". *Language and Literature* 6: 163–80.
Ochs, Elinor
　1979　"Planned and unplanned discourse". In Givón 1979: 51–80.
Ochs, Elinor
　1986　*The Pragmatics of Affect: A Special Issue of Text.* Berlin: Mouton.
Ochs, Elinor and Schieffelin, Bambi
　1986　"Language has a heart". In Ochs 1986: 7–25.
Ohmann, Richard
　1972　"Speech, Literature and the Space Between". *New Literary History* 4: 32–63.
Ohmann, Richard
　1973　"Literature as Act". In *Approaches to Poetics: Selected Papers from the English Institute*, Seymour Chatman (ed..), 81–107. New York: Columbia University Press.
Olson, Richard D. and Hildyard, Angela
　1983　"Writing and Literal Meaning". In Martlew 1983: 41–65.
Ong, Walter J.
　1982　*Orality and Literacy: The Technologizing of the Word.* London: Methuen.
Osgood, Charles
　1980　*Lectures on Language Performance.* New York: Springer.
Östman, Jan-Ola
　1982　"The symbiotic relationship between pragmatic particles and impromptu speech". In *Impromptu Speech: a Symposium*, Nils Erik Enkvist (ed.), 147–77. Åbo: Research Institute of the Åbo Akademi Foundation.
Östman, Jan-Ola
　1995　"Pragmatic particles twenty years after". In *Organization in Discourse: Proceedings from the Turku Conference* [= Anglicana Turkuensia 14], Brita Wårwik, Sanna-Kaisa Tanskanen and Risto Hiltunen (eds.), 95–108. Turku: University of Turku.
Otunnu, Olara A. and Doyle, Michael W. (eds.)
　1998　*Peacemaking and Peacekeeping for the New Century.* Lanham: Rowman and Littlefield.
Pagnini, Marcello
　1987 [1980]　*The Pragmatics of Literature.* Bloomington: Indiana University Press.
Parnell, Thomas
　1779　"Dr. Donne's Third Satire Versified". In *The Works of the English Poets. With Prefaces, Biographical and Critical, vol. 44*, Samuel Johnson (ed.), 99–104. London: J. Rivington.

Payne, Michael (ed.)
  1993   *Working Through Derrida*. Evanston: Northwestern University Press.
Perkins, Judith
  1982   "Literary History: H.-G. Gadamer, T.S. Eliot and Virgil". *Arethusa* 14: 241–9.
Perkins, Michael R.
  1983   *Modal Expressions in English*. London: Pinter.
Petrey, Sandy
  1990   *Speech Acts and Literary Theory*. London: Routledge.
Pilkington, Adrian
  1991   "Poetic Effects: A Relevance Theory Perspective". In Sell 1991a: 44–6.
Pilkington, Adrian
  1994   "Against Literary Reading Conventions". In Sell and Verdonk 1994: 93–106.
Pilkington, Adrian
  1996   "Introduction: Relevance Theory and Literary Style". *Language and Linguistics* 5: 157–162.
Plasa, Clara
  1991   "Reading Tennyson in *Four Quartets*: the Example of 'East Coker'". *English: The Journal of the English Association* 40: 239–58.
Pope, Alexander
  1747   "To the Right Honourable Robert Earl of Oxford and Earl Mortimer". In *Poems on Several Occasions. Written by Dr. Thomas Parnell, Late Arch-Deacon of Clogher*. Alexander Pope (ed.), A2r.-A3v.. London: H. Lintot, J. & R. Tonson and S. Draper.
Pope, Alexander
  1963   *The Poems of Alexander Pope*, John Butt (ed.). London: Methuen.
Pope, Alexander
  1963 [1733–1734]   *An Essay on Man*. In Pope 1963: 501–47.
Pope, Alexander
  1963 [1714]   *The Rape of the Lock* [2nd ed.]. In Pope 1963: 217–42.
Pope, Alexander
  1963 [1735]   "The Second Satire of Dr. John Donne, Dean of St. Paul's, Versifyed". In Pope 1963: 676–87.
Pound, Ezra
  1963   Interview with Grazia Levi. *Delta* 22: 3–4.
Pratt, Mary Louise
  1977   *Toward a Speech Act Theory of Literary Discourse*. Bloomington: Indiana University Press.
Prince, Ellen E.
  1981   "Toward a Taxonomy of Given-New Information". In Cole 1981: 233–55.
Pulkkinen, Lea
  1989   "Progress in Education for Peace in Finland". In Hinde and Parry 1989: 88–101.

Pupesinghe, Kuman
    1998   *Civil Wars, Civil Peace*. London: Pluto Press.
Putnam, Hilary
    1981   *Reason, Truth and History*. Cambridge: Cambridge University Press.
Puttenham, George
    1904 [1589]   *The Arte of English Poesie*. In *Elizabethan Critical Essays: Vol. 2*, G. Gregory Smith (ed.), 1–193. Oxford: Oxford University Press.
Rainsford, Dominic
    1997   *Authorship, Ethics and the Reader: Blake, Dickens, Joyce*. Basingstoke: Macmillan.
Randall, Marilyn
    1985   "Context and Convention: The Pragmatics of Literariness". *Poetics* 14: 415–31.
Randall, Marilyn Joan
    1987   "Le Contexte de la Littérarité: Vers une Pragmatique Lecture d'Hubert Aquin et de Réjean Ducharme". Diss., University of Toronto.
Randall, Marilyn
    1996   "Pragmatic Plagiarism". In de Faria 1996: 830–41.
Raphael, Linda
    1994 [1989]   "A Re-vision of Miss Havisham: Her Expectations and Our Responses". In *New Casebooks: Great Expectations*, Roger D. Sell (ed.), 216–32. Basingstoke: Macmillan.
Rawson, C.J.
    1972   *Henry Fielding and the Augustan Ideal under Stress*. London: Routledge and Kegan Paul.
Reichart, John
    1977   *Making Sense of Literature*. Chicago: University of Chicago Press.
Rice, Philip and Waugh, Patricia (eds)
    1996   *Modern Literary Theory: A Reader: Third Edition*. London: Arnold.
Richards, I.A.
    1924   *Principles of Literary Criticism*. London: Routledge and Kegan Paul.
Richards, I.A.
    1929   *Practical Criticism: a Study of Literary Judgement*. London: Routledge and Kegan Paul.
Richards, Christina
    1985   "Inferential Pragmatics and the Literary Text". *Journal of Pragmatics* 9: 261–85.
Ricks, Christopher
    1994   *T.S. Eliot and Prejudice*. London: Faber.
Rimmon-Kenan, Schlomith
    1983   *Narrative Fiction: Contemporary Poetics*. London: Methuen.
Rogers, Pat
    1975   *An Introduction to Pope*. London: Methuen.
Rushdie, Salman
    1997   "Tell me, what is there to celebrate?". *The Observer*, 10th August, 14–15.

Rutherford, Jonathan (ed.)
    1990   *Identity: Community, Culture, Difference.* London: Lawrence and Wishart.
Rytövuori-Apunen, Helena
    1990   *Peace Research in Scandinavia, 1959–86* Aldershot: Avebury.
Sadrin, Anny
    1988   *Great Expectations* [Unwin Critical Library]. London: Unwin Hyman.
Said, Edward
    1993   *Culture and Imperialism.* London: Vintage.
Schaar, Claes
    "On Free and Latent Semantic Energy". Sell 1991a: 164–78.
Schegloff, Emanuel, A.
    1981   "Discourse as an Interactional Achievement: Some Uses of 'uh huh' and Other Things that Come between Sentences". In Tannen 1981: 71–93.
Schmidt, Siegfried J.
    1976   "A Pragmatic Interpretation of Fictionality". In van Dijk 1976: 161–78.
Schmidt, Siegfried J.
    1982   *Foundations for the Empirical Study of Literature: The Components of a Basic Theory.* Hamburg: Buske.
Searle, John
    1975   "The Logical Status of Fictional Discourse". *New Literary History* 6: 319–92.
Searle, John
    1969   *Speech Acts: An Essay in the Philosophy of Language.* Cambridge: Cambridge University Press.
Sell, Roger D.
    1974   *The Shorter Poems of Sir John Beaumont: A Critical Edition with An Introduction and Commentary* [Acta Academiae Aboensis vol. 49]. Åbo: Åbo Akademi University.
Sell, Roger D.
    1980   *Robert Frost: Four Studies* [Acta Academiae Aboensis vol. 57 no. 2]. Åbo: Åbo Akademi University.
Sell, Roger D. (ed.)
    1985a   *Robert Frost: Two Unpublished Plays:* **In an Art Factory** *and* **The Guardeen** *with an introduction. The Massachusetts Review* 26: 265–340.
Sell, Roger D.
    1985b   "Tellability and 'Politeness in 'The Miller's Tale': First steps in Literary Pragmatics". *English Studies* 66: 496–512.
Sell, Roger D.
    1985c   "Politeness in Chaucer: Suggestions towards a Methodology for Pragmatic Stylistics". *Studia Neophilologica* 57:175–185.
Sell, Roger D.
    1986   "Dickens and the New Historicism: the Polyvocal Audience and Discourse of *Dombey and Son*". In *The Nineteenth Century British Novel*, Jeremy Hawthorn (ed.), 63–79. London: Arnold.

Sell, Roger D.
1987 "The Unstable Discourse of Henry Vaughan: A Literary-Pragmatic Account". In *Essential Articles for the Study of Henry Vaughan*, Alan Rudrum (ed.), 311–32. Hamden: Archon.
Sell, Roger D. (ed.)
1991a *Literary Pragmatics*. London: Routledge.
Sell, Roger D.
1991b "The Politeness of Literary Texts". In Sell 1991a: 208–224.
Sell, Roger D.
1991c "How Can Literary Pragmaticists Develop Empirical Methods? The Problem of Modal and Evaluative Expressions in Literary Texts". In *Empirical Studies of Literature: Proceedings of the Second IGEL-Conference*, Elrud Ibsch, Dick Schram and Gerard Steen (eds), 138–45. Amsterdam: Rodopi.
Sell, Roger D.
1992 "Literary Texts and Diachronic Aspects of Politeness". In Watts, Ide and Ehlich 1992: 43–69.
Sell, Roger D.
1993 "The Difficult Style of *The Waste Land*: a Literary-Pragmatic Perspective on Modernist Poetry". In *Twentieth-Century Poetry: From Text to Context*, Peter Verdonk (ed.), 134–58. London: Routledge.
Sell, Roger D.
1994a "Literary Gossip, Literary Theory, Literary Pragmatics". In Sell and Peter Verdonk 1994: 221–41.
Sell, Roger D.
1994b "Postdisciplinary Philology: Culturally Relativistic Pragmatics". In *English Historical Linguistics*, Francisco Fernández, Miguel Fuster and Juan José Calvo (eds), 29–36. Amsterdam: Benjamins.
Sell, Roger D. (ed.)
1995a *Literature Throughout Foreign Language Education: The Implications of Pragmatics* [= *Review of English Language Teaching* 5:1]. London: Modern English Publications in association with The British Council.
Sell, Roger D.
1995b Review of Fludernik 1993. *Journal of Pragmatics* 24: 557–63.
Sell, Roger D.
1999 "*Henry V* and the Strength and Weakness of Words: Shakespearian Philology, Historicist Criticism, Communicative Pragmatics". *Neuphilologische Mitteilungen* 100: 535–63.
Sell, Roger D. and Verdonk, Peter (eds)
1994 *Literature and the New Interdisciplinarity: Poetics, Linguistics, History*. Amsterdam: Rodopi.
Semina, Elena
1992 Review of Sell 1991a. *Journal of Literary Semantics* 21: 77–80.
Shakespeare, William
1996 [1609] "Sonnet 19" In *The Sonnets*, G. Blakemore Evans (ed.) [The New Cambridge Shakespeare], 42. Cambridge: Cambridge University Press.

Shakespeare, William
  1951   *William Shakespeare: The Complete Works*, Peter Alexander (ed.). London: Collins.
Shakespeare, William
  1951 [1600]   *Henry V*. In Shakespeare 1951: 551–88.
Shakespeare, William
  1951 [1623]   *The Winter's Tale*. In Shakespeare 1951: 377–413.
Shklovsky, Victor
  1965   "Sterne's *Tristram Shandy*: Stylistic Commentary". In Lemon and Reis 1965: 25–57.
Shusterman, Richard
  1988   *T.S. Eliot and the Philosophy of Criticism*. London: Duckworth.
Shusterman, Richard
  1990   "Reaction meets radical critique: Eliot and contemporary culture criticism". In Laura Cowan (ed.), *T.S. Eliot: Man and Poet, I*, Laura Cowan (ed.), 367–93. Orono: National Poetry Foundation, University of Maine.
Shusterman, Richard
  1992   *Pragmatist Aesthetics: Living Beauty, Rethinking Art*. Oxford: Blackwell.
Shusterman, Richard
  1993   "Don't Believe the Hype: Animadversions on the Critique of Popular Art". *Poetics Today* 14:101–22.
Sidney, Sir Philip
  1973 [1595]   "A Defence of Poetry". In *Miscellaneous Prose of Sir Philip Sidney*, Katherine Duncan-Jones and Jan Van Dorsten (eds), 59–121. Oxford: Clarendon Press.
Simpson, Paul
  1989   "Politeness Phenomena in Ionesco's *The Lesson*". In *Language, Discourse and Literature: An Introductory Reader in Discourse Stylistics*, Ronald Carter and Paul Simpson (eds), 171–93. London: Unwin Hyman.
Sinclair, Melinda
  1993   "Are Academic Texts Really Decontextualized? A Pragmatics Perpsective on the Role of Context in Written Communication". *Text* 13: 529–58.
Smith, Olivia
  1984   *The Politics of Language 1791–1819*. Oxford: Clarendon Press.
Smoker, Paul, Davies, Ruth and Munske, Barbara (eds.)
  1990   *A Reader in Peace Studies*. Oxford: Pergamon.
Snow, C.P.
  1959   *The Two Cultures* [published version of the 1959 Reid Lecture, "The Two Cultures and the Scientific Revolution"]. Cambridge: Cambridge University Press.
Snow C.P.
  1993 [1963]   "The Two Cultures: A Second Look". In his *The Two Cultures*, Stefan Collini (introd.), 53–100. Cambridge: Cambridge University Press.
Sokal, Alan and Bricmont, Jean Bricmont
  1998 [1997]   *Intellectual Impostures: Postmodern Philosophers' Abuse of Science*. London: Profile Books.

Soyinka, Wole
    1988   *Art, Dialogue and Outrage: Essays on Literature and Culture*. Ibadan: New Horn Press.

Sperber, Dan and Wilson, Deirdre
    1986   *Relevance: Communication and Cognition*. Oxford: Blackwell.

Sperber, Dan and Wilson Deirdre
    1995   *Relevance: Communication and Cognition* [2nd ed.]. Oxford: Blackwell.

Srivastava, Narsingh
    1988   "T.S. Eliot's Theory of Poetic Personality and Belief: a Study in Reconciliation". *Language Forum* 14: 94–104.

Stanhope, Philip Dormer [= 4th Earl of Chesterfield]
    1817 [1749]   Letter, 21st August, 1749 [printed in *The World*, 30th October, 1755]. In *British Essayists*, A. Chambers (ed.), 28 : 229–30.

Sternberg, Meir
    1991   "How Indirect Discourse Means: Syntax, Semantics, Poetics, Pragmatics". In Sell 1991a: 62–93.

Sternberg, Meir
    1983   "Deictic Sequence: World, Language and Convention". In *Essays on Deixis*, Gisa Rauh (ed.), 277–316. Tübingen: Gunter Narr.

Sterne, Laurence
    1903 [1759–67]   *The Life and Opinions of Tristram Shandy Gentleman*. London: Oxford University Press.

Stomfay-Stitz, Aline M.
    1993   *Peace Education in America, 1829–1990: Sourcebook for Education and Research*. Metuchen: Scarecrow Press.

Stone, Harry
    1979   *Dickens and the Invisible World: Fairy Tales, Fantasy and Novel-Making*. Bloomington: Indiana University Press.

Storey, J.
    1995   "F.R. Leavis". In *The A-Z Guide to Modern Literary and Cultural Theorists*, Stuart Sim (ed.), 254–7. London: Prentice Hall.

Stubbs, Michael
    1983   *Discourse Analysis: The Sociolinguistic Analysis of Natural Language*. Oxford: Blackwell.

Svarny, Erik
    1988   *"The Men of 1914": T.S. Eliot and Early Modernism*. Milton Keynes: Open University Press.

Swirski, Peter
    1996   "Literary Studies and Literary Pragmatics: The Case of 'The Purloined Letter'". *SubStance: A Review of Theory and Literary Criticism* 25:3 [= 81]: 69–89.

Talbot, M.M.
    1998   "Relevance". In *Concise Encyclopedia of Pragmatics*, Jacob L. Mey (ed.), 775–8. Amsterdam: Elsevier.

Tallis, Raymond
    1988a *Not Saussure: A Critique of Post-Saussurian Literary Theory.* Basingstoke: Macmillan.
Tallis. Raymond
    1988b *In Defence of Realism.* London: Arnold.
Tallis, Raymond
    1995 *Newton's Sleep: Two Cultures and Two Kingdoms.* Basingstoke: Macmillan.
Tallis, Raymond
    1997 *Enemies of Hope: A Critique of Contemporary Pessimism, Irrationalism, Anti-Humanism and Counter-Enlightenment.* Basingstoke: Macmillan.
Tambling, Jeremy
    1983 "Death and Modernity in *Dombey and Son*". *Essays in Criticism* 43: 308–329.
Tannen, Deborah (ed.)
    1981 *Analyzing Discourse: Text and Talk.* Washington DC: Georgetown University Press.
Tannen, Deborah (ed.)
    1982 *Spoken and Written Language: Exploring Orality and Literacy.* Norwood, N.J.: Ablex.
Tannen, Deborah
    1986 "Introducing constructed dialogue in Greek and American conversational and literary narrative". In *Direct and Indirect Speech*, Florian Coulmas (ed.), 311–332. Berlin: Mouton de Gruyter.
Tannen, Deborah
    1992 "How is conversation like literary discourse? The role of imagery and details in creating involvement". In *The Linguistics of Literacy*, Pamela Downing, Susan D. Lima and Michael Noonan (eds.), 31–46. Amsterdam: Benjamins.
Taylor, Charles
    1994 "The Politics of Recognition". In Gutman: 1994: 25–73.
Taylor, Charles
    1976 "Responsibility for the Self". In *The Identity of Persons*, Amélie Oksenberg Rorty (ed.), 281–7. Berkeley: University of California Press.
Tennyson, Alfred Lord
    1987 [1854] "The Charge of the Light Brigade". In *The Poems of...*[2nd ed.], Christopher Ricks (ed.), vol. 2, 511–3. London: Longman.
Tobin, Dav Ned
    1985 *The Present of the Past: T.S. Eliot's Victorian Inheritance.* Ann Arbor: UMI Research Press.
Todorov, Tzvetan
    1990 [1978] *Genres in Discourse.* Cambridge: Cambridge University Press.
Toolan, Michael (ed.)
    1992 *Language, Text and Context: Essays in Stylistics.* London: Routledge.

Toolan, Michael
    1994   "On Recyclings and Irony", in Sell and Verdonk 1994: 79–92.
Trilling, Lionell
    1967   *Beyond Culture: Essays on Literature and Learning.* Harmondsworth: Penguin.
Trilling, Lionel
    1965   "The Fate of Pleasure". In his *Beyond Culture: Essays on Literature and Learning* 62–86. Harmondsworth: Penguin, Harmondsworth.
Trotter, David
    1988   *Circulation: Defoe, Dickens, and the Economies of the Novel.* London: Macmillan.
Tynyanov, Yury
    1978 [1924]   "Rhythmn as the constructive factor of verse". In Metejka and Pomorska 1978: 125–35.
UNESCO
    1991   *UNESCO Yearbook on Peace and Conflict Studies 1988.* Paris: Unesco.
Vachek, J.
    1973   *Written Language: General Problems of English.* The Hague: Mouton.
van Dijk, Teun A.
    1972   *Some Aspects of Text Grammars.* The Hague: Mouton.
van Dijk, Teun A.
    1976   "Pragmatics and Poetics". In van Dijk 1976: 22–57.
van Dijk, Teun A.
    1981   "The Pragmatics of Literary Communication". In his *Studies in the Pragmatics of Discourse*, 243–63. The Hague: Mouton.
van Dijk, Teun A. (ed.)
    1976   *Pragmatics of Language and Literature.* Amsterdam: North-Holland.
van Stapele, Peter
    1990   "The Analysis of Deixis as a Basis for Discourse Analysis of Dramatic Texts". In *Learning, Keeping and Using Language*, M.A.K. Halliday, John Gibbons and Howard Nichols (eds.), 333–48. Amsterdam: Benjamins, Amsterdam, 1990.
van Tieghem, Paul
    1938   "La question des genres littéraires". *Helicon* 1: 95–101.
Vendler, Helen
    1992   Interview with John Ashbery. *Oxford Poetry* 6: 61.
Ventola, Eija
    1987   *The Structure of Social Interaction: A Systemic Approach to the Semiotics of Service Encounters.* London: Pinter.
Verschueren, Jef
    1987   "Pragmatics as a theory of linguistic adaptation". *Working Documents #1.* Antwerp: International Pragmatics Association.
Wadman, Karen L.
    1983   "'Private Ejaculations': Politeness Strategies in George Herbert's Poems directed to God", *Language and Style* 16: 87–106.

Wales, Katie
    1991   Review of Sell 1991a. *Modern Language Review* 89: 166–7.
Walker, Cheryl
    1991   "Persona Criticism and the Death of the Author". In Epstein 1991: 109–21.
Wall, Barbara
    1991   *The Narrator's Voice: The Dilemma of Children's Literature.* Basingstoke: Macmillan.
Wallace, Stephen
    1982   "Figure and Ground: The Interrelationships of Linguistic Categories". In Hopper 1982: 201–23.
Warnke, Georgia
    1987   *Gadamer: Hermeneutics, Tradition and Reason.* Cambridge: Polity Press.
Warton, Thomas
    1762   *Observations of the Fairy Queen of Spenser: The Second Edition: Corrected and Enlarged*, 2 vols. London and Oxford: R.& J. Dodsley and J. Fletcher.
Watts, Richard J.
    1981   *The Pragmalinguistic Analysis of Narrative Texts: Narrative Cooperation in Charles Dickens's "Hard Times".* Tübingen: Gunter Narr.
Watts, Richard J.
    1981   "Relevance and relational work: Linguistic politeness as politic behaviour". *Multilingua* 8: 131–66.
Watts, Richard J.
    1992   "Linguistic Politeness and Politic Verbal Behaviour". In Watts, Ide and Ehlich 1992: 43–69.
Watts, Richard J., Ide, Sachico and Ehlich Konrad (eds)
    1992   *Politeness in Language: Studies in its History, Theory and Practice.* Berlin: Mouton de Gruyter.
Waugh, Patricia
    1996   "Stalemates? Feminists, Postmodernists and Unfinished Issues in Modern Aesthetics". In *Modern Literary Theory: A Reader: Third Edition.* Philip Rice and Waugh (eds), 322–41. London: Arnold.
Webster, Richard
    1995   *Why Freud Was Wrong: Sin, Science and Psychoanalysis.* London: HarperCollins.
Weimann, Robert
    1976   *Structure and Society in Literary History: Studies in the History and Theory of Historical Criticism.* Charlottesville: University Press of Virginia.
Weinsheimer, Joel
    1985   *Gadamer's Hermeneutics: A Reading of* **Truth and Method**. New Haven: Yale University Press.
Weinsheimer, Joel
    1991   *Philosophical Hermeneutics and Literary Theory.* New Haven: Yale University Press.

Wellek, René
   1937   "Literary Criticism and Philosophy". *Scrutiny* 5: 375–83.
Wellek, René and Warren, Austin
   1963 [1949]   *Theory of Literature*. Harmondsworth: Penguin.
White, Hayden
   1978   "The Fictions of Factual Representation". In his *Tropics of Discourse*, 121–34. Baltimore: Johns Hopkins Press, Baltimore.
Wierzbicka, Anna
   1991   *Cross-Cultural Pragmatics: The Semantics of Human Interaction*. Berling: Mouton de Gruyter.
Wilson, Edmund
   1941   "Dickens: The Two Scrooges". In his *The Wound and the Bow*, 1–104. Boston: Houghton Mifflin.
Wimsatt, W.K.
   1970 [1955]   *The Verbal Icon: Studies in the Meaning of Poetry*. London: Methuen, London.
Winch, Peter
   1987   "Text and Context". In his *Trying to Make Sense*, 18–32. Oxford: Blackwell.
Witt, Richard
   1989   "The Death of Miss Havisham". *The Dickensian* 80:151–6.
Wittgenstein, Ludwig
   1978   "Lectures of Aesthetics". In his *Lectures and Conversations on Aesthetics, Psychology and Religious Belief*, Cyril Barrett (ed.), 1–40. Oxford: Blackwell.
Wollheim, Richard
   1992 [1980]   *Art and Its Objects: Second Edition: With Six Supplementary Essays*. Cambridge: Cambridge University Press.
Woodman, Thomas
   1983 "Parnell, Politeness and 'Pre-Romanticism'". *Essays in Criticism* 33: 205–19
Woodmansee, Martha
   1978   "Speech-Act Theory and the Perpetuation of the Dogma of Literature Autonomy". *Centrum* 6: 75–89.
Wordsworth, William
   1950 [1802]   Preface to *Lyrical Ballads*. In *The Poetical Works of William Wordsworth*, E. de Selincourt (ed.), 734–41. Oxford: Clarendon Press.
Yeats, W. B.
   1996 [1916]   "Easter 1916". In *Yeats's Poems*, A. Norman Jeffares (ed.), 287–9. Basingstoke: Macmillan.
Young, Andrew
   1998 [1933]   "An Old Road". In *Selected Poems: Andrew Young*, Edward Lowbury and Alison Young (eds), 14. Manchester: Carcanet.
Young, Edward
   1918 [1759]   *Conjectures on Original Composition*, Edith J. Morely (ed.). Manchester: Manchester University Press.

Name Index

A
Adams, Henry, 159, 268
Adams, Jon-K., 72
Addison, Joseph, 154
Adorno, Theodor, 262
Altieri, Charles, 78–80, 88, 116, 171
Alvarez, Al, 216
Appiah, K. Anthony, 10, 17, 20, 25, 95, 153–54, 159, 172, 210, 257, 270
Ariosto, Ludovico, *Orlando Furioso*, 184
Aristotle, 17, 34, 126, 130, 174, 231; *The Poetics*, 179, 182, 184
Arnold, Matthew, 161, 195, 273
Artaud, Antonin, 174
Ashbery, John, 233
Auden, W.H., 25
Augustine St, 159
Austen, Jane, 233, 238; *Emma*, 214; *Pride and Prejudice*, 166–69
Austin, J.L., 32, 49–53, 61, 79, 129, 147, 298–99
Ayer, A.J., 233, 290

B
Bakhtin, M.M., 42, 115, 153, 164, 270, 288
Balzac, Honoré, *Sarrasine*, 61–63
Banfield, Ann, 71–72
Barthes, Roland, 23 fn. 6, 24, 94, 106, 159, 163–64, 266, 289; "The Death of the Author", 89–91, 93, 199–200; *Sade/Fourier/Loyola*, 204–05; *S/Z*, 61–62;

Barzun, Jacques, 196
Bate, Jonathan, 93
Baudelaire, Charles, 199, 204
Baudrillard, Jean, 113
Baumgarten, Alexander Gottlieb, 146
Beaumont, Sir John, "Bosworth Field", 232
Bell, Ian A., 26, 151
Bell, Michael, 238
Ben-Porat, Ziva, 116, 137
Benveniste, Emile, 51, 53, 71
Bergonzi, Bernard, 105, 261, 272, 275, 279
Berkeley, George, *Alciphron*, 213
Berlin, Isaiah, 15–18, 20, 25, 26, 97, 153, 154, 157, 159, 279
Bernstein, Cynthia, 124
Betti, Emilio, 141
Bex, Tony, 73–74
Black, Max, 249
Blair, Hugh, *Lectures on Rhetoric and Belles Lettres*, 185
Blake, William, 9, 212, 238
Bloom, Harold, 19, 195, 261, 272, 275, 279
Bloomfield, Leonard, 40, 129, 299
Boileau, Nicholas Despreaux, 186
Booth, Wayne C., 160–61, 240–41, 243, 248; *The Rhetoric of Fiction*, 197
Boswell, James, 141
Bourdieu, Pierre, 243
Bowers, Fredson, 110
Brawne, Fanny, 161, 195
Brecht, Bertolt, 174

NOTE: *The name index does not include the names of characters in literary works*

Britten, Benjamin, *Peter Grimes*, 273
Brontë, Anne, 94
Brontë, Charlotte, 94
Brontë, Emily, 25, 94
Brooks, Cleanth, 23 fn. 5, 186
Brown, Penelope, 82, 209, 216–18, 293
Browning, Elizabeth Barrett, 58, 171
Browning, Robert, 58; "My Last Duchess", 124
Brunetière, Ferdinand, 184
Buchanan, Pat, 98–100, 230
Bultmann, Rudolf, 142, 181
Bunyan, John, 167
Byatt, A.S., *Possession*, 273

C

Caputo, John D., 147 fn. 16
Caraher, Brian, 113
Carlson, Lauri, 87
Carnap, Rudolf, 290
Carver, Raymond, "Little Things", 67–70, 123
Cassirer, Ernst, 34
Castiglione, Baldassare, 211
Caxton, William, 127
Cervantes Saavedra, Miguel de, 160
Chapman, George, 235
Chatman, Seymour, 45–46, 80, 292
Chaucer, Geoffrey, 25, 211; *The Canterbury Tales*, 221; "The Knight's Tale", 224–25; "The Miller's Tale", 222–25
Chesterfield, Philip Dormer Stanhope, 4th Earl of, 35, 214
Chesterton, G.K., 141
Chomsky, Noam, 42, 288
Christie, Agatha, 167
Cixous, Hélène, 287
Clark, Billy, 67–70, 123
Clark, Ian, 12
Coleridge, Samuel Taylor, 32, 34, 141, 174, 185–86, 292, 295
Connor, Steven, 9 fn.1, 275
Conrad, Joseph, 233, 238
Cortright, David, 11 fn. 2

Coulthard, Malcolm, 286
Cox, Geoff, 113–14
Croce, Benedetto, 185–86
Culler, Jonathan, 147 fn. 16

D

D'Aguiar, Fred, 26; *The Longest Memory*, 270; *Sweet Thames*, 269–70, 278
Dante, Alighieri, 127, 170, 229
Darwin, Charles, 41, 184
Davie, Donald, 233, 245
Davies, Ruth, 11 fn. 3
de Beaugrande, Robert, 43–45, 300
de Man, Paul, 50–51, 60, 136, 147 fn. 16
de Saussure, Ferdinand, 24, 25, 40, 129, 150, 299
Denham, Sir John, 232
Derrida, Jacques, 23 fn. 6, 32, 38, 50–51, 85, 115 fn. 12, 147, 281, 291, 293
Descartes, René, 150
Dewey, John, 34, 35, 79, 113, 134, 203; *Art and Experience*, 241–44
Dickens, Charles, 25, 92, 94, 116, 140, 142, 146, 155, 206, 238, 247–49, 260, 270; *David Copperfield*, 84, 155; *Dombey and Son*, 170, 215; *Hard Times*, 78, 80, 163; *Little Dorrit*, 214–15
Dickie, George, 186
Diller, Hans-Jürgen, 123–24
Dilthey, Wilhelm, 134, 141–42, 293
Dolitsky, Marlene, 132, 201
Donne, John, 180, 234–35, 243; "The Canonization", 165–66; "The Exstasie", 171; satires, 227–28
Doyle, Michael W., 11 fn. 2
Drakakis, John, 201–05, 266
Drayton, Michael, 235
Dreiser, Theodore, 70
Dressler, Wolfgang, 43–44
Dryden, John, 127, 232, 243; "To the Memory of Mr Oldham", 244
Du Bartas, Guillaume de Salluste, 212

du Maurier, Daphne, 140
Dubrow, Heather, 181
Duranti, Alessandro, 116
Dworkin, Ronald, 10

E
Edmondson, Willis, 81, 87, 286
Eichenbaaum, Boris, 297
Eisenstein, Elizabeth, 202
Elam, Keir, 174
Eliot, George, 80, 233, 238
Eliot, T.S., 23 fn. 5, 31, 84, 90, 103–06, 110, 127, 129, 156, 169–70, 173, 175, 195, 234, 247–49, 262–63, 268–69, 273, 292; *After Strange Gods*, 268; *Ash Wednesday*, 226; "Dirge", 104; "Gerontion", 105; "In Memoriam", 226, 229; *Poems 1920*, 104; the quatrain poems, 104; "Tradition and the Individual Talent", 91, 210; *The Waste Land*, 104 ("Death by Water"), 170, 197, 205, 208, 210, 215, 220, 229–30
Ellis, John, 147 fn. 16
Emerson, Caryll, 270
Emmet, Robert, 192
Empson, William, 36, 44–45, 127, 233, 295
Enkvist, Nils Erik, 300
Euthyphro, 275

F
Fairclough, Norman, 113, 286
Fanon, Franz, 294
Felperin, Howard, 147 fn. 16
Fielding, Henry, 128, 141, 219, 245, 279; *Amelia*, 213–14; "Essay on Conversation", 213, 218; *Tom Jones*, 211, 218
Firbas, Jan, 283
Firth, J.R., 42
Fish, Stanley, 47, 196, 297
Fitter, Chris, 273
Fitzgerald, Lord Edward, 192
Ford, Henry, 127

Foster, Hal, 9 fn.1
Foucault, Michel, 23 fn.6, 95–97, 108, 115 fn. 12, 136, 148, 163–64, 246, 266, 281, 289, 294
Fowler, Alastair, 181
Fowler, Roger, 78–80, 88
Freud, Sigmund, 117, 150, 195; "Inhibitions, Symptoms and Anxiety", 239–40
Frohnmayer, John, 100
Frost, Robert, 94, 196, 247–50, 268; "Spring Pools", 56–58; "The Subverted Flower", 205
Frye, Northrop, 186
Fuchs, Georg, 174
Fuller, John, "Valentine", 172–73

G
Gadamer, Hans-Georg, 38, 48, 97, 101, 127, 134, 137–45, 147–48, 153, 249, 264, 293
Gates, Henry Louis, 287
Gautier, Théophile, 105
Gelley, Alexander, 115
Genette, Gerard, 292
Gide, André, 141
Godwin, Charles, 116
Goethe, Johann Wolfgang, 262
Goffman, Erving, *The Presentation of the Self in Everyday Life*, 216–17
Goodman, Nelson, 34, 35, 79
Goody, J., 202
Gorbachev, Mikhail, 141
Graff, Gerald, 19, 96, 98, 147 fn. 16, 267–68
Gramsci, Antonio, 272, 273
Gray, Bennison, 73, 86–87
Greenblatt, Stephen, 108, 204, 245, 292
Greg, W.W., *Pastoral Poetry and Pastoral Drama*, 179
Gregory, Lady Isabella Augusta, 192, 216
Greville, Sir Fulke, 235
Grice, H.P., 51–52, 54, 65, 79, 81 fn. 8, 83, 222, 284, 297, 299

Grübel, Rainer, 71
Gunkel, Hermann, 181
Gutman, Amy, 97

H
Habermas, Jürgen, 11, 13, 19, 97, 98, 135, 293, 295
Hall, Stuart, 285
Halliday, Michael, 73, 81, 287
Halverson, J., 202
Hampshire, Stuart, 9, 13, 20, 97, 256, 269, 279
Hancher, Michael, 57–58
Hardy, Henry, 15 fn. 4
Hardy, Thomas, 94, 168, 206
Harpman, Geoffrey Galt, 238
Harris, Roy, 42
Harris, Wilson, 26, 157, 269
Hartman, Geoffrey H., 136–37, 147
Harvey, David, 9 fn.1, 270
Hausheer, Roger, 15 fn. 4
Havelock, E., 202
Hawkes, Terence, 202–03, 266
Hecht, Anthony, 99–101, 143, 233–34
Hegel, G.W.F., 183
Heidegger, Martin, 134, 142, 293
Heraclitus, 9, 13, 19, 97, 256, 279
Herder, Johan Gottfried, 134
Hill, Geoffrey, 232, 243–45; *Mercian Hymns*, 244; *Tenebrae*, 244
Hine, Robert A., 11 fn. 3
Hintikka, Jaako, 87
Hirsch, E.D., 37, 141
Hitchcock, Alfred, 140
Hobbes, Thomas, 12, 182, 214, 243
Hobsbawm, Eric, 273 fn. 22
Hoby, Sir Thomas, 211
Hoggart, Richard, 285
Holland, Norman, 152, 297
Holsti, Kalevi J., 13
Homer, 126, 231; *The Iliad*, 184
Horace, 174, 179
Hoy, David, 138 fn. 15
Hughes, Ted, *Tales from Ovid*, 273
Hume, David, 146, 148–49, 180

I
Ionesco, Eugène, 71
Irigaray, Luce, 287
Iser, Wolfgang, 47, 124, 140, 297

J
Jacob, Giles, 232
Jakobson, Roman, 34, 44, 77, 245, 300
James, Henry, 84, 197, 233, 238
James I, 232
James, William, 50, 134, 203, 296
Jameson, Fredric, 9 fn.1, 292
Jaspers, Karl, 152
Jauss, H.R., 47, 296
Johnson, A.W., 115 fn. 12
Johnson, Samuel, 31, 31 fn.7, 35, 87, 131, 141, 168–69, 214, 263, 279
Jolles, André, 180
Jonson, Ben, 127
Joyce, James, 161, 169, 238; *A Portrait of the Artist as a Young Man*, 197–98, 205–06
Julius, Anthony, 103–06, 110, 129, 143, 234
Jung, Carl Gustav, 150

K
Kant, Immanuel, 10, 30, 32, 33, 43, 54, 74, 75, 114, 145–46, 148, 153, 180, 186, 231–33, 241–43, 276
Karpenko, Tatyana, 35
Katz, Jerrold, 51, 53
Keats, John, 14, 161, 195, 259
Kermode, Frank, 26, 148–51, 154–55, 159, 261, 268, 272, 275, 279
Kristeva, Julia, 23 fn. 6, 163–64, 281, 287, 289
Kuhn, Thomas, 259

L
Labov, William, 52, 59, 80
Lacan, Jacques, 281
Lakoff, Robin, 222
Lane, Sir Hugh, 192

Langer, Susan K., 34
Lanser, Susan Sniader, 78–80, 88, 171
Larkin, Philip, 195
Lasserre, P., 90
Lawrence, D.H., 141, 238; *The Plumed Serpent*, 225
Leavis, F.R., 36, 44–45, 127–28, 136, 141, 143, 156, 162, 179–80, 225, 233–38, 240, 243, 245, 247–48, 264, 270, 279, 295; *The Common Pursuit*, 236; *The Great Tradition*, 233–34, 236–37; *Revaluation*, 234–35; *Scrutiny*, 261
Leech, Geoffrey N., 35, 44–45, 81–83, 125, 209, 220, 222
Leitch, Vincent, 147 fn. 16
Lemon, Lee T., 23 fn. 5
Lessing, Doris, 169
Lévi-Strauss, Claude, 24, 25, 150–51, 281, 292
Levin, Samuel, 54, 55, 72, 78
Levinas, Emmanuel, 26, 152
Levinson, Stephen, 82, 209, 216–18, 284, 293
Lewis, C.S., 143, 162–63, 240; *An Experiment in Criticism*, 264
Linell, Per, 41, 301
Lofton, Ramona (= Sapphire), 143; "Wild Thing", 99–101, 230
Longinus, 186
Lubbock, Percy, *The Craft of Fiction*, 197
Lyotard, Jean-François, 9 fn.1, 113, 135, 295

M
MacBride, John, 191
MacDonagh, Thomas, 191
Machiavelli, Niccolò, 12
Macleod, Norman, 116
Maingueneau, Dominique, 115, 124
Malinowski, B., 184
Markiewicz, Constance, 191
Marlowe, Christopher, 94
Maurras, Charles, 90

McGann, Jerome J., 110–13, 137, 192
Meckier, Jerome, 140
Merquior, J.C., 96
Meuller-Vollmer, Kurt, 138 fn. 15
Mey, Jacob, 174
Miller, John Hillis, 96–98, 101, 102, 238–40, 243, 246, 248, 270
Mills, Sara, 172–73
Milton, John, 37–38, 63, 127; *Paradise Lost*, 184, 225
Moerman, Michael, 263 fn. 20
Molière, 60–61, 63, 71
Montagu, Lady Mary Wortley, 141
Montrose, Louis, 292
Morris, Charles, 34, 64, 108–10, 113, 115, 295–96
Munske, Barbara, 11 fn. 3
Mukařovský, Jan, 34–35

N
Napoleon, 112
Nealon, Jeffrey T., 147 fn. 16
Newton, Isaac, 185
Nietzsche, Friedrich Wilhelm, 183–84
Noll, Richard, 150

O
O'Leary, John, 192
Ohmann, Richard, 55–56, 60
Ong, Walter J., 83–85, 91, 184
Otunnu, Olara A., 11 fn. 2
Owen, Wilfrid, "Dulce et Decorum Est", 192, 193

P
Pagnini, Marcello, 163
Parnell, Charles Stewart, 192
Parnell, Thomas, 212–14, 230; "The Hermit", 212–13; "Night Piece", 212–13; versions of Donne's satires, 227–28
Parry, Donald A., 11 fn. 3
Pascal, Blaise, 226
Pater, Walter, 197, 205
Payne, Michael, 147 fn. 16

Pearse, Patrick, 191
Peirce, Charles S., 49, 295–96
Perkins, Judith, 138 fn. 15
Petrey, Sandy, 50–51, 60–63, 71, 147 fn. 16
Pilkington, Adrian, 67
Plato, 32, 35–37, 63
Pope, Alexander, 16–17, 127, 210, 226–28, 230, 232; *An Essay on Criticism*, 186; *An Essay on Man* 17; *The Rape of the Lock*, 16–17, 208, 228; versions of Donne's satires, 227–28
Pound, Ezra, 105, 156, 233–34; "Envoi (1919)", 244; *Hugh Selwyn Mauberley*, 216; *The Cantos*, 223, 233, 245
Pratt, Mary Louise, 59–60, 80
Propp, Vladimir, 292
Pupesinghe, Kuman, 11 fn. 2
Putnam, Hilary, 268
Puttenham, George, 181

R
Rabelais, François, 169, 240–41
Rainsford, Dominic, 238
Randall, Marilyn, 133
Ransom, John Crowe, 292
Reichart, John, 77–8, 80, 88, 90, 255
Reis, Marion J., 23 fn. 5
Richard III, 232
Richards, Christine, 132–33
Richards, I.A., 36, 44–45, 79, 127–28, 179, 233, 237, 295; *Practical Criticism: A Study of Literary Judgement*, 128–29
Richardson, Samuel, 141
Richmond, Henry Tudor, Earl of, 232
Ricks, Christopher, 103
Rimmon-Kenan, Schlomith, 46
Rogers, Pat, 226–28
Rorty, Richard, 50, 134, 203, 259, 297
Rosenblatt, Louise M., 297
Rousseau, Jean-Jacques, 10, 12, 50, 60, 136, 145
Rushdie, Salman, 26, 159, 267–68; *The Satanic Verses*, 269

Russell, Bertrand, 42, 290
Rutherford, Jonathan, 9 fn.1

S
Said, Edward, 19, 20
Scaliger, J.C., 174
Schegloff, Emanuel, A., 86
Schleiermacher, Friedrich D.E., 141–42, 293
Schlick, Moritz, 290
Schmidt, Siegfried J., 38, 72
Scott, Sir Walter, 169
Searle, John, 45, 51, 53–54, 55, 58, 62, 63, 79, 82, 299
Sedgwick, Eve Kosofsky, 288
Sell, Roger D., 114 fn. 10 & fn. 11, 221 fn. 17, 222 fn. 18, 223 fn. 19
Shaftesbury, Anthony Ashley Copper, 3rd Earl of, 212, 215
Shakespeare, William, 60–61, 63, 71, 94, 127, 186, 201–04, 279; "Devouring Time, blunt thou the lion's paws", 56–58; *Hamlet*, 211; *Henry V*, 131; *Pericles*, 93; "Shall I compare thee to a summer's day?" 250; *The Winter's Tale*, 131
Shelley, Percy Bysshe, "The Defence of Poetry", 241
Shklovsky, Victor, 186, 297
Short, Mick, 44, 220
Showalter, Elaine, 287
Shusterman, Richard, 241, 244–45, 269 fn. 21, 274
Sidney, Sir Philip, 34–36
Simpson, Paul, 71
Smart, Christopher, 212
Smith, Adam, 92
Smoker, Paul, 11 fn. 3
Snow, C.P., 236–37
Socrates, 275
Solomon, 67
Soyinka, Wole, 26, 269
Spenser, Edmund, 126–27
Sperber, Dan 65–66, 68, 74, 120, 297
Stalin, Joseph, 142
Steele, Richard, 154

Sterne, Laurence, *Tristram Shandy*, 130, 186
Stevens, Wallace, 149
Stomfay-Stitz, Aline M., 11 fn.3
Stone, Harry, 140
Storey, J., 235
Swift, Jonathan, 169
Swirski, Peter, 187, 190

T
Tallis, Raymond, 11, 24, 25, 96, 150, 237, 245
Tambling, Jeremy, 92
Tannen, Deborah, 74
Taylor, Charles, 10, 153, 159, 161
Tennyson, Alfred Lord, 228–29; "The Charge of the Light Brigade", 110–12, 187–88, 190–93, 194; *In Memoriam*, 223, 229; "The Princess", 223
Thackeray, William Makepeace, 94
Thomas, Edward, 206
Todorov, Tzvetan, 115
Tomashevsky, Boris, 297
Tone, Wolfe, 192
Toolan, Michael, 67
Trilling, Lionel, 227
Trollope, Anthony, 239–40
Trotter, David, 92, 146
Tschaikovsky, Peter Iliitch, 199, 204
Tynynanov, Yuri, 297

V
van Dijk, Teun, 72–73
van Gogh, Vincent, 199, 204
van Tieghem, Paul, 180
Vaughan, Henry, 132, 145, 247–49, 273
Vendler, Helen, 115, 233
Ventola, Eija, 81, 82
Verschueren, Jef, 115–16
Vico, Giambattista, 134
Virgil, *The Aeneid*, 184

W
Waletsky, Joshua, 59, 80
Walker, Cheryl, 26, 151

Waller, Edmund, 232
Walton, Isaac, 243
Warnke, Georgia, 138 fn.15
Warren, Austin, 23 fn. 5, 179, 195, 237
Warton, Thomas, *Observations on the Fairy Queen of Spenser*, 126–28, 179, 182, 185, 231
Waterman, Lewis Edson, 240
Watson, John W., 281
Watts, Richard J., 78, 80, 87, 88, 163, 197, 218
Waugh, Patricia, 135 fn. 14, 147 fn. 16
Webster, Richard, 150
Weimann, Robert, 78
Weinsheimer, Joel, 138 fn. 15
Wellek, René, 23 fn. 5, 136, 179, 195, 237
Whorf, Benjamin Lee, 156
Wilde, Oscar, 25, 197, 205, 232
Williams, Raymond, 285
Wilson, Deirdre, 65–66, 68, 74, 120, 297
Wilson, Edmund, "Dickens: The Two Scrooges", 260
Wimsatt, William, 31–2, 45
Winch, Peter, 231
Wittgenstein, Ludwig, 42, 49, 78, 79, 146, 180, 187, 275, 290
Wollheim, Richard, 143–44, 186–87, 275
Woodman, Thomas, 212–13
Woodmansee, Martha, 58, 171
Woolf, Virginia, *To the Lighthouse*, 111, 187; *The Waves*, 198
Wordsworth, William, 113, 206, 259; *Lyrical Ballads*, 223, 228–29; "Ode — Intimations of Immortality from Recollections of Early Childhood", 136; Preface to the *Lyrical Ballads*, 182–83, 185, 228; "She dwelt among untrodden ways", 93, 147
Worsthorne, Peregrine, 204
Wotton, Sir Henry, 243

Y
Yeats, W.B., 206, 216, 228; "Easter 1916", 187–95, 210; "September 1913", 192–93

Young, Andrew, "An Old Road", 205–06
Young, Edward, *Conjectures on Original Composition*, 185

Subject Index

A
a-historical de-humanization, 23, 29–75, 135–36, 155–56, 293
absence/presence, 3, 27, 85–86, 209, 253
Absolon (in "The Miller's Tale"), 223
Action Française movement, the, 90
aesthetic impressions, the discussability of, 180
aesthetic reading convention, the notion of an, 72–73
aesthetic theory, 230–31
Aestheticism, 23, 125, 128, 179, 185, 195–97, 232, 289–90
Alisoun (in "The Miller's Tale"), 223
allusion, 94, 164, 169, 194, 200
American literature, 266
Amy Dorrit (in *Little Dorrit*), 215
Anne of Geierstein (in *Anne of Geierstein*), 169
anti-Semitism, 103–06, 195, 233–34, 245
Antony and Cleopatra, 32, 35–36
Apollonian/Dionysiac, 184
applied linguistics, 87–88
Arcite (in "The Knight's Tale"), 224
art
  as an institution, 186–87, 271–2, 275–76
  as co-adaptation, 187, 190, 228–30, 243, 243
art museums, 242
artistic ethics, the bi-dimensionality of, 231, 241

Augustan scholars and critics, 126–27, 231–32
author biography and biographical criticism, 22, 30, 62, 140, 144, 163, 193–207
author-reader bonding, 167–71
authorial intention, 31, 38–39, 44, 48, 61, 62, 73, 78–79, 133, 139

B
Barthesian criticism, 89–97, 107, 136–37, 141, 146, 157–58, 199–204, 209, 248, 255, 281
behaviouristic attitudes in linguistics, 23, 42–49, 64, 231, 281–82
Bible, the, 181
binary terminologies, 3, 7
Blifil (in *Tom Jones*), 218
bodily aesthetics, 244, 274
books, 88, 207, 266
  holy books, 85
  prayerbooks, 85
British-Irish Council, the, 12

C
catharsis, 179, 182
Centre for Contemporary Cultural Studies (Birmingham University), 285
children's literature, 114 fn.11, 171
Chorus (in *Henry V*) 131
classic texts, 63, 100, 229, 275–77
classroom talk, 87
Cold War, the, 13
comedy, 182

NOTE: *The subject index includes characters in literary texts.*

common sense, 26, 96–97, 145–54, 158–60, 291
communication, 2–4, 117–18, 120, 138, 282–83
communicative dynamism, 222–23, 283
communicative faith, 246, 251, 254, 276
communicative parity, 70, 125, 133, 143–44, 175, 195, 245, 248, 253, 283
communicative personae, 32, 45–47, 56–59, 78–79, 84, 88, 90, 158–75, 206, 254, 283
communicative situations, 2–3, 61, 63, 122–23, 253
comparative philology, 40, 41, 117, 155, 283
composition and reading, 87–88
compromizers, see "pragmatic particles"
confessional writing, 138, 159, 196, 199, 216
context, 119–20, 284
  communication-internal context, 121–22
  contextual disparities, 3–4, 7, 21, 26, 38–39, 47, 61, 63, 107, 117, 119–45, 229, 231, 247–49, 251, 253, 262
  implied contexts, proliferation of, 130–31
  real-world junctures of receiving, proliferation of, 131–45
conversation analysis, 80, 82, 284
cooking recipes, 85
Coriolanus (in *Coriolanus*), 60–61
corpus linguistics, 40–41, 52, 80–81, 285
Cousin Felix (in *Dombey and Son*), 215
Crimean War, the, 112
critical discourse analysis, 80, 113, 286
cultural anthropology, 24, 88
cultural materialism, 5, 19, 47, 88, 95, 129, 136, 231, 245, 255, 273, 285
cultural purism, 100, 130, 143, 207, 262, 285
cultural structuralism, 23–24, 77, 88–106, 117, 129, 135, 148–52, 154, 155, 245, 285

cultural studies, 47, 136, 271–75, 285
culture wars, the, 19, 30, 94, 96, 114, 201, 236

D
David Copperfield (in *David Copperfield*), 144, 155
death of the author, the, 24, 89, 151, 248
deixis, 64, 122, 122 fn. 13, 164–66, 224, 286
  discourse deixis, 224–25
deconstruction, 31, 50, 133, 136–37, 146–47, 172, 245
dependency strucures (syntactical), 84
detective stories, 168
deviant literary syntax, the notion of, 71–72
Dickens Fellowship, the, 140
Dickensian: A Magazine for Dickens Lovers, The, 140
discourse analysis, 80, 222, 285
dissensus, 96, 136, 239, 246, 251, 270
Don Juan (in Molière's *Don Juan*), 60–61
Don Quixote (in *Don Quixote*), 211
drama
  actor-audience relationship in, 123–24
  the duplicity of, 124
  the perlocutionary dimension in, 174
  unities of time, place and action in 130–31
dramatic monologues, 124

E
e–mail, 85
Easter Rising, the, 192–93
Elizabeth Bennet (in *Pride and Prejudice*), 168
Emelye (in "The Knight's Tale"), 224
emic differentiality, 24, 94–95, 299
Emma Woodhouse (in *Emma*), 214
emotive and evaluative expressions, 166–67, 286
English Theophrastus: or, The Manners of the Age, The, 213, 216
Enlightenment, the, 11, 134, 215

Subject Index

epic, 184; oral epic, 84, 184, 243
epithalamia, 181, 184, 185
Estella (in *Great Expectations*), 140
ethnic criticism/studies, 5, 19, 47, 89, 95, 129, 231, 245, 255, 287
exhortations, 243
explication de texte, 199

F

feminist criticism/studies, 5, 19, 47, 88, 95, 129, 134–35, 142, 151, 231, 245, 255, 272, 287
fiction, 3, 32–33, 54, 72–74, 80, 138, 159, 253
film criticism, 151
folktales, 243
form-historical theology, 181
frame/scenario/schema, 222
Frank Churchill (in *Emma*), 214
free indirect discourse, 170
French Revolution, the, 214
Freudian criticism, 117, 239–40, 254
functional linguistics, 80–81, 287; Prague school of, 85

G

game theory, in mathematics 187; in semantics, 87
gay and lesbian criticism/studies, 5, 19, 47, 88, 95, 129, 231, 245, 255, 288
generative grammar, 42, 49, 54, 136, 288
genres and genre criticism, 47, 73, 74, 82, 144, 176–93, 198
globalization, 12, 266
Goneril (in *King Lear*), 14
Good Friday Agreement of 1988, the, 11, 191

H

Hercule Poirot (in Agatha Christie's novels), 167
hesitations, 85
heteroglossia, 164, 288
historical criticism, 22
historical positivism, 30

historical purism, 21, 27, 100, 130, 143, 203, 207, 262, 288
historically human, the, 77–118, 288
historicist assumption, the (= sociohistorical determinism), 4, 7, 20–21, 91–95, 146–58, 219, 288–89
histrionic sampling/experimental histrionics, 159, 175, 248, 277
Holocaust, the, 106, 129
Home Rule Bill, 192
human beings,
 as social individuals, 25, 37, 48, 82, 108, 113, 117, 145–58, 219, 228–29, 254, 255, 298
 the sameness-that-is-difference of their condition, 18, 28, 71, 101, 157, 180, 191, 246, 276, 297
 their co-adaptations/co-adaptability/co-adaptivity, 7–8, 17–18, 21, 82, 103, 106, 108, 115, 116, 145–58, 154–55, 186–87, 190, 220, 228–30, 251, 282
 their critical self-distancing, 4, 37, 58–59, 148, 175
 their empathetic imagination, 4, 13–15, 18, 25, 37, 46, 58, 90, 95, 97, 101, 139, 153, 156–57, 158–75, 180, 193, 248, 251, 254, 277
 their individuation, 136, 153, 159–62, 248, 254, 256, 277
 their mental flexibility, 4, 13–15, 18, 20, 24, 46, 58, 75, 90, 95, 101, 153, 193, 230, 255
 their potentiality for change, 2–3, 26, 63, 86, 101, 108, 146, 154, 161–62, 220, 246, 254
 their relative autonomy, 4, 7, 18, 25, 27, 108, 148, 151, 155, 208, 254, 277
 their sense of identity, 161–62, 248
 their sociocultural positionality, 3–4, 7, 22, 24, 117, 146, 175, 277
 their temperament, 25, 70, 90, 98, 101–02, 150, 152, 155, 210–11, 254, 277

I

Imagists, the, 91
implied reader, see "communicative personae"
implied writer, see "communicative personae"
India, 267
inferencing, 38, 51, 64–65, 67–70, 109, 132–33, 137, 139, 164–70, 194, 203, 286, 296, 297
influences, 94, 106, 164, 193–207
interdisciplinarity, 4–8, 22, 23, 43–48, 53, 67, 77–78, 123, 237, 278
International Court of Justice, the, 11
Internet, the, 265, 273
interpersonal dimensions
 of language use in general, 40–43, 52, 80–83, 137–38, 176–77, 253
 of literature, 2, 25, 29, 36–39, 54–55, 58–60, 63, 77–80, 105, 107, 114–15, 158–75, 176–251, 256, 260
 of written language use in general, 83–88
interpretative indefiniteness, 38–41, 47–48, 73, 262, 276
intertextuality, 90, 94, 107, 140, 163, 169, 191–92, 194, 198, 200, 207, 255, 289
introspective evidence, 15, 101–2, 152–53
irony, 46, 82 fn. 8, 167, 171
 dramatic irony, 167–69, 286
Israeli poetry, 116

J

Jacobins, the, 10, 145
Jane Bennet (in *Pride and Prejudice*), 168
job interviews, 86–87
Junggrammatiker, the, 41, 283
justice, 9, 13, 28, 62, 97, 103, 202, 271, 279

K

King Lear (in *King Lear*), 14

L

Ladislaw (in *Middlemarch*), 80
laissez faire economic theory, 92
language competence, 42
language performance, 42
langue, 40, 42, 49, 50, 129
laws, 85
letters, 35
 business letters, 85
 love-letters, 85
lexical density, 84
liberal humanism, 7–8, 20–21, 24, 108, 145–46, 151, 255, 289
liberal philosophy, 8–11
literariness, ideas of, 5, 33, 54, 71–74, 78, 179
literary aesthetics and communicational theory, 74–75, 114–15, 276
literary canons, 100, 238, 251, 257, 271–72, 275
literary criticism and theory, 1, 7, 21, 259–61
literary formalism, 5, 22–23, 29–39, 43–48, 65, 67, 70–80, 90, 125, 135–36, 155, 200, 248, 254, 289–90
literary gossip, 141–42
literary history, 21, 100, 110, 138 fn. 15, 178–79, 182, 194, 198–99, 207, 229, 231–32, 258
literary pragmatics, 1–2, 117, 187, 194, 290
 a historical yet non-historicist theory of, 22–28, 107–118, 230, 251, 253–56
 Åbo Symposium on, 114 fn. 10
 and general pragmatics, 6–8, 22, 29, 39, 46, 117–18, 246
 formalist accounts of, 23, 64–74, 77, 123, 162–63, 220–21, 254
 intradiegetic pragmatics, 71, 220–221
 and literary pragmatism, 203
literary scholarship and ideology, 5, 262, 266–79
literary structuralism, 31, 38, 172, 203, 245, 248

literature, 290
  its future, 271–77
  and power, 271–73
  as a source of inspiration, 146–51, 277
litigation narratives, 243
logical atomism, 23, 43, 290
logical positivism, 23, 43, 233, 290
logocentricism, 50–51, 134–35, 146–48, 291
Lynch (in *A Portrait of the Artist as a Young Man*), 197–98
lyric writing, 60, 93, 138, 196, 199, 205–06, 226, 270

M
macro-structure/sectional boundary, 222
Madame Bovary, 72
Manchester United, 273
Marxist/post-Marxist critics, 30, 88, 129, 231, 245, 255, 294
meaning-making, 38–39
mediating criticism 1–4, 8, 19–21, 24, 114, 155, 175, 193, 207, 230, 246–48, 250–51, 253–79
  and conflict, 266–71
  and judgement, 263–64
  its main aims, 256
  its own medium of communication, 265–66
  and mental flexibility, 258–68
  trajectories, ethnographical and talent-scouting, 257–58
mediation 1–4, 65, 144, 291
  positive mediation, 12–18, 19, 25, 127, 237, 251, 278
metaphor, 52; as itself a metaphor for human interaction, 249–50
Metaphysical poets, the, 127
Miss Havisham (in *Great Expectations*), 140, 141
Miss Mowcher (in *David Copperfield*), 84
modal expressions, 166–67, 209, 291
Modernism, 9 fn.1, 23, 29–39, 40, 44, 84, 90, 93, 105, 108, 125–28, 135, 170, 179, 185, 195–98, 200, 209–10, 216. 226–27, 229, 231–33, 245, 247–48, 262
moral philosophy, definition of terms in, 211–12
Movement, the, 216
Mr Allworthy (in *Tom Jones*), 211
Mr Bingley (in *Pride and Prejudice*), 168
Mr Darcy (in *Pride and Prejudice*), 168
Mr Dombey (in *Dombey and Son*), 215
Mr Knightley (in *Emma*), 214–15
Mr Ramsay (in *To the Lighthouse*), 111–12, 187–88
Mrs Bennet (in *Pride and Prejudice*), 168
Mrs General (in *Little Dorrit*), 215
mutual knowledge hypothesis, the, 66, 109, 120, 292
myth, 243
myth criticism, 117, 245, 254

N
narratee, see *"communicative personae"*
narratology, 45–46, 77, 117, 245, 292
  "showing" versus "telling", 197–98
narrator, see *"communicative personae"*
National Endowment for the Arts, the, (= NEA), 98–100
negative capability, 14
neo-Aristotelian critics (of Chicago), 184–85
New Age, 245
New Criticism, 23 fn. 5, 30–39, 40, 42, 45, 84, 90–91, 100, 115, 115 fn 12, 136, 172, 175, 179, 186, 195–96, 231–32, 245, 292
new historicism, 5, 19, 88, 95, 128, 129, 231, 245, 255, 292
new liberal economics and social policy, 279
Nicholas (in "The Miller's Tale"), 223–24
nihilism, 47, 97, 134, 147, 157, 271

Nobel Prize for Literature, the, 100
non-automatic inferencing, 132, 201

O
obeying an order, 88
objective correlative, 30, 292
orality/literacy, 27, 31, 60–61, 66, 81–88, 91, 141, 200–04, 253, 273
   the residual orality of writing, 84, 91
   the covertly dialogic nature of writing, 86–88

P
Palamon (in "The Knight's Tale"), 224
parody, 94
parole, 40, 42, 49, 50, 52, 129
Paul Dombey (in *Dombey and Son*), 215
Peace Studies, 11, 13
persona criticism, 151
pessimistic sociocultural determinism, 95–106, 150, 251, 255
phatic communication, 121
philosophical hermeneutics, 48, 97, 134, 136, 137–45, 158, 173, 293
phonocentric attitudes of linguists, the, 43, 83–86, 120, 125, 209, 293
point of view, 78–79
politeness, 59, 81 fn.8, 82, 85, 115, 175, 208–30, 256, 293–94
   face, 217–20
   face-threatening act (FTA), 217–20
   generation gaps and changes, 220–21, 226, 227, 229
   horizons of politeness expectations, 210, 216
   politeness spectrum, 217–20
   presentational politeness, 221–22
   selectional politeness, 221
   strategic impoliteness, 210, 219, 223–24
   strategies in writing, 209–210
   styles of politeness, 224–25
political correctness/incorrectness, 16–17, 25, 98–102, 107, 136, 143, 219, 230, 236, 251, 255, 267, 278, 294
politics of recognition, 9–11

polivalence reading convention, the notion of a, 73
popular culture, 272–75
   pop videos, 273; rap, 274
postcolonial criticism/studies, 5, 19, 47, 88, 95, 129, 136, 157, 231, 245, 255, 269, 294
postcolonial literature, 269–70
postitive discrimination, 10
postmodernism, 9 fn.1
postmodernity, 2, 5, 8–12, 20–22, 27, 47, 65, 74, 88–106, 114, 152, 201–04, 215, 219, 249, 251, 271, 273, 276, 294–95
poststructuralism, 23–24, 32, 50, 77, 88–106, 117, 133, 135, 148, 151, 154–56, 199, 203
practical criticism, 128–29, 179, 260, 295
pragmatic paradoxes, 219, 223–24
pragmatic particles, 85, 87
pragmatics (*see also literary pragmatics*), 1–2, 4, 50, 64–67, 81, 113, 243, 295–96
   anthropological approaches to, 80, 116, 151, 163, 175, 243, 255
   of cultural interfaces, 137, 193
   historical approaches to, 6–8, 193, 231, 255
pragmatism, 32, 47, 49–50, 97, 113, 134, 146, 203, 241–43, 296
pragmatist semiotics, 34, 35, 79, 136, 244
literary pragmatism, 203
Prague Linguistic Circle, the, 34, 283
presuppositions, 26, 65, 68, 122, 131, 132–33, 139, 166
Princeton University Center for Human Values, 97–98
productive hypocrisy, 159, 161
psycholinguistics, 222, 250
psychological aesthetics, 36, 79, 233
pyschoanalysis, 150, 159
   psychoanalytical criticism, 117, 239–40, 245, 253

Q
quick of life, the, 155–57

R
rationalality/rationalism 47, 134–35, 157, 213, 215, 271
reader-response criticism, 46–47, 55, 124, 140, 152, 164, 297
Realism, 84, 197
realpolitik, 13
reasonable disagreement, 13, 19–20, 135, 180, 263, 265, 270–71
reception aesthetics, 46–47, 55, 296–97
Regan (in *King Lear*), 14
relevance theory, 65–70, 74, 109, 132–33, 297
Renaissance and Neo-Classical poeticians and rhetoricians, 130–31, 179, 181, 184
Restoration comedy, 213–14
reviewers, 206–07
rhetoric of blame, the, 19, 24, 102, 115, 129, 136, 143, 234, 251, 265
role models and public scripts, 10, 159–60
Romanticism, 32, 47, 127, 179, 183, 185, 186, 195, 232, 259
Russian Formalism, 23, 23 fn.5, 35, 44, 45, 71, 115, 179, 191, 195, 297

S
salience and foregrounding, 222
Scriblerus Club, the, 212
semiosis, 23, 38, 89, 136, 139, 147, 148, 281, 298
service encounters, 81
short story, the, 179
significant other, the, 153, 159, 250
sincerity/insincerity/"sincerity gap", 45, 58, 171–72, 186, 220
Sister Western (in *Tom Jones*), 211
sociosemiotics, 73, 81
Somme, the battle of the, 192
Sophia Western (in *Tom Jones*), 211
sources, 94, 164, 194–95, 200
Spectator, The, 212
speech act theory, 32, 49–53, 77, 80–82, 147, 298–99
  conversational implicature, 51–52, 54
  the cooperative principle, 51, 59, 65, 81 fn. 8, 83, 222, 284–85
  the descriptive fallacy, 51
  felicity conditions, 51, 54, 60, 219
  illocutionary acts, constative and performative, 3, 49–51, 53
  indirect speech act, 49–50, 52, 218, 221
  locutionary acts, 49
  the maxims of manner, quality, quantity, and relation, 51, 65, 81 fn.8
  perlocutionary acts, 3, 50, 174, 219
speech act theory of literature, 49, 53–64, 72, 77, 123, 174, 254
Stephen Dedalus (in *A Portrait of the Artist as a Young Man*), 197–98
structuralist linguistics, 5, 24, 25, 40–43, 117, 129, 136, 145, 155, 299–300
stuttering, 85
styles, high/middle/low, 182
stylistics, 44–45, 77, 117, 220, 300
Sublime, the, 186
Supreme Court opinions, 243
Symbolism, 23, 38, 40–41, 73, 91, 125, 128, 179, 185, 190–91, 195–96, 232, 289–90
synchronic focus of linguistics, the, 129

T
tape recorders, 85
telephone directories, 85
telephones, 85
text-linguistics, 43–44, 77, 117, 222, 224, 300
textualization-cum-contextualization, 122, 130, 163, 164–67, 254, 300
The carpenter (in "The Miller's Tale), 223–24
The Miller (in *The Canterbury Tales*), 221

The Reeve (in *The Canterbury Tales*), 221
"the" *versus* "this/that", 85
Theory of Literature (Warren and Wellek), 179, 195, 237
Time (in *The Winter's Tale*), 131
Tityvillus (devil in morality play), 124
tragedy, 179, 182, 184
trickster tales, 243
Trobriand Islanders, 184
truth, 32–33, 47, 50, 51, 60, 74, 134–36, 138, 142
　episodic and specific truth, 33–34, 287, 298
　general and moral truth, 34, 54, 253, 288, 291

U
unitary context assumption, the, 65–71, 106, 109, 119–45, 183, 193, 234, 300

United Nations, the, 11

V
verse/prose, 179
Vienna Circle, the, 290

W
Waverley (in *Waverley*), 169
Wheel of Virgil, the, 182
Whig supremacy, the, 214
William Dorrit (in *Little Dorrit*), 214
Woman in White of Berners Street, the, 140
written-language bias of linguistics, the, 40–41, 43, 66, 120, 125, 301

In the PRAGMATICS AND BEYOND NEW SERIES the following titles have been published thus far or are scheduled for publication:

1. WALTER, Bettyruth: *The Jury Summation as Speech Genre: An Ethnographic Study of What it Means to Those who Use it.* Amsterdam/Philadelphia, 1988.
2. BARTON, Ellen: *Nonsentential Constituents: A Theory of Grammatical Structure and Pragmatic Interpretation.* Amsterdam/Philadelphia, 1990.
3. OLEKSY, Wieslaw (ed.): *Contrastive Pragmatics.* Amsterdam/Philadelphia, 1989.
4. RAFFLER-ENGEL, Walburga von (ed.): *Doctor-Patient Interaction.* Amsterdam/Philadelphia, 1989.
5. THELIN, Nils B. (ed.): *Verbal Aspect in Discourse.* Amsterdam/Philadelphia, 1990.
6. VERSCHUEREN, Jef (ed.): *Selected Papers from the 1987 International Pragmatics Conference. Vol. I: Pragmatics at Issue. Vol. II: Levels of Linguistic Adaptation. Vol. III: The Pragmatics of Intercultural and International Communication* (ed. with Jan Blommaert). Amsterdam/Philadelphia, 1991.
7. LINDENFELD, Jacqueline: *Speech and Sociability at French Urban Market Places.* Amsterdam/Philadelphia, 1990.
8. YOUNG, Lynne: *Language as Behaviour, Language as Code: A Study of Academic English.* Amsterdam/Philadelphia, 1990.
9. LUKE, Kang-Kwong: *Utterance Particles in Cantonese Conversation.* Amsterdam/Philadelphia, 1990.
10. MURRAY, Denise E.: *Conversation for Action. The computer terminal as medium of communication.* Amsterdam/Philadelphia, 1991.
11. LUONG, Hy V.: *Discursive Practices and Linguistic Meanings. The Vietnamese system of person reference.* Amsterdam/Philadelphia, 1990.
12. ABRAHAM, Werner (ed.): *Discourse Particles. Descriptive and theoretical investigations on the logical, syntactic and pragmatic properties of discourse particles in German.* Amsterdam/Philadelphia, 1991.
13. NUYTS, Jan, A. Machtelt BOLKESTEIN and Co VET (eds): *Layers and Levels of Representation in Language Theory: a functional view.* Amsterdam/Philadelphia, 1990.
14. SCHWARTZ, Ursula: *Young Children's Dyadic Pretend Play.* Amsterdam/Philadelphia, 1991.
15. KOMTER, Martha: *Conflict and Cooperation in Job Interviews.* Amsterdam/Philadelphia, 1991.
16. MANN, William C. and Sandra A. THOMPSON (eds): *Discourse Description: Diverse Linguistic Analyses of a Fund-Raising Text.* Amsterdam/Philadelphia, 1992.
17. PIÉRAUT-LE BONNIEC, Gilberte and Marlene DOLITSKY (eds): *Language Bases ... Discourse Bases.* Amsterdam/Philadelphia, 1991.
18. JOHNSTONE, Barbara: *Repetition in Arabic Discourse. Paradigms, syntagms and the ecology of language.* Amsterdam/Philadelphia, 1991.
19. BAKER, Carolyn D. and Allan LUKE (eds): *Towards a Critical Sociology of Reading Pedagogy. Papers of the XII World Congress on Reading.* Amsterdam/Philadelphia, 1991.
20. NUYTS, Jan: *Aspects of a Cognitive-Pragmatic Theory of Language. On cognition, functionalism, and grammar.* Amsterdam/Philadelphia, 1992.

21. SEARLE, John R. et al.: *(On) Searle on Conversation*. Compiled and introduced by Herman Parret and Jef Verschueren. Amsterdam/Philadelphia, 1992.
22. AUER, Peter and Aldo Di LUZIO (eds): *The Contextualization of Language*. Amsterdam/Philadelphia, 1992.
23. FORTESCUE, Michael, Peter HARDER and Lars KRISTOFFERSEN (eds): *Layered Structure and Reference in a Functional Perspective. Papers from the Functional Grammar Conference, Copenhagen, 1990*. Amsterdam/Philadelphia, 1992.
24. MAYNARD, Senko K.: *Discourse Modality: Subjectivity, Emotion and Voice in the Japanese Language*. Amsterdam/Philadelphia, 1993.
25. COUPER-KUHLEN, Elizabeth: *English Speech Rhythm. Form and function in everyday verbal interaction*. Amsterdam/Philadelphia, 1993.
26. STYGALL, Gail: Trial Language. *A study in differential discourse processing*. Amsterdam/Philadelphia, 1994.
27. SUTER, Hans Jürg: *The Wedding Report: A Prototypical Approach to the Study of Traditional Text Types*. Amsterdam/Philadelphia, 1993.
28. VAN DE WALLE, Lieve: *Pragmatics and Classical Sanskrit*. Amsterdam/Philadelphia, 1993.
29. BARSKY, Robert F.: *Constructing a Productive Other: Discourse theory and the convention refugee hearing*. Amsterdam/Philadelphia, 1994.
30. WORTHAM, Stanton E.F.: *Acting Out Participant Examples in the Classroom*. Amsterdam/Philadelphia, 1994.
31. WILDGEN, Wolfgang: *Process, Image and Meaning. A realistic model of the meanings of sentences and narrative texts*. Amsterdam/Philadelphia, 1994.
32. SHIBATANI, Masayoshi and Sandra A. THOMPSON (eds): *Essays in Semantics and Pragmatics*. Amsterdam/Philadelphia, 1995.
33. GOOSSENS, Louis, Paul PAUWELS, Brygida RUDZKA-OSTYN, Anne-Marie SIMON-VANDENBERGEN and Johan VANPARYS: *By Word of Mouth. Metaphor, metonymy and linguistic action in a cognitive perspective*. Amsterdam/Philadelphia, 1995.
34. BARBE, Katharina: Irony in Context. Amsterdam/Philadelphia, 1995.
35. JUCKER, Andreas H. (ed.): *Historical Pragmatics. Pragmatic developments in the history of English*. Amsterdam/Philadelphia, 1995.
36. CHILTON, Paul, Mikhail V. ILYIN and Jacob MEY: *Political Discourse in Transition in Eastern and Western Europe (1989-1991)*. Amsterdam/Philadelphia, 1998.
37. CARSTON, Robyn and Seiji UCHIDA (eds): *Relevance Theory. Applications and implications*. Amsterdam/Philadelphia, 1998.
38. FRETHEIM, Thorstein and Jeanette K. GUNDEL (eds): *Reference and Referent Accessibility*. Amsterdam/Philadelphia, 1996.
39. HERRING, Susan (ed.): *Computer-Mediated Communication. Linguistic, social, and cross-cultural perspectives*. Amsterdam/Philadelphia, 1996.
40. DIAMOND, Julie: *Status and Power in Verbal Interaction. A study of discourse in a close-knit social network*. Amsterdam/Philadelphia, 1996.
41. VENTOLA, Eija and Anna MAURANEN, (eds): *Academic Writing. Intercultural and textual issues*. Amsterdam/Philadelphia, 1996.
42. WODAK, Ruth and Helga KOTTHOFF (eds): *Communicating Gender in Context*. Amsterdam/Philadelphia, 1997.

43. JANSSEN, Theo A.J.M. and Wim van der WURFF (eds): *Reported Speech. Forms and functions of the verb.* Amsterdam/Philadelphia, 1996.
44. BARGIELA-CHIAPPINI, Francesca and Sandra J. HARRIS: *Managing Language. The discourse of corporate meetings.* Amsterdam/Philadelphia, 1997.
45. PALTRIDGE, Brian: *Genre, Frames and Writing in Research Settings.* Amsterdam/Philadelphia, 1997.
46. GEORGAKOPOULOU, Alexandra: *Narrative Performances. A study of Modern Greek storytelling.* Amsterdam/Philadelphia, 1997.
47. CHESTERMAN, Andrew: *Contrastive Functional Analysis.* Amsterdam/Philadelphia, 1998.
48. KAMIO, Akio: *Territory of Information.* Amsterdam/Philadelphia, 1997.
49. KURZON, Dennis: *Discourse of Silence.* Amsterdam/Philadelphia, 1998.
50. GRENOBLE, Lenore: *Deixis and Information Packaging in Russian Discourse.* Amsterdam/Philadelphia, 1998.
51. BOULIMA, Jamila: *Negotiated Interaction in Target Language Classroom Discourse.* Amsterdam/Philadelphia, 1999.
52. GILLIS, Steven and Annick DE HOUWER (eds): *The Acquisition of Dutch.* Amsterdam/Philadelphia, 1998.
53. MOSEGAARD HANSEN, Maj-Britt: *The Function of Discourse Particles. A study with special reference to spoken standard French.* Amsterdam/Philadelphia, 1998.
54. HYLAND, Ken: *Hedging in Scientific Research Articles.* Amsterdam/Philadelphia, 1998.
55. ALLWOOD, Jens and Peter Gärdenfors (eds): *Cognitive Semantics. Meaning and cognition.* Amsterdam/Philadelphia, 1999.
56. TANAKA, Hiroko: *Language, Culture and Social Interaction. Turn-taking in Japanese and Anglo-American English.* Amsterdam/Philadelphia, 1999.
57 JUCKER, Andreas H. and Yael ZIV (eds): *Discourse Markers. Descriptions and theory.* Amsterdam/Philadelphia, 1998.
58. ROUCHOTA, Villy and Andreas H. JUCKER (eds): *Current Issues in Relevance Theory.* Amsterdam/Philadelphia, 1998.
59. KAMIO, Akio and Ken-ichi TAKAMI (eds): *Function and Structure. In honor of Susumu Kuno.* 1999.
60. JACOBS, Geert: *Preformulating the News. An analysis of the metapragmatics of press releases.* 1999.
61. MILLS, Margaret H. (ed.): *Slavic Gender Linguistics.* 1999.
62. TZANNE, Angeliki: *Talking at Cross-Purposes. The dynamics of miscommunication.* 2000.
63. BUBLITZ, Wolfram, Uta LENK and Eija VENTOLA (eds.): *Coherence in Spoken and Written Discourse. How to create it and how to describe it.Selected papers from the International Workshop on Coherence, Augsburg, 24-27 April 1997.* 1999.
64. SVENNEVIG, Jan: *Getting Acquainted in Conversation. A study of initial interactions.* 1999.
65. COOREN, François: *The Organizing Dimension of Communication.* 2000.
66. JUCKER, Andreas H., Gerd FRITZ and Franz LEBSANFT (eds.): *Historical Dialogue Analysis.* 1999.

67. TAAVITSAINEN, Irma, Gunnel MELCHERS and Päivi PAHTA (eds.): *Dimensions of Writing in Nonstandard English.* 1999.
68. ARNOVICK, Leslie: *Diachronic Pragmatics. Seven case studies in English illocutionary development.* 1999.
69. NOH, Eun-Ju: *The Semantics and Pragmatics of Metarepresentation in English. A relevance-theoretic account.* 2000.
70. SORJONEN, Marja-Leena: *Recipient Activities Particles nii(n) and joo as Responses in Finnish Conversation.* n.y.p.
71. GÓMEZ-GONZÁLEZ, María Ángeles: *The Theme-Topic Interface. Evidence from English.* n.y.p.
72. MARMARIDOU, Sophia S.A.: *Pragmatic Meaning and Cognition.* 2000.
73. HESTER, Stephen and David FRANCIS (eds.): *Local Educational Order. Ethnomethodological studies of knowledge in action.* 2000.
74. TROSBORG, Anna (ed.): *Analysing Professional Genres.* 2000.
75. PILKINGTON, Adrian: *Poetic Effects. A relevance theory perspective.* 2000.
76. MATSUI, Tomoko: *Bridging and Relevance.* n.y.p.
77. VANDERVEKEN, Daniel and Susumu KUBO (eds.): *Essays in Speech Act Theory.* n.y.p.
78. SELL, Roger D. : *Literature as Communication. The foundations of mediating criticism.* 2000.
79. ANDERSEN, Gisle and Thorstein FRETHEIM (eds.): *Pragmatic Markers and Propositional Attitude.* 2000.
80. UNGERER, Friedrich (ed.): *English Media Texts – Past and Present. Language and textual structure.* n.y.p.
81. DI LUZIO, Aldo, Susanne GUNTHER and Franca ORLETTI (eds.): *Culture in Communication. Analyses of intercultural situations.* n.y.p.
82. KHALIL, Esam N.: *Grounding in English and Arabic News Discourse.* 2000.
83. MARQUEZ-REITER, Rosina: *Linguistic Politeness in Britain and Uruguay. A contrastive study of requests and apologies.* n.y.p.
84. ANDERSEN, Gisle: *Pragmatic Markers and Sociolinguistic Variation. A relevance-theoretic approach to the language of adolescents.* n.y.p.
85. COLLINS, Daniel E.: *Reanimated Voices. Speech reporting in a historical-pragmatic perspective.* n.y.p.
86. IFANTIDOU, Elly: *Evidentials and Relevance.* n.y.p.
87. MUSHIN, Ilana: *Evidentiality and Epistemological Stance. Narrative Retelling.* n.y.p.
88. BAYRAKTAROGLU, Arin and Maria SIFIANOU (eds.): *Linguistic Politeness Across Boundaries. Linguistic Politeness Across Boundaries.* n.y.p.